The Early Jesus Movement and Its Gospels

The Early Jesus Movement and Its Gospels

Four Major Parties, Four Major Gospels

Harry W. Eberts, Jr.
Paul R. Eberts

YBK Publishers
New York

YBK Publishers, Inc.
39 Crosby Street
New York, NY 10013
www.ybkpublishers.com

The Early Jesus Movement and Its Gospels:
Four Major Parties, Four Major Gospels

ISBN 978-1-936411-29-0

Library of Congress Cataloging-in-Publication Data

Eberts, Harry W., 1926-
  The early Jesus movement and its gospels : four major parties, four
major gospels / Harry W. Eberts, Jr., Paul R. Eberts.
      pages cm
  Includes bibliographical references and index.
  ISBN 978-1-936411-29-0 (pbk.)
  1. Bible. Gospels–Criticism, interpretation, etc. 2. Jesus Christ–
Biography. 3. Christianity–Origin. I. Eberts, Paul R. (Paul Robert), 1932-
II. Title.
  BS2555.52.E24 2013
  226'.06–dc23
                                        2013027333

Manufactured in the United States of America
or in the United Kingdom or Australia
when distributed elsewhere

13-08

"Jesus Christ, as he is attested for us in
Holy Scriptures, is the one Word of God,
which we have to hear
and which we have to trust
and obey in life and in death."

—*The Theological Declaration of Barmen,
Germany,* May, 1934:

Contents

Detailed Outline
of Chronology
# of Jesus' Ministry

Part Two of this book presents a chronology of Jesus' ministry. Chronologies are seldom explicit among contemporary New Testament scholars. Most agree that events reported in the New Testament are authentic, but do not organize them into a chronology. John's gospel provides the basis for such a chronology.

The gospels agree that Jesus' ministry begins with John the Baptist in Judea, possibly after a feast-day celebration in Jerusalem which Jesus attended. They concur that Jesus returns to Galilee to take up his ministry. The next Passover reported in Matthew, Mark, and Luke (called the Synoptic Gospels because Matthew and Luke use Mark's basic outline for events in Jesus' life) culminates in Jesus' death and resurrection. That chronology in the Synoptic Gospels gives Jesus a ministry of well less than a year.

John's gospel alone, as seen below, reports that Jesus went back and forth between Galilee and Jerusalem during two Passover seasons in addition to his final one. This gives Jesus a ministry of nearly three years instead of less than one (as reported in the Synoptics). We believe John's Gospel is accurate in these reports.

An important demonstration in this chronology is that, in John's Gospel, Jesus was in Jerusalem often enough and for long enough to gather several group of followers there—from Hellenist Jews, Hebrew Jews (Brethren), and, possibly, newly arrived Hellenist Jews (Apostles) who were not known to those in Galilee until after Jesus' resurrection. Certain events become clearer using this thesis. The brief titles added to the sub-sections of Part Two, below, show how, with a few exceptions, key events in Jesus' ministry fit together into a single timeline.

The Early Jesus Movement and Its Gospels

Part One

Introduction to the Study of the Gospels

Chapter One

Our Approach to Studying the Gospels

The greatest treasure accumulated by the early Jesus movement was its four Gospels. At the same time, these Gospels present certain challenges. Who wrote them? For what purpose? Why four? How dependent are they on one another? Christians have struggled with these mysteries since the Gospels were composed.

We will not resolve all these questions. But we believe an extension of the general theses developed in our two earlier volumes *The Early Jesus Movement and Its Parties* (2009) and *The Early Jesus Movement and Its Churches* (2011) provides certain new clues about the production and content of each Gospel. Briefly, our thesis is that each Gospel was produced under the auspices of one of the four major parties in the early Jesus movement—Disciples, Brethren, Hellenists, and Apostles. They were party documents more than individuals' documents. We believe the authors were individuals who were writers but also compilers or editors, choosing from a variety of stories about Jesus which each party found meaningful to them as representative of their party's beliefs. On the number of stories to choose from, the Gospel of John says, *"There are also many other things which Jesus did; were every one of them to be written, I suppose that the world itself could not contain the books that would be written"* (John

21:25). This book is designed to examine carefully each Gospel in order to show distinctive marks that each of these parties put on its Gospel. Such an outcome would be expected if each Gospel "spoke" from and to a different constituency.

As reported in our first book (2009), these constituencies and parties are reasonably well-identified in The Acts of the Apostles and Paul's Letters. For instance, the Disciples are seen as separable from the Apostles after Paul's conversion on the road to Damascus. *"For several days he [Paul] was with the disciples at Damascus"* (Acts 9:19). *"And when he had come to Jerusalem he attempted to join the disciples; and they were all afraid of him, for they did not believe that he was a disciple"* (9:26). Then Acts distinguishes a second grouping. *"But Barnabas took him, and brought him to the apostles"* (9:27). Acts also distinguished between *Hebrews* (Acts later calls them the *Brethren* or *Brothers*) and *Hellenists*. *"The Hellenists murmured against the Hebrews because their widows were neglected in the daily distribution"* (6:1). Our first book followed these leads in Acts and Paul's first letter to the Corinthians where Paul laments, *"Each one of you says, "I belong to Paul," "I belong to Apollos," "I belong to Cephas," and, "I belong to Christ." Is Christ divided? Was Paul crucified for you? Or were you baptized into the name of Paul?"* (1:12-13). From such evidence it became possible to delineate a great many differences among the four parties. Some differences are discussed in this book but they do not cover all differences denoted in our previous books (2009, 2011).

We believe the Gospels reflect these four parties. The Disciples are readily identified with the Twelve and other followers from Galilee, described in some detail in the Gospel known as Mark. Brethren struggled with Pharisees in Jerusalem and Galilee; these struggles are described in detail in the Gospel of Matthew. Hellenist Christians struggled with their fellow Hellenist Jews; the Gospel of John gives Christian interpretations to typical Hellenist concepts such as *"word," "light," "love,"* and *"eternal life,"* words less frequently found in the other three Gospels. The Apostles struggled with both Hebrews and Hellenists in Diaspora cities and also with Hellenist Gentiles as shown in Paul's letter to the Galatians and in our 2011 book. Luke was a colleague of Paul, the Apostle (Acts 16:9-10, passim). Since the parties' constituencies differed geographically and ethnicly, their Gospels reflect these differences.

All four Gospels focus on Jesus of Nazareth as, in Greek, the *Christos*, the Christ, the "Anointed of God," what he said, what he did, and why he said or did certain things. The Gospels differ largely in explaining Jesus' beliefs and actions so their constituencies could understand the Christ more adequately. We will demonstrate many of these differences in this book.

Six Tasks for this Book

Based on the dynamics underlying what was happening to and in the four parties in the early Jesus movement, six tasks emerge.

First, to describe in some detail the social, economic, political, and religious conditions where Jesus undertook his ministry, in Galilee, Judea, and Jerusalem. This description includes certain issues in what was happening within Judaism, especially in Jerusalem, as well as among the rulers of the area, the Sanhedrin, Herodians, and Romans. The Romans were the ultimate authorities and had final "say" on things. But they decentralized certain decisions to the Herodians and the Sanhedrin, sometimes with disastrous consequences for ordinary people. The next chapter addresses these issues.

Second, to develop a comprehensive chronology of Jesus' ministry based primarily on the Gospels of Mark and John. The parties agreed that Jesus ministered in both Galilee and Judea. Most scholars also agree that Mark was written first, probably in Rome, probably based on memories of one or more of his remaining Galilean disciples or their close associates, and probably just after the halfway point of the first century CE. Mark's Gospel depicts Jesus' ministry as taking place within a duration of less than one year. Matthew and Luke depend heavily on Mark's writings for their chronologies, each adding or subtracting certain details. John's Gospel differs considerably. John's Gospel posits that Jesus' ministry was spread over several years, alternated locations between Judea and Galilee, and celebrated not one but three Passovers. To comprehend these differences among the Gospels requires a new overall chronology for Jesus' ministry. This chronology is presented in Part Two.

Third, to recognize dangers Jesus faced during his ministry. Because of what he said and did, Jesus can be seen as under close surveillance by those who had status and power in Judea and Galilee (the Sadducees, Sanhedrin, Pharisees, Herodians, and Romans). The Gospels explicitly report on Jesus' conflicts with these powerful groups. Questioning of him by Scribes and Pharisees was a form of surveillance. These men reported Jesus' beliefs and actions to the Sanhedrin, Sadducees, and high priests in Jerusalem (Caiaphas and Ananias). On the basis of such reports, powerful leaders of these groups came to consider Jesus dangerous, especially because the beliefs espoused by Jesus and his followers threatened the beliefs, privileges, and prerogatives of these high-status groups. From the moment Jesus emerged from the shadow of John the Baptist and especially after he *"cleansed the Temple,"* he was a man marked for punishment and eventual execution. Such dangers to Jesus are noted in the chronology.

Fourth, to examine each Gospel (and its underlying oral tradition) in its uniqueness—how each one represents a party's geographic and socio-political-religious environment. Although each Gospel presents similar features in Jesus' life and work, each differs in certain details that both complement and occasionally contradict one another. These details usually stem from a party's basic concerns. Part Three examines these details.

Fifth, to deal with the most important question posed by the New Testament—who is the Jesus of the Early Jesus Movement? The four Gospels (and various Letters in the New Testament) provide a wide range of sometimes inconsistent materials through which to understand Jesus as a central historical figure who affected so many cultures, especially in Western Europe. In Part Four, we will sort through the Gospels' contents to determine where they converge. From this analysis a reasonably complete picture of Jesus, the central figure of the early Jesus movement, emerges.

Sixth, based on perspectives presented in this book, we conclude with an Afterword that addresses some of the glaring issues facing contemporary Christians today.

Chapter 2

Socio-Political, Economic, and Religious Conditions During Jesus' Life and Ministry

The four Gospels in the contemporary New Testament clearly agree that Jesus of Nazareth was an historical figure who lived and ministered in a particular time and place. But the Gospels are less clear on the nature of the historical circumstances of his time or how these circumstances affected key decisions in his ministry. Major contributions to Jesus' decisions were, first, his understanding of how the God of Hebrew Scriptures wanted people to respond to one another; second, the various responses being made to the God of these Scriptures by major status groups among his contemporaries; and, third, how social, economic, political, and religious conditions in Galilee and Judea constrained both him and his contemporaries in their responses.

"Jesus came into a world of irrepressible conflict" (Neusner, 1984: 32). Tumultuous social, economic, political, and religious conditions in Galilee and Judea deeply affected Jesus and his followers before, during, and after his ministry. Jesus saw how his contemporaries were responding to their circumstances. He saw people suffering from a variety of maladies; he saw people violently using weapons against one another; he saw people crucified for such violence; he saw people indifferent to these conditions; he saw concerned people struggling to figure out appropriate responses to their circumstances; he saw concerned people making ineffective responses to their ideals; he saw that circumstances in heavily rural Galilee were different from those in urban Jerusalem; he saw divided and ineffective leadership in dealing with these circumstances.

Such conditions explain in part why the four Gospels vary from one another. Our previous two books looked at certain of these social conditions in considerable detail (2009, 2011). At least three sets of social conditions heavily affected these parties—those experienced by Jesus before and during his ministry in Galilee and Judea (5-30CE); the conditions the parties' key followers experienced before and during their ministries (30-66CE); and those experienced by the authors of the four Gospels (50-85CE). We summarize the first of these conditions here in four sections. The others will be considered in the book's various Parts (Two, Three, and Four).

1. Social Conditions in Galilee and Judea before and during Jesus' ministry
2. Romans, Herodians, and Hellenism as they affected Jesus' ministry
3. Jewish Parties in Judea and Galilee during Jesus' Ministry
4. Early Jesus-Movement Parties and their Changes

Galilee and Judea—Lands, History, and Social Condition in Jesus' Lifetime

Jesus of Nazareth, the central figure in all four Gospels, grew up in Galilee and, as a faithful Jew, by age twelve traveled for several days by foot to and from Jerusalem for major Jewish festivals and learning from rabbis in the Temple during these journeys. As he grew, he became a student of Jewish history through the Scriptures—Torah Laws, kings, psalms, prophecies—and the importance of his surroundings in this history. He came to know Abraham, Moses, Joshua, Saul, David, Solomon, Amos, Jeremiah, Isaiah, and so on, the places where they spent their lives, and the circumstances of their lives.

From stories about contemporary events, Jesus surely heard about the destruction of Sepphoris (8-9 miles northwest of Nazareth—see Figure 1, Map) when he was a child in Nazareth. At Herod's death in 4BCE, Herod's palace in Sepphoris was first ransacked by Jewish "bandits," "bandits" who could actually have been Zealots (Josephus, 94; Sepphoris, 2012). Then in a retaliatory search-and-destroy mission, Roman troops from Damascus completely destroyed Sepphoris and certain neighboring villages, killing and crucifying many urban and rural Jews.

Soon after, the Tetrarch Herod Antipas reconstructed Sepphoris to become his capital in Galilee. Even though Sepphoris is not mentioned in the Gospels, Jesus' father, living near Sepphoris and being a carpenter, might have worked in Sepphoris to help in its restoration. In Jesus' youth, Sepphoris was a Greek-Hellenist dominated city which Jews visited largely for official business as in paying taxes. During these times Jesus probably became increasingly aware of the many social, political, economic, and religious disruptions, including tax revolts by peasants (aided by Zealots) in Galilee. The Gospels show that Jesus ministry, from 27-29CE, included followers both from Hellenists and Hebrews in Galilee but also Judea and Jerusalem, who would have known about these disruptions.

A major influence on many Israelite historical events was the "Fertile Crescent" trade route as it went through Galilee. This trade route, established by 2000BCE (before the patriarch Abraham drove donkey caravans over it into Canaan), linked powerful kingdoms on the eastern crescent-shaped Euphrates River (Ur, Babylon, Assyria) from the Persian Gulf

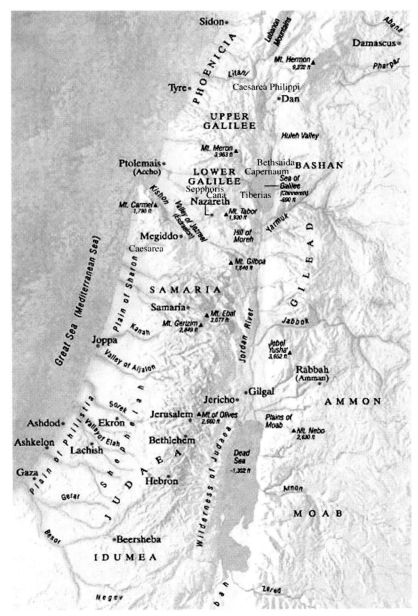

Figure 1. Map of Galilee and Judea during Jesus' Ministry

to northern Syria. From Syria, the route (the handle of the crescent) then went southeast to Damascus and Galilee, west to the Mediterranean Sea, then southwest to the Nile (and Egypt).

The Euphrates, Tigris, and Nile rivers had similar flood ecologies that provided extensive amounts of moist, fertile land on their banks due to Spring flooding, which provided abundant food for their dense and large populations and extremely large and rich kingdoms with diversified products. In Galilee, the trade route could take several paths to the Mediterranean coastal kingdoms of Philistia and Phoenicia, and the Plain of Sharon near the coast on which Ceasarea Maritima would be built which became the largest city in the whole area and seat of Roman government. The least mountainous route went from the confluence of the Jordan and Yarmuk Rivers, west along the Galilee-Samaria border, through the very fertile Plain of Esdraelon (also called Megiddo or Jezreel, Hebrew for Esdraelon), and then through one of several low mountain passes to the Mediterranean Sea (see map, Fig 1). Nazareth, Cana, and Sepphoris were on a northern ridge of the Plain of Esdraelon.

The good agriculture in the fertile Plain of Esdraelon and the trade route through it became increasingly problematic for Hebrew tribes on its path. As long as the Hebrews lived in tribal structures with no standing army, they were comparatively less well organized militarily and thus more easily exploited by powerful kingdoms to their west (Philistia and Phoenicia) as well as southwest (Egypt) and northeast (especially Babylon, Assyria, and, later, Persia).

After Moses and Joshua took the city of Jericho (1450-1250BCE), the twelve Hebrew tribes, guided by Torah Laws, tended to treat one another with reasonable respect and equality. Egyptians loosely ruled most of the entire region from Jerusalem up to about 1050BCE and constantly had to deal with "rebels" in the Galilee area (Veen, 2013: 44). These rebels were probably members of Israel's twelve tribes. From the Israelite point of view, they were attacked by the powerful Egyptian empire or their vassals and allies, such as the Philistines (see 1 Samuel, passim), possibly due to disputes over the fertile land in the Plain of Esdraelon or because the attackers thought, perhaps with good reason, that Hebrews were raiding caravans in the Galilean-Samarian part of the Fertile Crescent trade route (Veen, 2013: 45).

Such attacks induced the Israelites, somewhat reluctantly, to form a kingdom (1 Samuel:chs 8-11). They called the kingdom "Israel," named after the man they considered the progenitor of their twelve tribes, Jacob, who was also called Israel. Saul was its first king. Eventually, David defeated the Philistines, Egyptians, and their allies, forced them to withdraw, and secured the inland valley from the Sea of Galilee to the Dead Sea. Then the Israelites extended the kingdom into northern Galilee and southern Idumea. But even Israelite kings, starting with Solomon, did what kings and their elite supporters always tend to do—they accumulated wealth and power for themselves and, despite warnings by many prophets such as Amos, Hosea, Isaiah, Jeremiah, and Micah, to their ultimate detriment the kings neglected widows, orphans, and the poor, including "small" farmers. A result was that, when war came from peoples of the East, the divided Israelites did not respond effectively.

The timeline in Figure 2 underscores these events and what happened next. After surviving relatively unscathed under various kings for almost 300 years, the Israelites experienced two devastating defeats over the next 600 years. Shortly after Solomon's reign, Israel divided into two parts, the fertile agricultural north, Galilee and most of Samaria, as a Northern Kingdom, called Israel, and the mountainous Southern region, called Judah, named for its largest Israelite tribe. Both kingdoms developed typical kingly status hierarchies that favored the rich over the poor. The northern kingdom, Israel, based on agriculture (with an "agri-cultural" God, Elohim), lasted until 722BCE when Assyria, whose capital was in the Tigris River valley north of Babylon, destroyed it. The less wealthy Southern Kingdom, Judah with moun-

2000 BCE	Trade (facilitated by donkey caravans like ones driven by Abraham) among tribes and kingdoms along the "Fertile Crescent" of the Euphrates River from eastern kingdoms on the Tigris River to the southwestern kingdoms on the Nile (Egypt and Ethiopia) which also passed through the confluence of the fertile Yarmuk River valley and the even more fertile Plain of Esdraelon in southwestern (Lower) Galilee.
Prior to 11th century	Israelites' twelve tribes initially led by Moses then by Joshua lived in relative equality, peace, and mutual respect but sometimes (if not often) raided trade caravans.
11th century BCE– 930 BCE	To defend themselves more adequately from incursions by neighboring kingdoms (Egypt, Philistia), the 12 Hebrew Tribes formed a kingdom of Israel under Saul, David, and Solomon, that included Galilee, Samaria, Judea, and Idumea.
930 BCE– 722 BCE	The Israelite Kingdom split in two; Galilee and Samaria (with their better agriculture) formed the independent Northern Kingdom (Israel) with Samaria as its capital; the Southern Kingdom, with more defensible Jerusalem as its capital, took the name Judah.
722 BCE	Kingdom of Israel (and its ten tribes in Samaria and Galilee) was defeated by Assyria; Israel's leaders were killed and the people were scattered throughout the Assyrian Empire.
586 BCE– 539 BCE	Assyria and Judah were defeated by Babylonian Empire and Galilee, Samaria, Judah became a province of Babylon.
539 BCE– 332 BCE	Babylon Defeated by Persia; the area became a Persian province.
457 BCE	Aided by Persian King Ataxerxes, Ezra and Nehemiah returned to Jerusalem from Babylon and re-built its walls and temple.
332 BCE– 305 BCE	Galilee, Samaria, and Judah became a province in the Macedonian Empire of Alexander the Great who defeated the Persian Empire.
305 BCE– 198 BCE	Galilee, Samaria, and Judah became a Province in the Greek-Egyptian Ptolemaic Empire; Greek culture introduced in the region.

Figure 2   Brief Timeline of Jewish History from Abraham through Destruction of Jerusalem and Subsequent Domination by the Roman Empire.

198 BCE – 141 BCE	Judah, Galilee, and Samaria became a Province in the Greek-Seleucid Empire when Ptolemies were defeated by the Seleucids near Damascus.
141 BCE – 63 BCE	The Hasmonean family called Maccabees ("hammerers") established an Independent Jewish Hasmonean state (Judah).
63 BCE – 37 BCE	Roman Empire defeated Hasmoneans; Israel again a province, this time under the Romans; Greek culture persisted.
37 BCE – 70 CE	Herodian Dynasty ruled Galilee, Samaria, and Judea with oversight by Roman governors.
6-2 BCE to 29-30 CE	Jesus of Nazareth matriculated in Galilee and Judea.
70 CE	Romans end "Jewish Revolt"; Jerusalem and its Temple destroyed.
135 CE	Emperor Hadrian defeats another revolt led by Bar Kochba, re-naming the area "Syria Palaestina," a name originally used by historian Herodotus based on the name of Israel's ancient enemy, the Philistines; Jews forbidden to live in Jerusalem.

Figure 2 *(continued)*   Brief Timeline of Jewish History from Abraham through Destruction of Jerusalem and Subsequent Domination by the Roman Empire.

tainsides, rough terrain, few natural resources other than sheep, olives, figs, and salt from the Dead Sea, and its "herding-cultural" God, Yahweh, lasted another 140 years. Partly due to its remote location and defensible capital, Jerusalem, Judah lived until 586BCE before it was destroyed by a powerful resurgent Babylon. Babylon was then captured by the Persian Empire, which itself was defeated by the Macedonians and Greeks under Alexander the Great. The Jews were without autonomy in their "promised land" for another 450 years until the Hasmonean family dynasty took control in Galilee, Samaria, and Judea in 141BCE.

When the Greek-Seleucid Empire, ruling from Babylon, was collapsing, the Jewish Hasmonean family violently reestablished Israel's independence again in 141BCE. This dynasty lasted for less than 80 years—Romans took their independence away in 63BCE. As was their custom, in 37BCE Rome gave routine control over the territory to local leaders, in this case to an Idumean named Herod, later called "The Great." This "Jewish" kingdom was the largest in area for a Jewish state since Kings David and Solomon.

While Herod the Great held the governorship, he engaged in a huge public works program throughout Palestine brought on in part by a large earthquake in 31BCE. These building projects continued after his death and gave some stimulus to Judean and Galilean economies.

Social Conditions and Changes in Fertile (Lower) Galilee

Herod the Great died in 4BCE. Upon his death, Herod's sons (raised in Rome) induced considerable palace intrigue as they vied for the Roman Emperor Augustus' approval to rule in Galilee and Judea. Eventually the region was subdivided among Herod's three oldest sons. Herod Antipas became tetrarch in the most fertile parts of Galilee west of the Sea of Galilee, the area surrounding the southern part of the Jordan River on the important pilgrimage route from Galilee to Jerusalem, and much of the arid wilderness of Perea east of the Lower Jordan valley. Herod Phillip became tetrarch in areas east and north of the Sea of Galilee (Upper Galilee), including the Golan Heights (Gaulinitis). Archelaus, the oldest son, was given the important region of Judea and Jerusalem (Herod Antipas, 2012). But, among other cruelties, after brutally putting down what he considered a Pharisee sedition that killed 3,000 of them, Archelaus was deposed in 6CE and replaced by Roman military governors. Pontius Pilate was one of these governors (26-36CE).

Herod the Great was not universally loved by "his" people, especially in rural Galilee. After he died, the Zealot "Judas the Galilean" (or perhaps Judah ben Hezekiah, another "bandit" according to Josephus [94] a historian who previously was a Jewish war commander [66-70CE] but became part of the entourage of the Roman Emperor Hadrian) organized a raid on Herod's palace in Sepphoris in 4BCE (Padfield, 2012; Strange, 2001, 2012; see Acts 5:37). Rome was incensed. Its Syrian Governor's search-and-destroy follow-up to this event featured the killing, enslavement, or crucifixion of many citizens of Sepphoris and surrounding villages and burning Sepphoris to the ground.

Since this palace was to have been the seat of Herod Antipas' Galilean government, Herod Antipas moved to re-build Sepphoris. Later, in 17CE, a new Roman Emperor, Tiberius, built Antipas a more grand capital, named Tiberias, on the Sea of Galilee's western shore about twenty or so miles from Sepphoris. Living so close to Sepphoris and Tiberias, Jesus and his father might have plyed their carpenter's skills in them as they were being built. Jesus might have learned about Hellenist culture and to speak Greek from such experiences.

Most Jews lived in Galilee's 204 small villages that ranged in size from a dozen families to a few thousand (Josephus, 78CE; Horsley, 1996: 215 ff). Settlements generally occupied from two to five acres, with 40 to 60 people per acre to average fewer than 300 people per village. Family size would vary, but probably averaged three or four adults and four to seven or eight children (Jesus had four brothers and at least two sisters), or, roughly, 30-35 families per village. Although no definitive estimate is available, Galilee's total rural-village population, then, was probably slightly over 60,000 Galileans. The fishing villages of Capernaum and Bethsaida probably added about 2,500 people each (Horsley, 1996: 218; Crosson, 1998: 220). The Herodians' government centers of Sepphoris and, later, Tiberias probably added between 8,000-12,000 each (Crosson, 1998: 220 f, uses Reed's estimates, 1992: 15, which doubles these sizes for Sepphoris and Tiberias, but Reed did not account for land used by public facilities in his estimates).

Within a rural village each family lived in a small house, consisting of a room or two (ca 9 by 12 feet) that opened onto a courtyard shared with other families. Each village also had a shared oven, millstone, cistern, and wine- and olive-presses. Nazareth probably had 450-500 Aramaic-speaking people and was within daily walking distance from both Sepphoris to the northwest and Cana to the northeast. Cana was Jesus' mother's hometown (Padfield, 2012). In his maturity, after Jesus started his ministry, he attended a wedding in Cana where he turned water into wine (John 2:3-10).

Galilee and Samaria were not fully Jewish (Neusner, 1984: 28-30). The Assyrians overran Galilee in 722BCE, destroying its capital city, also named Samaria, taking away its leaders *"in chains and fishhooks"* (Amos 4:2) and scattering the Northern Kingdom's Jewish secondary leaders and people to the far reaches of the Assyrian Empire. The Assyrians then re-settled Assyrian sub-elites and peasants into Galilee's villages who lived free of Jewish influences for five centuries. Many became well-established in various fertile valleys and plains in Esdraelon and Samaria and worshiped pagan agricultural "fertility" gods such as Mithra (Lenski and Lenski, 1987: 135; Mithra, 2013).

Galilee only became "Jewish" again under Hasmonean rule. But this rule lasted for only 80 years (141-63BCE) before Rome conquered the region. Neusner (1984: 29) maintains that "the Hasmoneans used Judaism imperially, as a means of winning the loyalty of pagan Semites... But in a brief period of three or four generations deeply-rooted practices of Semitic natives...could not have been greatly changed merely by receiving 'Judaism,' which meant in the beginning little more than submitting to the knife of the circumciser rather than to the sword of the slaughterer."

Horsley disagrees with Neusner. In many Galilean villages, the ancient covenant between God and people through Moses continued as the most important religious influence (but less so the "kingly" Davidic covenant—see Eberts 2011: 25-30). "Judging from the use of Aramaic and Hebrew—and almost complete lack of Greek inscriptions, the villages of... Galilee maintained a traditional Israelite culture...without much interference from the imperial authorities who were interested primarily in the taxes" (Horsley, 1996: 89, 106). Both Jews and those committed to other religions were subject to the harsh and exploitative rule of the Herodians and the Romans.

Galilee's rulers traditionally looked on these villages as fertile land, literally, for taxation and tribute. Agricultural lands and their products were easily countable and easiest properties to tax. From Galilean peasants, both priests in Jerusalem and the Herods exacted taxes, including those paid in tribute to Rome. Since Herod left intact the Temple and high priesthood with their imposed Temple tax of one-half shekel for each male, it meant that in 60 years Galilee's people went from one layer of taxation, the Hasmonean, to three—Herodian government, Roman tribute, priesthood and Temple. All were apparently collected by the Herodians. According to Josephus (who might be exaggerating), annual revenues supporting these rulers came to around 900 talents, an enormous amount to be generated from a small population (Horsley, 1996: 21-34). One talent was worth 3,000 shekels and one shekel equaled 2 denarii (two days at a laborer's wage of one denarius per day; see Weights and Measures, 2013).

The math *using these estimates* shows that about 5.4 million denarii (=900 talents times 6000 denarii), or man-days of labor, annually went in taxes, roughly 60 denarii per person annually (on a population base of 90,000 as estimated above). Even though taxes were surely not paid on a per capita basis, the amount of taxes families would pay would be equivalent to a per capita basis. Since over half of the 90,000 people were children (many people in these kinds of societies reproduced near their biological maximum; Lenski and Lenski, 1987: 178) and women did not work outside the home, approximately 40,000 heads of families or single males were responsible for the taxes. By these calculations, Jesus' family of a married couple (Mary and Joseph), two adult children still at home (Jesus and James), and five other children (three more brothers and at least two sisters, as noted in Mark 6:3) would pay 540 denarii (=9 people times 60 denarii per person) per year in Herodian taxes. The family carpentry business would have to muster this cash income. The burden would fall on the three adult males, Joseph, Jesus, and James (assuming the latter two are at least in their middle to late teens when the final child is born), who would do most of the work; with five younger children at home, Mary would only marginally participate in the business. The Temple tax is one-half shekel (1 denarius) per year on every adult male (age 13+). Total taxes for Jesus' family, then, would come to 543 denarii, the bulk going to the Herodians. These tax estimates may or may not include the graft put into tax collections by the publicans collecting the taxes nor unpaid-tax equivalents among unemployed males when unemployment could be quite high. All these taxes were probably collected by the Herodians, then partly re-distributed to the Romans, priests, and Temple.

A reasonable assumption is that each male living in a rural area made a minimum wage of one denarius per work day per person (see Crosson, 1998: 346, and Lenski, 1966: 278, who believe that rural artisans—such as carpenters—made about the same wages as peasants). Since Jewish families were forbidden to work on the Sabbath (52 days) and on Feast Days (Passover, Tabernacles, "First Fruits"—*Pesach, Sukkoth, Shavuoth*—plus at least 6 days time, at a rather fast pace, to walk to and from Jerusalem for each of three Feasts plus an average of three days staying in Jerusalem each Feast), the base calculation of days of work available is probably closer to 290 rather than 365 (and the 290 could be high). Three times 290 denarius gives Jesus' family an income of 870 denarii a year at a minimum wage (it could be more if a fourth "person" among the kids, combined, worked). Percentage of taxes to income for Jesus' family, then, is (=543/870) 62 percent (bordering on 2/3rds) of income paid in taxes.

Although making other assumptions than those presented here (on "exchange rates" or days worked, for instance) could change the numbers in the various calculations, the tax burden on most families would still be high and for some confiscatory. There is little wonder that peasants were the same, or worse off than Jesus' family. Extended unemployment of key earners could put many families into serious debt. Little wonder that such people would resent the Herodians, Romans, priests, and Temple!

Such burdensome taxation resulted in some Galilean families losing their lands (for instance in "drought years") to richer land-owners who paid taxes for them but, in return, took their land, reducing former owners to tenant farmers or sharecroppers. In places around the Sea of Galilee, Herod's building programs induced a little economic, employment, and population growth due to building projects in Sepphoris and Tiberias, agricultural and manufacturing diversification, and Hellenist elites building estates near richer rural villages. But these initiatives increased inequalities between exploiting richer, urban-based, largely Greek-speaking people and exploited, Aramaic-speaking serfs, peasants, small farmers, small businessmen, and artisans, including carpenters (Jensen, 2012: 45). Such people recognized their relative deprivations, fueling frustrations and aggressive tendencies (see Eberts and Schwirian, 1968), with a subsequent rise of the Zealot movement. The Zealot movement aided many Galilean peasants as they fought, often violently, against their tax-collecting rulers (Zeitlin, 1988: 30 ff).

These conditions follow from what happened frequently when a dominant power routinely oversees a subdued rural population in societies like the one in which Jesus lived. "Accomplishments," such as income and population growth, could produce political and socioeconomic unrest due to higher taxes, widespread administrative corruption, and increased inequality as publicans collected taxes on a "highest bidder" status for Roman tribute. Josephus (94) mentioned that over a dozen "rebel bands," like those of "The Egyptian" and "Judas the Galilean," developed in Galilee. Judas the Galilean and his family of nascent Zealots provided leadership in the tax revolts. The insurgent Zealot movement envisioned an independent Israel once again. Starting in rural Galilee, the peasants and Zealots upset social relations among themselves and their Roman-Herodian rulers, and Temple priests and officials. Overall conditions became increasingly tense and disruptive.

An example of a tax revolt came in 6CE, when Jesus was nearing his teen years (he was an adult according to people of his times) and Romans tried to take a population census in order to raise taxes. Again, Judas the Galilean, among others, resisted. Many Galilean peasants saw this Judas as a patriot who preached that Jews should have an independent nation and not pay any taxes to Rome (Judas the Galilean, 2012). When Judas was killed, his sons and grandsons carried on, joined by many peasants. Horsley (2011: 181-182) estimated that Roman crucifixions were in the thousands as the 66-70 rebellion approached and increased until the Zealot-led Jewish uprising was finally quelled. Consistent with Roman practices, most crucified bodies were left hanging to rot along Galilee's main roadways to remind others of their fate should they dare revolt against the Herods and Rome. Jesus could see firsthand the pain and anguish of crucifixion. Galilee, seemingly quiescent for centuries, became a hotbed for violent Zealot resistance to Rome and its puppet governments of Herodians, Sadducees, Sanhedrin, and priests. Throughout Jesus' life, politically, socially, and religiously Galilee was a tumultuous and chaotic region.

Social, Political, and Religious Conditions in Jerusalem

In Jesus' time, Jerusalem was a one-industry town with religion as its economic base. With 30,000-40,000 permanent residents, Jerusalem was the smaller of Judea's two major cities. The Temple was the seat of Jewish authority. Over the years, the Herod family rebuilt Jerusalem's Temple into the most beautiful building between Antioch and Alexandria. It attracted people from the entire Empire, especially during the chief religious festivals (Passover, Tabernacles, "First Fruits"—*Pesach, Sukkoth, Shavuoth*). Many householders maintained facilities for Jewish pilgrims coming to these religious festivals, when the population swelled to about 100,000 people. Levite priestly families lived on the heights near the Temple along with rich merchants who served the Temple by selling animals for Temple sacrifices. The bulk of the population, including many Pharisees, scribes, shopkeepers, tradesmen, and laborers, lived in its lower levels.

In Jerusalem, despite a minority Hellenist-Jewish population, Rome let the Sanhedrin, a large Hebrew-Jewish Council, become its local government (Neusner, 1984: 30-31). The Sanhedrin, a self-coopting group of 71 Jewish higher-status men—elders, high priests, Sadducees, and certain Pharisees, presided over by the high priest—reached its pinnacle of importance just before Jerusalem's destruction in 70CE (Sanhedrin, 2012).

The Sanhedrin had a series of responsibilities. It

- legislated all aspects of Jewish religious and political life within parameters laid down by Roman law and Scriptural and Rabbinic traditions;
- administered Roman laws, meted out punishments, and recommended to the Roman governor certain criminals for capital punishment (the Sanhedrin lost the authority for capital punishment just before Jesus' ministry);
- judged accused lawbreakers (but did not initiate arrests), including adulterous wives, after a minimum of two witnesses testified against a suspect; neither prosecutors nor defendant had attorneys—an accusing witness stated the offense in the presence of the accused and the accused could call witnesses on his own behalf. The court could question the accused, accusers, and witnesses. It also held proceedings connected to discovery of a corpse; and

- resolved irregularities in ritual law and tithes; collected Biblical levies; dealt with matters pertaining to secular, religious, and Temple rituals; prepared Torah Scrolls for the king and the Temple; and drew up the official calendar (Sanhedrin, 2012).

Although the Sanhedrin was important in Jewish life, ultimate power of life and death was in Roman hands. Both the Herodians and Sanhedrin collaborated with the Romans to maintain law and order. Usually only during feast days were the Roman troops physically present in Jerusalem. In their absence, the Sanhedrin was mainly responsible for law and order in Jerusalem.

Romans, Herodians, and Hellenists

After Rome conquered the Hasmonean Dynasty and even during Jesus' lifetime, the entire region of Galilee, Samaria, and Judea were informally partitioned into about equal land sizes of about 25 by 50 miles. Judea was an area with a Jewish majority. Majorities in Samaria and the Fertile-Crescent trade-route coastline were predominantly Greek-speaking and Hellenistic. Jews in Galilee were a larger minority but still a minority (Galilee, 2013). Tensions between Galilean Jews and Samaritans were so high that Galilean Jews tended to avoid Samaria when traveling the Jordan River route to and from Jerusalem.

The major seat of Roman and Herodian power over the entire region was in Caesarea on the Samarian coast (see Fig 1, Map). It was a Greek city of about 100,000 people, three times the size of Jerusalem. This Caesarea (later scholars added the name "Maritima" to distinguish it from Caesarea Philippi, north of the Sea of Galilee, named for Herod Philip) was built by Herod the Great to be his capital and named it for his patron, Caesar Augustus (Padfield, 2012). With streets designed in a Greek-grid pattern, it featured a large marble temple to Augustus, magnificent palaces and public buildings, a hippodrome, an amphitheater seating 45,000 spectators on the city's southern edge facing the sea, and a beautiful 40-acre artificial harbor with breakwaters 200 feet wide in a graceful arc 600 yards long that extended 250 yards into the sea. This superb and busy city, located near the main caravan route from the Fertile Crescent and Phoenicia to Egypt, made it attractive to settlers. The city's culture mixed both minority Jews, who clung to the worship of "one God" and abhorred the presence of pagan idols, with a majority Greco-Roman population which used idols in their religious practices. During the horrendous battles of the Jewish-Roman War of 66 to 70CE, Jews killed many Greeks there but were ultimately annihilated by the Greeks and Romans.

In Caesarea the Roman governor commanded about 3,000 well-trained Roman troops. More troops could be supplied, as needed, by his superior, the Roman governor of Syria. During each Jewish pilgrimage feast, the governor and Roman legionnaires occupied Jerusalem, billeted at one end of the Temple plaza in the Fortress Antonia. For a people who celebrated God's promise of equality, freedom, and justice (*"Let my people go!"* Exodus 5:1) in their annual Passover Festival, this reminder of Roman power and authority was a continuing source of irritation to leading and ordinary Jews alike (Crosson, 1998: 575 ff, Epilogue). Galilean and Judean citizens in their daily routines rarely saw Romans. Herodians were the visible political entity. Jews mainly saw tax collectors (*"publicans"*), whom they considered corrupt and *"sinners"* (Luke 3:13), as the most visible sign of Rome's power and authority. But every Jew knew that Rome was the source of wealth, cruelty, inequality, and problems in the Jewish state.

Most Jews recognized that Jerusalem's Sanhedrin collaborated with the Romans in maintaining law and order. This recognition also fueled the insurgent Zealot movement. In 66CE a full-scale Jewish revolt against the Sanhedrin and Rome broke out, resulting in widespread destruction by its end in 70CE. The war fell into two distinct phases. The Roman General Vespasian, soon to become the next Roman Emperor, first, wanted to obliterate revolt in Galilee so that Judea and Jerusalem, his ultimate targets, could not be reinforced from there. In 68CE, the death of the Emperor Nero delayed these plans. A year of civil war in Rome ensued between the forces of three different individuals who sought the emperorship. In this time, Zealot forces united in the Temple district with Jewish insurrectionists from all over the area. Vespasian's son, Titus, led the final siege, then destruction, of the Temple and Jerusalem.

Following the final Jewish-Roman War ending in 135CE, the name, Judah (Judea, in Greek; in Hebrew, *Yehud Medinata*), which had existed through Persian and Hellenistic to Herodian and Roman times, was re-designated to *Syria Palaestina*. Judea as a geographical location was lost until officially revived in the 20th century as part of the Israeli district name for most of the West Bank, Judean, and Samarian areas.

Hellenism in Galilee, Judea, Samaria, and the Early Jesus Movement

Hellenist civilization in the Near East was created by the conquests of Alexander the Great near the end of the fourth centuryBCE. Within 20 years after his premature death in 323BCE, his generals divided the empire into three large jurisdictions, which extended from Greece to India and Egypt. One major area that survived intact into the first centuryBCE was the Seleucid kingdom. It ranged from Assyria on the upper Tigris River to Babylon (its overall capital), to Syria, Galilee, and Judea. Another major area was the Ptolemaic kingdom in Egypt, established in 305BCE. It continued until Caesar Augustus conquered it in 31BCE. Since Judea, Samaria, Galilee, and the Fertile Crescent trade routes were located at the end-points of these two powerful kingdoms, the three small Jewish provinces near their western (to the Seleucids) or northern (to the Ptolemies) borders were often in contention by these two powers or their allies. Hellenistic culture, however, remained a staple in both empires.

Leaders in the Seleucid and Ptolemaic kingdoms thought Hellenistic ideas provided the basis for the greatest of all civilizations. Greek language, philosophy, law, and rationality in politics, science, literature, poetry, drama, medicine, and so forth were considered the finest the world had ever seen. The Seleucids and Ptolemies never ceased in shaping their worlds around these ideas and ideals, including even the designs of cities into grid patterns with wide avenues and many columns, a variety of public buildings, and open spaces for market-places (in Greek, *agoras*) and other uses.

Hellenism also impacted Jewish culture. By the second centuryBCE Jews in Ptolemaic Alexandria translated Hebrew Scriptures into Greek, producing the Septuagint, a translation which greatly influenced Jews living in other predominantly Hellenistic cities. The Septuagint, read daily in Hellenist-Jewish synagogues, made it easier for "Hellenist Hebrews" to accommodate to a Greek-dominated society largely endorsed by the Roman Empire. Hellenist Jews in Caesarea (Maritima), for instance, also attended theatrical productions, symposia, "games," and other Greek-oriented events.

In Alexandria, Philo (ca 20BCE to 50CE) was an example of the intense Hellenization of Judaism. He was a philosopher and Scriptural interpreter trying to effect a synthesis between Scripture and Platonic and Stoic philosophy (among others, Philo, 2013). He believed that the Scriptural word of God, the logos, the divine reason, a Platonist idea, was conceived as being in the mind of God. To this Platonist philosophical model he added a Stoic one, the immanent rationality of the world, built upon the Stoic idea that reason constitutes the inner working of the world. The Hebrew meanings of both God and humankind, then, were restated in terms of Platonist and Stoic philosophy. His theology greatly affected the prologue to John's Gospel.

Hellenism in Judaism was often an occasion for conflict. The Hasmonean family led a revolt against Jewish Hellenism that lasted for the eight decades of their rule (141 to 63BCE). This outward revolt was quelled by the Romans when their legions took charge in Jerusalem. At least three Hellenist synagogues remained in Jerusalem (Acts 6:9). The revolt's effects simmered through Christian ministry down to the final total destruction of Jerusalem in 135CE and the expulsion of all Jews from the province.

Conflicts broke out in the Jesus movement when the Hellenist-Christian Stephen was brought before the Sanhedrin to have his beliefs reviewed. The Sanhedrin condemned them as blasphemy and Stephen was stoned to death in Jerusalem. A conflict continued when Saul (later Paul) volunteered to go to Damascus to root out remnants of "The Way," one of the names for the Hellenist-Christian party, that had lodged in the Seleucids' provincial capital city (Acts 6-9).

Previously, Jesus personally recruited Hellenists from the highest ranks of Jerusalem society—Nicodemus the Pharisee who was a member of the Sanhedrin, Joseph of Arimathea who had to be wealthy in order to own a large tomb, the family of Lazarus of Bethany and Jerusalem who owned houses in both places, possibly also Mary Magdalene whose family in Galilee owned a fish-processing plant. All these people were residents in Jerusalem when Jesus was crucified. Hellenists in the Jesus movement were confident enough in their status to form one of the four major parties in the movement and to establish permanent governance for its party in the persons of the Seven (Acts 6:3). Stephen and one of the Galilean-Twelve, Philip, were members of the Seven (Acts 6:5). They gave leadership to the movement's Hellenist segment just as the Twelve and Jesus' brother James gave leadership to the Hebrew parties. They enshrined their position in the Jesus movement through Stephen's impassioned speech recorded in Acts 6 and 7, for which he was condemned to death, through the statements of their ideas in the Gospel of John and the "Letter to the Hebrews," and through their missions into Samaria, Gaza, Egypt, Ephesus, Corinth, and probably Rome itself (see Eberts 2011, passim).

Jewish Parties in Jerusalem and Judea during Jesus' Ministry

Due to these chaotic conditions, as Jesus started his ministry a key issue was, "Given these times, what was next for Israel—what does its one God intend for the Jews?" The various Jewish religious groups in Jerusalem had differing answers to this question. Most sought some version of living in accord with traditional Jewish Torah Law. But they contended with one another on how to interpret the Torah during the Roman version of imposed "peace," *Pax Romana*. All disagreed with Jesus' interpretation.

As typical in Roman and other agriculturally-based societies, Jerusalem was dominated by major status groups (Romans, Herodians, Hebrew Sadducees, Temple priests, Pharisees, Scribes, Hellenists). Among the Jews, Sadducees were in the top status and generally seen as either explicitly or tacitly collaborating with Roman rulers in keeping law and order. Pharisees were another high-ranking influential group. The Essenes largely ignored the top status groups and Roman rulers. Two others (Zealots and Sicarii) violently opposed the Romans and their collaborators. Each status group was "closed" in that much socializing went on *within* each one but with little mixing *among* them (except for official or semi-official transactions). The *Herodians*—sons, relatives, cousins, close friends, and officials of Herod the Great—were Rome's stand-in secular rulers. Their bureaucracy included tax collectors, accountants, scribes, family servants, overseers of peasants on the Herods' extensive land-holdings, police, and a small militia (Romans were the main military force). The unorganized peasantry, "the people" of the Gospels, were the lowest status grouping.

Sadducees were richer highest-status Hebrew Jews who administered affairs through the Temple priesthood (many Sadducees were from priestly Levite families) and the Sanhedrin. They collaborated with Romans and Herodians to impose law and order and subdue hostilities with Rome. The priests with their huge, magnificent, golden Temple, constructed largely by Herod the Great, were supported by a thriving Temple commerce for sacrifices and a Temple tax on all Jews—in Jerusalem, Judea, and Galilee, which extended to even distant Diaspora cities (Horsley, 2011: 134).

Much Sadducean wealth was inherited but other wealth came from Temple functions. Priests presided over Temple worship and, for a fee, administered various kinds of animal sacrifices, with appropriate ritualized ceremonies, before the Sabbath and during week-long "Feast" days. Merchants openly sold animals to worshipers in the Temple's outer courts. Especially when a high priest entered the Holy of Holies, the Temple's inner sanctum for communing with God, the priests believed they represented all Jews.

Pharisees were primarily laymen, well-educated in and deeply committed to Torah Law, while trying to reconcile it with its various interpretations. They looked forward to a time when God's reign would be vindicated and Judea and Galilee would be at peace. To prepare for this and to live their lives righteously, they kept Jewish Torah Law in detail in their daily routines. Jesus might initially have studied to be a Pharisee but eventually differed from them on key issues (Zeitlin, 1988: 11 ff). The Gospels record that Pharisees were aggressively trying to bring all Jews under such religious authority and thus often came in conflict with Jesus and his followers when their ideas diverged. After Jesus' resurrection, a small but identifiable group of Pharisees either converted to the "Brethren" party within the early Jesus movement or became a Pharisee-Christian party on their own (Acts 15:5).

Scribes, possibly the only people in Jerusalem who could read and write in Greek, Hebrew, and Aramaic, were a clearly recognizable group in this complex mix of people in Jerusalem and Judea. They aligned themselves with those who used their skills, primarily the Sadducees, priests, and Sanhedrin, as well as Pharisees (Mt 2:4). Matthew's Gospel, especially, noted that *"Scribes and Pharisees"* were frequently together questioning Jesus about his beliefs and intents (Mt 5:20, 12:38, 15:1, etc).

Essenes lived apart from those who did not hold their beliefs, in one of several communes, and devoted their lives wholly to God (Zeitlin, 1988: 24 ff). Qumran, a site on the cliffs overlooking the Dead Sea but within walking distance of both Jericho and Jerusalem, was probably their largest commune (Qumran, 1998, 2013). Essenes believed their monastic, communal, prayerful, non-violent lifestyle prefigured the coming Kingdom of God. Their exclusive community was composed only of able-bodied adult Jewish males. The blind, lame, diseased, or females, need not apply. They sought righteousness according to their interpretations of Judaism's historical traditions. They maintained their population sizes through welcoming adult males and healthy orphans into their communes. Since his parents were quite old when he was born, John the Baptist may have been such an orphan. Jesus was the Essenes' antithesis—he lived and worked within Jewish communities and throughout his ministry healed the blind, lame, and diseased, whether male or female.

Resident *Hellenist Jews* were recognized in Acts (6:1) as a set of relatively well-off and well-organized resident minorities in Jerusalem. Having their own synagogues in Jerusalem according to the regions where their extended Diaspora families lived (Acts 6:9) made Hellenist Jews less well-integrated with one another than if they would have had just one Hellenist synagogue. They all spoke Greek in their daily lives and used the Septuagint, the official Greek Scriptural translation, in their worship services and education programs. Such practices set them apart from resident Hebrew Jews. Hellenist Jews recognized Jerusalem as the center of Jewish religious life while differing from Hebrew Jews in their theologies and ethics (Acts 6, 7). Hellenist Jews questioned the Temple's legitimacy—previous to the "first" Temple of King David, the Ark of the Covenant traveled from place to place—and even whether Torah Law came directly from

God. They were much less committed to the letter of Torah Law than Hebrew-Jews.

Such beliefs conflicted with Jerusalem's Hebrew majority. These conflicts bubbled up occasionally within the early Jesus movement, most notably soon after the resurrection. A proximate outcome of deep-seated socio-religious differences between Hellenists and Hebrews resulted in the stoning of Stephen (Acts 7:58-60). After his death, Hellenist, Galilean, and some Hebrew-Brethren followers of Jesus were banned from Jerusalem and *"scattered"* to rural Judea, Samaria, and other places in the eastern Mediterranean (Acts 8:1-2). An unintended but significant consequence of this scattering was the spread of the Jesus movement throughout the Roman Empire.

Zealots and Sicarii, identified by Josephus as a "fourth sect" (with Sadducees, Pharisees, and Essenes), believed Jews could only follow the Law if they had political independence (Zeitlin, 1988: 29 ff; Crosson, 1998; Horsley, 1985, 1996, 2011). They felt the *religious* duty of all Jews was to fight, literally, for such independence from Rome (or any other oppressor). Such beliefs led the Zealots to prepare for war and conspire to see that it happened. Many Jews responded to this call even when Romans considered the Zealots traitors and crucified them. Among his closest chosen disciples, Jesus included a Zealot (Simon the Zealot) and probably a Sicarii (Judas Iscariot).

Sicarii were Zealot terrorists who used a short knife called a *sicarius*, hidden under their robes, to kill Roman soldiers and Jewish collaborators when they found them alone and unaware of the danger. Zealot and Sicarii commitments, policies, and strategies eventually engaged nearly all Jews in the war with Rome in 66CE. Although it started in Galilee, by 70CE this conflagration resulted in destroying Herod's great and beautiful Temple and much of Jerusalem.

Such destruction devastated Judaism. Its leaders were killed, enslaved, or fled. To continue their faith, remaining rabbis looked to discover a new form of Judaism, which became known as rabbinic Judaism (Neusner, 1984: 30). The early Jesus movement was deeply affected by both the war and this movement. Due to the war, the Brethren-Christian party based in Jerusalem was scattered throughout the eastern Mediterranean, most notably to Egypt where the Gospel of Matthew was probably composed.

"The people of the land," as in most Roman and other similar "patron-client" societies, were the largest but lowest status group of all (Grant, 1975; Lenski and Lenski, 1987: 205 ff). They were a disparate, non-cohesive, and powerless majority that included peasants, serfs, slaves, laborers, lower-status craftsmen, small-hold farmers and their families, orphans, widows, the lame and diseased, and those dependent on others for their livelihoods whose dominant religious beliefs were probably based on Moses' Covenant (see Eberts, 2011: ch 2). People from Galilee were given an even lower status than those from Judea. As "guileless" Nathanael remarked near the beginning of John's Gospel (1:46), *"Can any good come out of Nazareth [in Galilee]?"*

These status groups and parties composed the basic social hierarchy in Judea and Galilee in Jesus' time. Each believed it had the answer to what God intended for the Jews. Jesus came into conflict with each one. The odds were stacked against Jesus' physical survival in these conflicts. The prevailing message was, "Kill the messenger and the message will die!" (see John 11:47-50). Who among the various status groups would rescue him or even defend him? Not the Romans; not the Herodians; not the Sanhedrin; not the Eleven; not even Peter and the Twelve. The future looked bleak indeed.

Social Conditions of Four Major Jesus-Movement Parties

Initially after Jesus' resurrection according to Acts, all of Jesus' followers were in basic agreement (1:14). But Acts also records that they soon devolved into four major, reasonably well-organized "parties." Our first book (2009) identified their appearances in Jerusalem and our second book (2011) demonstrated their diffusion throughout the eastern Roman Empire. A first distinction was between Hellenists and Hebrews (Acts 6:1-3). The early-Jesus Hebrews from Jerusalem (later known as the Brothers of Jesus, the Brethren, possibly because its leader, James, was probably Jesus' blood brother) came into conflict with Hellenists over their interpretations of Jewish history (Acts 6, 7). Acts also distinguished between Disciples, Apostles, and Hellenists (9:26-27). First Corinthians identified four parties according to their leaders. *"Each one of you says, 'I belong to Paul,' 'I belong to Apollos,' 'I belong to Cephas (Peter),' and, 'I belong to Christ'"* (1:12). Paul's party was the Apostles (Acts 9:26-27); Apollos was from Hellenist Christians in Alexandria (Acts 18:24; 1 Cor 16:14); Peter was the Disciple's leader; the "Christ" party probably referred to the Brothers (Brethren).

Although the parties' constituencies were all initially Jews living in Jerusalem after the resurrection, they were distinguished by two basic criteria. One criterion was the primary ethnic background of the members' parties, whether wholly Hebrew or whether Hellenist Jews where their Jewishness mixed culturally with Greek Hellenists. The second criterion was the geographic location from which the parties' original followers came, whether having come from inside Jerusalem (Brethren and resident Hellenists) or from outside it (the Twelve Galilean Disciples and the Apostles, including sons of non-resident Hellenist-sympathetic Jews in Diaspora places). The Brethren (Brothers) and Hellenist Christians emerged from Jesus' followers who lived most of their lives in Jerusalem. The Twelve, Disciples, lived most of their lives in Galilee. The Apostles party was formed by followers who initially lived in smaller Hellenist-dominated Eastern Mediterranean cities but came to Jerusalem separate from their families (Paul was from Tarsus, Barnabas from Cyprus, and, later, Luke from northern Asia Minor).

Figure 3 offers a general outline of these four parties. It shows their different emphases, including in their basic theologies. Key was how the four parties interpreted Jewish history. Galileans and Brethren tended to emphasize Jesus' close continuity with Jewish history whereas Hellenists and Apostles tended to see Jesus as showing less such continuity and more "universal" appeal to all Roman and Greek Hellenists. From these different theologies stemmed other differences as in their ethical prescriptions and the very vocabularies used in their Gospels as they interpreted Jesus' life to their fellow constituents (see Eberts 2009, *The Early Jesus Movement and Its Parties*; Figure 3 on the next page; and Figure 5 in Part Two that follows). Although Jesus' followers eventually went to *"all nations"* to explain Jesus Christ's importance to all Jews and Gentiles, the Brethren tended to go primarily to Diaspora Hebrew Jews, the Disciples to Diaspora Jews who had accommodated with Hellenist culture, the Hellenists to Hellenist-Jews in Diaspora cities, and the Apostles to Greek-Hellenists. Table 2 in Chapter 2 of our 2011 book cites 43 different cities or towns in the Roman Empire where followers of at least one of the four parties were found by 60cE. Such differences were consistent with how these four parties represented a different constituency and perspective. Later, from the struggles these constituencies faced, each party produced a Gospel aimed at its primary constituency. In doing this, each party left distinctive marks on its Gospel (the subject of the present book).

The *Brethren (Brothers)* party was initially a Jerusalem-based party of Hebrew-Christians whose theology saw them in a renewed covenant with God (Fig 3). Its leader, James, has traditionally been identified as Jesus' blood brother but certainly a "brother in fellowship" (the Greek word *adelphos* could refer to either). From its beginning, the Brethren believed that, since Jesus was a Jew, possibly even a Pharisee, the Brethren closely followed Torah Law and its exclusionary practices of separating women from men and Jews from Greeks in many ways (Acts 15). The Brethren consolidated

	Twelve	**Brethren**	**Hellenists**	**Apostles**
Primary leader	Peter	James	Philip and the "Beloved Disciple"	Barnabas and Paul
Primary constituency	Galileans and Judeans living near the Coast	Torah-observant Hebrews in Jerusalem	Hellenist-Jews, initially in Jerusalem, then Diaspora cities	Diaspora synagogues and their Gentile friends
Primary goal of party	To bring spirit of Jesus to Galileans, Gazans, and other nearby "coastal" communities	To turn Torah-observant Jewish synagogues into Jesus-observant synagogues	To convert Hellenist-Jewish synagogues into Hellenist-Christian synagogues	To build communities of "the Body of Christ... [where] neither Jew nor Greek, slave nor free, men and women... free from the yoke of law... [could be] new creations."
Basic Theology	Successors to Israel	Renewed Covenant	Entirely "New Covenant"	People "in Christ"
Gospel	Mark	Matthew	John	Luke
Source: Eberts and Eberts, 2009: 91, Figure 5				

Figure 3. Overview of the Four Major Parties in the Early Jesus Movement, their Primary Leaders, Constituencies, and Overall Goals.

their power by successfully converting more formerly-Hebrew synagogues to Christianity in Jerusalem and other key Roman Empire cities and towns than any other party (see Eberts, 2011, Table 2.2). When Peter was imprisoned in, then escaped and fled from, Jerusalem, James took charge of the Jesus movement there and considered the Brethren's exclusionary practices normative for all within the entire Jesus movement (Acts 12:17 ff). Brethren even rebuked Peter, Paul, and Barnabas for breaking the Law when they ate with Gentiles (Acts 11:1-3, 14, 15). In a major conference of leaders about 50CE, James made a significant concession to the other parties when he, other Brethren, and even a Pharisee-Christian party acquiesced in accepting Gentiles into the movement without first being circumcised. Yet the Brethren insisted that all followers must strictly adhere to other Torah Laws, including laws on food, marriage, and keeping the commandments (Acts 15:20-21).

Hellenist Christians (called Hellenists in Acts 6, 7), initially Greek-speaking Jews who resided permanently in Jerusalem, apparently began their party during Jesus' three-year ministry in Jerusalem and Judea and remained in Jerusalem after Jesus' resurrection, trying to take their place beside James and other Hebrew-Christians. But, Acts reported that Hebrews and Hellenists were in tension with one another (*"the Hellenists murmured against the Hebrews because their widows were neglected in the daily distribution,"* 6:1). Stephen's defense of Hellenist Christianity shows that the tensions were deeper than daily distributions suggest. Hebrews and Hellenists differed on the importance of the Temple and Torah Law in Jewish life which indicates deep differences in their basic theologies. The Hellenist Stephen's speech in Acts 6 and 7 demonstrated a belief that God was not limited to a single Temple but, as with the Ark of the Covenant among earlier Hebrew tribes, moves from one place and one ethnic group to another. Such a belief seemed to surprise Hebrew Jews who thought and acted as if all Jews believed the great and beautiful Temple in Jerusalem was God's primary residence. The Hebrews resented such Hellenist beliefs to the point that they stoned the Hellenist Stephen to death.

How could Hebrew and Hellenist Jews with such contrasting theological views live side by side in Jerusalem and not recognize, or take steps to resolve, such differences? Probably the main reason was that each group seldom interacted outside its own "status-exclusive" grouping—each had its own synagogue (Acts 6:9) and probably did not mix much socially or even commercially. Hebrew Jews mostly talked with other Hebrews about theology and ethics and Hellenist Jews talked with other Hellenists on these topics. The twain apparently seldom met. Mutual understanding, trust, and tolerance of differences between them were low. In any case, as noted above, a deadly rift grew between them that resulted in Stephen's death by stoning (Acts 6-7) and the subsequent expulsion of the whole Hellenist-Christian party, and perhaps Hellenist Jews, from Jerusalem (Acts 8:1).

The Jesus movement verged on dissolution. But the scattering sent followers to major and minor cities throughout the eastern Mediterranean region where they spread their understanding of how God was in Christ. Rome, Ephesus, Alexandria, Corinth, Antioch, and Damascus were key recipients of the emigrants. From their Greek backgrounds, Hellenist Jews were comfortable in dealing with Greek Gentiles and the wide range of ideas and concepts Greeks used. More than the other Gospels, the Hellenists' Gospel of John used key Hellenist concepts, such as *"word," "truth," "life," "love," "darkness," "light," "eternal life," "the way,"* in their oral and written traditions. Hellenist Christians in giving Christian emphases to traditional Greek concepts played significant roles in converting the wider world of Greek-Gentiles into the Jesus movement (as in Paul's "Letter to the Philippians," in Eberts, 2011, ch 6).

Jews raised from childhood outside Jerusalem had different experiences from those raised inside Jerusalem. They often lived in places dominated by Hellenists in cities such as Sepphoris and Tiberias and towns such as Capernaum and Bethsaida, in effect forcing them to interact with Greek Gentiles on a wide variety of issues. Jews in such settings had to do business with Greek Gentiles and handle political issues with them. Smaller places, as in Galilee, would have only one synagogue that facilitated dealings among Hebrew- and Hellenist-Jews. Such instances helped them to be sympathetic to, and even trust, people from different backgrounds who espoused a wider variety of beliefs not their own. Jews inside Jerusalem who lived, relatively, as "isolated masses" or "isolated blocs," worked with and trusted mainly those from similar backgrounds to their own—their "own people" (see Flora and Flora, 2003).

The *Twelve* Disciples included both Hebrew and Hellenist Jews from towns in Galilee—Andrew, Philip, Thaddeus, and even Peter had Greek names. Peter became the de facto leader of the *Twelve* and, according to Acts, Philip later became a leader in the Hellenist party (6:5). But even the Twelve lived under repressive social and economic conditions imposed by Herodian collaborators of Roman rulers. The Herodians were mostly Hellenists who dominated both Hebrew and Hellenist Jews in Galilee. Most Galileans lived in small villages that have always been subject to intimidation by outside forces. Some Galilean Jews remembered a better time when they were citizens of an all-Jewish state and now continued to fight, literally, for it. Jesus and his Disciples eschewed violence. They stood for principles that responded to meeting people's immediate distresses directly, including healing the sick, lame, and blind, and feeding the hungry. In contrast, Jerusalem's Sanhedrin tended to collaborate with Romans and Herodians in exacting Temple and land taxes from Galileans while neglecting their downtrodden and in the process creating greater inequality. Still, the mixing of Hebrew and Hellenist Jews in Galilee contributed to the Twelve's ability to understand Hellenist modes of life more fully, which helped them as they extended the Jesus movement beyond Galilee.

The *Apostles* were Jews from both Greek-Hebrew and Hebrew-Hebrew families who came from Diaspora cities which usually had overwhelming Hellenist majorities (Cyprus, Tarsus). The Apostles undoubtedly had non-Jewish Hellenist friends and acquaintances in these cities so that they, too, were more likely to understand Hellenist beliefs and traditions, including obvious status inequalities. They were newcomers in Jerusalem who became Jesus' followers, some before, others soon after, his resurrection.

Perhaps being composed of idealistic young men who built on Jesus' inclusiveness and equal treatment for all in his beliefs and practices, initially the Apostles, Peter, and others perhaps intended to form a community similar to Qumran's, in which each participant contributed his property to the community in return for lifetime care of each member's necessities (*"And all who believed were together and had all things in common; and they sold their possessions and goods and distributed them to all, as any had need"*; Acts 2:44-45). Such a community would be very different from male-only Qumran with its exclusionary policies. It would include both men and women, husbands and wives, free and slaves, diseased and well, and, eventually, Jew and Gentile (Galatians 3:28).

But it did not work out in practice. Two older neophytes, Ananias and Sapphira, husband and wife, promised to give their entire property to the community but then reneged (Acts 5:1 ff). Under intense questioning by community leaders, first Ananias and then Sapphira suddenly collapsed and died. Chastened, the Apostles settled into practices similar to those of the Disciples and Brethren. They preached in the Temple and, when arrested on trespass charges, went to prison as part of their witness to Christ. But they also continued fellowship meals where all were welcome which facilitated an understanding of people from various backgrounds (Crosson, 1998: 433-441, calls them "communal meals"). Such actions were essential in successfully spreading the Jesus movement throughout the Roman world.

The aftermath of Paul's journey to Damascus elucidated the extent of differences among the parties in the early Jesus movement. Saul went toward Damascus with the Sanhedrin's approval to "root out" Hellenist Christians (known as *"followers of the Way"*; Acts 9:2). But on his way he encountered Christ and became convinced that Christ had very different plans for him (prompting him, among other things, to change his name to Paul). In Damascus he was helped by Disciples, so when he returned to Jerusalem, he tried to join the Disciples party. But they refused him. The Apostle Barnabas, from Cyprus, interceded and invited Paul to join the Apostles (Acts 9:26-28). While Hellenist Christians, among others, were thrown out of Jerusalem following Stephen's stoning, the Apostles were not thrown out (Acts 8:1). Still, Paul along with Barnabas soon left Jerusalem voluntarily and returned thereafter only occasionally to meet with the Disciples' Peter and the Brethren's James regarding his mission. Such inter-party tensions within the Jesus movement persisted among the parties (see Eberts, 2011).

Changes in Early Jesus-Movement Parties Stemming from their Socioeconomic, Political, and Religious Situations

Most changes in the four parties of the early Jesus movement were due to early Jesus-movement followers working with Greek Gentiles. Since Alexander the Great, Hellenistic culture dominated the Mediterranean world outside Jerusalem. Each party encountered it, even if in different ways. The Gospels tell the stories of the ministry of Jesus of Nazareth as viewed from four different socio-religious-geographic parties that responded positively to him.

The *Twelve,* Galilean Jews, whose lifestyles delineated their differences from Hellenist pagans around them placed great importance on the Passover—eating the meal celebrating God's deliverance of, and promises to, them. They kept the Torah Law as they understood it, which included circumcision and eating only certain foods with other Jews, making them an exclusive community through which they found support and comfort in their chaotic world.

Early after Jesus' resurrection, the restored Twelve (Judas Iscariot having committed suicide) faced a crisis. In Caesarea (Maritima), its leader Peter was invited to the house of the Roman centurion, Cornelius, who had heard about Jesus of Nazareth and wanted to learn more about him. As Peter and Cornelius spoke, they became aware that something new and exciting was happening to them. The spirit of the

Christ seemed to flow from their conversations. Cornelius asked to be baptized, and Peter replied, *"'Can any one forbid water for baptizing these people who have received the Holy Spirit just as we have?' And he commanded them to be baptized in the name of Jesus Christ"* (Acts 10:47-48). What was forbidden was that, under Torah Law, Cornelius was baptized without first being circumcised. This "first" within the Jesus movement was, to the Brethren party's James in particular, a serious departure. Peter and Cornelius also ate a meal together, another departure from Torah Law which prohibited Jews from eating with Gentiles. After Peter left Cornelius and traveled to Antioch, there again he ate meals with Gentiles. On the arrival of James' Brethren party's followers, who believed that all Jesus' followers should *strictly* adhere to Torah Law, they reprimanded Peter for what he was doing. Peter then *"pulled back"* (Galatians 2:11-12). Such changes challenged the Disciples as they sought to bring their practices into accord with Jesus' spirit.

The *Apostles* party also changed. Originally composed of Diaspora Jews living in Jerusalem, the Apostles were the only party not thrown out of Jerusalem after the stoning death of the Hellenist-Christian Stephen (Acts 8:1). But Barnabas and Paul soon left voluntarily to return to Cyprus, Barnabas' ancestral homeland. While preaching in synagogues there, they recognized, to their surprise, that Gentiles as well as Jews responded positively to what they were saying (Acts 13:16; Eberts, 2009: 47-48). Encouraged, they preached their gospel elsewhere, such as in Antioch. They returned to Jerusalem and met with Peter and James, who gave them permission to preach to and convert Gentiles. Then, formulating their message to include women, men, slaves, freedmen, Greeks, and Jews (Gal 3:28), they took their gospel into Asia Minor, Macedonia, and Greece. They welcomed everyone into their communities, called *ekklesia*, "assemblies set apart." Physically, they moved from Jerusalem to Greece, culturally they moved from being encapsulated in Judaism to becoming full participants in the Hellenistic world (Eberts, 2011: ch 8).

Hellenist Christians, who had been summarily thrown out of Jerusalem, also changed. The Hellenist-Christian leader Philip, once a member of the Twelve, fled to Samaria where he successfully preached the gospel to Greek-oriented Samaritans. On a trip to Gaza, he met an Ethiopian eunuch and showed him that the difficult passage in Scripture about "the servant who suffers" was fulfilled in Jesus Christ. Philip settled in Caesarea Maritima, where he raised a family of four daughters. Fearing the spread of violent hostilities with Rome (the beginning of the 66-70CE insurrection), Philip fled, moving to Ephesus. There, with its message of God's love as revealed in Jesus Christ, the Hellenist-Christian party flourished, eventually writing its Gospel of John there.

Even the *Brethren* party changed. Its initial exclusionary practices of Torah Law separated Jews from Greeks and women from men. After Peter's arrest, escape, and self-imposed exile from Jerusalem, James and his party considered themselves in charge of the entire Jesus movement and set their practices as normative for all in the movement, whether they lived in Jerusalem or not. But when James was arrested and executed prior to the 66-70 war (Josephus, 94: 598), the Brethren underwent a major crisis. The party's new leadership could not exert James' authority. The war with Rome that resulted in destroying Jerusalem's Temple made most Brethren flee from Jerusalem in terror. Some went east over the Jordan River into Perea, others northwest to Antioch, Ephesus, and Greece, others southwest to Egypt. In Ephesus the Brethren's John the Seer later wrote Revelation (in the 90sCE) during his grueling slavery—for not sacrificing to the goddess Roma—in the blistering heat of Rome's granite mines on Patmos Island. This John insisted that Christians by all means should resist the Roman Empire. Yet, probably in Egypt, Brethren's experiences helped the party restate and moderate many of its previously rigidly exclusionary positions as it wrote their Gospel of Matthew. The Brethren's theological and ethical stances were radically different in the early 80sCE (when they probably wrote their Gospel) from what they were in 50ce (of Acts 15).

Although the Jesus movement was imperiled by being *"scattered"* from Jerusalem (Acts 8:1), this major challenge gave the early Jesus movement an opportunity to deal with all kinds of people in large and small Roman Empire places outside Jerusalem, Judea, and Galilee. Another major challenge was that during the late 50s and early 60sce the movement's first generation of leaders was passing away, some by natural causes but many by Roman hands. Eyewitnesses' first-hand accounts from knowing Jesus personally were increasingly rare in the parties' *ekklesia*. Some of these key informants' testimonies were saved through oral statements and others through letters written by individuals to congregations with which they worked. But soon followers in the four parties began to write longer documents about Jesus, from his early life to his death and resurrection. Eventually some of these writings were formed into Gospels. They were not 21st century biographies. They were written by people who strongly believed Jesus was God's anointed but who were also members of different parties telling the "good news," the gospel, as they understood it, to their colleagues and constituents. Because the Gospels were written by key informants in different parties, they saw Jesus through differing lens. Similarities, differences, and various "meanings," even of the same event as it is presented in each Gospel, are key topics in the remainder of this book.

Part Two

A Chronology of the Ministry of Jesus of Nazareth

Mark's Gospel, probably written between the late 50s to early 70sCE, was the first to circulate. Both Matthew and Luke used Mark as a basic source for their Gospels. Due to their agreement, these three are called the Synoptic Gospels. Such agreement made it seem logical that Jesus' ministry began in Galilee where Jesus lived.

Chronologically, however, all four Gospels agree that Jesus' ministry began when Jesus heard John the Baptist preach in Judea, with John's Gospel providing details not found in the other Gospels on Jesus' relationship to John the Baptist and his ministry. Mark's accounts supplement John's narrative in providing details on Jesus' Galilean ministry not found in John. The accounts overlap mainly at the critical point when Jesus enters Jerusalem during his last Passover and goes to his death on the cross. Even here the Gospels give similar but not identical accounts of events.

The late C. H. Dodd (1963) at the University of Cambridge in England made the most compelling case for the authenticity of historical traditions in the fourth Gospel. Despite that the Gospel writer John worked his materials into a somewhat contrived event-dialogue-monologue form found frequently in his Gospel, Dodd is so certain of John's authenticity that he devoted over 87 pages to details separating John's work from the others (1963: 64-151). Dodd concludes, "The basic tradition on which this Evangelist was working was shaped in a Jewish-Christian environment still in touch with the synagogue, in Palestine, at a relatively early date, at any rate before the rebellion in AD 66" (1963: 426). Dodd suggests three distinct traditions found in John's Gospel that differ from those found in the other Gospels.

First, John had teaching materials drawn from sources, "key informants," different from those in the Synoptic Gospels of Matthew, Mark, and Luke.

Second, John's Gospel demonstrates knowledge of the culture, geography, and topography of Judea and Jerusalem seldom found in the other Gospels. He gave Hebrew or Aramaic names to places known by those names in Jesus' time. He frequently supplied a Greek equivalent for a Hebrew name, as he did with *Gabbatha* (the high ground from which Fortress Antonia could oversee the whole Temple area), *Golgatha* (the *Calvary* of the crucifixion), *"Rabbi' (which means Teacher)"* (John 1:38), and *"We have found the Messiah (which means Christ)"* (Jn 1:41). John's Gospel also provides an urban perspective that contrasts with the others' focus on Jesus' rural-village Galilean ministry.

Third, John reports events in Jesus' arrest, trial, execution, and reunion with his followers that are independent of those in the other Gospels.

In contrast, Mark's Gospel, set primarily in Galilee and environs, delivers layers of information about Jesus' ministry there—his healings (Mark 1:21-2:12) and his controversies about fasting, Sabbath, forgiveness, and the kingdom of God (Mk 2:13-3:35, 4:1-34). When John the Baptist is killed, Mark's

Gospel traced Jesus' sequential activities during his trips outside Galilee (6:35-9:50), which John does not report. To receive a full picture of Jesus' ministry, the events narrated in Mark's Gospel cannot be ignored. While each incident in Mark is probably authentic in Jesus' ministry, these acts do not offer irrefutable insight into the timeline in which an event occurred.

By putting the sequential acts in Mark and John together, we can see a plausible chronology of Jesus' ministry. We cannot claim ours is *the* chronology of Jesus' life and times. We see Jesus only through the eyes of *different* friends and followers in Galilee and in Judea. These followers did not write a biography. They wrote about the good news brought by Jesus. But from these accounts a series of events occur that at least simulate a chronology of Jesus' ministry. We invite our readers to examine this chronology to see if it matches their own understanding of Jesus' ministry based on the textual materials at hand.

Since John's Gospel has a longer timeline than Mark's, we begin our chronology of Jesus' ministry with events according to John's Gospel. Then we integrate them with events in Mark's Gospel, ending with comparisons and contrasts between these two Gospels on what happened during Jesus' final Passover in Jerusalem.

When did Jesus' ministry actually begin? A line in John's Gospel provides a clue for when Jesus "cleansed the Temple" and another line in Luke's Gospel confirms the same time period. Jews who opposed Jesus' action said to him, *"It has taken forty-six years to build this temple"* (Jn 2:20). Work on the Temple began in 20-19BCE. Forty-six years after this date would be 26-27CE as the date when Jesus' cleansing act took place. More precisely, on 13th Nisan, the day before the Passover festival when Jews "purified" their houses by removing leaven from them. On this date Jesus "purified" his Father's house (MacGregor, 1959, on Jn 2:13). "Year One of Jesus' Ministry" begins in late 26CE or early 27CE. This latter date also fits with Luke's reckoning, who says that Jesus was baptized by John the Baptist *"in the fifteenth year of the reign of Tiberius Caesar"* (Lk 3:1). Since Tiberius' rule started in 14CE, this would set a date of 29CE for the beginning (and end) of Jesus' earthly ministry according to Luke. The two dates are compatible because John's Gospel gives Jesus a two-plus year start over Luke in determining the date of Jesus' ministry. Luke, following Mark's Gospel, gave Jesus a ministry of less than one year. Both put Jesus in Jerusalem in the Spring of 29CE to celebrate what became Jesus' final Passover.

Chapter 3

Year One of Jesus' Ministry

John's Gospel opens with a prologue, possibly a hymn used in worship services by Hellenist Jews, that briefly summarizes the meaning of Jesus' ministry for the world. This prologue does not refer specifically to Jewish history or traditions. It is intended for all people in all nations. It starts, *"In the beginning was the Word, and the Word was with God, and the Word was God..."* and includes *"And the Word became flesh and dwelt among us..."* and ends with *"No one has ever seen God; the only Son, who is in the bosom of the Father, he has made him known"* (1:1, 5, 14, 18). After presenting this creed, John proceeds to tell of Jesus' ministry.

This Chronology tells the story of these events. Almost every act in Jesus' ministry presented a challenge to civil or religious authorities, or both. An event's context, then, enables us to estimate the danger to Jesus from Jewish and Roman authorities occasioned by it. These dangers, too, are noted for each event.

In Judea: Jesus' Ministry Starts with John the Baptist (John 1:28-42; Mark 1:1-12; Matthew 3:1-17; Luke3:1-22)
Danger to Jesus in this episode: Low to Moderate—Herod Antipas did not arrest John's disciples, or Jesus, when he arrested John

All four Gospels describe the beginning of Jesus' ministry as taking place in Judea in Jesus' encounter with John the Baptist. As told in John's Gospel, John the Baptist was baptizing *"in Bethany beyond the Jordan"* when he saw Jesus coming toward him (Jn 1:28-29). *"Bethany beyond the Jordan"* is not to be confused with the Bethany where Mary, Martha, and Lazarus lived. The latters' Bethany was a small town outside Jerusalem over the Mount of Olives on the road to Jericho that could not be seen from Jerusalem. The Bethany where John the Baptist worked was east of the Jordan River in the desert on an important trade route to the towns east of Jericho.

The Baptist in John's Gospel contrasts with John the fiery preacher in the other Gospels. Here he serves two roles—to prepare the way for the coming one, Jesus, and to introduce this *"one who is to come"* to the world. While the Synoptic Gospels tell a longer story about the Baptist—Luke includes the Baptist's words to his followers and his imprisonment—after the Baptist introduces Jesus to others, the Baptist, somewhat curiously, disappears from John's Gospel.

When Jesus approached, John the Baptist said, *"Behold, the Lamb of God, who takes away the sin of the world! This is he of whom I said, 'After me comes a man who ranks before me, for he was before me'"* (Jn 1:29-30). In John's Gospel, John the Baptist admitted that he did not know Jesus beforehand but adds that for this reason he came baptizing, that this one *"who ranks before me"* might be revealed to Israel. John attested to his witness, *"I saw the Spirit descend as a dove from heaven, and it remained on him. I myself did not know him; but he who sent me to baptize with water said to me, 'He on whom you see the Spirit descend and remain, this is he who baptizes with the Holy Spirit. And I have seen and have borne witness that this is the Son of God'"* (Jn 1:32-34).

Mark also opens his Gospel with an account of Jesus' baptism by John the Baptist and proceeds to tell of Jesus' temptation in the wilderness. Mark's Gospel says that the Baptist *"preached, saying, 'There comes one mightier than*

I after me, the ties of whose shoes I am not worthy to stoop down and unloose'" (Mk 1:7). How did the Baptist know this about Jesus? Had Jesus already started his ministry and had a reputation for it prior to being baptized by John and prior to calling disciples to follow him? The Gospel of Luke gave an answer. Luke says, *"The disciples of John told [the Baptist] of all these things. John, calling to him two of his disciples, sent them to the Lord, saying, 'Are you he who is to come, or shall we look for another?'... In that hour Jesus cured many of diseases and plagues and evil spirits and on many that were blind he bestowed sight. He answered them, 'Go and tell John what you have seen and heard: the blind receive their sight, the lame walk, lepers are cleansed, the deaf hear, the dead are raised up, the poor have good news preached to them. Blessed is he who takes no offense at me'"* (Lk 7:18-23).

Previous to meeting the Baptist, then, Jesus practiced a ministry that included compassion for the disadvantaged, healing, and collecting followers. Certain of Jesus' followers, among them Simon, Andrew, James, John, and Philip of Bethsaida, initially followed the Baptist. But when the Baptist pointed out that Jesus was the one who was to come, they became Jesus' disciples.

"The kingdom of God is at hand" declared Jesus. Jesus' understanding of God's kingly rule centered not on keeping the Torah Law in detail as among the Pharisees, nor on Temple worship as among the Sadducees.

In John's Gospel the Baptist's witness begins a process of "naming Jesus" that continued throughout this Gospel. John's Gospel supplied various names for him. The Baptist calls Jesus

- the Lamb of God, who sacrifices himself to take away the sin of the world
- a man who ranks before me, for he was before me
- the one on whom the Spirit descends and remains
- the one who baptizes with the Holy Spirit
- the Son of God.

From Judea to Galilee: Initial Disciples in the Jesus Movement (John 1:35-51)
Danger: Low

"The next day," John told two of his disciples that Jesus was the coming one. Jesus saw these two following him and said to them, *"What do you seek?"* The process of "naming" continued. They said to him, *"'Rabbi' (which means Teacher), where are you staying?"* *"Rabbi,"* another name for Jesus, could also have meant "my greatness," a term of honor for one who taught the Torah to fellow Jews. Jesus fulfilled the role of revered teacher for his followers. Unlike other rabbis, however, Jesus took the initiative in calling followers to him. He said to them, *"Come and see."* They came and saw where he was staying and stayed with him that day, *"for it was about the tenth hour."*

One of the two whom the Baptist directed to Jesus was Philip and the other Andrew. Andrew was to play a prominent part in Jesus' ministry by calling others to Jesus. Andrew's first act was to call his brother, Simon Peter (called by the Greek name *Cephas* in Paul's Letters). Simon Peter soon became a leader among Jesus' followers. These two continue the process of naming Jesus.

Andrew said to his brother Simon, *"We have found the Messiah"* (Jn 1:41). *"Messiah"* denoted *"the anointed one."* Greek *christos* and Hebrew *mashi'a* mean *"to be rubbed in, to be anointed,"* referring to the oils and salves of anointing. Although Greeks did not use *"Christos"* as a title, to Jews the word was an honorable designation reaching deep into Israel's history. Inaugural ceremonies in consecrating a king (1 Kings 1:39), priest (Exodus 30:30), or prophet (1 Kings 19:16) included pouring sacred oil on the designee's head, thereby setting the person apart for official duties. In the Old Testament it came to mean *"the son of David who will sit again on the throne of Israel."* This expectation began with Isaiah of Jerusalem 700 years before Jesus, then used by other prophets. To make Jesus consistent with Scripture was a deep concern to all the Gospel writers. To put the concept of Messiah front and center, in his very first chapter, the writer John was giving a scriptural basis for who Jesus was.

When Jesus was born, hope for a messiah was widespread. The Pharisees hoped for someone who would inaugurate a new age of God's reign of law over all the earth. The Sadducees saw the Messiah as one who would turn all hearts to Jerusalem, so that all the world would worship at God's Temple. The Zealots longed for a military leader to drive the Romans out of the sacred land. To certain Jews these hopes began to center on Jesus. That Jesus of Nazareth came to be known among his followers as *"the Messiah"* meant they recognized him as the one delegated and empowered by God's Spirit to deliver God's people and establish God's kingdom.

The disciples Andrew and Philip have purely Greek names. Shime'on/Simon, the next man called, bore the most frequently used name in Galilee and Judea. This name recalled the successful Maccabean brother who founded the Hasmonean dynasty and won independence for it. That Simon, Andrew, and Philip came from Bethsaida (1:44) also had historical value. Herod's son Philip refounded this place before 2BCE. Bethsaida was remarkedly "Hellenized" compared to surrounding villages. These three men, each in turn, played significant roles in the early Jesus movement's ministry.

Andrew brought to Jesus his brother Simon Peter (1:40-43). Andrew searched the crowd by the seaside for food and found a lad who had five barley loaves and two fish to set in motion the feeding of five thousand men (6:9). When Jesus last entered Jerusalem, Andrew found Greeks who had come to Jerusalem for the Passover and brought them to Jesus (12:20). This precipitated Jesus' "last temptation," said this Gospel. Although the issue is not crystal clear from the context, traditionally the question was, Should Jesus go to Greece to teach Greeks in a philosopher's shaded groves or should he go to the cross? Andrew's skill was bringing others to Jesus.

The first time we see Philip, he is doing what Andrew did so well—he brought Nathanael to Jesus (1:45). Philip also figures in Jesus' later ministry. He was the first person Jesus asked concerning what he should do when he saw the big hungry crowd approaching. All Philip did at this time was to offer a counsel of despair, *"Two hundred denarii would not buy enough bread for each of them to get a little"* (6:7). Philip also was the one who sought out Andrew to bring the Greeks to Jesus (12:21-22). Up to this point in John's Gospel there is little about Philip that makes him as attractive a disciple as Andrew.

But during Jesus' final supper in Jerusalem, Philip raised a leading issue, *"Lord, show us the Father, and we shall be satisfied"* (Jn 13:8). Jesus' countered sharply, *"Have I been with you so long, and yet you do not know me, Philip? He who has seen me has seen the Father; how can you say, 'Show us the Father'? Do you not believe that I am in the Father and the Father in me? The words that I say to you I do not speak on my own authority; but the Father who dwells in me does his works. Believe me that I am in the Father and the Father in me; or else believe me for the sake of the works themselves… Truly, truly, I say to you, he who believes in me will also do the works that I do; and greater works than these will he do, because I go to the Father"* (13:9-12). Philip says nothing in response. In John's Gospel, this is all Philip does.

In The Acts of the Apostles Philip did some of these *"greater works."* He soon became the de facto leader of the Hellenist-Christian party. He was with the Twelve when they met together in a room in Jerusalem when the risen Christ left them (Acts 1:13). He was one of the Seven chosen to help lead the Hellenist party in the early Jesus movement (along with Stephen) and the only one from the Twelve to be chosen for this leadership (6:5). After Stephen laid out the Hellenists' position before Hebrews, Disciples, and Apostles, Philip became the de facto leader of the Hellenist party. Philip escaped the ensuing persecution by going to Samaria and there presented the message of Christ to *"multitudes."* They were astonished by the *"signs"* he did. He preached good news about God's kingdom in the name of Jesus Christ.

He baptized many of them, both men and women (Acts 8:5-6, 11). Philip met an Ethiopian official on the Gaza Road as this official was returning to Ethiopia after having worshipped in Jerusalem. This man was puzzling over the passage in Isaiah that talked about a suffering servant. Philip's interpretation that Jesus was the suffering servant satisfied the Ethiopian and Philip baptized him into the community of Jesus Christ (8:26-39). After this, Philip preached the gospel in many towns before he went to the region's Roman capital, the Hellenist city of Caesarea (8:40).

Acts recorded that the Apostle Paul visited Philip in Caesarea (21:8-9). Paul also noted that Philip had four unmarried daughters, who *"prophesied"* in Christ's name. Before the war of 66-70CE came to the Caesarea area, Philip gathered his daughters and took them to Ephesus, a leading center for Hellenist-Christian thought. Philip undoubtedly contributed his leadership skills and knowledge of Jesus to Hellenist Christians there. He might have been in Ephesus when the Gospel of John was written.

Simon Peter also gave skilled leadership to the Jesus movement's development, especially in Galilee. In our 2009 book (pp. 33 f), we see Peter in the following ways.

- Peter was the first one in Galilee called to follow Jesus—Peter the called.
- He offered Jesus a place to stay in his own home—Peter the host.
- He saw Jesus teach, heal, and cause the dead to rise—Peter the witness.
- He sat among those whom Jesus fed in the wilderness and at the table of the Last Supper—Peter the privileged.
- He was the first to call Jesus "the Christ"—Peter the insightful.
- When Jesus was transfigured, Peter was the one who wanted to erect three tents for visitors to stay in—Peter the practical.

- When Jesus told his disciples they would desert him in his hour of greatest need, Peter protested that he would remain faithful—Peter the impetuous.
- He joined Jesus in his prayer in Gethsemane—Peter the prayerful.
- He was the first to fall asleep that night—Peter the exhausted.
- When Peter was outside the courtroom in Jerusalem, three times he denied that he knew the man on trial—Peter the denyer.
- After he denied his Christ, he broke down and wept—Peter the forgiven.

Peter was the initial leader of the whole early Jesus movement (Acts 2:14-5:42). He preached, prayed, healed, and was arrested. After escaping from prison, except for Paul's note that he and his wife were in Corinth (1 Cor 1:12, 3:22, 9:5), he disappeared from further New Testament accounts (see Eberts, 2009: ch 2, on the party history of the Twelve).

In Galilee: With Nathanael (John 1:43-51)
Danger: High. Jesus deliberately restates an important text in historic Judaism

After his baptism, Jesus decided to go to Galilee. On the way he found Philip and invited him to become a follower (1:40-44). Like Andrew and Peter, Philip lived in Bethsaida. Philip introduced Jesus to a man called Nathanael who was sitting under a fig tree meditating on the Torah. Jesus said of him, *"Behold, an Israelite indeed, in whom is no guile!"* Nathanael asked how Jesus knew him and Jesus responded with a perplexing statement, *"I saw you under the fig tree before Philip called you."*

Jesus' response to Nathanael alluded to several Old Testament passages. The vision of *"every man under his vine and under his fig tree"* (1 Kings 4:25, Micah 4:4, Zechariah 3:10) referred to the coming of a messianic figure called the *"Branch"*

(Zech 3:8-10). Evidence from the Dead Sea scrolls shows that Jewish exegeses in Jesus' time identified the Branch foretold by Zechariah and Jeremiah as Messiah, Son of God, and King of Israel. Against this background, Nathanael immediately bestowed royal titles on Jesus. Nathanael says to Jesus, *"Rabbi, you are the Son of God! You are the King of Israel!"* (Hengel, 1989: 16).

A second part to this conversation was based on Jesus' perception that Nathanael was meditating on Genesis 28, the story about the guileful-deceiver Jacob and his vision. The vision was of a ladder set up on earth whose top reached into the heavens on which God's angels were ascending and descending. Jacob declared, *"The Lord is in this place"* (Gen 28:17). Jesus tells Nathanael that, if you stay with me, you will not depend on a vagrant dream in the wilderness to see God but you will experience the true vision of God. *"Truly, truly, I say to you* [Jesus frequently uses this phrase when re-interpreting Scripture], *you will see heaven opened and the angels of God ascending and descending on the Son of humankind."* The Greek for humankind is not *aner*, meaning "man," as in *uios tou aner*, "Son of Man" (in the Revised Standard Version), but *uios tou anthropos* "Son of all human beings," shortened here to "Son of Humankind." When this title is used in the New Testament, it is always *"uios tou anthropou"* not *"uios tou aner."* Jesus was saying to Nathanael, "Live with this vision and, unlike Jacob, you will become a true Israelite, an Israelite in whom there is no need for guile." By this early in Jesus' ministry, six characterizations of Jesus in John's Gospel have been introduced— Lamb of God, Rabbi, Son of God, King of Israel, Son of Humankind, Messiah-Christ (1:45-51).

In Galilee: The Wedding in Cana (John 2:1-12; not in the other Gospels)
Danger: Lowest in any event of Jesus' ministry

In Jewish peasant life during Jesus' time, weddings were the most festive celebrations of all. Peasants' lives were hard. Their meager diet seldom included meat or poultry that required killing one of their few precious animals. A wedding celebration meant momentary release from unremitting labor to enjoy copious amounts of food and wine, accompanied by music and dancing. By placing this wedding event near the beginning of Jesus' ministry, John's Gospel gave the story particular significance in showing Jesus inaugurating his ministry with a vivid enactment of a happy, convivial event and the gift he could offer.

During the festivities, a crisis occurred—the wine was running out. Noting this, Jesus' mother said to the servants, *"Do whatever he [Jesus] tells you to do"* (Jn 2:5). Her words echo Pharaoh's words to Joseph in which Pharaoh expresses total confidence in Joseph's ability to resolve scarcity during an Egyptian drought (Gen 41:55). Jesus' mother's words do the same. She believes her son can do something about the deficit of wine. When he seemed to demure at her request, she was still certain Jesus would fulfill it. *"Do whatever he says,"* she said to the servants.

Six stone jars used for Jewish purification rites were standing nearby, each large enough to hold twenty or thirty gallons. Jesus said to the servants, *"Fill the jars with water."* They filled them to the brim. Then he said, *"Now draw some out and take it to the steward of the feast."* So they took it to the steward who, when he drank it, was amazed. He said to the bridegroom, *"Every man serves the good wine first and, when men have drunk freely, then the poor wine; but you have kept the good wine until now"* (Jn 2:6-10).

Among the prophets of old, abundance of good wine is a sign of the joyous arrival of God's new age (Amos 9:13; Joel 3:18). This wedding event suggests this story is more than the inauguration of Jesus' ministry—it fulfilled Old Testament hopes. This event points beyond itself to God's promised salvation. Such "pointing beyond itself" is the reason John's Gospel called this event a "sign" and not a "miracle." A "miracle" is an act in which human possibilities are expanded through healing or new insight into a human situation—a leper is cleansed, a son is restored to his father. A "sign" points to significance beyond the moment, a continuing marvel of abundance, extravagance, transformation, and new possibilities.

A Jewish person hearing this story would have been struck by one discordant note—Jewish weddings did not have an official designated *"Steward of the feast."* But Hellenist weddings did. This fact points to the Gospel's composition. In the original story Jesus dealt with servants as his mother requested. As the story was orally repeated in Hellenist-Christian synagogues before it was written down, one servant was called *"Steward of the feast"* and has remained such in Christian circles ever since.

After the wedding, Jesus went to Capernaum with his mother, brothers, and disciples and stayed there for a few days (2:12). This was Jesus' last happy moment with his family. Following this quick visit, the writer John reports Jesus went to Jerusalem for Passover.

In Jerusalem: Passover; "Cleansing the Temple" (John 2:13-22)
Danger: Very high; during and after this event, both priests and rulers joined together to do away with Jesus

When Jesus first arrived at Jerusalem's Temple preceding the Passover season, in one daring moment Jesus challenged the legitimacy of Jerusalem's religious establishment and, at least indirectly, Rome's right to rule Jewish people. He wanted to replace both Temple and Roman authorities with a religion and government more attuned to human needs and dignity. This action shaped Jesus' ministry from then on.

John's Gospel describes Jesus going to Jerusalem to celebrate Passover. Jewish tradition was for pilgrims to go first to the Temple. There vendors sold oxen, sheep, and pigeons for sacrifices and moneychangers did their usual business. Jesus was incensed. He made a whip of cords, began driving

the animals out of the Temple, followed by screaming vendors, overturned moneychangers' tables, coins flying everywhere, and said, *"Take these things away. You shall not make
my Father's house a house of trade."*

Jerusalem's Temple was Herod's chief architectural triumph. Built of gleaming white marble overlaid with gold and
jewels high on a summit in Jerusalem, it was a spectacular
sight to pilgrims coming over the top of the Mount of Olives
on the Jericho road. People said of it, "Whoever has not seen
Herod's Temple has seen nothing beautiful."

To build the Temple, Herod acquired a thousand wagons
and oxen to transport quarry stones to the building site. He
hired 10,000 skilled workmen for the construction. So as not
to desecrate the Temple by the presence of profane men,
priests were taught necessary carpentry and masonry skills
to work on the sanctuary and Court of Priests—priests alone
were allowed into this part of the Temple (Lev 14, 15; Num
19; Josephus, 94, 15.11.2: 389-90). The construction began
about 20BCE and lasted until 63CE, just seven years before the
Romans destroyed it. But most work was completed earlier
rather than later. Josephus said the inner court (*ho naos*)
was completed in a year and a half, while the *stoa* and outer
courts took eight more years (Josephus, 94, 15.11.5-6: 420 f).
Josephus also claims that, when the inner court was under
construction, no rain fell during the day but only at night, so
as not to hinder progress (94, 15.11.7: 425).

When the Romans destroyed the city and Temple in 70CE,
they left the Temple walls standing. Some still stand today
and support the present Muslim holy place, The Dome of
the Rock. Most stones in surviving walls weigh between two
and five tons, but some, especially the cornerstones, are
even larger—one is 12 meters long and weighs almost 400
tons. These huge stone blocks were fit together with ramps
and pulleys (ben-Dov, 1985: 84). The Roman historian Tacitus (116) described the Temple as "possessing enormous
riches," which is credible since the Jews had only one Tem-

ple—all their resources were directed to this structure alone (116CE, 5.8.1).

Josephus described the Temple's layout (94, 2.8: 103-109). Each of its four courts had restrictions on who could enter. The outer court was open to all, including non-Jews, except menstruating women. The second court allowed all Jewish men and menstrually-clean Jewish women. Only Jewish men could enter the third court. The fourth court was restricted to properly attired priests, which meant priests on-duty. Only the High Priest attired in high-priest raiment could enter the inner sanctuary (*adytum*), the holy of holies.

Support for Temple ministries affected nearly every area of Jewish life (Sanders, 1993: 255). Temple taxes, agricultural tithes, minor agricultural offerings, redemption of first-born sons and animals, sin and guilt offerings, offerings of animals to provide food for banquets and festivities, and festivals themselves—all took place in the Temple.

The Passover, which Jesus and his fellow Jews celebrated, had originally been two separate festivals, one for shepherds and one for farmers, both called Passover. These two similar celebrations existed before the Israelites began to celebrate their own feast. A *"Passover of the Lord"* combined the celebration of farmers, who brought fresh bread to eat, with that of shepherds who offered their lambs (Exodus 12:11, 27). Israel's festival denoted God's intervention in human affairs by liberating Hebrew people from Egyptian slavery. The Hebrew word *pasach* (from which *Pesach, Passa,* and *Passover* are derived) refers to the *"passing over"* of Hebrews by the Lord who then smote Egyptians' first-born. This *"passing over"* act by God is uniquely *"remembered"* in Passover.

The Hebrew Passover was initiated when the tribes under Moses departed from Egypt but no evidence exists that the Passover was celebrated while God's people were with Moses in the wilderness. Joshua reintroduced it only after Israel entered the Promised Land (Josh 5:10). Even after Joshua, Passover did not become an annual affair. King Hezekiah restored the rite, sometime after 700BCE (2 Kings 23). Under Hezekiah, the Passover animal could be slaughtered and eaten in any Jewish community. When the Law of Deuteronomy was rediscovered during the time of King Josiah (ca 622), the Passover sacrifice was centralized in Jerusalem. During Jesus' time, Passover groups assembling in Jerusalem annually slaughtered approximately 10,000 lambs.

The meal itself was not celebrated in the Temple but in festival rooms, furnished with couches. It was similar to a Greek festival meal, called a symposium. One great, gloriously outfitted chair was set for Elijah, with a huge cup of wine standing ready for its occupant. All vestiges of leavened food were removed from the house. Each household participant was prescribed at least four cups of wine. Doors and windows were left open to welcome the expected messenger of the end time. Passover denoted a hope for something better in life. The feast looked forward to a time when God would grant freedom to all nations and each of its members.

During this celebration, Jesus performed his signatory act of "cleansing the Temple." The action took place in the Court of the Gentiles, the large outer enclosure surrounded by colonnades accessible to both Jews and Gentiles where animals and birds were sold for required sacrifices. Here Jesus overturned the tables of those who changed Roman coins for Tyrian shekels in which the annual Temple tax was paid. Jesus brandished a whip, *phraggelion*—a word used only here in the New Testament. It referred to a "scourge, lash, or prod used in driving cattle" (Barrett, 1978: on 2:15). MacGregor (1959) noted that John 2:15 is phrased to suggest that tradesmen themselves were not subject to violence. Jesus did not drive them out because they were, for example, cheating. He acted because they were buying and selling, *"turning the Father's house into an emporium* [the exact Greek word], *a house of merchandising"* (2:16).

Jesus had precedence for what he did. Jeremiah said the house of the Lord would be destroyed if the people did not mend their ways (Jer 7:1-20). Kings Hezekiah and Josiah had cleansed the temple of foreign impediments when they took office. Armitage Robinson said that cleansing the temple was Jesus' deliberate starting point to fulfill Malachi's program, *"The messenger of the Lord coming suddenly to his temple"* (1962: 40-46). Jewish tradition held that, when the Messiah came, he would bear a lash to chastise evildoers (MacGregor, 1959). In other words, significant Israelites had previously spoken about cleansing the Temple as a necessity.

Jesus was fulfilling his predecessors' words and acts. The Lord had indeed come suddenly and unexpectedly to his Temple. Like Jeremiah, Jesus declared that the Temple will be destroyed so that not one stone will be standing on another (Mk 13:2). Like Hezekiah and Josiah, Jesus cleansed the temple of foreign impediments, the cattle and coins used for sacrifices designed to bring God's presence and God's forgiveness to the people. "Not so," declared Jesus, "Too mechanical." Jesus said that forgiveness comes when one is reconciled with his or her neighbor. *"If you are offering your gift at the altar, and there remember that your brother has something against you, leave your gift there before the altar and go, first be reconciled to your brother, and then come and offer your gift"* (Matt 6:23-24). Jesus claimed that God's forgiveness came through actions like those in his ministry, not through priestly ministrations in a temple. He drove away the cattle; he upset the tables of the money changers; he cleansed the temple.

Beyond the precedents provided for him, Jesus cleansed the Temple for at least three reasons.

First, Jesus performed this act in accord with contemporary beliefs. The Hellenists, as represented by their leader Stephen, did not believe that God lived in the Temple (Acts 6:44-51). There was no temple in the wilderness, Stephen said, when God directed the people from Egypt to the Promised Land. God met them only in the tent of witness. This simple structure was so important to Israel that the tribes brought it with them when they crossed into the Land of Promise. *"Our fathers brought it in with Joshua when they dispossessed the nations which God thrust out before our fathers.*

So it was until the days of David, " said Stephen, *"who found favor in the sight of God and asked leave to find a habitation for the God of Jacob."* But God did not grant permission to David to build it. *"It was Solomon who built a house for him."* Stephen went on, *"The Most High does not dwell in houses made with hands; as the prophet says, 'Heaven is my throne, and earth my footstool. What house will you build for me, says the Lord, or what is the place of my rest? Did not my hand make all these things?' You stiff-necked people, uncircumcised in heart and ears, you always resist the Holy Spirit. As your fathers did, so do you."* God gave no authorization to build a temple. *"The Most High does not dwell in houses made with hands."*

Second, Jesus cleansed the Temple because it failed to meet the spiritual needs of people who came there for spiritual sustenance. Jesus told this story (Luke 18:10-14), *"Two men went up into the temple to pray, one a Pharisee and the other a tax collector. The Pharisee stood and prayed thus with himself, 'God, I thank thee that I am not like other men, extortioners, unjust, adulterers, or even like this tax collector. I fast twice a week, I give tithes of all that I get.' But the tax collector, standing far off, would not even lift up his eyes to heaven, but beat his breast, saying, 'God, be merciful to me a sinner!' I tell you, this man went down to his house justified rather than the other."* The promised forgiveness of God was not bestowed upon everyone who worshipped there. The Pharisee, performing the appropriate rituals, claimed to receive it. The one who did receive God's mercy was not even aware of it, as his prayer seemed so out of place amidst the showy Temple rituals. *"God, be merciful to me a sinner!"*

Third, Jesus cleansed the Temple because, with its constant demand for money, its operation contributed to oppress the poor. Mark's Gospel describes how one day Jesus sat down opposite the treasury of the Temple, the repository for gifts to the Temple. He watched the multitude putting money into the treasury. Many rich people put in large sums. A poor widow came and put in two copper coins, which made a penny. Jesus called his disciples to him and said to them, *"Truly, I say to you, this poor widow has put in more than all those who are contributing to the treasury. For they all contributed out of their abundance; but she out of her poverty has put in everything she had, her whole living"* (12:41-43). Everything! Widows were the most vulnerable persons in Jesus' society, yet, without a second thought, the Temple took all her living and she had nothing left to feed and clothe herself and her family. The rich could afford it but for the widow it was oppression of the worst sort, oppression in the name of religion. No wonder Jesus was to say shortly after this incident that the Temple would be destroyed. *"As he came out of the temple, one of his disciples said to him, 'Look, Teacher, what wonderful stones and what wonderful buildings!' Jesus said to him, 'Do you see these great buildings? There will not be left here one stone upon another that will not be thrown down'"* (Mk 13:1-2).

As expected, Jews challenged Jesus for what he did. *"What sign have you to show us for doing this?"* Jesus answered, *"Destroy this temple and in three days I will raise it up."* The Jews replied, *"'It has taken forty-six years to build this temple, and will you raise it up in three days?'"* (Jn 2:20). John goes on to say, *"But Jesus spoke of the temple of his body. When Jesus was raised from the dead, his disciples remembered what he had said, and they believed the scripture and the word which Jesus had spoken"* (Jn 2:21-22).

By this act of cleansing, Jesus challenged the legitimacy of both the high priests, Judaism's religious authorities who operated the Temple and received its benefits, and the house of Herod, proud builders of the Temple. Both were Roman collaborators and the ruling political powers in Judea and Galilee. New entities responsive to a loving God needed to replace both, signaled Jesus. The spirit in which these new entities would act was the spirit of the crucified and risen Lord, the Temple of Jesus' body. After Jesus' initial act of detoxification of the Temple, these two powers joined hands to violently destroy the otherwise non-violent Jesus. His initial public act in cleansing the Temple concluded with Roman officials and Jewish priests collaborating publicly and violently to nail Jesus to a cross.

In Jerusalem: Nicodemus (John 3:1-17)

Danger: Very High—Nicodemus, a member of the Jewish Sanhedrin, could make Jesus suspicious of him and what might transpire

"There was a man of the Pharisees, named Nicodemus, a ruler of the Jews. This man came to Jesus by night" (3:1-2). This story is in the Gospel writer John's usual format of event-dialogue-monologue (reflection). From the start, it raises several questions. A first is why would Nicodemus, *"a ruler of the Jews"* (which probably meant that he was a member of the Great Sanhedrin, Jerusalem's ruling body), want to see Jesus? John's Gospel might have included this story because of the Sanhedrin connection. Was Nicodemus coming to really find out more about Jesus for purposes of understanding and perhaps becoming a follower or was he coming for some other reason such as to trap Jesus in some way? In any case, he came and Jesus received him. Only later does John let us know that Nicodemus was probably sincere in seeking Jesus in order to understand and follow him (Jn 7:50, 19:39).

A second question is where did they meet? Up to this point, the writer John has not told us that, when Jesus went to Jerusalem with his disciples to celebrate a feast day, they often set up camp in a place called Gethsemane on the hillside called the Mount of Olives, on the other side of the brook Kidron (Jn 8:1, 18:1). Nor does John mention, even if Luke in Acts does mention it, that Jesus' followers frequently met in houses in Jerusalem after the resurrection (among others, Acts 2:2). Apparently Jesus had a set of Jerusalem followers whom he trusted enough to stay with them. In such a house is probably where Jesus met Nicodemus.

"This man came to Jesus by night." A usual interpretation of the phrase *"by night"* is that Nicodemus was in the dark about spiritual matters. Such an interpretation is consistent with

seeing John's Gospel as primarily a spiritual document given
to double meanings that require parsing words and passages
to discover hidden lessons. Although such double meanings
occur throughout this Gospel, certain words can be taken at
face value. *"At night"* can be taken literally. Yet for a man to
be out at night was unusual and often unsafe. Without street
lights, a person could easily lose his way at night when moving through Jerusalem's tangled streets. Nighttime was also
dangerous—thieves, robbers, and sicarii were about looking
for quarries and Herod's ubiquitous secret police were looking for any kind of threat. Jesus' action at the Temple made
him a marked man. Herod's police might be looking for him
or a man like the respected Pharisee, Nicodemus, who might
conspire with or against a suspect like Jesus. Perhaps because
Nicodemus came *"by night,"* Jesus might have been more open
to such a meeting. If things went wrong, Jesus too could fade
into the night. Further, prying eyes might more easily see the
two of them if they met "by day."

Nicodemus' first words were, *"Teacher, we know..."* (Jn
3:2). Nicodemus was a well-educated Jewish leader conver-
sant with the Law. In John's Gospel he was truly religious,
utterly sincere, but, like most Pharisees, rather complacent
about knowing God and God's will and not particularly open
to new ways of thinking about God. Nicodemus continued,
*"that you are a teacher come from God, for no one can do the
signs that you do unless God is with him."* Jesus responded,
*"Truly, truly...unless one is born anew, he cannot see the king-
dom of God."* Such a response was astounding. By these
words, Jesus made quite a jump over several intermediate
steps, so that Nicodemus grew confused. Citing his age, he
asked, *"How can a man be born when he is old?"* Jesus responded, *"Unless one is born of ... the Spirit, he cannot enter
God's kingdom... that which is born of flesh is flesh and that
which is born of spirit is spirit."* Nicodemus asked, *"How can
this be?"*

A key to this conversation is probably the Greek word
anothen. It could accurately be translated as either "born

anew" or "born from above." "Born from above" could mean "born from heaven," where "heaven" can be a substitute word for God. The writer John undoubtedly recognized both meanings when he used this word. Nicodemus took the first meaning, Jesus the second. A person filled with the spirit descends from and ascends to heaven (3:13). Apparently a little irritated, Jesus finally said to him, *"Are you a teacher of Israel and yet do not know these things?"* (Jn 3:10). The wisdom of God in Jesus Christ, John's Gospel often insisted, confounded the wisdom of the Jews.

This part of the conversation started with *"the kingdom of God"* and ended with *"spirit."* Such a starting place might have been expected, since John the Baptist stirred up the Jews by proclaiming the near approach of God's kingdom. Being born to a Jewish mother, according to Jewish Law, Nicodemus was a member of Israel's Covenant. But especially in John's Gospel, Jesus insisted that being born a *"child of Abraham"* alone, even though preparation for hearing God's Word, was inadequate for salvation (see 8:33-40).

Another double meaning comes from the word *"Spirit."* Both Hebrew and Greek had a single word, in Greek *pneuma*, meaning "spirit" or "wind." By using this word, Jesus implies that one does not need to know everything about the wind in order to enjoy its presence; nor does one need to know everything about the spirit to respond to its presence.

"As Moses lifted up the serpent in the wilderness, so must the Son of Humankind be lifted up, that whoever believes in him may have eternal life" (3:14-15). By this obscure phrase, Jesus again makes several jumps in his references. Since Nicodemus was an educated Pharisee, Jesus probably assumed that Nicodemus could understand the implications of this symbol. The Old Testament reference is to an act Moses performed in the wilderness while moving toward the Promised Land (Numbers 21:4-9). *"[As] they journeyed from the mountain Hor,...the people grew impatient. And the people spoke against God and against Moses. 'Why did you bring us up from Egypt to die in the wilderness? For there is no water*

and we loathe the wretched bread.' The Lord sent against the people viper-serpents, they bit the people, and many people died. The people came to Moses and said, 'We have offended against the Lord...Pray to the Lord that he take the serpents away from us...' The Lord said to Moses, 'Make you a viper and put it on a standard, so whoever is bitten will see it and live.' Moses made a serpent of bronze and put it on a standard, and so, if the serpent bit a man, he looked on the serpent of bronze and lived" (Altar's translation, 2004: 789-790).

"So must the Son of Humankind be lifted up." The writer John once again uses one phrase to mean two things. The first meaning is that Jesus will be lifted up on the cross in death. But it also means that because of this "lifting up in death" Jesus will be lifted up in glory and exalted above all persons. The bronze serpent was venerated in Egypt as a healing object and adopted by Israel on Moses' orders. It continued in Israel until Hezekiah destroyed it when he cleansed the temple. Jesus' point of comparison is that, as healing came to the snake-bitten Israelites by looking at the bronze serpent hanging from a pole, so life is given to those who look with eyes of faith on the Son of Humankind hanging on the cross. Jesus was thinking of desperate people in his world, dying in multitudes, beset by loathsome creatures from which there was no escape in their ailing, sinful, foolish world where people lived like a primitive barbaric tribe that has lost its way while holding on to nasty little customs as the only possible rules of life. But deliverance was possible for them, too. If only they keep looking at the up-lifted Jesus on a cross, deliverance would come to those who still survived—heavenly things dark to them now will dawn on them and the glory of God will come home to them.

To have found such an obscure Scripture as this and make an important point through it, clearly indicated that Jesus, Nicodemus, and the Gospel writer John knew their ancient Scriptures intimately. The images in this passage also imply that Jesus surely foresaw his crucifixion as a *fait accompli*. He knew his act of *"cleansing the Temple"* aroused various authorities enough for them to endeavor to eradicate him. The public display of crucifixion was how Rome usually accomplished such an endeavor.

The conversation continued. Jesus (or the writer John) reflected on what he said. *"For God so loved the world that he gave his only Son, that whoever believes in him should not perish but have eternal life. For God sent the Son into the world, not to condemn the world, but that the world might be saved through him"* (3:17). These calming words interpreting the Nicodemus event were consistent with the writer John's understanding of who Jesus was and what he stood for as expressed in his prologue.

"The world," *kosmon* (root, *kosmos*), is not only one of creation, order, beauty, and marvels. In John's Gospel, the *kosmon* refers to "human life organized to keep God out," as H. Richard Niebuhr implied (1951, and stated explicitly in his courses, 1950, 1954). Jesus was born in Bethlehem, the Gospels say, but they also say that human society had no place for him at his birth—his mother gave birth in an inhospitable stable. Jesus came to Jerusalem to proclaim his message and *"the world"* put him on a cross. All this is summed up in John's cutting phrase in the Gospel's prologue, *"He came to his own, and his own did not receive him."* (1:11). This phrase previews Jesus' lifestory, for it goes on to say, *"But to all who received him, who believed on his name, he gave power to become sons of God, born not of blood or the will of the flesh or the will of man, but of God"* (1:12-13).

"Believed," *pisteuon,* was not giving assent to a set of propositions about Jesus. *"Believed"* means to make a commitment to Jesus, to trust him, to have confidence in his leadership, to give oneself wholeheartedly to him and his mission.

"Only son," *monogenai,* this word, literally, means "only born." It also denotes one who has "power of attorney" for someone else. God bestowed on Jesus God's power of attorney. Jesus, both in flesh and in spirit, acted for God, spoke for God, bound persons to contracts in God's name. Jesus had God's power and authority.

"Life eternal," zoe aionion, "life to come," to the average Hebrew was not a place of eternal bliss, where souls communed with one another. Hebrews pictured the life to come as living with God where God lives, in ages beyond ages. *"Life eternal"* meant living with God in God's abode. This key phrase in John's Gospel therefore can be translated as "God so loved the world of humanity, organized to keep God out of human life, that God sent into this world the one bearing his power of attorney to show that he who trusts him will not perish but will enjoy life with God where God dwells now and in the ages yet to come."

Nicodemus appeared three times in John's Gospel, this first time secretly *"by night"* (3:2). The same Nicodemus also stood before the Sanhedrin's fellow councilmen to defend Jesus, an extraordinary act of courage on his part because the Sanhedrin immediately accused him of being Jesus' follower and perhaps subject to punishment (7:50-52). Nicodemus' response to this taunt is not recorded but the Gospel writer noted this was the same Nicodemus who previously came to Jesus, *"by night."* Still later, Nicodemus performed an even greater act of courage. Roman law condemned any person who touched the body of a crucified man to suffer the same punishment. Yet Nicodemus openly joined Joseph of Arimathea in removing Jesus' body from the cross (19:39-42). By doing this, Nicodemus did what Jesus had asked of him previously. Nicodemus *"lifted up"* Jesus in taking his body from the cross to place it in a tomb. Again John's Gospel noted who this man was—the same Nicodemus who first came to Jesus *"by night."* On that night, a confused Nicodemus came to the Light—he both saw the Light and walked in the Light (see Jn 3:21).

In Samaria: Jesus by Jacob's Well (John 4:1-42)
Danger: Surprisingly low, even if being in Samaria was always dangerous to Jews

Jesus' encounter with Samaritans began near the Samaritan city of Sychar. On his trip from Judea to Galilee, Jesus and the Twelve purposely took a shortcut through Samaria. Usually Jewish people did not go through Samaria. This region, separating Galilee from Judea, was composed largely of people who were relocated by previous regimes that had conquered Israel (Assyria, Babylonia, Persia, Greece, and Rome). Samaria included Caesarea (Maritima) on its western border, from which Romans and Herodians governed the entire region. For these reasons, Jews usually took a longer route between Jerusalem and Galilee, east of the Jordan River through Perea.

In this instance, when the disciples in Samaria came to a well, called Jacob's well, about the sixth hour, noon, in the heat of the day, Jesus asked a Samaritan woman for a drink of water. The request was deceptively simple. But in making this request, Jesus broke several traditional principles—of geography, gender, ethnicity, and religion. This Jacob's-well event came to embody great symbolic significance in reconciling Jesus' followers with Samaritans.

Jacob's well was ancient. Dug to a depth of more than a hundred feet, its shaft was seven and a half feet wide cut through a thick bed of soil and soft rock. Water filtered in through the sides, so that it was both a spring and a rain pit. The well was located near a field that, in tradition, the patriarch Jacob had given to his son Joseph (who was later sold into slavery in Egypt by his brothers). Although Jacob, a Jewish patriarch, had dug the well, for generations its use was denied to Jews. Water, then as now, was a precious commodity in parched areas of Judea, Galilee, and Perea, and water rights, then as now, were much contested.

Jesus, weary in the day's heat, sat down beside the well. A woman from nearby Sychar came to the well in the middle of the day, instead of earlier in the morning when other women came to the well. Perhaps, as indicated later in the story, she came at this hour because she had been ostracized from Sychar's society. Respectable Samaritan women wanted nothing to do with her, and if men wanted her it was not for respectable reasons. She was an outcast, a Samaritan pariah.

By asking this woman for a drink of water, Jesus violated a rabbinical principle that said, "A man should hold no conversation with a woman in the street, not even with his own wife, still less with any other woman, lest men should gossip." The general contempt in which women were held was expressed in a thanksgiving litany during a daily synagogue service. "Blessed art thou, oh Lord, who hast not made me a woman," said the men. The women responded from their segregated gallery, "Blessed art thou, oh Lord, who has fashioned me according to thy will."

The woman at the well, then, was greatly surprised that Jesus would ask her for a drink of water. She asked Jesus, *"How is it that you, a Jew, ask a drink of me, a woman of Samaria?"* Jesus responded, *"If you knew the gift of God, and who it is that is saying to you, 'Give me a drink,' you would have asked him and he would have given you living water."* The woman, in a practical manner, said to him, *"Sir, you have nothing to draw with and the well is deep; where do you get living water?"* She had another thought. *"You are not greater than our father Jacob, who gave us the well, and drank from it himself, and his sons, and his cattle—are you?"* Jesus answered her, *"Every one who drinks of this water will thirst again, but whoever drinks of the water that I shall give will never thirst; the water that I shall give will become a spring of water welling up to eternal life."* The woman, again practical as ever, said to him, *"Sir, give me this water, that I may not thirst, nor have to come here to draw."*

"Living water" was water running in a stream, not stagnant well water. In Asia Minor, the generic name for a spring is *Huda-Verdi*, "God has given." In desert country, running water is the most precious of God's gifts.

Jesus then turned the subject to another matter, saying to her, *"Go, call your husband and come here."* The woman answered him, *"I have no husband."* Jesus said to her, *"You are right in saying, 'I have no husband,' for you have had five husbands and he whom you now have is not your husband."* Possibly the five husbands were symbolic of the five non-

Israelite regimes that had ruled this region—Assyria, Babylon, Persia, Greece, and Rome (Campbell, 2012). Otherwise, how did Jesus know *"a woman with five husbands"* would come to the well at noon as she did on this day? But possibly she had *"five husbands"* at the same time, which would indicate she was a prostitute. Or, again, she might have been caught in a situation of Levitical marriage, where a woman was passed from one brother to another to provide a son for the first brother who had died. But, if this was the case, *"five husbands"* would exceed the Levitical limit of three such marriages. Had she been abused by being forced to marry two additional brothers? Had each husband died in her presence, resulting in a scandal in a small town like Sychar? We cannot answer such questions since neither Jesus nor the woman elaborated further on *"five husbands."*

The woman changed the subject, again, from ethics to religion. *"Sir, I perceive that you are a prophet. Our fathers worshiped on this mountain and you say that Jerusalem is the place where men ought to worship."* Jesus' response surprised her again. *"Woman, believe me, the hour is coming when neither on this mountain nor in Jerusalem will you worship the Father... But the hour is coming and now is when true worshipers will worship the Father in spirit and truth... God is spirit and those who worship him must worship in spirit and truth."*

The woman decided to close this increasingly uncomfortable conversation. She said to him, *"I know the Messiah is coming (he who is called Christ); when he comes, he will show us all things."* Jesus' next response really surprised her. Jesus said to her, *"I who speak to you am he."* In her great astonishment the woman left her water jar at the well (something no woman would ever do except under extreme circumstances), raced back to the city, and told these things to the very people who had ostracized her. *"Come see the man who told me all that I ever did."*

The Samaritans came and Jesus talked with them. Many Samaritans from Sychar believed in him because of the woman's testimony. So impressed were they with their conversations that they asked him to stay with them and many more believed because of his words. They said to the woman, *"It is no longer because of your words that we believe, for we have heard for ourselves and know that this is indeed the Savior of the world."* After two days Jesus departed toward Galilee.

The townspeople believed not just that Jesus was the Samaritan Messiah, the *Taheb*, but that he was indeed *"the savior of the world."* This title was sometimes given to human deliverers of Israel but most often to God himself. In the Hellenist world, the term was attributed to pagan gods and Roman emperors. Augustus Caesar was declared "savior of the world" (MacGregor, 1959: 114). Only very deserving men or high-ranking officials received this title which removed them from the ranks of ordinary humankind and placed them in a significantly higher position. Somewhat surprisingly, this title was not assigned to Jesus earlier, perhaps because *Jesus*, in Hebrew means "God is our Savior." But John's Gospel did not explain the term. The hearer or reader was left to gather from the tenor of the whole work in what sense Jesus was the world's *"savior."*

Before this conversation began, Jesus' disciples had gone into the city to buy food. When they returned, they marveled that he was talking with a woman, but none asked why. They simply said, *"Rabbi, eat."* Jesus replied, *"I have food to eat of which you do not know. My food is to do the will of him who sent me and to accomplish his work. Do you not say, 'There are yet four months, then comes the harvest?' I tell you, lift up your eyes and see how the fields are already white for harvest. He who reaps receives wages and gathers fruit for eternal life, so that sower and reaper may rejoice together. For here the saying holds true, 'One sows and another reaps.' I sent you to reap that for which you did not labor; others have labored and you have entered into their labor"* (Jn 4:31-38).

In Palestine as elsewhere, sowing winter wheat takes place in October or November and the harvest comes in April. At this time in Spring, Jesus was looking at the waving fields of wheat and barley in the rich plains of Mahneh, already ripe for the sickle. This scene suggested to Jesus the imminent harvest of souls in neighboring towns. Comparing the king-dom of God to a harvest was often made in the Old and New Testaments. *"The harvest"* was a figure of speech signifying the great event of the coming kingdom. Jesus saw the fields as ripe for harvest and likened it to his own situation. Al-ready, as Samaritans came then left to tell others, Jesus was reaping the first harvest in anticipation of greater harvests to be reaped by other disciples. Later, after the Resurrec-tion, when the Hellenist Philip preached to the Samaritans (the first such mission), he won many converts (Acts 8:5). Its precedence for reconciling Christians and Samaritans was set by Jesus in this event of "the woman at Jacob's well." This was the underlying meaning when Jesus said, *"Others have labored and you into their labor have come."*

An important aspect of this Samaritan mission came at the account's beginning (Jn 4:1-3). Jesus left Judea, says John's Gospel, because Pharisees heard that Jesus was baptizing more disciples than John the Baptist. Then a contradicting phrase is added to the account, stating bluntly, *"Jesus him-self did not baptize, but only his disciples"* (4:2) This unusual statement was unique to John's Gospel. The other Gospels assert that Jesus himself baptized his followers. This is-sue emerged prominently in the mid-50sCE in an argument between the Hellenist-Christian Apollos of Alexandria and the Apostle Paul's proteges, Priscilla and Aquila (Acts 18:24-19:7). When Apollos began preaching in the Asia Minor city of Ephesus, he did not baptize. He said that he did not know of baptism by Jesus but only the baptism of John the Baptist. Priscilla and Aquila set him straight, *"they expounded to him the way of God more accurately"* (Acts 18:26).

Paul was especially incensed that Apollos did not baptize, because this meant none of Apollos' followers had received the Holy Spirit, a central part of Paul's faith. On a trip to Ephesus, when Paul asked these Hellenist-Christians if they had ever heard of the Holy Spirit, they replied that they had not. Paul's follow-up question about their baptism revealed that they had only been baptized into John's baptism. Paul said, *"John baptized with a baptism of repentance but when the coming one, Jesus, came he would baptize with the Holy Spirit."* This Spirit would come through the baptism of Jesus. Paul then baptized these Hellenists and the Holy Spirit came upon them. Much tension between the two parties was then resolved. From this point on, Apostles and Hellenists in general and Paul and Apollos in particular tended to cooperate with one another with subsequent great benefits to Corinthian Christians especially (Acts 18:27, 19:1 ff; 1 Cor 3:16 and passim; Eberts, 2011: ch 8).

In Galilee: Healing the Official's Son (John 4:43-54)
Danger: Low; Jesus was safer in Galilee

"After the two days Jesus departed to Galilee. When he came to Galilee, the Galileans welcomed him, having seen all that he had done in Jerusalem at the feast, for they too had gone to the feast. He came again to Cana in Galilee, where he had made the water wine.

"At Capernaum there was an official whose son was ill. When he heard that Jesus had come from Judea to Galilee, he begged Jesus to come and heal his son, who was at the point of death. Jesus said, 'Go! Your son will live.' The man believed the word that Jesus spoke to him and went his way.

"As he was going down, his servants met him and told him that his son was living. He asked them when the boy began to mend. They said, 'Yesterday at the seventh hour the fever left him.' The father knew that was the hour when Jesus had said to him, 'Your son will live'; and he himself believed, and all his household. This was the second sign that Jesus did when he had come from Judea to Galilee" (4:43-54).

A first remarkable thing about this story is that Jesus did not see the boy before he healed him. We are told the boy was at the point of death. The father sought Jesus and begged him to heal his son. Jesus simply said to him, *"Go; your son will live."*

Second, this is the first healing by Jesus recorded in John's Gospel. Mark, Matthew, and Luke described Jesus as a healer of great reputation and reported that Jesus had hardly arrived in Capernaum after the arrest of John the Baptist before he healed multiple people (Mk 1:23-2:12). But in John only four recorded healings were reported—here, the beggar at the Pool of Siloam (5:2-15), the man born blind (9:1-41), and the raising of Lazarus from the dead (11:1-44). In John, healing was part of Jesus' ministry but no more so than encouraging disciples to follow him, attending a wedding, attacking merchants and moneychangers in the Temple, repeated conversations with many people, and contentious arguments with his Jewish compatriots.

The most remarkable aspect in the healing of the official's son is the trust this father invested in Jesus. Why would this "*official*" seek Jesus out as this father did? He was desperate—his son was dying. He had heard of Jesus, a holy man and holy men usually had reputations as healers. The man believed what Jesus said to him, to go home, and he went his way. The result was that the man "believed" and all his household joined him in his new life.

In Jerusalem: By the Pool of Siloam (John 5:1-47)
Danger: Very high; Jesus was almost killed over this incident

Jesus went to Jerusalem to celebrate an unnamed Jewish festival. Reading between the lines in John's Gospel, Jesus apparently went to such feasts frequently and addressed attendees while they were in Jerusalem. The text gives no clues as to which pilgrimage festival this might have been (Passover, Tabernacles, Dedication).

"*There is in Jerusalem by the Sheep Gate a pool, in Hebrew called Bethzatha...[where] lay a multitude of invalids, blind, lame, paralyzed*" (Jn 5:3, 5). Recent excavations in Jerusalem north of the Temple site have disclosed a large trapezoidal-shaped double pool divided in the middle by a broad wall. This corresponds to the description of the sheep pool. It had four columns surrounding it and a fifth post in the middle. Remains of pillars and balustrades further support the identification, and votive inscriptions suggest that ancient superstition ascribed healing virtue to the water (Wahlde, 2011). Two different place names are given in translations of the Gospel for the event. The New Revised Standard Version calls the place Bethzatha, and The New International Version calls it Bethsaida (which was also a place on the north shore of the Sea of Galilee). These differences result from variants in the textual tradition.

Blind, lame, and paralyzed invalids gathered there because an ancient legend said that, when the waters were stirred, even a little, the first person to jump into the pool's waters would be healed. The water rippling a little would produce a great frenzy—bed-clothes ripped off, reaching for canes and crutches, shouting, calls for help, clawing, pushing and shoving—to be first in the healing water.

Wahlde (2011), an excavator of the Pool of Bethzatha, said that this passage indicates the writer John's real knowledge of Jerusalem. "The excavators of the large Pool of Siloam, close to where Jesus cured the blind man, have interpreted it as a public *mikveh,* a place for ritual washings by festival crowds. The same was true of the Pool of Bethesda (Bethzatha). These are in fact the two largest *mikvdot* in Jerusalem That both of these pools are mentioned only in John's Gospel reflects John's and Jesus' intimate knowledge of Jerusalem. Jesus frequented sites as these because large numbers of people would be there."

One man in particular caught Jesus' attention. He had been an invalid *"for thirty-eight years." Thirty-eight years* corresponds to the period the Israelites wandered in the wilderness before they came into the Promised Land and the number of centuries, according to Jewish theology in Jesus' time, that Israel had waited for the coming of the messiah. Certainly the Gospel writer had these ideas in mind as he wrote *"thirty-eight years."*

"When Jesus saw him and knew that he had been lying there a long time, he said to him, 'Do you want to be healed?'

The sick man answered him, 'Sir, I have no man to put me into the pool when the water is troubled, and while I am going another steps in front of me.' Jesus said to him, 'Rise, take up your pallet, and walk.' At once the man was healed and he took up his pallet and walked" (5:5-9). The man appeared friendless. Lying there for 38 years, the only people the man knew were his fellow sufferers who were not about to help him in the quick competition for a place in the pool. Jesus came to his aid. He told this man to get up and walk. No mention is made about stepping into the pool. Under Jesus' influence, the lame man simply rose from where he lay and walked away.

There is self-pity in the man's voice—he was helpless to get to the pool. This sense of victimhood turned up in the last things he said to the crowd. When some Jews, quoting their Law, said, *"It is a Sabbath; it is not lawful for you to carry your pallet,"* the man played the victim. He was not responsible for breaking Sabbath law; the man who told him to walk was the one responsible. They pressed him further. *"Who is the man who said to you, 'Take up your pallet and walk?'"* The now-healed man said he did not know for certain because Jesus had already moved on into the crowd. Afterward, Jesus found the man in the Temple and said to him, *"See, you are well! Sin no more, that nothing worse may befall you."*

But the healed man went to the Jewish authorities and told them that Jesus was the one who had healed him. This victim in life's events, perhaps naively rather than maliciously, told the authorities the identity of the person, Jesus, who had healed him. For such a man Jesus, who also knew Sabbath Law, was willing to die, if need be.

The ensuing discussion between Jesus and Jewish authorities centered on *"Sabbath."* Since the text has no definite article before *"Sabbath,"* it may well be that this was not a seventh-weekday Sabbath when Jews emulated God's *"day of rest."* But Sabbath Laws were in effect on all feast days— every such day was Sabbath. Jews considered them based on divine example and surely Jesus knew this.

Here the argument between Jesus and Jewish authorities took an unexpected turn. Scribes and Pharisees had long recognized that the living God must still be doing something on the seventh day. To reconcile the idea of continuous divine activity with the ideal of Sabbath rest, Jews separated God's work as creator from his work as judge. On the Sabbath day, God rests from physical work but eternally works in his judgments, condemning the wicked and conferring life on the just. Jesus' answer speaks directly to the problem, *"My Father is working still and I am working."*

Jesus adds, *"The father loves the son and shows him all that he himself is doing."* Dodd (1953) commenting on John 5:20 says that this described how a son fulfilled his apprenticeship in his father's shop. In near-eastern, and Jewish, trades, especially specialized ones such as weaver, metalworker, carpenter, and scribe, a son ordinarily followed a father's trade. To become a master workman a son closely watched his father. If Jesus was a carpenter's son, the passage may be a recollection of Jesus' years spent learning this trade in Joseph's shop at Nazareth.

But Jewish authorities gave Jesus' statement another interpretation. They said that Jesus was making himself equal with God (5:19). To this charge Jesus replied, *"I do nothing without God's prompting"* (Barrett, 1978). Jesus insisted that he was totally dependent on God in that he was doing the work God himself does (5:20-22, 26).

- The father loves the son and shows him all the things he is to do (20).
- The father raises the dead and gives life to the disabled; so does the son (21).
- The father judges and the son judges by the father's will (22).
- The father has life in himself; so the son has life in himself (26).

Jesus continued, *"I can do nothing on my own authority; as I hear, I judge; and my judgment is just, because I seek not my own will but the will of him who sent me. If I bear witness to myself, my testimony is not true; there is another who bears witness to me, and I know that the testimony which he bears to me is true. The works which the Father has granted me to accomplish, these very works which I am doing, bear me witness that the Father has sent me. And the Father who sent me has himself borne witness to me"* (5:30-37).

At the discussion's beginning, Jewish authorities laid charges against Jesus. At its end, Jesus turns the tables on his antagonists and lays charges against them. *"You do not have his word abiding in you, for you do not believe him whom he has sent. You search the scriptures, because you think that in them you have eternal life; and it is they that bear witness to me; yet you refuse to come to me that you may have life. I do not receive glory from men. But I know that you have not the love of God within you. I have come in my Father's name and you do not receive me; if another comes in his own name, him you will receive. How can you believe, who receive glory from one another and do not seek the glory that comes from the only God? Do not think that I shall accuse you to the Father; it is Moses who accuses you, on whom you set your hope. If you believed Moses, you would believe me, for he wrote of me. But if you do not believe his writings, how will you believe my words?"* (5:38-47). In effect, Jesus says, "In your quest to understand what God wants of you, you Jews search the Scriptures. But you do not seek me who is telling you, based on Scriptures, what God wants you to do."

On this contentious note, we believe Year One of Jesus' ministry ends just before Jesus' second Passover during his ministry.

Chapter 4

Year Two of Jesus' Ministry

(John 6:1–10:42)

In Galilee: The Meal for 5,000 by the Seaside (John 6:1-13)
Danger: Very high

Following this sharp discussion, Jesus and his disciples left Judea and journeyed back to the *"other side of the Sea of Galilee"* (the Gospel writer John used the Roman name *"Sea of Tiberias"*). A multitude of people followed him, more than 5,000 men. This year Jesus did not go to Jerusalem to celebrate Passover but instead ate a meal with 5,000 men, some of whom were perhaps Passover pilgrims, on the east side of the Sea of Galilee.

When Jesus saw the crowd was hungry, Jesus asked Philip, *"How are we to buy bread, so that these people may eat?"* Philip had no answer. *"Two hundred denarii,"* he said in despair, *"would not buy enough bread for each of them to get a little."* A denarius was a day's wage for a peasant's work. Jesus and his followers did not have this much money. Andrew, Simon Peter's brother, made a quick survey of the crowd and told Jesus, *"There is a lad here who has five barley loaves and two fish."* This seemed hopeful but then Andrew added, *"What are they among so many?"* Jesus said, *"Make the people sit down."* Now, says the Gospel, there was much grass in the place, so everyone sat down.

The "lad," *paidarion*, was a child or youth, or possibly a young slave. The word is used no place else in the New Testament. The denarius, a common Roman silver coin first issued around 19CE, was a typical day's wage. It pictured Emperor Tiberius (14BCE–37CE) and read "Tiberius Caesar, son of the Deified Augustus and himself Augustus." The reverse side showed Livia, Tiberius' mother, represented as Pax, the goddess of peace. A denarius was mentioned at least eight times in the Gospels (Mt 20:2, 22:19; Mk 6:37, 12:15, 14:5; Lk 7:41, 10:35; and Jn 12:5). The word used for "fish," *opsaria* (plural), meant specifically "fish boiled or roasted to be eaten with bread" (Culpepper, 2005).

Jesus took the fish and loaves and, when he had given thanks, distributed them to the crowd. The people ate as much as they wanted. After they ate their fill, Jesus told his disciples to gather up the left-overs so nothing would be lost. When gathered, the leftovers filled twelve baskets from the original five barley loaves and two fish.

What did this episode signify? Dodd (1963) and Barrett (1978) see this event as John's rendering of the Lord's Supper that became a usual part of a Hellenist-Christian fellowship meal after the Resurrection. In the Synoptic Gospels, the Last Supper happened during Passover season when Jesus had a last meal with his disciples, which became the Lord's Supper in many churches. Jesus also performed a ritual in taking the loaves and fish, giving thanks for them, and distributing them to those assembled. These things were also associated with the Lord's Supper.

Compared to descriptions in the Synoptic Gospels, if it would be the Lord's Supper, John omitted several things from his account.

- He omits "looking up to heaven."
- He omits "the breaking of the bread."

- He describes the bread as "barley loaves," the poorest form of bread.
- He distributes fish rather than wine.
- Jesus distributes the food rather than his disciples doing so.

Despite these differences from the Synoptic Gospels, John's account could reflect a communal supper held by Hellenist Christians. At the time John's Gospel was written, life in the Jesus movement had no standard requirements for a specified ritual during a meal—elements in a fellowship meal were flexible. Hellenist Christians could use poorer bread than the kosher bread used during Hebrews' sacred meals and fish could be substituted for another element— bread, or fish, or wine, or all three. Rather than strict ritual, the thing that mattered most to Hellenist Christians was the sense that Jesus was presiding over the fellowship meal and personally distributing food to his followers.

This story certainly continues the theme of abundance from God that comes to people through Christ. Sometimes the abundance is wine, as in the wedding at Cana; sometimes abundance is water as with the Samaritan woman at Jacob's well; sometimes abundance is spirit, as in the conversation with Nicodemus; sometimes abundance is life, as when Jesus healed the official's son. Here abundance is of bread and fish. John's Gospel indicates the abundant life is offered by God to all people.

The "feeding of the 5,000" also brought in themes not previously considered. Since it was Passover season, this gathering of Jewish men might not have been from Galilee alone but perhaps from the entire Mediterranean world. The east side of the Sea of Galilee would have been an appropriate place for pilgrims to congregate before proceeding down the safer side of the Jordan River into Jerusalem for Passover.

Another distinctive mark in this account was the number of men involved—five thousand. Such a large meeting with a man like Jesus was forbidden by Roman law. The Herods, with their spies and informers all over Judea and Galilee, were certain to find out that many men met with Jesus in Galilee in this openly clandestine way. With their routine fear of insurrection, the Herods would want to question many of these men and its leader, Jesus. By this meeting, Roman nails were sharpened to pound into Jesus' hands and feet.

In Galilee: Jesus Invited to be King (John 6:14-15)
Danger: Potentially very high

When the people saw the sign Jesus had done in feeding the 5,000, they said, *"This is indeed the prophet who is to come into the world!"* Certain people in Galilee and Judea, especially the Zealots, were always hunting a strong, charismatic man to lead an armed rebellion against the Romans. Apparently after Jesus successfully fed 5,000 men and especially because so many people had come to him there, they wanted to make Jesus leader for an uprising. That some people wanted such a leader depicts the volatile character of the social conditions during Jesus life. But Jesus was not to be a political messiah. *"Perceiving then that they were about to come and take him by force to make him king, Jesus withdrew again to the hills by himself"* (Jn 6:15). He refused the kingly role and departed from them.

This event showed Jesus as a magnetic, charismatic leader drawing others to him—"star quality" some might say today. People recognized his confidence in his abilities to accomplish tasks he set for himself and his enormous courage, fearlessness, and outspokenness in a way that challenged them to move beyond their present mundane lives to something better. Why not make this dramatic, articulate man their leader?

But it was not to happen. Jesus' hour to bring in a kingdom had not yet come. When the hour came, it would not be as leader of a violent guerilla band. It would come in a show of power. But the power was of love not war. His life and death would benefit not Jewish people alone but all humankind. As a lone man on a cross, others would look up to him as they looked to the bronze serpent in the wilderness. He would bear their grief, carry their sorrows; by his sufferings sins would be forgiven and healing would come. Jesus recognized these things and rejected people's entreaties to be their mundane king. In the next episode of his life, he would show the people who he really is.

In Galilee: Who Jesus Really Is (John 6:16-21)
Danger: Low from the Herods, high from the priests

Jesus had been alone on the mountain for a number of hours and his disciples were searching for him. When dusk came, his despairing disciples went down to the sea, got into a boat, and started rowing across the sea to Capernaum. A strong wind was blowing and waves arose. When the disciples rowed three or four miles, they saw Jesus walking on the sea, drawing near the boat.

Barrett (1978), among others, pointed out that Jesus may not have miraculously walked on the water. He may have simply been walking on the beach either in the lapping water or beside it—as soon as the disciples' boat reached him, it also reached shore. Translating the Greek word *epi* could be either "on" or "near." Barrett's translation is, *"They wished to take him into the boat, but found...that they had reached the shore."* When Mark's Gospel reported the same incident, it left less doubt that Jesus walked on and not by the sea (Mk 6:43-51).

The disciples were frightened, but Jesus said to them, *"It is I; do not be afraid"* (Jn 6:20). The phrase in Greek is *"ego eimi,"* "I am." This key phrase shows that Jesus identified himself with God. In the Septuagint, the Hebrew Bible's Greek translation, *"ego eimi"* are the exact words God used in identifying himself to Moses in the wilderness after he left Egypt (Exodus 3:13-14). Hellenists routinely heard these words when reading from the Septuagint in their synagogues. In later chapters of John's Gospel, Jesus used these same words to describe himself, his work, and his relationship to God. Here Jesus used them to identify himself to his followers.

In Galilee: Discussion in Capernaum's Synagogue (John 6:22-65)
Danger: Certain Jews grew increasingly hostile

Hellenist Christians were ritually flexible in practicing the Lord's Supper. But, in the discussion between Jesus and Jewish men in the synagogue at Capernaum, John's Gospel demonstrated a theological rigidity.

Some of the 5,000 people who met Jesus on the east side of the Sea of Tiberias, in territory ruled by a reasonably tolerant Herod Philip, wanted to know more of what Jesus would say and do. The next day they looked for him but neither Jesus nor his disciples were around. When boats from Tiberias came near the place where they had eaten, seeking Jesus they got into the boats and went to Capernaum. Capernaum was on the north shore of the Sea of Galilee in territory ruled by Herod Antipas, who had imprisoned and executed John the Baptist. The people disembarked at Capernaum, went into the synagogue, and found Jesus.

Tiberias, on the west-central shore, was a new city in Galilee, built in 17-20CE by the Emperor Tiberius to become Herod Antipas' capital city of Galilee (see Fig 1, Map; Hengel, 1989: 39). Since Jewish authorities did not want Herod Antipas to build another temple, in Tiberias he copied the era's greatest synagogue, the one in Alexandria with its five naves. He also directed Tiberias to mint its own coins and have its own constitution with a *boule* (assembly) headed by an *archon* (leading man or governor). The city was supervised by two officials appointed by the Tetrach Herod, a police officer (*huarchos*) and the market overseer (*agoranomos—nomos*, law, plus *agora*, market).

By this time, some people who had eaten the meal by the sea began to equate the meal with an earlier *"meal in the wilderness"* that they knew about from Scripture (Exodus 16). Moses was recorded as hearing the hungry people murmuring against God and against Moses' leadership. God responded to this murmuring by delivering them quail and *manna*. *"Manna"* meant simply, "what is it?" The Hebrew word was *"manhu."* Exodus described *manhu* as *"morning dew and, when the layer of dew lifted, on the surface of the wilderness was flaky stuff, fine as frost on the ground"* (Alter's translation of Exodus 16:14, 2004: 408). Jewish theologians regarded the giving of *manna* as the miracle *par excellence*, a difficult miracle for even the Messiah to accomplish. Rabbis held that the Messiah would prove his authority by repeating miracles by which, they said, Moses had proved his. "As was with the first redeemer so shall it be with the final redeemer; as the first redeemer caused manna to fall from heaven, even so shall the second redeemer cause the manna to fall" (MacGregor, 1959, on Jn 6:26-34).

The dialogue between Jesus and these Jews went like this. *"When they found him…, they said to him, 'Rabbi, when did you come here?' Jesus answered them…, 'You seek me, not because you saw signs, but because you ate your fill of the loaves.' Then he added, 'Do not labor for food which perishes, but for the food which endures to eternal life, which the Son of Humankind will give you, for on him has God the Father set his seal.' They said to him, 'What must we do, to be doing the works of God?' Jesus answered them, 'This is the work of God, that you believe in him whom he has sent'"* (Jn 6:25-29).

This did not satisfy these Jews, so they went on, *"Then what sign do you do, that we may see, and believe you?"* They also referred to Exodus 16. *"Our fathers ate the manna in the wilderness…' Jesus replied, 'Truly, truly, I say to you'* [Jesus again re-interpreting Scripture], *'it was not Moses who gave you the bread from heaven; my Father gives you the true bread from heaven. For the bread of God is that which comes from heaven and gives life to the world.' They said to him, 'Lord, give us this bread always.' Jesus said to them, 'I am the bread of life. He who comes to me shall not hunger and he who believes in me shall never thirst. This is the will of my Father, that every one who sees the Son and believes in him should have eternal life'"* (6:30-35).

If the conversation had stopped there, these Jews might have been satisfied, and two thousand years of controversy over the meaning of the next comment might have been avoided. But Jesus added a sacramental note. *"Your fathers ate the manna in the wilderness, and they died. I am the bread of life..., the bread which comes from heaven that a man may eat and not die. I am the living bread...from heaven; if any one eats this bread, he will live for ever; and the bread which I shall give for the life of the world is my flesh"* (6:48-51).

The Jews who heard this disputed among themselves. *"How can this man give us his flesh to eat?"* Jesus said to them in his most authoritative way, *"Truly, truly, I say to you, unless you eat the flesh of the Son of Humankind and drink his blood, you have no life in you. He who eats my flesh and drinks my blood has eternal life, and I will raise him up at the last day. For my flesh is food indeed, and my blood is drink indeed. He who eats my flesh and drinks my blood abides in me, and I in him"* (6:52-56). In Judaism, "flesh and blood" referred to one's "whole self." Perhaps Jesus' reference to flesh and blood was simply metaphoric for "follow me, closely." But possibly he was already thinking about the "flesh and blood" as a way to commemorate his life and death in "the Lord's Supper." Jesus' flesh and blood had multiple meanings for people's lives.

Churches still disagree on how to interpret these words. Catholics and Orthodox priests take the words literally. In the Mass, the bread and wine used in their congregations are miraculously changed into the actual body and blood of Jesus. Protestants tend to interpret these words figuratively. As they eat the bread and drink from the cup, Jesus Christ is present among them in a spiritual way.

Other parties in the early Jesus movement did not interpret the "eating and drinking" nearly so boldly. Mark emphasized the covenantal aspect of the supper more than the sacrificial and depended on another story in Exodus to do this, the story of the original sealing of the covenant. *"Moses built an altar at the foot of the Mount [Sinai] and he erected twelve pillars for each of the twelve tribes of Israel. The young men of Israel sacrificed bulls to the Lord, for a communion sacrifice. Moses put half the blood in a basin. This half of the blood he threw upon the altar. Then he took the book of the covenant and read it to the people. They said, 'All that the Lord has spoken we will heed.' Then Moses took the remaining blood and threw it on the assembled people and said, 'Behold the blood of the covenant which the Lord has made with you'"* (Ex 24:4-8). In this way, their covenant was sealed in blood. Mark had this Exodus passage in mind when he described the Lord's Supper. *"As they were eating, Jesus took bread, and blessed, and broke it, and gave it to them, and said, 'Take; this is my body.' He took a cup and when he had given thanks he gave it to them, and they all drank of it. And he said to them, 'This is my blood of the covenant, which is poured out for many'"* (Mk 14:22-24). Matthew followed Mark's wording until the end, when he said, *"This is my blood of the covenant, which is poured out for many for the forgiveness of sins"* (Mt 27:26-28).

Luke changes the ritual considerably. *"Jesus took a cup and when he had given thanks he said, 'Take this, and divide it among yourselves, for I tell you that from now on I shall not drink of the fruit of the vine until the kingdom of God comes"* (Luke 22:17-18). Luke mentions two cups. The first cup emphasizes the fellowship aspect of the meal. The disciples had frequently eaten together and each time, following Jewish custom, they passed a cup from hand to hand to indicate the depth of their fellowship. But in this meal Jesus does not drink from the cup that is passed around. He was telling them that their fellowship was about to be broken by his death. Then Luke repeated the ritual as he had learned it from the other Gospels. *"Jesus took bread, and when he had given thanks he broke it and gave it to them, saying, 'This is my body which is given for you. Do this in remembrance of me.' Likewise the cup after supper, saying, 'This cup which is poured out for you is the new covenant in my blood'"* (Lk 22:19-20). The words "new covenant" come from

Jeremiah (31:32), *"I will make a new covenant with the house of Israel and the house of Judah."* Each of these acts is described as coming from Jesus. Each of the four major parties in the early Jesus movement made its own interpretation of what Jesus had said.

John's Gospel completes his account when Jesus says, *"As the living Father sent me and I live because of the Father, so he who eats me will live because of me. This is the bread which came from heaven, not such as the fathers ate and died; he who eats this bread will live for ever. This [Jesus] said as he taught in the synagogue at Capernaum"* (Jn 6:57-59).

In Galilee: Revolt of Many Galilean Disciples (John 6:66-71)
Danger: Very high; certain Jews are incensed with Jesus; after this they sought to kill him; many Galilean disciples deserted him

When they heard what Jesus had asserted in Capernaum's synagogue, many followers said, *"This is a hard saying; who can listen to it?"* Jesus recognized that his disciples murmured at it. The Hebrews in the wilderness also murmured (the sound made by a large and discontented crowd) against Moses (Exodus 16:2 ff). Jesus said to them, *"Do you take offense at this? Then what if you were to see the Son of Humankind ascending where he was before? It is the spirit that gives life, the flesh is of no avail. The words that I have spoken to you are spirit and life. But there are some of you that do not believe... This is why I told you that no one can come to me unless it is granted him by the Father. [Since] so many followers drew back, Jesus said to the Twelve, 'Do you also wish to go away?' Simon Peter answered him, 'Lord, to whom shall we go? You have the words of eternal life and we have believed, and have come to know, that you are the Holy One of God.' Jesus answered them, 'Did I not choose you, the twelve, and one of you is a devil?' He spoke of Judas, the son of Simon Iscariot, for he, one of the twelve, was to betray him."*

The Twelve had not been mentioned before in John's Gospel and are not mentioned again until the resurrection ap-

pearance to Thomas who is identified as one of the Twelve
(Jn 20:24). Nor is there a place in John's Gospel where Jesus calls the Twelve, nor does the writer John ever name all
Twelve. Yet, this discussion takes place in Galilee which was
the home of the Twelve. The writer John knew of the Twelve
and of this event and inserted this incident in his narrative
because it seemed appropriate at this point. Along with all
the Gospel writers, John had a store of material other than
what he used (see Jn 21: 25).

Instead of embracing Peter's confession, Jesus raises the
question of selection and choice. *"Did I not choose you, the
twelve, and one of you is a devil?"* The verb *eklegomai,* "to
choose" or "to select," refers exclusively to Jesus' selection
of his followers (see Jn 6:70; 13:18; 15:16, 19). But even selection into the special group of Twelve was no guarantee
of a faithful response because one member of the Twelve is
"a devil." To speak of Judas (6:71) as a devil (see 13:2, 27)
means that Judas is drawn to evil more than to God (3:19-21).
By alluding to the devil among the Twelve, Jesus warns his
readers that their faith will always be tested and is always in
jeopardy. Selection has to be followed by a decision of faith.

A note of pathos can be detected in this passage. Large
numbers of Jesus' Galilean followers were deserting him
and Jesus asked the Twelve if they also wanted to leave.
Although Peter answers with memorable words—*"Lord,
to whom shall we go? You...are the Holy One of God"*—the
writer John seems to have let his guard down for a moment
to reveal a discouraged Jesus. By saying what he did, Jesus
alienated many Galilean followers. The writer John is frank
to tell about this despairing moment for Jesus.

In Galilee, then Jerusalem: Feast of Tabernacles (John
7:1-8:1, 8:12-59)
Danger: Very High

*Near the time for the Feast of Tabernacles ("Feast of Suk-
kot") in the Fall, Jesus was still in Galilee with his brothers.*

The brothers said to him, *"Leave here and go to Judea, that your disciples may see the works you are doing. For no man works in secret if he seeks to be known openly. If you do these things, show yourself to the world."* His brothers wanted Jesus to become more widely known for the good he was doing. Jesus said, *"My time has not yet come. Go to the feast yourselves. I am not going up to this feast, for my time has not yet fully come."* So, he remained in Galilee.

The Feast of Tabernacles was a week-long celebration dedicated to remembering what God had done for the Hebrews during their exodus from Egypt. The day before the festival, people built booths to live in during this feast—on their houses' roofs, in the courtyards, in streets and squares, on roads and in gardens. The only requirement was to build them within a Sabbath day's journey of the Temple. Since their ancestors lived in similar circumstances in the wilderness, Jews were to eat and sleep in these booths for the seven days of the feast. On the early autumn evening of the 14th day of the seventh Jewish month *Tishri* (which shifted between September and October), blasts from the priests' trumpets on the Temple Mount announced to Israel the feast's advent.

Tabernacles began on 15 *Tishri*, just as Passover fell on the 15th day of the first month. Tabernacles was the happiest of all Israel's festivals. Fruits and crops were gathered and stored. The land awaited softening by refreshing "latter rain" to prepare it for a new winter wheat crop.

Part of Tabernacles' symbolism was of the water given to the Hebrews from the rock in the desert in their time of need. On each of the Festival's seven days a golden pitcher full of water was carried in a procession from the Siloam Pool to the Temple to symbolize the people's thirst during their desert journey and God's provision of water for them. On the Feast's last and great day, this ritual was changed to celebrate the Hebrews' entrance into the Promised Land with its springs and rivers. God had now provided for all their needs; they no longer needed to carry water with them.

Jerusalem's Siloam Pool from which the water was drawn still exists. The small pool, measuring 33 feet by 19 feet by 19 feet deep, was built by Israel's King Hezekiah due to a water emergency arising in 705BCE from a threat posed by Assyrian King Sennacherib. Prior to this pool, a chief source of Jerusalem's water supply was the Spring Gihon in an undefended part of the Kidron valley. Citizens who filled their water jars at this spring were vulnerable to enemy attack. So Hezekiah's engineering staff conceived the idea of bringing this water to a more protected site. Laborers began to dig from both ends of the project. In order to dodge huge rocks and Kings' Tombs, they dug 583 yards to traverse 366 yards. Scratched on the wall of the Siloam tunnel is a famous inscription seen today in the Turkish Museum in Istanbul, "This is the story of the tunnel while...the axes were against each other and while three cubits were left to cut...the voice of a man...called to his counterpart,...and on the day of the tunnel [being finished] the stonecutters struck each man towards his counterpart, ax against ax and water flowed from the source to the pool." Water still flows through the Siloam tunnel into the Siloam pool, which means *"Sent"* because the water was sent from one place to another.

After his brothers left for the Feast, Jesus decided to go, too, privately. At the Feast, the Jews' chief priests were looking for him saying, *"Where is he?"* The people *"muttered"* about him but, fearing the Jewish authorities, no one spoke openly about him.

Near the middle of the Feast, Jesus went into the Temple and taught. Ordinary Jews marveled, saying, *"How is it that this man has learning, when he has never studied?"* Jesus apparently did not study the Torah with rabbis. But, as a well-raised Jewish boy, he was taught in his hometown synagogue and by his family. Jesus replied, *"My teaching is not mine, but his who sent me."* Jesus referred to an incident that had happened a few days back. *"I healed one man and you all marvel at it. But you tell me I should not have done this because I healed the man on a Sabbath. Think of this,"* Jesus said, *"Moses gave you circumcision, and you circumcise a man on the Sabbath. If on the Sabbath a man receives circumcision so that the law of Moses may not be broken, are you angry with me because on the Sabbath I made a man's whole body well? What do you say to this?"* (7:14-24). John added a theological note, *"not that circumcision is from Moses but from the father."*

Some people said, *"Is not this the man whom they seek to kill? Yet here he is speaking openly and they say nothing to him! Can it be that the authorities really know that this is the Christ?"* But they still had a problem that needed to be re-solved before they could proclaim that Jesus was Messiah. *"We know where this man comes from; but when the Christ appears, so we are told, no one will know where he comes from."* *"True,"* said Jesus. But he went on, *"you know me, and you know where I come from. But I have not come of my own accord. He who sent me is true and him you do not know. I know him for I come from him and he sent me."* Jesus was again insisting he had a special relationship with God that no one else ever had, not even the revered Moses. So Jewish authorities sought to have him arrested. But, says the writer John, no one laid hands on him because his hour had not yet come. Many people were still convinced that he was the Christ and said, *"When the Christ appears, will he do more signs than this man has done?"* (Jn 7:25-31).

Jesus spoke again to ordinary Jews *"on the last day of the feast, the great day"* when worshippers would march seven times around the altar. After the priest returned from Siloam with his golden pitcher of water and for the last time poured its contents at the base of the altar, the worshippers sang the *"Hallel"* to the sound of a flute and priests blew their silver trumpets three times. The mass of worshippers waved a forest of leafy branches towards the altar and chanted the last words of Psalm 118:24-29.

> *This is the day which the LORD has made;*
> *let us rejoice and be glad in it.*
> *Save us, we beseech thee, O LORD…!*
> *Thou art my God, and I will give thanks to thee;*

thou art my God, I will extol thee.
O give thanks to the LORD, for he is good;
for his steadfast love endures forever!

On this day amidst these circumstances, the writer John says, *"Jesus stood up to preach"* (Jn 7:37). Standing to preach was unusual. Most teachers of his time sat while teaching. But so more people could hear his message, Jesus stood. Jesus quoted Scripture to them, *"Out of his heart shall flow rivers of living water"* (Jn 7:38), distinguishing, as he did with the Samaritan woman at Jacob's well, between water from wells ("dead water") and water from rivers ("living water," moving water). In effect, Jesus was repeating a promise he made to this Samaritan woman, *"If any one thirsts, let him come to me and drink."* Jesus perceived that people thirst to find that which sustains life and fills their souls' emptiness. Jesus was a truly refreshing source of fulfilment. He offered his "living water" not as a symbol of water given in the desert but as living water for the soul, abundant, overflowing, and satisfying.

This living water flows from the Spirit of Jesus Christ. But this Spirit will not be fully released into the world until Christ has been *"glorified"* (Jn 7:39). *"Glorified"* in John's Gospel means Jesus' death on the cross followed by his resurrection. Through this selfless dedication, powers were released that were not operative before the event. When Jesus is glorified, then his Spirit will be fully available to all.

Jesus' words and actions divided his listeners. Some said, *"This really is the prophet."* Others said, *"This is the Christ."* But some said, *"The Christ is not to come from Galilee, is he? Has not the scripture said that the Christ is descended from David and comes from Bethlehem, the village where David was?"* Some people sought to arrest Jesus. But no one laid hands on him (7:40-43).

Some Pharisees heard the crowd muttering, so the chief priests and Pharisees sent officers to arrest Jesus. Jesus said, *"I shall be with you a little longer and then I go to him who sent me. You will seek me and you will not find me."* The

Jews said to one another, *"Where does this man intend to go that we shall not find him?"* The officers went back to the chief priests and Pharisees, who said to them, *"Why did you not bring him?"* The officers answered, *"No man ever spoke like this man!"* The Pharisees replied, *"Are you led astray, you also? Have any of the authorities or of the Pharisees believed in him?"*

Actually, one had. The Pharisee, Nicodemus, believed in him. He had talked with Jesus earlier *"at night"* and was both Jesus' follower and a Sanhedrin councilman. In attempting to defend Jesus, he said to them, *"Does our law judge a man without first giving him a hearing and learning what he does?"* But others on the Sanhedrin dismissed this argument with scorn. *"Are you from Galilee too? Search and you will see that no prophet is to rise from Galilee"* (7:44-52). Apparently the writer John, despite his many informants on Jesus' life, did not know the story of Jesus' birth in Bethlehem, the city of David.

John reports that *"each went to his own house, but Jesus went to the Mount of Olives"* to pray and sleep (7:53-8:1). Probably most Hellenist followers of Jesus lived in Jerusalem so that at night *"each went to his own house."* Early in the morning Jesus came again to the Temple. The people also came and Jesus sat down and taught them, *"I am the light of the world; he who follows me will not walk in darkness but will have the light of life."*

The words, *"I am the light of the world,"* pointed to another elaborate ceremony which took place at the Feast of Tabernacles. The Feast's first day concluded with worshippers descending to the Court of the Women. Four golden candelabras were there, each with four golden bowls against which rested four ladders. Four young Levites held a pitcher filled with oil. Priests' wornout clothes served as wicks in these lamps. Every courtyard, every house in Jerusalem was lit up by the light in *"the house of water-pouring."* Men danced with flaming torches while singing hymns and songs of praise. Levites, with harps, lutes, cymbals, and trumpets stood on the fifteen steps leading down from the Court of Israelite Men to the Court of the Women, singing fifteen Songs of Approach from the Book of Psalms. Two priests with trumpets at the upper gate blew them three times as day dawned, then proceeded down the steps. When reaching the tenth step, they blew another threefold blast. Then entering the court itself, they blew another threefold blast while advancing to the Beautiful Gate that opens to the east. As they came to this gate, they turned westward to face the Holy of Holies, saying, "Our fathers who were in this place turned their back on the Sanctuary of the Lord, and their faces toward the east and worshipped towards the rising sun; but as for us, our eyes are towards the Lord."

The light shining from the Temple into the surrounding darkness was a symbol both of the *Shechinah* (the light of God) which once filled the Temple and the *"great light"* which *"the people who walked in darkness"* were to see, and which was to shine *"upon them that dwell in the land of the shadow of death"* (Isaiah 9:2). Jesus referred to this ceremony in the words he spoke that day in the Temple at the Feast of Tabernacles. *"I am the light of the world; he who follows me shall not walk in darkness but shall have the light of life"* (Jn 8:12).

Jesus went on in his sermon. *"When you have lifted up the Son of Humankind, then you will know that I am he (ego eimi) and that I do nothing on my own authority. I speak as the Father taught me. He who sent me is with me. He has not left me alone, for I always do what is pleasing to him."* The Jews said, *"Abraham died, as did the prophets; and you say, 'If any one keeps my word, he will never taste death.' You are not greater than our father Abraham who died, are you? And the prophets died! Who do you claim to be?"* Jesus answered, *"It is my Father who glorifies me, of whom you say that he is your God. You have not known him. I know him. Your father Abraham rejoiced that he was to see my day. He saw it and was glad."* The Jews said to him, *"You are not yet fifty years old, are you, and you have seen Abraham?"* Jesus said to them, *"I say to you, before Abraham was, I am (ego eimi)."* So they took up stones to throw at him; but Jesus hid himself, and went out of the Temple (8:12-59).

In Jerusalem: The Woman Caught in Adultery (John 8:2-11)
Danger: Very high

The story about the woman caught in adultery is an "orphan." No one knows where it fits into Jesus' chronology. May (1988) said bluntly, "This famous story was not originally a part of the Gospel of John." The oldest and best copies of the Greek New Testament do not have it. Some scholars reassign it to Luke's Gospel. The Revised Standard Version has it in a footnote and the New Revised Standard Version puts it in brackets. In order not to divide the account of Jesus at the Feast of Tabernacles (as in both versions above), we see this story as part of Jesus' ministry in Jerusalem.

Scribes and Pharisees must have been on dawn patrol if they caught this woman in the act of adultery *"early in the morning."* We have no indication of the circumstances of her adultery. The online *Jewish Encyclopedia* gives details of Jewish law on adultery in Jesus' time. "The crime can be committed only by and with a married woman; for the unlawful intercourse of a married man with an unmarried woman is not technically adultery in the Jewish law. Under Biblical law, the detection of actual sexual intercourse was necessary to establish the crime (Lev. 18: 20; Num. 5:12, 13, 19)... Ancient Jewish law, as well as other systems of law which grew out of a patriarchal society, does not recognize the husband's infidelity... Although in ancient society and law adultery was regarded as a private wrong committed against the husband, later public law exercised control of its investigation and punishment—organized society was considered impossible unless it punished this crime, which saps the very root of the social life. *'Thou shalt not commit adultery'* is not merely a command that prohibits tampering with the domestic affairs of another; it is also a warning to refrain from unsettling the foundations of society… Law and morality went hand in hand to prevent the commission of this crime. For those who were deaf to the warnings of law and reason, the punishment of death was ordained. Both the guilty wife and her paramour were to be put to death (Deut. 22:22). The punishment for this crime was stoning to death at a place of public execution (Deut. 22:24)."

According to the story, Jesus was teaching outside the Temple when some scribes and Pharisees brought a woman who had been caught in adultery. *"Teacher,"* they said, *"this woman was caught in the very act of committing adultery. Now in the law, Moses commanded us to stone such women. What do you say?"* (8:3-5). As noted in the *Jewish Encyclopedia* above, they do not include the man in this accusation. The story is clear on one point, The writer John says, *"This they said to test him, that they might have some charge to bring against him"* (8:6). Later (18:31), the writer John says that the Romans had denied Jewish courts the right to impose the death penalty and yet the scribes and Pharisees were suggesting that Jesus approve this very thing. This trick question put Jesus in a difficult dilemma—if he followed Roman law, he could not say that she should be put to death; if he followed Mosaic law, he must say that she should be put to death. To answer their question Jesus appeared to have to disobey one law or the other. Regardless of his answer, Jesus could be reported to the appropriate authorities as having broken the law.

Jesus dealt with the question in an intriguing way, *"Jesus bent down and wrote with his finger on the ground."* When they continued to question him, he gave his famous reply, *"Let anyone among you who is without sin be the first to throw a stone at her"* (8:6-8).

What Jesus wrote remains a mystery, perhaps nothing interpretable. One possible explanation of why he wrote on the ground is that it was a feast day and Sabbath laws applied to feast days. Writing was proscribed on a Sabbath, with one exception. According to the Mishnah, the oldest rabbinic legal compilation (about 200CE), writing that left no lasting mark was permitted on a Sabbath. One could write with fruit juice, dirt on the street, or writer's sand' (*Shabbat* 12:5). This law seemed broad enough to permit Jesus to write on the ground. By doing this, Jesus demonstrated to his attackers both that he was well versed in Jewish law and that he was a good Jew. What he wrote we do not know. We do know it fulfilled the law according to the Mishnah. His writing "did not leave a lasting mark" (see May, 1998).

"*One by one beginning with the oldest, the scribes and Pharisees wandered off. When Jesus and the adulterous woman were alone, he asked her, 'Has no one condemned you? 'No one, sir,' she said. Jesus told her, 'Neither do I condemn you. Go, and do not sin again'"* (8:9-11). We do not know whether she obeyed Jesus' admonition.

In Jerusalem: Jesus and the Man Born Blind (John 9:1-42)
Danger: Very high

As Jesus left the Temple and his near escape from arrest, he saw a man blind from birth. His disciples asked him, *"Rabbi, who sinned, this man or his parents, that he was born blind?"* Jews at this time believed everything hurtful in the world had to be the result of sin. Jesus corrected them. *"It was not that this man sinned, or his parents, but that the works of God might be made manifest in him. We must work the works of him who sent me, while it is day; night comes, when no one can work. As long as I am in the world, I am the light of the world."*

By mentioning the *"light of the world"* the writer John reminds his readers of first creation, when God created light. By making the blind man see, Jesus recreated primal creation. He put clay on the man's eyes and commanded him, *"Go, wash in the pool of Siloam,"* the pool from which the water for the Feast of Tabernacles had been drawn. So the man went, washed, and came back seeing.

But his neighbors could not agree whether he was the blind beggar who sat daily by the pool or not, so they took him to the Pharisees, who again asked how he had received his sight. The formerly blind man said, *"He put clay on my eyes, and I washed, and I see."* The Pharisees then asked, *"What do you say about him, since he has opened your eyes?"* The formerly blind man said, *"He is a prophet."*

The Pharisees then went to the blind man's parents and asked them, *"Is this your son, whom you say was born blind? How then does he now see?"* His parents answered, *"We know that this is our son and that he was born blind. How he now sees we do not know, nor do we know who opened his eyes. Ask him. He is of age, he will speak for himself."* According to Jewish law to be *"of age"* (Greek, *likian*) was someone at least thirteen years old. Then he was able to make a legal response. His parents said this because they feared the Jewish authorities, for they had already agreed that, if any one should confess him to be Christ, he was to be put out of the synagogue.

They again called the man before them. Unlike the earlier man whom Jesus healed, this man refused to denigrate Jesus. Instead he said, *"Never since the world began has it been heard that any one opened the eyes of a man born blind. If this man were not from God, he could do nothing."* They answered him, *"You were born in utter sin, and you would teach us?"* They then cast him out.

Jesus came to him as he had gone to the other beggar whom he had healed and said, *"Do you believe in the Son of Humankind?"* This man answered, *"Who is he, sir, that I may believe in him?"* Jesus said to him, *"You have seen him and it is he who speaks to you."* He said, *"Lord, I believe."* And he worshiped him.

The man's words had terrible consequences for him. He was cast out of the synagogue and the Temple, which meant being shunned, cut off from family, friends, Torah, and Sabbath. When reading this story as simply another healing, one could easily miss the loneliness in its final scene when Jesus and the man converse outside the synagogue. The story's tragedy comes from the underlying pathos of being cut off from all practicing Jews and their community, religiously, socially, and commercially, while waiting on God to write a new ending to his life. Many Christians must have experienced such loneliness.

In Jerusalem: Jesus Names Himself the Good Shepherd
(John 10:1-21)
Danger: Increasingly High

To Jewish authorities, the huge unanswered question in previous encounters was, "Who are you, Jesus? When we deal with you, with whom are we dealing, really?" Jesus made one final attempt to answer this question. To do so he resorted to an Old Testament image of a shepherd. He knew Psalm 23, *"The Lord is my shepherd."* He also knew Ezekiel 34. Among other prophets, Ezekial accused Israel and its leaders, kings, princes, priests, and elders of being bad shepherds, of not caring properly for the sheep. Ezekiel declared that to replace these evil shepherds, God himself would become Israel's shepherd.

"Son of Humankind," says the Lord to his prophet, *"prophesy against the shepherds of Israel, prophesy, and say to them..., 'Thus says the Lord GOD: Ho, shepherds of Israel who have been feeding yourselves! Should not shepherds feed the sheep? You eat the fat, you clothe yourselves with the wool, you slaughter the fatlings; but you do not feed the sheep. The weak you have not strengthened, the sick you have not healed, the crippled you have not bound up, the strayed you have not brought back, the lost you have not sought, and with force and harshness you have ruled them. So they were scattered, because there was no shepherd; and they became food for all the wild beasts.*

"Therefore, you shepherds, hear the word of the LORD:... Behold, I am against the shepherds...; I will rescue my sheep from their mouths, that they may not be food for them...

"Behold, I myself...will seek the lost and I will bring back the strayed and I will bind up the crippled and I will strengthen

the weak and the fat and the strong I will watch over; I will feed them in justice. I will save my flock, they shall no longer be a prey. I will make with them a covenant of peace... And they shall know that I, the LORD their God, am with them and that they... are my people" (Ezekiel 34:1-31).

"I am the door of the sheep; I am the good shepherd" (Jn 10:7, 11). Jesus' words recall the context of Ezekiel's prophesy but also of shepherding practices in Judea at the time. The sheepfold was a walled enclosure without a roof but with a heavy door watched by a gatekeeper. Shepherds gave their sheep names as farmers tend to do with their animals. A name is proof of individual knowledge and affection. The regular custom was not to follow the sheep but to walk in front of them as their guide. The sheep knew the voice of their shepherd. Three or four shepherds would go together to a sheepfold where herds would mix with one another. Although flocks would move independently of one another, they often became mixed while pasturing. After the sheep had time to graze, shepherds went to different sides of a valley, called out in his specific tones, and sheep of each drew from the herd to their own shepherd. The flocks passed on as orderly as they had come (MacGregor, 1959).

Jesus is *"the good shepherd."* The Greek word, *kalos,* translated "good," is nearly untranslatable by a single word. *Kalos* combines the ideas of beautiful, fit, competent, excelling, and deeds of power and moral excellence that result in health and well-being. It implies "model" or "true." Jesus fit the meaning of the Greek word *kalos,* good. But, after Jesus came, the word had a new referent. John's Gospel firmly asserts Jesus is *the* model for *"the good."* *"The good shepherd"* knows the sheep by name and they know him. The good shepherd lays down his life for his sheep. He does not run away when the wolf attacks but protects the sheep even at the cost of his own life. The writer John pushes this point to its conclusion. The relationship between shepherd and sheep is like the relationship between the Father and the Son. The Son knows the Father's will, and the Father knows the Son's. What is good is what Jesus did. What is true about life is the way Jesus lived.

"I have other sheep not of this fold but I must bring them in also." This thought could refer to Jewish people, Gentiles, Hellenists, generations yet to come, or all of them. When they heed the voice of Jesus Christ, they as individuals also become part of a flock with one shepherd.

Jesus is both the *"shepherd"* and the *"door of the sheep."* Jesus as the *"gate"* referred to Jesus as the "gateway to life." Jesus as the *"good shepherd"* is the one who leads the way to life (Hellenist Christians were often called followers of *"the Way"*). Jesus is both guardian and liberator of the flock, protecting it by night and leading it by day. To seal his purposes, Jesus declared that the choice to lay down his life is his own. *"I have the power to lay it down,"* Jesus says, *"and I have the power to take it up again"* (Jn 10:18). But he adds, *"This charge I have from my father."* Jesus' decision accords with the Father's will for him. All this he said between the Feast of Tabernacles (September, October) and the Feast of Dedication (December). Both Jewish people and their leaders understood what he said.

In Jerusalem: Feast of Dedication—"I and the Father are One" (John 10:22-42)
Danger: Very High

It was winter, the time of the Feast of the Dedication in Jerusalem. Jesus was walking in the portico of Solomon on the Temple's east side, the warmest spot on this cold winter day. Jews gathered around him and said, *"How long will you keep us in suspense? If you are the Christ, tell us plainly."* Jesus answered, *"'My sheep hear my voice and I know them; they follow me and I give them eternal life, and they shall never perish, and no one shall snatch them out of my hand. I and the Father are one.' The Jews took up stones again to stone him."* Jesus protested to them, *"If I am not doing the works of my Father, then do not believe me. But if I do them, even though*

*you do not believe me, believe the works, that you may know
and understand that the Father is in me and I am in the Father."*
Again officials tried to arrest him but somehow he escaped
and *"went away across the Jordan to the place where John at
first baptized and stayed there"* (10:40).

John's Gospel, and presumably the Hellenist-Christian
community, presented Jesus as someone who increasingly
saw himself as *"one with God."* John's Prologue stated, *"And
the Word became flesh and dwelt among us"* (Jn 1:14). Jesus'
clearest statement occurred at the Feast of Dedication in
December when he responded to a gathering of Jews who
asked, *"How long will you keep us in suspense? If you are the
Christ, tell us plainly."* Jesus told them plainly, *"I and the Father are one"* (10:30). The Jews clearly did not want to hear
this. *"The Jews took up stones again to stone him."* Jesus
again escaped.

John's narrative breaks at this point. Possibly the writer
John was speaking of a considerable length of time in which
he had no information about Jesus until Jesus came back
to Jerusalem. Jesus went to a familiar area where he was
first called into his ministry by John the Baptist, *"beyond the
Jordan,"* northeast of Jericho. We speculate this incident is
more than it appears. In John's Gospel, Jesus remained there
for some time. More likely, unbeknown to the writer John,
Jesus went back to Galilee where he learned that John the
Baptist was arrested by Herod Antipas and, soon after, executed by him.

In Galilee: Overview of Events after John Was Executed
(John 11:1-13:16, 18:1-21:19; Mark 11:1-16:8)
Danger: High

Up to this point in the chronology, we have exclusively
followed the narrative in the Gospel of John. But part of
the chronology in Mark's Gospel seems appropriate to consider here. Beginning with the execution of John the Baptist,
Mark's chronology followed Jesus as he traveled through the

area ruled not by Herod Antipas, John's executioner, but by his brother, Herod Philip, who was apparently more tolerant of Jesus' ministry.

When John was executed, Jesus left Capernaum in the territory of Herod Antipas, who had executed John the Baptist, and went *"across the river"* (the Upper Jordan River that flows from Lake Samechontis due south to the Sea of Galilee), to Bethsaida in the territory of Herod Philip (Mk 6:30). With his disciples he then proceeded north into Caesarea Philippi, Herod Philip's capital city, and even farther north and west into the region of Tyre and Sidon. We surmise Jesus was struggling over decisions of what to do next. His decisions focused on, first, whether to go to Jerusalem where he undoubtedly recognized he would face the death penalty since he knew political and religious leaders there were out to get him, and, second, whether to take the Twelve with him with possible similar consequences for them as well. From these northern places of refuge, Jesus decided to go boldly back to Jerusalem, with his disciples, for his arrest, trial, and death.

Jesus' northward journey and return could easily fit into the space provided in John's Gospel. The interval in question is from the Feast of Dedication (Hanukkah) in December (Jn 10:1-38) to the Feast of Passover in the spring. John's Gospel, based on reports by Hellenist-Christians who lived in Judea and Jerusalem, told only a little about Jesus' ministry in Galilee, whereas Mark's Gospel, based on his Galilean disciples' memories, knew little of Jesus ministry in Judea. Jesus was in Jerusalem for the Feast of Dedication. John was arrested around this time. Going north out of Jerusalem, Jesus stopped in the place *"across the Jordan where John had baptized"* and then, unbeknown to informants for John's Gospel, proceeded north to Galilee, then to Caesarea Philippi and onward. Eventually he retraced his steps down the Jordan Valley and came to Bethany, Lazarus' hometown, just before Passover and went on to his final days in Jerusalem as narrated by Mark, the other two Synoptics, and John.

Such an account provides a way to connect events in Mark's Gospel with those in John's Gospel.

According to Mark's Gospel, when Jesus returned to Galilee after his baptism, he went to Capernaum where he called four fishermen to be his disciples—Simon Peter, Andrew, James, and John (Mk 1:16-20). He began a series of astonishing healings, including a man with an unclean spirit, Simon Peter's mother-in-law, and others who were ill with various diseases and demons. He left Capernaum and went throughout Galilee, preaching in synagogues, healing the ill, and casting out demons (Mk 1:40-45).

Jesus withdrew with his disciples to the Sea of Galilee, and a great multitude followed him. They came from Galilee, Judea, Jerusalem, Idumea, Tyre, Sidon, and from beyond the Jordan (3:8). He went up on the mountain, where he appointed Twelve to be with him (3:13-19). He sent them out to preach in Galilean villages and have authority to cast out demons. *"Then he went home; and the crowd came together again, so that they could not even eat"* (3:20).

Scribes and Pharisees came down from Jerusalem to investigate his ministry (3:22-30). Standing by the sea to preach, Jesus attracted a very large crowd. He got into a boat and spoke while the crowd sat beside the sea on the land (4:1). When evening came, he said to his disciples, *"Let us go across to the other side."* Leaving the crowd, Jesus and his disciples got into a boat and left. Other boats followed them. On the sea a great storm arose and Jesus calmed the sea for everyone (3:35-41).

Jesus was now approaching the zenith of his healing ministry. He went to the country of the Gerasenes and healed a powerful man who had multiple mental problems, *"unclean spirits"* Mark's Gospel calls them, a legion of them. Mark went on to say that the unclean spirits begged Jesus not to expel them from the country but to send them into a nearby herd of two thousand pigs, which Jesus did. The pigs immediately rushed down a steep bank and drowned in the sea. Of course, Jews did not eat pigs' meat. Possibly the disturbance made by the young man during his healing startled the pigs so that, despite pleas from their Gentile herdsmen, they fled the spot (5:1-20). Not being allowed to eat pigs' meat, Jewish listeners might have chuckled on hearing this story.

When Jesus crossed the sea by boat, he again faced a great crowd. A ruler of a synagogue, Jairus by name, sought Jesus out to heal his 12-year old daughter who was at the point of death (5:21). As Jesus went with him, a woman who had a flow of blood for 12 years came up behind him in the crowd and touched his garment. Immediately the hemorrhage ceased and the woman believed she was healed. Jesus felt power go out of him, looked around, and asked, *"'Who touched my garments?' The woman confessed and Jesus said, 'Daughter, your faith has made you well. Go in peace and be healed of your disease.'"* At the same time, word came to the ruler of the synagogue that his little girl was dead. Jesus went to the child and took her hand. The girl immediately got up and walked. All present were amazed (5:22-43). Building on these successes, Jesus sent out the Twelve to expand his work (Crosson 1998: 280, and Horsley 1989: 50, argue that Jesus sent out the disciples to revitalize "local community life" in Galilee's villages). They were successful, casting out many demons and, by anointing with oil, many sick people were healed (6:7-13). *"The apostles returned to Jesus and told him all they had done and taught"* (6:30).

The time period covered by these foregoing events was actually quite short. Mark emphasizes this shortness by his frequent use of the word *"immediately,"* eutheos in Greek, very little time passing between one event and another. Mark's Gospel uses this word 35 times. Mark did not mentioned any Passover prior to the final one, nor even that Jesus celebrated any of the three pilgrimage feasts of Judaism in Jerusalem. In Mark's Gospel, Jesus' ministry in Galilee possibly covered only three or four months between Hanukkah in December and Passover in the Spring when Jesus went to Jerusalem for the final time. All this contrasts with accounts in John's Gospel, which mentions that Jesus attended three Passovers and several other Feasts.

Mark noted the special relationship between Jesus and John the Baptist (Mk:8, 9). Jesus' disciples asked him, *"Why do the scribes say that first Elijah must come [before the Messiah]?"* (Malachi 4:5). Jesus said to them, *"Elijah does come first to restore all things. And how is it written of the Son of Humankind, that he should suffer many things and be treated with contempt? But I tell you that Elijah has come, and they did to him whatever they pleased, as it is written of him"* (Mk 9:11-13). In brief, following a simple formula, Jesus could have thought that John the Baptist's death meant that his own death was imminent.

Baptist = Elijah = he was killed
Jesus = Messiah = he will be killed

Although this formula might explain Jesus' thinking, it masks his deep emotions over it. Jesus was facing the loss of the Baptist, his cousin, mentor, exemplar, friend. Further, John's unnecessarily brutal death, by beheading with the head paraded before a crowd of revelers, signified the contempt and rejection Jerusalem's Herodian and priestly officials held for what John and Jesus stood for. Jesus came to an agonizing recognition that his own death would be extremely painful. Jesus' quietly discerning remark, *"Come away by yourselves and rest a while,"* concealed the avalanche of emotion that surrounded it (6:31).

In Galilee: The Execution of John the Baptist (Mark 6:14-29)
Danger: High; Having killed John, Herod Antipas could turn his attention to Jesus

We have two stories about the death of the Baptist. One is told in Mark's Gospel and the other by Josephus (94), the first century historian of Jewish affairs. Mark reported that Tetrach Herod Antipas decided to throw a birthday party for himself and by the time it was over, he had executed John the Baptist. This deed changed the course of Jesus' ministry.

Because of the execution, Jesus had to decide when, or even whether, he would return to Jerusalem.

The party was apparently a loud and boisterous affair. Mark reported that Herodias, Antipas' wife, was earlier incensed about John. She had been married to Antipas' brother Philip but, after an affair with Antipas in Rome, divorced Philip and married Antipas. For these acts, John called Herodias an adulteress according to the Law. Antipas then had the Baptist arrested. Herodias' opportunity to deal a fatal blow to the Baptist came during this party. Herodias' daughter, Salome, danced for the assembled guests and so pleased the drunken Antipas that he vowed to give her anything she wanted, even up to half his kingdom. Egged on by her mother, Salome requested the head of John the Baptist on a platter. The king felt he could not back down from his vow. He sent a guard with orders to bring John's head. The soldier complied. He brought the Baptist's head on a platter and gave it to Salome. She gave it to her mother. When John's disciples learned of the murder, they took his body and buried it in a tomb (Mk 6:17-29).

Josephus, the Jewish historian, told quite another story about the affair. The action in Josephus' story took place at Fortress Machaerus, an Antipas' stronghold southeast of Jerusalem on the eastern side of the Dead Sea. Josephus also reported that Antipas had married his brother's divorced wife. But in marrying Herodias, Antipas had to divorce his previous wife, the daughter of Aretus IV, a powerful Nabatean king. Nabatea was a formidable kingdom south and east of Judea whose capital was the famed Petra. When the king's daughter returned to her father's house in disgrace, Aretus gathered his army and invaded Judea. Many of Antipas' soldiers were killed and Antipas was debased by the action. John the Baptist, acting as a prophet, spoke for the Lord against unjust actions by Antipas, who then arrested John and, while he was in prison, executed him.

We have no way of knowing which account is closer to fact but in either case John the Baptist was executed by

Herod Antipas, Roman-appointed Tetrach, ruler of Galilee and Perea, because Herod considered him a menace to his rule.

Neither account was dated. The date for the party suggested in John's Gospel was near the end of the "Feast of Dedication" (actually a boisterous celebration of a re-dedication of the Second Temple during the Maccabean Revolt; 10:40). This feast, otherwise called Hanukkah, was the most unruly of Hebrew feasts, a time for drinking, carousing, shouting, and stomping designed to drown out the villain Haman's name. Some rabbis even instructed people to get drunk in the celebration which was similar to a Jewish Mardi Gras or a Christmas office-party where alcohol runs freely. Such settings fit the description of Herod's "birthday" party.

Putting these two facts together may give us a date for the beheading. Mark tells of a disorderly party. John tells that Jesus left Jerusalem shortly after the Feast of Dedication, Hanukkah, and then Jesus disappeared briefly from John's story until he emerged again just before Passover, three months later, at the spot where the Baptist had ministered. From there, according to John's Gospel, Jesus proceeded to Jerusalem and the cross.

In Galilee: From Capernaum to Caesarea Philippi to Tyre and Back (Mk 1:1-10-52)

We suggest that in this three month period from Hanukkah to Passover, Jesus engaged in a journey described in Mark. This journey was unknown to John, who knew little about Jesus' activities in Galilee. Our suggestion is that, when John the Baptist was executed during Hanukkah, Jesus returned to Galilee. Then he went beyond Galilee to Caesarea Philippi, Tyre, Sidon, and returned to the Capernaum-Bethsaida area (see Fig 1, Map). Jesus then journeyed south to Jericho, Bethany, Bethpage, the Mount of Olives, and emerged in Jerusalem just as the Passover was about to be celebrated. We believe Jesus' long walking tour was a journey of decision.

After the Baptist was executed, Jesus took the extensive journey for at least two reasons, first, to avoid Antipas' territories and, second, to think things through on what course of action to follow. His trip included crossing the "Upper Jordan" river that empties into the northern shore of the Sea of Galilee between Capernaum on the west side of this river, in Herod Antipas' jurisdiction, and Bethsaida on the east side, in the more moderate Herod Philip's jurisdiction (6:45). But when people kept crowding around him, he moved farther north toward Tyre and Sidon (7:24), returned to Bethsaida, then went into the Decapolis region (ten independent Greek-speaking towns southeast of Bethsaida), and again returned to Bethsaida. There, crowds gathered around Jesus. Jesus then took his disciples north, to villages near Philip's capital city, Caesarea Philippi in Upper Galilee, where there were comparatively few Jews (8:27).

In Galilee: Jesus Feeds 5,000 Followers (Mark 6:31-44)
Danger: Low

In the first part of his journey, Mark recorded one of the most important events in Jesus' ministry. After receiving word of the Baptist's death, Jesus decided to go with his disciples to a *"lonely place"* where they could rest and pray. The crowd that had been with Jesus earlier had a good idea of where he was going, so they preceded him to this deserted spot. The crowd was composed of five thousand men (6:44). Although John's Gospel also recorded the event (see above, Jn 6:1-14), John's report significantly differs from Mark's account.

Brueggemann (1999: 346-347) brilliantly catches the sense of this extraordinary event. "The feeding of the multitudes, recorded in Mark's Gospel, is an example of the new world coming into being through God. When the disciples, charged with feeding the hungry crowd, found a child with five loaves and two fishes, Jesus *took, blessed, broke, and gave* the bread to the people. These four italicized verbs are decisive in Christians' sacramental existence. Jesus conducted a Eucharist, a gratitude. He demonstrated that the world is filled with abundance and freighted with generosity. If bread is broken and shared, there is enough for all. Jesus is engaged in the sacramental, a subversive re-ordering of public reality.

"The profane is the opposite of the sacramental. 'Profane' means flat, empty, one-dimensional, exhausted. Market ideology wants us to believe that the world is profane—life consists of buying and selling, weighing, measuring and trading, and then finally sinking into death and nothingness. But Jesus presents an entirely different kind of economy, one infused with the mystery of abundance and a cruciform kind of generosity. Five thousand are fed and twelve baskets of food are left over—one for every tribe of Israel. Jesus transforms the economy by blessing the bread and breaking it beyond self-interest. From broken Friday bread comes Sunday abundance. Here, people do not grasp, hoard, resent, or act selfishly. They watch as the juices of heaven multiply the bread of earth."

In Galilee: Jesus Leaves Galilee For a Northward Trip To Make a Decision; the Syro-Phoenician Woman (Mark 7:24-37)
Danger: Moderately High

A committee of Pharisees traveled to Galilee to investigate Jesus' credentials and were unsatisfied by what they learned (Mk 7:1-23). After these discussions, Jesus no longer felt safe to stay in Galilee. He withdrew farther north than he had ever been before. He went as far as Tyre and Sidon, a territory not congenial to Jews—Josephus described its inhabitants as "notoriously our bitterest enemies" (Grundy-Volk, 1995: 161). Farmers living outside these cities, many of whom were Jews, produced food for the city-dwellers and these urbanites consumed so much that farmers had little left over for themselves. Being in Tyre and Sidon was a dangerous place for a Jew like Jesus to be wandering about.

Shortly after arriving there, a most unusual woman confronted Jesus. She was "*a Greek woman, a Syro-Phoenician by birth,*" a Gentile. She begged Jesus to have mercy on her daughter who was severely possessed by a demon. This woman was desperate; for no other reason would she approach a Jew to heal her daughter. Nor would any woman have approached any man unless she was so desperate. In no culture of the day did women address men they did not know and certainly not on an open street. But there she was, imploring the Jewish Jesus to help her. In her need, she was breaking the human-constructed barriers that kept her from her daughter's healing.

Jesus' reaction might seem strange, "*Let the children be fed first. It is not fair (kalon) to take the children's bread and throw it to dogs*" (Mk 7:27). *Kalon* might also mean "good" or "right." As noted earlier, much of Greek philosophy was a quest to discover what was good, right, appropriate, *kalon.* Jesus' action may not have been so strange from the point of view of his Hebrew followers, as represented by James the brother of Jesus. This party in the early Jesus movement believed from the very beginning that Jesus' mission was only to Jewish people and Jesus' statement reflects their belief. The woman was not satisfied with this response. She answered immediately, "*Yes, sir, yet even the dogs under the table eat the children's crumbs.*" In effect, she was saying, "Could I not have a 'crumb' from your ministry to heal my daughter?" Jesus was duly impressed. "*For saying that, you may go,*" he said. "*The demon has left your daughter.*" The daughter was healed instantly.

Having healed a man who was deaf, and having again fed a large crowd that gathered to see him, Jesus left the region of Tyre, went through Sidon to the Sea of Galilee, then to the Decapolis region. He had not succeeded in removing himself from crowds' attentions nor perhaps from Herod Antipas' attention. He probably also experienced some of the discrimination about which Josephus had written.

He returned again to Bethsaida when Pharisees accosted him once again and people brought a blind man to him to be healed. Jesus took the blind man out of the village and there restored his sight. Seeking the solitude that seemed to be denied them, Jesus and the Twelve again turned northward.

In Galilee: Jesus Is Called "Messiah" (Mark 8:27-38)
Danger: Moderate

Jesus went with his disciples from Bethsaida to villages around Caesarea Philippi. This newly built capital of Herod Philip, son of Herod the Great and brother of Herod Antipas, was equidistant east of Tyre on the Mediterranean Sea and north of the Sea of Galilee, outside Herod Antipas' territory.

There Jesus asked his disciples a significant question. *"Who do people say that I am?"* They gave him the answers they had heard on street corners, in market places, and at synagogues. *"You are John the Baptist come back from the dead..., you are Elijah, you are one of the prophets."* These were dangerous things to say about Jesus. John the Baptist was killed by Herod Antipas. Elijah was the enemy of kings and ruling powers. Prophets had opposed kings of Israel and Judah and taken strong stands against their policies. If Jesus were any of these, he would indeed be Herod Antipas' enemy.

Jesus then asked the next question, *"Who do you say that I am?"* Peter answered him, *"You are the Christ [the anointed, the Messiah]"* (Mk 8:28). This insight on Peter's part recognized that Jesus was more in stature than any of those mentioned by people in general. He was the one promised by God who would free God's oppressed people.

What the messiah would actually do was a matter of great debate among Jews. Was he to be Judaism's great spiritual leader who would free people from their sins? Or was he, as many within Galilee and Judea considered him, a political leader who would free their small nation from Rome's power? If the latter was how the land's rulers were seeing the title, for Jesus to acknowledge that he was messiah would be extremely dangerous. No wonder Jesus said to his disciples, *"Tell no one about this."*

"Jesus began to teach his disciples that the Son of Humankind (uios tou anthropou) must suffer many things, and be rejected by the elders, chief priests, and scribes, be killed, and after three days rise again. He said this plainly. Peter took him aside, and began to rebuke him. Turning and seeing his disciples, he rebuked Peter, 'Get behind me, Satan! For you are setting your mind not on divine things but on human things'" (Mk 8:31-33).

Jesus, in describing himself in terms of the Son of Humankind, links him with a description in the book of Daniel, *"I looked, and there before me was one like a Son of Humankind, coming with the clouds of heaven"* (7:13). A *"cloud of heaven"* is the great symbol of the Old Testament for God. A cloud led the Israelites through the wilderness. *"The Son of Humankind coming in a cloud"* relates Jesus with God himself. God is seen in Jesus Christ and Jesus Christ as his son has God's power of attorney to act for God in God's dealings with human beings. A cloud was at Jesus' baptism, transfiguration, and ascension (Acts 1:9-11).

Jesus knew now that suffering was in his future and began to state it plainly. He knew he would be rejected by his people's elders and leaders. This was not a prophetic insight but a practical application of Jesus' situation. The elders, priests, and Sanhedrin, had already taken stands against him. His disagreements with the Pharisees indicated they would be unlikely to defend him. Jesus now announced that all these would conspire to kill him. The forces of religion and government did away with John the Baptist. Why would Jesus not suffer a similar fate?

What was new was Jesus' announcement that he would rise again. The disciples did not understand this pronouncement. When Jesus died, they did not stand around his tomb waiting for him to rise. Instead, they deserted him and fled.

"Peter took Jesus aside and began to rebuke him." Peter thought that Jesus' ministry should go from triumph to tri-

umph. Jesus should be honored for healing the sick, giving sight to the blind, helping the lame to walk. Why should he die, why should he talk about his death? Peter thought of the glories of Christ's ministry, not the minister's suffering. At this point, Peter's was a theology of personal glory not of crucifixion.

But Jesus rebuked Peter, *"Get behind me, Satan! For you are setting your mind not on divine things but on human things."* Saying that Peter was allied with Satan was harsh. But Jesus had fought this dark, evil, and intricate power since he went into the wilderness after his baptism. Anything that turned Jesus from his determined course toward Jerusalem was a suggestion that came from the powers of darkness. Jesus' theology was of the cross not of his own glory—his glory was the cross.

In villages near Caesarea Philippi, danger and destiny met in Jesus' life and destiny won. His destiny was under God and he accepted this destiny. *"Jesus called to him the multitude with his disciples, and said to them, 'If any man would come after me, let him deny himself and take up his cross and follow me'"* (Mk 8:34).

From his boyhood on, Jesus knew crucifixion was how Romans dealt with people whom they considered a menace to even Jewish law and order, no less Rome's (Cahill, 1999). He did not seek crucifixion. It would be thrust on him by the authorities due to his outrageous claim that he and God were one and the same.

"Crucifixion was the ultimate form of Roman humiliation and, to understand it properly, we have to imagine a grove of huge poles set up near a central thoroughfare where any day as we pass by we may see fellow citizens pinned to the poles with great iron nails, pierced through their joints that were ripped open and left to be drained of blood as if they were animal carcasses. Every day freshly crucified victims appear on the poles as old victims expire and are carted off for burial. The crucified men, twisted, bloody torsos stripped for all to see, anti-Adonises, writhe and grimace most horribly in their pain. Delicate citizens pass by quickly with averted eyes, while the more sportive and cruel…taunt the naked men, in the same way that…people always gathered eagerly in ages past to witness public executions. We spit on the pierced men and tell them how happy their pain makes us, how richly they deserve it, that our only wish is to see their dying last as long as possible… The public, physical humiliation—beginning with the flogging of Jesus by Roman centurions, the mock crowning with thorns pressed down into Jesus' skull, and all that followed—this was a trauma not only to Jesus' followers but to Jesus, to his soul as well as his body" (Cahill, 1999: 286-287).

It was to this to which Jesus was calling his disciples when he said, *"Take up your cross and follow me."*

In Galilee: Jesus' Transfiguration (Mark 9:2-9)
Danger: Low

"After six days Jesus took with him Peter, James, and John, and led them up into a high mountain apart by themselves and he was transfigured before them. His garments glistened, dazzling white as snow, as no one on earth can bleach them. And there appeared Elijah and Moses talking with Jesus. Peter said to Jesus, Teacher (Rabbi), it is well we are here; let us make three tents (booths), one for you, one for Moses, and one for Elijah. He did not know what to say, for they were terrified. And a cloud overshadowed them and a voice came out of the cloud, saying, 'This is my beloved Son; listen to him.' And suddenly, looking around, they no longer saw anyone with them except Jesus. And as they were coming down the mountain, he charged them to tell no one what they had seen, until the son of humankind has risen from the dead."

This is a strange story. Its significance may relate to Jesus' previous statement. *"Truly I tell you, there are some standing here who will not taste death until they see that the kingdom of God has come with power."* *"Truly I tell you"* is the New Testament equivalent to the Old Testament command, *"Thus says the Lord."* In this solemn announcement Jesus said that some standing here will not die until they see the kingdom of God come with power. The "some" surely included Peter, James, and John, who went with Jesus onto the mountain and received the assurance that *"the kingdom of God [will] come with power."*

"Peter, James, and John" were three favored disciples, who gave primary leadership to key groups in the mission to the world after Jesus' resurrection. Having seen Jesus in his transfigured state prepared them to see him in his resurrected state.

"Jesus led them up a high mountain apart by themselves." In the Bible, revelations of God often took place on mountains. God came to Moses on a mountain in the desert. God came to Elijah when he sought the same mountain in his moment of greatest need. Now these three disciples were on a mountain with Jesus.

"Jesus was transfigured before them." The Greek word, *metamorphosis*, transfiguration, meant a complete and total change of one's being. With tales of people turning into animals and gods turning into people, the poet Ovid had recently introduced the word into Roman literature. For the first time, these three, Peter, James, and John, saw Jesus in his transcendent glory. Prior to this, they had seen him only as Jesus of Nazareth doing wondrous things. Now they began to see him as the son and beloved one of God.

"His clothes became dazzling white, such as no one on earth could bleach them." When the Messiah arrives, Jewish lore said, he will radiate like the sun. Jesus now fit this vision.

"There appeared to them Elijah and Moses talking with Jesus." These were the two greatest men among Hebrew people. Moses saved them from perpetual slavery and gave the law and covenant to Israel. Elijah (whose name combined the Elohim as God was known in the Northern Kingdom of Israel with the Yahweh of the Southern Kingdom of Judah) was their prototype prophet. Who greater than these could God

summon at this moment? The great men of the past stand at Jesus' side, testifying to the character of his life and mission.

"*Peter said to Jesus, 'Rabbi, it is good for us to be here. Let us make three tents, one for you, one for Moses, and one for Elijah.'*" Mark adds, "*He did not know what to say, for they were terrified*" (9:6). Was Peter speaking only in embarrassment, as some scholars suggest, to cover his complete lack of understanding of what was happening before him? Perhaps Peter wanted only to retain the vision of Jesus' healing power rather than to see him going to his cross when Jesus said earlier, "*Deny yourself, pick up your cross, follow me.*" Peter was repelled by seeing Jesus as a suffering servant who goes to the cross.

Was Peter recalling that tents were extremely important in Jewish life. The Greek word "dwelt," *eschenosen*, actually means "tabernacled," "pitched a tent." A main feature of the Jewish Feast of Tabernacles was pitching a tent. For a week Jewish people lived in tents to commemorate their time in the wilderness when God cared for them while they could not care for themselves. Or possibly Peter was recalling the "tent of meeting" that Israel erected in the desert in order to meet God. Initially, unlike other gods, Israel's God had no temple, no regular place in which to meet with his people (see Stephen's speech, Acts 7:48). So in the desert Israel built a tent in order to meet God. Peter did not suggest they build "shrines" to Moses, Elijah, and Jesus. He suggested they build tents, where, away from the day's heat and bystanders' prying eyes, all could meet God as God had come to them this day. Peter volunteered to build such a tent, a booth, another tent of meeting.

"*Then a cloud overshadowed them.*" A cloud is the visible form of the governing, guiding, yet hidden form of God in the Old Testament. A cloud reveals shapes and forms but also hides them. The cloud stood for God both hidden and revealed. The word for "overshadowed" suggests a vaporous cloud that casts a shadow, a shining cloud surrounding and enveloping persons with its brightness. "Enveloping them in the brightness of the presence of God" is what it could have meant. The cloud represented the creative energy of the immediate presence and power of God.

"From the cloud came a voice, 'This is my Son, the Beloved. Listen to him.'" In Psalm 2:7, God says to the newly crowned king of Israel, *"You are my son. Today I have begotten you."* This does not denote physical generation from God; there is nothing in this statement that indicates that God is the king's physical father. It says, instead, that God has chosen this particular person, this human being, to rule God's people in God's name. This voice may have represented Jesus' enthronement as regent of God, king of God's people. He is God's "beloved one." The beloved knows the father's will, hopes, and dreams, the word of the father. *"Listen to him"* recalls the words of Moses enshrined in the most important creedal statement of Israel, *"Hear, O Israel, the Lord our God is one Lord. And you shall love the Lord your God with all your heart and with all your mind and with all your strength"* (Deut 6:4). Jesus' disciples are to give the same attention to Jesus. He is the father's will and word; they are to attend to him with their whole being.

"Suddenly" it was over. *"When they looked around, they saw no one with them any more except Jesus."* Jesus remained when Moses and Elijah disappeared. As they moved down this mountain, not only had Jesus changed, metamorphosized, in their presence but they too had changed, all their world had changed. They now saw Jesus, a rabbi from Nazareth, in a completely new light and nothing was ever the same again.

In Galilee: Announcement Of Coming Events—Jesus' Irrefutable Decision is Made (Mark 9:30-32)

When Jesus and his disciples arrived in Galilee after these momentous events, Jesus told his disciples of the decision he made while they were wandering about. *"The Son of Humankind is to be betrayed into human hands, and they will kill him. Three days after being killed, he will rise again."* This was his destiny and he accepted it. From this moment on, there was no more hesitation on Jesus' part, no more going here and there with no apparent purpose. Jesus now set his course toward Jerusalem. He would die there and there he would rise from the dead.

Chapter 5

Year Three of Jesus' Ministry: From Capernaum to Jerusalem and the Final Passover of His Ministry

(John 10:40-19:42; Mark 10:1-15:47;
Matthew 26:20-27:66; Luke 22:14-23:56)

From Capernaum to "beyond the Jordan" into Judea (Mark 10:1-45)
Danger: High

On the way from Capernaum down the Jordan route to Judea, local Pharisees raised the question of divorce. *"Is it lawful for a man to divorce his wife?"* It was a loaded question. The Herods had divorced one another and John the Baptist was executed because he had railed against their divorces. Were they trying to set Jesus up for the same punishment? Jesus' answer was forthright. *"'What did Moses command you?' They said, 'Moses allowed a man to write a certificate*

125

of divorce and put her away.' Jesus said to them, 'For your hardness of heart he wrote you this commandment. From the beginning of creation, God made them male and female. For this reason a man shall leave his father and mother and be joined to his wife, and the two shall become one flesh. So they are no longer two but one flesh. What therefore God has joined together, let not man put asunder'" (10:8-12).

A young man came to him , *"What must I do to inherit eternal life?"* Hellenists raised questions like this, not Jews. A Jew would have sought resurrection from the dead. Jesus replied, *"You know the commandments: Do not kill, Do not commit adultery, Do not steal, Do not bear false witness, Do not defraud, Honor your father and mother."*

The young man's response must have astonished Jesus. He said to him, *"'Teacher, all these I have observed from my youth.' Jesus looking upon him loved him and said to him, 'You lack one thing; go, sell what you have, and give it to the poor, and you will have treasure in heaven; and come, follow me.' At this saying his countenance fell and he went away sorrowful; for he had great possessions. And Jesus looked around and said to his disciples, 'How hard it will be for those who have riches to enter the kingdom of God.' And the disciples were amazed at his words"* (Mk 10:17-24).

From this time on, as Mark says, *"They were on the road going up to Jerusalem, and Jesus was walking ahead of them. They were amazed, and those who followed were afraid. Taking aside the Twelve again, he told them once more what was to happen to him, 'Behold, we are going up to Jerusalem. The Son of Humankind will be delivered to the chief priests and the scribes. They will condemn him to death and deliver him to the Gentiles. They will mock him, and spit upon him, and scourge him, and kill him. After three days he will rise'"* (Mk 10:32-34).

As they were walking together, James and John, the sons of Zebedee, came forward to him and said, *"'Teacher, we want you to do for us whatever we ask of you.' Jesus said to them, 'What do you want me to do for you?' They replied,*

'Grant us to sit, one at your right hand and one at your left, in your glory.' Jesus said to them, 'You do not know what you are asking. Are you able to drink the cup that I drink or to be baptized with the baptism with which I am baptized?' They of course responded, 'We are able.' Jesus said to them, 'The cup that I drink you will drink; and with the baptism with which I am baptized, you will be baptized; but to sit at my right hand or at my left is not mine to grant, but it is for those for whom it has been prepared.'" Then Jesus gave his prescription for leadership. *"You know that those who are supposed to rule over the Gentiles lord it over them, and their great men exercise authority over them. But it shall not be so among you; but whoever would be great among you must be your servant, and whoever would be first among you must be slave of all. For the Son of Humankind came not to be served but to serve and to give his life as a ransom for many"* (10:35-45).

In Jericho: Blind Bartimaeus (Mark 10:46-53)
Danger: High

Jesus' journey down the Jordan Valley took him to Jericho. The streets of this ancient city, one of the oldest continuously inhabited towns on earth, were narrow, twisting, and filled with people. Jesus and his disciples had to shoulder their way through the noisy crowds that surrounded them. As they were leaving the city, an incident occurred that caught the Gospel writer Mark's attention.

Bartimaeus, a blind beggar, was sitting by the side of the road. He heard the crowd as it approached. He even heard the name of Jesus of Nazareth called out. He heard some call *"Teacher,"* others call *"Christ,"* and still others called out *"Son of David."* This last title spoke to the blind beggar. Solomon, son of David, had been a healer. He cast out demons—his "wisdom" consisted of this healing ability. Bartimaeus needed healing. So he cried out, *"Jesus, Son of David, have mercy on me!"* He was addressing Jesus as a healer of men and women.

Many around him rebuked him. Why should he call on Jesus? He was a nobody, he didn't even have a name, he was simply "Bar-Timaeus," son of Timaeus; he was a worthless beggar sitting on a street filled with beggars. But Bartimaeus was not going to be put off by mere rebukes. He called again, *"Jesus, Son of David, have mercy on me."* Through the clamor and clatter of voices around him, Jesus heard his call and stopped. On his way to Jerusalem, Jesus stopped at the call of a single voice, and the whole parade of people shook to a halt along with him. *"Call him,"* said Jesus. The crowd echoed Jesus' call, *"Take heart,"* said one. *"Rise,"* said another. *"He is calling you."*

Blind Bartimaeus sprang up, throwing off his garment. In his haste and anxiety, he simply threw it away. It was all he owned and Bartimaeus cast it aside when Jesus called. The rich man who had approached Jesus just days before could not do this. He had too many possessions to throw them aside and follow Jesus. Not Bartimaeus. He cast aside all he owned to be healed as he went to Jesus.

"What do you want me to do for you?" Jesus asked him. *"Master,"* said Bartimaeus, *"let me receive my sight."* Jesus said to him, *"Go your way. Your faith has made you well."* Jesus did not make a spittle of clay nor lay his hands on the man. Jesus had no system for healing; each healing was unique. He simply said, *"Go your way."* But Bartimaeus did not go his way. He went Jesus' way. He followed Jesus on the way to Jerusalem. Blind Bartimaeus was freed to become a disciple and follow Jesus to the cross, on the way that liberated him.

Approaching Passover—From Jericho to Jerusalem (John 10:40-11:55; Mark 10:1-11:11)
Danger: Extremely High

Jesus now passed the point where the chronology in John's Gospel left him, *"across the Jordan to the place where John had baptized"* (10:40). Leaving Jericho, Jesus started to climb the mountain road to Jerusalem. At this point, John's Gospel entwines with Mark's Gospel. They are two similar yet independent narratives on the conclusion of Jesus' ministry. The accounts reflect but do not mirror each other. Even if one omits something the other knows, each account has its own integrity. Each account follows Jesus as he moves to Jerusalem.

Figure 4 shows the main features when comparing Mark's account of Jesus' arrest, trial, and death with that in John's Gospel. Both accounts are complete, even if some event or story is not known or reported by the other. For instance, Mark indicates that Jesus spent a week in Jerusalem. *"Day after day I was with you in the temple teaching, and you did not seize me"* (Mk 14:49). John, as he presents his version of events, does not note this passage of time *"in the temple teaching"* during this final Passover. John believed that Jesus in his ministry had celebrated at least three different Passovers whereas Mark reports only this one Passover.

As differences between Mark and John multiply, it becomes clear that Mark and John had different informants regarding important events in Jesus' ministry. Both Gospels probably resulted from a consensus among reports from a network of informants who themselves had different sources of information—some from informants directly, others from second- and third-hand accounts. Most informants cannot be identified; only a few are known. Each of the four major parties undoubtedly had different informants. This chronology is limited mostly to differences between the Gospels of Mark and John. All four Gospels saw the crucifixion and resurrection as clearly central in their understandings. The four major parties and their four Gospels will be treated separately in Part Three of this book.

(continues on page 135)

Gospel of John

"Jesus went away again across the Jordan to the place where John at first baptized, and there he remained" (Jn 10:40)

Mary, Martha, and Lazarus in Bethany (11:1-44)

Council condemns Jesus to death (11:47-53)
"Jesus no longer went about openly among the Jews. He went to the country near the wilderness, to Ephraim, where he stayed with the disciples" (11:54)

"Now the Passover of the Jews was at hand" (11:55)

"In the temple he found those who were selling oxen and sheep and pigeons, and the money-changers at their business. And making a whip of cords, he drove them all, with the sheep and oxen, out of the temple; and he poured out the coins of the money-changers and overturned their tables" (2:14-15)

Mary, sister of Martha and Lazarus, anoints Jesus as Messiah (12:1-8)
"The next day a great crowd who had come to the feast heard that Jesus was coming to Jerusalem. So they took branches of palm trees and went out to meet him, crying, 'Hosanna! Blessed is he who comes in the name of the Lord, even the King of Israel!' And Jesus found a young ass and sat upon it; as it is written, 'Fear not, daughter of Zion; behold, your king is coming, sitting on an ass's colt' " (12:12-15)

Gospel of Mark

Jesus and his disciples went to *"the region of Judea and beyond the Jordan"* (Mk 10:1)

"They drew near to Jerusalem, to Bethpage and Bethany, at the Mount of Olives" (11:1a)

Entrance into Jerusalem (11:1b-11a)
Return to Bethany (11:11b)

And they came to Jerusalem.

"In the temple he found those who were selling oxen and sheep and pigeons, and the money-changers at their business. And making a whip of cords, he drove them all, with the sheep and oxen, out of the temple; and he poured out the coins of the money-changers and overturned their tables" (2:14-15)

Questioning Jesus (11:27-12:40) re
... Authority
... Render to Caesar
... Resurrection

"While he was at Bethany in the house of Simon the leper, as he sat at table, a woman came with an alabaster flask of ointment of pure nard, very costly, and she broke the flask and poured it over his head" (14:3)

Figure 4. Jesus going to and in Jerusalem according to the Gospels of John and Mark.

"Now among those who went up to worship at the feast were some Greeks. So these came to Philip, who was from Bethsaida in Galilee, and said to him, 'Sir, we wish to see Jesus.' Philip went and told Andrew; Andrew went with Philip, and they told Jesus. Jesus answered them, 'The hour has come for the Son of Humankind to be glorified. Unless a grain of wheat falls into the earth and dies, it remains alone. If it dies, it bears much fruit. He who loves his life loses it, and he who hates his life in this world will keep it for eternal life. If any one serves me, he must follow me. Where I am, there shall my servant be also. If any one serves me, the Father will honor him'" (12:20-26)
"Now is my soul troubled. And what shall I say? 'Father, save me from this hour?' No, for this purpose I have come to this hour" (12:27)

"Now before the feast of the Passover, when Jesus knew that his hour had come to depart out of this world to the Father, having loved his own who were in the world, he loved them to the end" (13:1)

"On the first day of Unleavened Bread, when they sacrificed the Passover lamb, his disciples said to him, 'Where will you have us go and prepare for you to eat the Passover?' He sent two of his disciples, and said to them, 'Go into the city, and a man carrying a jar of water will meet you. Follow him, and wherever he enters, say to the householder, The Teacher says, Where is my guest room, where I am to eat the Passover with my disciples? He will show you a large upper room furnished and ready. There prepare for us'" (14:12-15)

Knew Judas would betray him (13:2,21-27)

Judas' betrayal (14:10, 18-21, 26-27)

"Jesus rose from supper, laid aside his garments, and girded himself with a towel. Then he poured water into a basin, and began to wash the disciples' feet, and to wipe them with the towel with which he was girded" (13:4-5)

"As they were eating, he took bread, and blessed, and broke it, and gave it to them, and said, 'Take; this is my body.' He took a cup, and when he had given thanks he gave it to them, and they all drank of it. And he said to them, 'This is my blood

of the covenant, which is poured out for
many. I shall not drink again of the fruit
of the vine until that day when I drink it
new in the kingdom of God.' When they
had sung a hymn, they went out to the
Mount of Olives" (14:22-26)

Jesus' long discourse with disciples
(13:31-17:26)
  "Wash one another's feet" (13:14)
  "I go to prepare a place for you" (14:2)
  "I am in the Father and the Father in
me" (14:10)
  "If you ask anything in my name, I will
do it" (14:14)
  If you love me, you will keep my commandments" (14:15)
  "The Father will send the Counselor, the
Holy Spirit, in my name" (14:26)
  "I am the true vine, and my Father is the
vine dresser" (15:1)
  "As the Father has loved me, so have I
loved you; abide in my love" (15:9)
  "This is my commandment, that you love
one another as I have loved you. Greater
love has no man than this, that a man lay
down his life for his friends" (15:12-13)
  "They will put you out of the synagogues;
indeed, the hour is coming when whoever
kills you will think he is offering service to
God" (16:2)
  "The hour is coming, indeed it has come,
when you will be scattered, every man to
his home, and will leave me alone. Yet I
am not alone, for the Father is with me"
(16:32)
  "Be of good cheer. I have overcome the
world" (16:33)
  "This is eternal life, that they know thee,
the only true God, and Jesus Christ whom
thou hast sent" (17:3)
  "As thou didst send me into the world, so
I have sent them into the world" (17:18)
  "That they may all be one, even as thou,
Father, art in me, and I in thee, that they
also may be in us" (17:21)

"When Jesus had spoken these words, he went forth with his disciples across the Kidron valley, where there was a garden, which he and his disciples entered" (18:1)

"They went to a place which was called Gethsemane. He said to his disciples, 'Sit here, while I pray.' He took with him Peter and James and John, and began to be greatly distressed and troubled. He said to them, 'My soul is very sorrowful, even to death; remain here, and watch.' Going a little farther, he fell on the ground and prayed that, if it were possible, the hour might pass from him. He said, 'Abba, Father, all things are possible to thee; remove this cup from me; yet not what I will, but what thou wilt.' He came and found them sleeping, and he said to Peter, 'Simon, are you asleep? Could you not watch one hour? Watch and pray that you may not enter into temptation; the spirit indeed is willing, but the flesh is weak'" (14:32-38)

Judas brings the police (18:2-3)

"Judas came, one of the Twelve, and with him a crowd with swords and clubs, from the chief priests and the scribes and the elders. The betrayer had given them a sign, saying, 'The one I shall kiss is the man; seize him and lead him away under guard.' When he came, he went up to him at once, and said, 'Master!' And he kissed him. They laid hands on him and seized him. One of those who stood by drew his sword, and struck the slave of the high priest and cut off his ear. They all forsook him, and fled" (14:43-47,50)

Jesus arrested (18:4-12)

Peter cuts off Malchus' right ear (18:10)

Peter denies him (14:56-73)

Hearing before Annas (18:13-24)
Tried before Caiaphas (18:24-28)
Peter denied him (18:25-27)
Brought to Pilate (18:28-40)
Pilate and Jesus on kingship and truth (18:33-38)
Pilate had Jesus scourged (19:1)

"As soon as it was morning the chief priests, with the elders and scribes, and the whole council held a consultation. They bound Jesus and led him away and delivered him to Pilate. Pilate asked him, 'Are you the King of the Jews?' He answered him, 'You have said so.' The chief priests accused him of many things. The crowd came up and began to ask Pilate to do as he was wont to do for them. He answered them, 'Do you want me to release for you the King of the Jews?'

They cried out again, 'Crucify him'"
(15:1-15) "The soldiers led him away inside the palace (that is, the praetorium);
and they called together the whole bat-
talion. They clothed him in a purple cloak,
and plaiting a crown of thorns they put it
on him. They began to salute him, 'Hail,
King of the Jews!' They struck his head
with a reed, and spat upon him, and they
knelt down in homage to him. When they
had mocked him, they stripped him of
the purple cloak, and put his own clothes
on him. And they led him out to crucify
him" (15:16-20)

Crown of thorns and purple robe
(19:2)
Jesus sentenced on the sixth hour of
the day of Preparation of the Passover
(19:14)

"They compelled a passer-by, Simon of
Cyrene to carry his cross. They brought
him to the place called Golgotha. They
offered him wine mingled with myrrh; but
he did not take it. They crucified him"
(15:21-24)

"They divided his garments among them,
casting lots for them. It was the third
hour, when they crucified him" (15:25)

"Standing by the cross of Jesus were his
mother, and his mother's sister, Mary the
wife of Clopas, and Mary Magdalene.
When Jesus saw his mother, and the
disciple whom he loved standing near, he
said to his mother, 'Woman, behold, your
son!' Then he said to the disciple, 'Behold,
your mother!' From that hour the disciple
took her to his own home" (19:25-27)
Jesus said (to fulfil scripture), 'I thirst.'
When Jesus had received the vinegar,
he said, 'It is finished'; and he bowed his
head and gave up his spirit" (19:30)

"When the sixth hour had come, there
was darkness over the whole land until
the ninth hour. At the ninth hour Jesus
cried with a loud voice, 'Eloi, Eloi, la'ma
sabachthani?' which means, 'My God,
my God, why hast thou forsaken me?'"
(15:33-34)

"Jesus uttered a loud cry, and breathed
his last" (15:37)

"The curtain of the temple was torn in
two, from top to bottom. When the centurion saw that he breathed his last, he
said, 'Truly this man was the Son of God!'
There were also women looking on from
afar, among whom were Mary Magdalene, and Mary the mother of James

the younger and of Joses, and Salome"
(15:38-40)

"Since it was the day of Preparation, in order to prevent the bodies from remaining on the cross on the Sabbath, the Jews asked Pilate that their legs might be broken, and that they might be taken away. The soldiers came and broke the legs of the first, and of the other who had been crucified with him. When they came to Jesus and saw that he was already dead, they did not break his legs. One of the soldiers pierced his side with a spear, and at once there came out blood and water" (19:30-34)
Joseph of Arimathea, who was a disciple of Jesus…, asked Pilate that he might take away the body of Jesus, and Pilate gave him leave. He took away his body. Nicodemus also came bringing a mixture of myrrh and aloes… They took the body of Jesus, and bound it in linen cloths…" Because it was the day of Preparation, as the tomb was close at hand, they laid Jesus there" (19:38-42)

"When evening had come, since it was the day of Preparation, that is, the day before the Sabbath, Joseph of Arimathea, a respected member of the council, who was also himself looking for the kingdom of God, took courage and went to Pilate and asked for the body of Jesus. Pilate wondered if he were already dead. Summoning the centurion, he asked him whether he was already dead. When he learned from the centurion that he was dead, he granted the body to Joseph. He bought a linen shroud, and taking him down, wrapped him in the linen shroud, and laid him in a tomb which had been hewn out of the rock; and he rolled a stone against the door of the tomb. Mary Magdalene and Mary the mother of Joses saw where he was laid" (15:42-47)

In Bethany: The Raising Of Lazarus (John 11:1-44)
Danger: Extremely High

Both John's and Mark's Gospels present the same geographic path from Galilee to Jerusalem—down the Jordan River to Jericho, then to Bethany on the east side of the Mount of Olives, and west over the Mount to Jerusalem.

But only John's Gospel includes the story of Lazarus' resurrection. Lazarus lived in Bethany with his sisters Mary and Martha. Bethany was located where it could not be seen from Jerusalem because it was over the lip of the Mount. When Jesus was in Jerusalem and Judea, he, apparently, sometimes stayed with this family.

If an investigative reporter from the 21st century would be dealing with the account we call "The Resurrection of Lazarus," he might have written it up as follows (see Jn 11:1-54).

Lazarus of Bethany Raised from the Grave
Sisters and friends celebrate his return to life
Jesus of Nazareth credited with his resurrection

Jerusalem Daily, *a week before Passover*

Filed in Bethany of Judea

The sisters of Lazarus, a wealthy landowner in Bethany with holdings both in this village and in Jerusalem, reported yesterday that their brother was raised from the grave. They credit Jesus of Nazareth with having accomplished this unique task.

"Our brother Lazarus was very ill," they told this reporter. "For three weeks he had a fever, and each day the fever grew worse. We sent a message to his friend, Jesus of Nazareth, to come to minister to him, but Jesus did not come right away. When he finally arrived in Bethany, Lazarus was already dead."

Martha said that she went out to meet Jesus and said to him plaintively, "Lord, if you had been here, my brother would not have died." Jesus said to her, "Your brother will rise again." Martha thought Jesus meant, "He will rise again in the resurrection on the last day." But Jesus corrected her, "I am the resurrection and the life," she reported him as saying. "He who believes in me, though he die, yet shall he live." Martha insists that these are Jesus' exact words.

Friends of Mary and Martha, who came to console them, joined the sisters at the grave. Jesus saw the sisters weeping and friends who came with them were also weeping. Jesus appeared deeply troubled in spirit. He said, "Where have you laid him?" They said, "Lord, come and see." And Jesus wept, too.

Jesus came to the tomb, they said. It was a cave and a fitted stone blocked the entrance. Jesus said, "Take away the stone." Martha said to him, "Lord, by this time there will be a stench. He has been dead four days! We watched the grave for three days to make sure that the one buried was really dead, but this is already the fourth day." Jesus insisted that they take away the stone. So they took away the stone.

"Jesus stood before the tomb," they said, "and he cried with a loud voice, 'Lazarus, come out.'" And Lazarus did come out! His hands and feet were bound with bandages and his face wrapped with a cloth. Jesus said, "Unbind him and let him go."

"I have heard of many supposed 'raisings from the dead,'" said one witness, "and this one is more credible than most. But I have questions. There was no odor from the tomb when the stone was rolled away. Was Lazarus simply in a deep coma and at the sound of his friend's voice, he woke from his sleep? I need more proof than merely a report like this!"

Later, the reporter might later have filed this report.

Sanhedrin Met Yesterday
Serious issue to deal with
People saying that Jesus of Nazareth actually raised a certain Lazarus from the dead

Jerusalem Daily, *less than a week before Passover*

Filed in Jerusalem of Judea

We have a report that the Sanhedrin met yesterday in Jerusalem. "What shall we do?" was the question put to them by their presiding officer, Caiaphas the high priest. "This man Jesus of Nazareth," says a credible witness who was present at the meeting, "performs many signs. If we let him go on like this, every one will believe in him, and the Romans will come and destroy both our holy place and our nation. Is it not expedient then that one man should die for the people so that the whole nation should not perish?"

So they took counsel how to put him to death. If the eyewitnesses to the event in Bethany were not certain what had occurred that day, the Council in Jerusalem was. Jesus had raised Lazarus from the dead and he needed to be executed for the act.

In a separate action, they also declared that Lazarus should die. As long as he was alive, they said, people would recall what Jesus had done.

Then, the reporter might have filed a related third story.

Jesus of Nazareth Executed This Day
Nailed to a cross on the hill called Golgotha
Hung there until he died

Jerusalem Daily, *one day before Passover*

Filed in Jerusalem of Judea,

Jesus of Nazareth, called "King of the Jews" (a sign on his cross said this in three languages) was crucified today on the Hill of a Skull. As by Roman Law, only a few people other than a Roman contingent were present. The authorities are seeking to find and execute a man named Lazarus, an alleged close acquaintance of this Jesus, as well.

Only at the end of the account about Lazarus in John's Gospel is it indicated that the chief priests wanted to execute Lazarus as well as Jesus. As long as Lazarus lived, as one raised from the dead, he was a symbol of Jesus' power and a threat to the priests' power. The other Gospels do not mention anything about Lazarus.

In Bethany: Jesus Anointed as Messiah (John 11:1-44, 12:1-11; Mark 14:3)
Danger: Extremely High

At dinner in the house of Mary, Martha, and Lazarus, an unusual event occurred. Mary took an expensive jar of perfume, anointed Jesus' feet with it, then wiped the excess perfume from his feet with her hair. Judas Iscariot complained about the waste of money, though the Gospel is quick to point out that he did not care about the poor. Jesus responded that he should leave Mary alone.

The perfume was expensive indeed—Judas said it was worth 300 denarii. A denarius was the usual wage paid for one day's work. This perfume therefore would have cost a village workman close to a year's wages. The nard mentioned was Syrian Nard, a prized ingredient for any unguent. It may have been obtained from an herb grown in the high pasture land in the Himalayan Mountains. This distant source would explain its high cost.

Even more remarkable was what Mary did. She anointed Jesus' feet with the oil and wiped them with her hair. To do this she had to unbind her hair, something only a harlot would do in those days. Pouring ointment on the feet, not on the head, is strange but to wipe it with her hair was extremely unusual.

Jesus' response to Judas provides a clue to what Mary was doing. Whatever her intention, she had anointed Jesus. Now he was indeed the Messiah, the Christ, the anointed one. Judas recognized the significance of the act. Soon he made arrangements with Jesus' enemies to have him arrested and executed as "the Christ, the anointed one." When it became widely known that Jesus had been anointed as Messiah, the Romans joined with his Jewish enemies to kill him.

Mark tells a similar story. "*While Jesus was at Bethany in the house of Simon the leper, as he sat at table, a woman came with an alabaster flask of ointment of pure nard, very costly, and she broke the flask and poured it over his head... Jesus said, 'Let her alone; why do you trouble her? She has done a beautiful thing to me... Truly, I say to you, wherever the gospel is preached in the whole world, what she has done will be told in memory of her'*" (Mk 14:3-9). Both events occur in Bethany, but details differ. In John's Gospel, the woman is the sister of Lazarus; in Mark's, she is an unknown woman. In John, the event takes place in the house of Lazarus where Mary anoints his feet; in Mark, in the house of Simon the leper the unknown woman anoints his head. Both agree that a woman anointed him and both agree that the anointing had vast consequences. Jesus now has been publicly anointed as Messiah, the Christ. When the anointing became widely known, the Romans joined with his Jewish enemies to kill him.

John's Gospel also underlined its very low esteem of Judas. He did not care for the poor, said the writer. He also was stealing from the common purse he held in behalf of all the disciples. And he was about to betray Jesus. He had no advocate in John's Gospel.

In Jerusalem: Jesus' Entry (John 12:12-19; Mark 11:1-10)
Danger: Extremely High

The incident with Lazarus introduced John's account of Jesus' entry into Jerusalem. *"The next day a great crowd who had come to the feast heard that Jesus was coming to Jerusalem. So they took branches of palm trees and went out to meet him, shouting, 'Hosanna! Blessed is he who comes in the name of the Lord, even the King of Israel!' And Jesus found a young donkey and sat upon it; as it is written, 'Fear not, daughter of Zion; behold, your king is coming, sitting on a donkey's colt!' His disciples did not understand this at first; but when Jesus was glorified, then they remembered that this had been written of him and had been done to him"* (Jn 12:12-16). Jesus had come as Messiah and King into the sacred city of Jerusalem, where he would be sacrificed like a lamb, then raised from the dead.

Waving palm branches, reported the Gospel writer John, people went out to welcome Jesus as Messiah and King into Jerusalem. Palm branches were conscious symbols of Jewish nationalism and resistance to Roman occupation. As noted in chapter 2, in Galilee, ruled by Herod Antipas, the Jews once won a small victory. Most Roman coins of the time were imprinted with the Roman emperor Tiberius' face on them. This contravened Jewish laws against graven images. The Jews insisted that the coins be changed. They were. Coins found in Galilee from about 24CE show they were re-struck with a palm branch imprinted over Caesar's face. Palm branches at Jesus' entry indicated that, to many fellow Jews, Jesus was both a spiritual and political savior (Fleming, 1996). Such an image was probably not lost on Herodian and Roman officials.

Jesus was welcomed as *"the one who comes in the name of the Lord."* This welcome in John's Gospel echoes Nathanael's confession of Jesus given at the beginning of this Gospel, *"You are the Son of God. You are the King of Israel"* (Jn 1:49). John's Gospel pictures Jesus entering Jerusalem on the *"colt of a donkey."* Zechariah depicts the coming king as *"humble and riding on a donkey, on a colt, the foal of a donkey"* (9:9). The donkey symbolized a humble kingship, the kind of ruler who, before Solomon, never thought of oppressing his people in order to live an affluent life. Jesus was a humble king. He came not to oppress but to liberate his people. Songs attributed to the humble king in Zechariah fit the coming of Jesus. *"Rejoice greatly, O daughter Zion! Shout aloud, O daughter Jerusalem. Lo, your king comes to you. Triumphant and victorious is he, humble and riding on a donkey."*

John further says, *"His disciples did not understand these things at first, but when Jesus was glorified, then they remembered that these things had been written of him and had been done to him."* The disciples did not understand that only by his death would Jesus claim his own kingdom. To the writer John the word *"Glory"* refers to at least three sets of acts in Jesus' life—Jesus was glorified by his teachings, by his crucifixion, and by his resurrection. Jesus *"glorified God on the earth, having accomplished the work which God gave him to do"* (Jn 17:4). The glory of God is in Jesus Christ.

Mark's Gospel noted something not found in John's Gospel—that Jesus' entrance into Jerusalem began at a small village named Bethpage just over the mountain from Bethany on the Jerusalem side. Its significance was that Bethpage, unlike Bethany, was part of Jerusalem. By Jewish law, a Jew may not work on the Sabbath. In the Talmud, this law forbade a Jew from carrying anything from outside a city into a city on the Sabbath. Since Bethpage was inside the closed area of Jerusalem, Jesus could legally go there to pick up the animal he rode into the city. *"Jesus sent two of his disciples and said to them, 'Go into the village ahead of you, and immediately as you enter it, you will find tied there a colt that has never been ridden; untie it and bring it. If anyone says to you, 'Why are you doing this?' just say this, 'The Lord needs it and will send it back here immediately.' They went away and found a colt tied near a door, outside in the street"* (Mk 11:1-4).

According to the writer Mark, the Twelve considered that, since Jesus knew an animal would be tethered in this village street, Jesus had special insight about this. It happened as Jesus said it would. What might have happened is that Jesus, through his previous, probably Hellenist, connections in Bethany during his earlier two-year ministry in and around Jerusalem, had prearranged with its owner, possibly even Lazarus who apparently had a house in Bethpage, to use this animal to ride into the city. The signal for the pickup seems to have been the words Mark quotes, *"The Lord needs it and will send it back here immediately."* Taking the animal in this way was not unusual. Roman soldiers routinely requisitioned animal and human labor from Jewish people. But the story is unique in that Jesus promised to return the animal promptly. By doing this, Jesus differentiated what he did from how Romans took what they thought they needed.

"A colt that has never been ridden" (Mk 11:2) indicated Jesus' purpose in borrowing it. Such animals were used in sacred rituals. Jesus was acting out a plan to show people that his entrance into Jerusalem was a sacred and kingly act. Due to possible contamination and disease, a true king never chose an animal that had been ridden before and Jesus was "a true king." By riding the colt, Jesus indicated that he accepted being the messiah; he entered Jerusalem as messiah and king (Lightfoot, 1893: 44).

"As they were untying it, bystanders said to them, "What are you doing, untying the colt?' They told them what Jesus had

*said; and they allowed them to take it. Then they brought the
colt to Jesus and threw their cloaks on it; and he sat on it. Many
people spread their cloaks on the road, and others spread leafy
branches that they had cut in the fields. Then those who went
ahead and those who followed were shouting*

> *Hosanna!*
> *Blessed is the one who comes in the name of the Lord!*
> *Blessed is the coming kingdom of our ancestor David!*
> *Hosanna in the highest heaven! (Mk 11:1-10; see Jn 12:13)*

Contrary to law and custom, Jesus rode into the city on
a colt. People, including pilgrims, were expected to enter
the city on foot. Jesus' deliberate gesture was intended to
draw attention. It contrasted with the way Romans entered
a city, on their chariots with pomp and circumstance, em-
blazoned banners and trumpets blaring. Possibly the Romans were entering Jerusalem through a different gate on
the same day.

People coming to the city at this time recognized something unusual was happening. People spread their cloaks
before Jesus, as for a king. When Jehu came to Jerusalem to
be installed as king, people spread their cloaks before him
so that he might walk on them (2 Kings 9:13). The crowd
gathered branches as they approached the city and sang the
psalms for a festival as they entered the city. The writer John
said they were "palm branches." More likely they were *lulabs*,
green leaves and branches from palms, myrtle, and willows
that people often used when entering the city for festivals.
With their right hands they waved the *lulabs* and in their left
hand they carried an *etrog,* fruit or blossom. *Hosanna* means
"save" but its ritual meaning was *"Help Israel, O God"* (Psalm
118:25) and was used by pilgrims during festivals such as
Passover and Tabernacles.

> *"Blessed is the one who comes in the name of the Lord!*
> *Blessed is the coming kingdom of our ancestor David!"*

These two *"blessings,"* for messiah and king, may originally have been different acclamations brought together by Mark. The second one looked forward to the restoration of David's kingdom, a long-held belief in Judaism. The first was the fulfillment of Jesus' proclamation; at the beginning of his ministry Jesus said that the kingdom of God was near (Mk 1:15).

In Jerusalem: "Cleansing the Temple" (John 2:12-21; Mark 11:15-19)
Danger: Extremely High

The Gospels of Mark and John do not agree on the timing of Jesus' *"cleansing of the temple."* In Mark the cleansing takes place at the beginning of the week in which Jesus would be crucified but after *"he entered the temple and began to drive out those who bought and those who sold and overturned the tables of the moneychangers and the seats of those who sold pigeons"*(Mk 11:15). In John, Jesus confronts such enterprising men in the Temple in year one of his ministry when John recorded that Jesus first went to Jerusalem from Galilee for the Passover (Jn 2:12-21). This confrontation was followed by Jesus' two-year ministry in Judea and Galilee. Both accounts agree on one thing—cleansing the Temple was Jesus' first act when he arrived in Jerusalem from the north country during his ministry even if its timing varied by several years.

In John, Jesus is already condemned to death by the Jerusalem Council, the Sanhedrin, for raising Lazarus from the dead before he arrived in the city (Jn 11:47-53). In Mark, Jesus is condemned to death by Pilate after a brief trial the same week the cleansing took place (Mk 15:15).

In Jerusalem: Date of the Day of Passover and Crucifixion (John 13:1, 19:31,42; Mark 14:12)

The two Gospels disagree on the exact date of the arrest and crucifixion. Part of the confusion arises because a day among the Jews of Jesus' time differed from a day in our timeframe today. By Jewish reckoning a "day" began at sunset and went to the next sunset, not from midnight and to the next midnight. Their day was semi-darkness followed by light to semi-darkness. Our day is from deep darkness to deep darkness. Passover had a distinct ritual at this time. Passover lambs were killed on the day before the feast (equivalent to our Thursday). Passover itself began with the day of the Feast of Unleavened Bread (our Thursday evening but their Friday), then continued for a week.

John said Jesus' crucifixion occurred on Thursday (that started with what is our Wednesday evening), *"the Day of Preparation for the Passover"* when the sacrificial lambs were slain (Jn 19:31). According to John, Jesus did not eat the Passover meal with his disciples. Instead Jesus' last meal with his disciples came *"before the feast of the Passover"* (Jn 13:1). All the events of the trial and execution were compressed into this day—Wednesday evening, the night, and Thursday before sunset. It was still on the Jewish day of Preparation that Jesus was laid in the tomb (19:42).

Mark's account is somewhat different and a little confusing. He said the critical day was *"the first day of Unleavened Bread when they sacrificed the passover lamb"* (Mk 14:12). This would also be Thursday as in John's Gospel. But, Mark's Gospel says, on this day the disciples went into the city to find a place to eat the Passover meal. They celebrated the meal (the Last Supper) within hours of this, probably just after sunset on their Thursday evening, *"when evening had come, since it was the day of Preparation, that is, the day before the sabbath."* During this day from darkness through the light to darkness again, Jesus' arrest, various trials, sentencing, and execution occurred. After the next sunset, the next day, which would be Passover Friday, he was taken from the cross by Joseph of Arimathea and was buried (Mk 16:42). The confusion came because Passover, which is the equivalent of a sabbath, started on the equivalent of our Thursday evening through Friday, which then carries over to the sabbath on Saturday. But no activity was to occur on any Sabbath (as seen earlier in a confrontation between the Pharisees and Jesus) and especially not a crucifixion. This "dating" issue between Mark and John is, however, moot. The important issue is that Jesus had a last meal with his disciples and then was taken from the Garden by armed officials, suffered through several trials, and then was crucified just before Passover all in one day in 29ce.

In Jerusalem: Arrangements for the "Last Supper" (John 13:1-2, 23; Mark 11:1-6, 14:12-17, 15: 42-47)
Danger: Extremely High

Some confusion also applies to Jesus' instructions about preparing for his last meal. Mark said, *"On the first day of Unleavened Bread his disciples said to him, 'Where will you have us go and prepare for you to eat the Passover?' Jesus sent two of his disciples and said to them, 'Go into the city, and a man carrying a jar of water will meet you. Follow him. Wherever he enters, say to the householder, The Teacher says, Where is my guest room, where I am to eat the Passover with my disciples? There prepare for us.' When it was evening Jesus came with the Twelve"* (14:12-17). The anomaly in Jesus' statement is that men did not normally carry a jar of water. How did Jesus know that one such man would appear and lead them where they needed to go? The disciples, the members of the Twelve, believed that this too was a moment of Jesus' amazing foreknowledge of events.

But, as with the use of a donkey's colt on entering the city, another interpretation of these events is possible. The story about *"the man with the jar"* directing the disciples to a *"guest room"* was another instance of a possible coded message set by Jesus' friends in Judea and Jerusalem. Again, these friends were possibly Hellenist party members that Jesus recruited during earlier visits to Jerusalem of which the Twelve were not aware. Jesus arranged for these friends to find the room before he got to Jerusalem with the Twelve. The codes about *"the man carrying a jar of water"* set the plan in motion. In this secret location, Jesus and his disciples ate the preparatory meal without revealing their presence to authorities.

Members of these two groups, the Twelve from Galilee and Hellenists in Jerusalem, were gathered earlier and independently by Jesus. They had not yet met and Mark's Gospel did not recognize that Jesus had separate followers in Jerusalem. John's Gospel did not record the events of the colt and of finding the room that Mark does. Another indirect support for the two-party distinction is that in John's Gospel a previously unknown disciple, the *"one…whom Jesus loved, lying close to the breast of Jesus"* at the last meal, appeared with the Twelve there (Jn 13:23). None of the Twelve had previously received this designation. Possibly this person was a Hellenist follower from Jerusalem, perhaps the same person who owned the room where the meal was being held.

In Jerusalem: The "Last Supper," Judas' Betrayal, the New Covenant (John 13:4-16; Mark 14:1-26, 15:1-5; see Matthew 26:20-29, 27:26-28; Luke 22:14-23)
Danger: Extremely High

Descriptions of Jesus' last meal with his disciples also vary widely in John and in Mark. The meal began with Jesus' dread pronouncement that one of the Twelve, one eating with them, would betray him. *"Woe to that man by whom the Son of Humankind is betrayed! It would have been better for him if he had not been born"* (Mk 14:21; see Jn 13:21).

After this dread pronouncement, Jesus turned to the meal itself. In contrast to John's Gospel, Mark sees the meal as Jesus' opportunity to renew the covenant God made with the people. *"As they were eating, he took bread and blessed it and broke it and gave it to them and said, 'Take; this is my body.' He took a cup, and when he had given thanks he gave it to them, and they all drank of it. Jesus said to them, 'This is my blood of the covenant, which is poured out for many. Truly, I say to you, I shall not drink again of the fruit of the vine until that day when I drink it new in the kingdom of God'"* (Mk 14:18-26). Most versions of Luke's Gospel added two phrases, *"new covenant..."* and *"Do this in remembrance of me"* (Lk 22:20). The word "remembrance" says, "Remember the 'new covenant' made here, Jesus' sacrifice for it, and the sacrifices those who partake in it will make in fulfilling a healing God's promises to his people."

"My blood of the covenant" refers to Moses' actions recorded in Exodus (24:1-8). Moses had received the covenant's commands from God, and *"When Moses returned to the people from the mountain of God, he built an altar at the foot of the mountain. Young men of Israel offered burnt offerings and sacrificed peace offerings of oxen on the altar. Moses took half of the blood and put it in basins, and half of the blood he threw against the altar. Then he took the book of the covenant and read it in the hearing of the people. They said, 'All that the Lord has spoken we will do, and we will be obedient.' Moses took the remaining blood and threw it upon the people, and said, 'Behold the blood of the covenant which the Lord has made with you in accordance with all these words.'"*

By similar words and actions, Jesus brought God and the disciples together into a solemn covenant. When Moses threw half the blood from the sacrificed oxen on the altar and half on the people, he bound them together in a covenant sealed by blood. Jesus' sacrifice, his blood shed on the cross, will also bring God and people together. When Jesus talked about bread and wine, *"This is my body, ...this my blood,* he was talking about his mortal sacrifice. Jesus was saying to them, "This is myself I am offering to you; as you take this food and drink it, let it remind you of the strong commitment we have made together." Jesus knew he was about to give himself for these others on his cross; in this meal he invited them to be bound in sacred covenant with him. This is the meal's importance as Mark describes it.

In John's Gospel, the meal signifies something else. One event in the story is similar—Jesus announced that one of them would betray him and it turned out to be Judas. After this pronouncement, every element of the two stories is different.

The "Beloved Disciple," whom we have identified as a leader of Jesus' Hellenist followers, was present at this meal. *"One of his disciples, whom Jesus loved, was lying close to the breast of Jesus"* (Jn 13: 23). Near the breast of the host was the favored spot in a meal. The disciples are pictured, in the style of a Greek meal, lying around the table, each one with his head close to the breast of his companion on his right. This "Beloved Disciple" was not present at the meal described by Mark.

"After the meal Jesus rose from supper, laid aside his garments, and girded himself with a towel. Then he poured water into a basin and began to wash the disciples' feet and to wipe them with the towel with which he was girded" (Jn 13:4-5). City streets in Jesus' world were very dirty places. All kinds of filth, human and animal, were simply thrown into the street and often carried into houses on the feet of those entering. Feet had to be washed, usually before, not *"after,"* a guest was properly prepared for the meal. Among Greeks and Romans, the foot washing was generally performed by a slave but here Jesus washes the invited guests' feet. That it took place *"after"* the meal only added emphasis to what Jesus was doing. Jesus concluded his act by saying, *"If I then, your Lord and Teacher, have washed your feet, you also ought to wash one another's feet. I have given you an example, that you also should do as I have done to you. Truly, truly, I say to you, a servant is not greater than his master; nor is he who is sent greater than he who sent him"* (Jn 13:14-16).

This foot washing event has become part of the Holy Week ritual in certain contemporary churches. But this is the only reference to the practice in the New Testament. John writes that Jesus then returned to his place at the table and spoke at length with his disciples. The other Gospels did not record a scene like this.

Jesus talks with his disciples, including the Beloved Disciple, and says,

... *"Wash one another's feet"* (Jn 13:14);

... *"I go to prepare a place for you"* (14:2);

... *"I am in the Father and the Father in me"* (14:10);

... *"If you ask anything in my name, I will do it"* (14:14);

... *"If you love me, you will keep my commandments"* (14:15);

... *"The Father will send the Counselor, the Holy Spirit, in my name"* (14:26);

... *"I am the true vine, and my Father is the vine dresser"* (15:1);

... *"As the Father has loved me, so have I loved you; abide in my love"* (15:9);

... *"This is my commandment, that you love one another as I have loved you. ... Greater love has no man than this, that a man lay down his life for his friends"* (15:12-13);

... *"They will put you out of the synagogues; indeed, the hour is coming when whoever kills you will think he is offering service to God"* (Jn 16:2);

... *"The hour is coming, indeed it has come, when you will be scattered every man to his home, and will leave me alone. Yet I am not alone, for the Father is with me"* (16:32; see Acts 8:1);

... *"Be of good cheer, I have overcome the world"* (Jn 16:33);

... *"This is eternal life, that they know thee the only true God, and Jesus Christ whom thou hast sent"* (17:3);

... *"As thou didst send me into the world, so I have sent them into the world"* (17:18);

... *"That they may all be one. Even as thou, Father, art in me, and I in thee, that they also may be in us"* (17:21).

When he had said these things, Jesus led his followers to a garden, to his trial, to his death. He went out to fulfill the will of God and to follow where God leads in these many ways.

John does not report Jesus praying in the garden. Nor does John report Jesus using the phrase, *"Abba, Father, all things are possible to thee. Remove this cup from me. Yet not what I will but what thou wilt"* (Mk 14:36).

In Jerusalem: What did Judas Betray? (Mark 15:1-5, 14:1-2, 21; John 18:1)
Danger: Immediate and Deadly

Both accounts speak of Jesus' betrayal by Judas. What did Judas betray? One or two things are suggested in the gospel accounts.

One could be Jesus' anointing as Messiah. Public or semi-public anointing was a sign to authorities that someone was the Messiah. To be Messiah was to be in revolt against Rome, treason, a crime punishable by death. Romans would take action against it. This charge was brought against Jesus in his trial before Pilate. *"As soon as it was morning the chief priests, elders, scribes, and the whole council held a consultation. They bound Jesus, led him away, and delivered him to Pilate. Pilate asked him, 'Are you King of the Jews?' Jesus answered, 'You have said so.' Again Pilate asked him, 'Have you no answer to make? See how many charges they bring against you.' But Jesus made no further answer"* (Mk 15:1-5).

The other information Judas may have revealed was the place Jesus and the Twelve slept at night while in Jerusalem for Passover. Pilgrims were mandated to spend nights within Jerusalem's precincts. But, with a total population size of 30,000 to 40,000, not enough housing was available within its walls to hold the 100,000 or so pilgrims who attended Passover each year. Temple authorities temporarily, then, extended the city's borders to include the west side of the Mount of Olives, which at night became filled with sleeping pilgrims. If officers were to arrest Jesus, they had to know the exact spot where Jesus and his followers stayed. Roman soldiers and Temple police wanted to avoid blundering randomly into campsites on the Mount that might disturb too many pilgrims. To avoid riots, they even decreed they would not arrest Jesus during Passover. *"It was now two days before the Passover and the feast of Unleavened Bread. And the chief priests and scribes were seeking how to arrest him by stealth, and kill him; for they said, 'Not during the feast, lest there be a tumult of the people'"* (Mk 14:1-2). But Judas knew the place in the Garden of Gethsemane where Jesus and his disciples spent each night while in Jerusalem during this Passover. No wonder his disciples fell asleep as soon as they arrived at Gethsemane—it was night and this was where they normally slept. Judas led the police and soldiers to this spot and they arrested Jesus.

The writer John did not identify the place. He said Jesus and his disciples went across the brook Kidron to a garden but does not name the garden (Jn 18:1). Hellenists who helped compose John's Gospel might not have known the exact place because most of them lived in or near Jerusalem and slept in their own homes at night.

In Jerusalem: Jesus Arrested in the Garden (Mark 14:32-52; Jn 18:1-14; see Matthew 26:36-46; Luke 22:40-46)
Danger: The Ending is Near

The report that, during Jesus' arrest, one disciple drew a sword and wounded a man of the arresting crew also shows a contrast between John and Mark. Mark reports it matter-of-factly, *"One of those who stood by drew his sword and struck the slave of the high priest and cut off his ear"* (Mk 14:47). John gives names to them—Simon Peter had and drew the sword that struck the high priest's slave and cut off his *"right ear."* The slave's name was Malchus. Which tradition is more accurate? Did John actually know the name of the person whose ear was cut off? Probably. John usually gives names in events, whereas Mark does not. In this incident John might have had more complete information than Mark.

Both accounts agree that a slave's ear was cut off. John reported that Jesus did not sanction this action. Is this a message from Jesus to his followers, such as Simon the Zealot and Judas Iscariot, who were trying to confront the Romans? The writer John has Jesus say to Peter, *"Put your sword into its sheath. Shall I not drink the cup which the Father has given me?"* (Jn 18:11). Also noteworthy is that Roman law forbade civilians from carrying a sword. Why then did Peter, an intimate follower of a man of peace, have a sword and especially during Passover? Where did he get it? How did he conceal it? This sounds like something a sicarii, an assassin, or perhaps Judas, might have done. But Peter? Why was he at least not arrested for carrying a concealed weapon or killed for drawing blood? Did this incident also make Peter a marked man? This part of the incident befuddles our understanding.

In Jerusalem: Peter's Denial (John 13:36-38, 18:17-25; Mark 14:53-72; see Matthew 26:57-75; Luke 22:54-71)
Danger: Extremely High for Peter

Although both accounts report that Peter denied that he knew Jesus, the details vary. John's account is, *"As the meal ended, Simon Peter asked Jesus, 'Lord, where are you going?' Jesus answered, 'Where I am going you cannot follow me now; but you shall follow afterward.' Peter said to him, 'Lord, why cannot I follow you now? I will lay down my life for you.' Jesus answered, 'Will you lay down your life for me? Truly, truly, I say to you, the cock will not crow, till you have denied me three times'"* (Jn 13:36-38).

John's Gospel extends the story as Jesus was put on trial. *"The maid who kept the door to the chambers of Annas said to Peter, 'You are not one of this man's disciples, are you?' Peter said, 'I am not.' The servants and officers warmed themselves around a charcoal fire that they had made. Peter joined them by the fire. They asked him the same question…and Peter gave the same answer… A servant of the high priest, a kinsman of the man whose ear Peter had cut off, asked, 'Did I not see you in the garden with him?' Peter again denied it. At once the cock crowed"* (Jn 18:17-18,25). As Jesus had said, three denials and the cock crowed. The cock may have been a rooster since poultry are often raised inside mid-east cities or it may have been a bugle call for getting soldiers up in the morning; reveille was sometimes called "the cock."

Mark's story contrasts slightly from John's. He wrote that after Jesus' arrest, *"Peter followed him at a distance, right into the courtyard of the high priest. He was sitting with the guards and warming himself at the fire. One of the maids of the high priest came by. She looked at Peter and said, 'You also were with the Nazarene, Jesus.' He denied it, saying, 'I neither know nor understand what you mean.' He went out into the gateway. The maid saw him again and said to the bystanders, 'This man is one of them.' Again he denied it. A short time after, again the bystanders said to Peter, 'Certainly you are one of them, for you are a Galilean.' But Peter invoked a curse on himself and swore, 'I do not know this man of whom you speak.' Immediately the cock crowed a second time. Peter remembered how Jesus had said to him, 'Before the cock crows twice, you will deny me three times.' Peter broke down and wept"* (Mk 14:54-72).

Both stories are credible. Either (or neither) could have been the original. John adds a note of authenticity to his story by saying there was another man with Peter, who, presumably, could vouch for the veracity of the event. *"Simon Peter followed Jesus and so did another disciple. As this disciple was known to the high priest, he entered the court of the high priest along with Jesus, while Peter stood outside at the door. So the other disciple, who was known to the high priest, went out and spoke to the maid who kept the door and brought Peter in"* (Jn 18:15-16). We have no idea who this *"other disciple"* might have been. John might have known but, perhaps for the man's safety, he failed to reveal his name.

In Jerusalem: Jesus' Hearings and Trial; Release of Barabbas (John 11:47-53, 18:39-40, 19:1-38; Mark 14:53-15:6-15, 21; see Matthew 26:57-27:32; Luke 22:54-23:32)
Danger: Ending Underway

In John a hearing and two trials were held for Jesus during the night. In Mark there was only one hearing (not described in detail) and a trial before Pilate.

John's Gospel reported a hearing held in the presence of Annas (or Ananus or Ananias). Annas (23/22BCE–66CE), son of Seth, was appointed High Priest of the Jerusalem Temple in 6CE by the Roman Legate Quirinius when Archelaus, first son of Herod the Great and Ethnarch of Judea, was deposed. Judea was then put under direct Roman rule with overall jurisdiction through the Syrian Legate in Damascus. The Legate appointed a Procurator (if of Senatorial status) or Prefect (if of Equestrian status) over Judea. Either the Legate or his designee appointed the High Priest. Annas was the first High Priest of the newly formed Roman province of Judea and officially served for ten years (6-15CE). Then at age 36 Annas was deposed by the Procurator Gratus "for imposing and executing capital sentences which had been forbidden by the imperial government" (Josephus, 94).

Although officially removed from office, Annas exercised great power over religious affairs in Israel by seeing that his five sons and son-in-law, Caiaphas, followed him in this office. In 16CE after Annas was deposed, Caiaphas became high priest and held the office at the time of Jesus' hearings and trial. Caiaphas was deposed by the Syrian Legate Lucius Vitellius in 36CE. Caiaphas was probably a puppet High Priest with Annas pulling the strings. Otherwise there is no reason why Jesus would have been brought before Annas to be questioned privately. After Pentecost, Annas presided over the Sanhedrin before which the disciples Peter and John were brought (Acts 4:6). Annas was assassinated in 66CE for advocating peace with Rome. The writer John, curiously, spoke of Caiaphas as the high priest *"in that year"* (11:49, 18:13), as if this office alternated every year. John, too, probably thought that, even while Caiaphas performed the High Priestly duties, he was mainly a stand-in for the real power, his father-in-law Annas.

Jesus' trial before Jewish authorities took place during the night of the Day of Preparation before twenty-three of the 71 members of the Sanhedrin, its executive-committee equivalent, over whom Caiaphas presided (Mt 26:57). Jesus' second trial was before Pontius Pilate. Historically, Pilate has been called "Procurator of Judea" but an inscription on a limestone block, known as the Pilate Stone, discovered in 1961 in the ruins of an amphitheater at Caesarea Maritima, refers to Pilate as "Prefect of Iudaea." He probably, then, held Equestrian, not Senatorial, status (the difference usually being extent of wealth). When Judea, Samaria, and Idumea were first amalgamated into the Roman Province of Iudaea about 6CE, officials of the Equestrian order (the lower rank) governed. They held the Roman title of Prefect until Herod Agrippa I was named King of the Jews in 41CE by Emperor Claudius. After Agrippa's death in 44CE, Iudaea reverted to direct Roman rule and the governor held the title Procurator.

The governor of Judea, in this case Pilate, controlled an auxiliary force of probably 3,000 locally recruited "Roman" soldiers stationed primarily in Caesarea Maritima. In most military situations Pilate yielded to his superior, the Syrian Legate, who would descend on Palestine with his legions as necessary (as on Sepphoris to destroy the revolt by rebels there on the death of Herod the Great in 4BCE). In this era Roman governors could pronounce death sentences on persons recommended for execution by local authorities (Josephus, 94). Prefects and Procurators were also responsible for collecting imperial taxes. Rome's usual practice was to let most civil and judicial matters in the hands of a local ethnic government or municipal council, such as the Sanhedrin and its presiding officer, the High Priest.

In performing his duties to keep order, Pilate traveled throughout the province from his primary residence in Caesarea Maritima. During Passover, a festival of deep national and religious significance to Jews, Pilate and his small legion would be in Jerusalem even if not usually visible to the throngs of worshipers.

According to Mark, the Sanhedrin arrested and questioned Jesus then took him to Pilate (15:1a). Mark asserts that the Sanhedrin was given answers by Jesus that they considered blasphemous under Mosaic law (14:64). But blasphemy was not a capital offense under Roman law. In Mark's Gospel Jesus says very little to his accusers. *"Pilate asked him, 'Are you the King of the Jews?'"* Jesus gave an ambiguous answer, *"You have said so. [Since] the chief priests accused him of many things, Pilate again asked him, 'Have you no answer to make? See how many charges they bring against you.' But Jesus made no further answer, so that Pilate wondered"* (Mk 15:2-5).

When taken before Pilate, the main charges against Jesus were for sedition against Rome for opposing the payment of taxes to Caesar and for calling himself a messiah and king. Fomenting tax resistance was a capital offense. Jesus had asked the tax collector Levi, at work in his tax booth in Capernaum, to quit his post and influenced Zacchaeus, *"a chief tax collector"* in Jericho, to resign. Jericho was in Pilate's tax jurisdiction. Still, Pilate's main question to Jesus was whether he considered himself *"King of the Jews"* and thus a political threat to Rome. The Jewish leaders explained to Pilate that, due to his claim to King David's throne as King of Israel in the royal line of David, Jesus presented a threat to Roman power and occupation. Pilate agreed and condemned Jesus to crucifixion (15:1b-15).

Following Roman custom, Pilate ordered a sign posted above Jesus on the cross stating *"Jesus of Nazareth, King of the Jews"* in Greek, Hebrew, and Latin. This was public notice of the legal charge against him for his crucifixion. The chief priests protested that the sign should read that *"Jesus claimed to be King of the Jews."* Weary of legalistic nit-picking, Pilate refused to change the posted charge, saying *"What I've written I've written"* (Jn 18:12-19:16).

John's Gospel gives more details about the dialogues that took place between Jesus and his accusers. After the soldiers and police led Jesus to Annas, Annas questioned Jesus about his disciples and teaching. Jesus said, *"I have spoken openly to the world. I have always taught in synagogues and in the temple, where all Jews come together. I have said nothing secretly. Why do you ask me? Ask those who have heard me, what I said to them. They know what I said."* After saying this, an officer standing by struck Jesus with his hand, saying, *"Is that how you answer the high priest?"* Jesus responded, *"If I have spoken wrongly, bear witness to the wrong. But if I have spoken rightly, why do you strike me? Annas then sent him bound to Caiaphas the high priest"* (Jn 19:13,19-24).

In John, little is said about Jesus' trial before Caiaphas, because, John reported, even before Jesus' arrest, Caiaphas and the Sanhedrin had already passed sentence on Jesus—the chief priests and Pharisees gathered a council before Jesus had even arrived in Jerusalem for the Passover (Jn 11:47 ff). *"They asked, 'What are we to do? This man performs many signs. If we let him go on, everyone will believe in him and the Romans will come and destroy both our holy place and our nation.' But one of them, Caiaphas, who was high priest that year, said to them, 'You know nothing at all. You do not understand that it is expedient for you that one man should die for the people and that the whole nation should not perish.'"* John added, *"He did not say this of his own accord but being high priest that year he prophesied that Jesus should die for the nation... From that day on they took counsel how to put him to death and they gave orders that if anyone knew where he was, he should let them know, so that they might arrest him"* (11:47-53,57).

At his trial before Pilate in John's Gospel, Jesus was also active in his own defense. *"They led Jesus from the house of Caiaphas to the praetorium... They themselves did not enter the praetorium, so that they might not be defiled but might eat the Passover. So Pilate went out to them and said, 'What accusation do you bring against this man?' They answered him, 'If this man were not an evildoer, we would not have handed him over.' Pilate said to them, 'Take him yourselves and judge him by your own law.' The Jews said to him, 'It is not lawful for us to put any man to death.' Pilate entered the praetorium again, called Jesus, and said to him, 'Are you the King of the Jews?' Jesus answered, 'Do you say this of your own accord, or did others say it to you about me?' Pilate answered, 'I am not a Jew, am I? Your own nation and the chief priests have handed you over to me. What have you done?'"*

John reported that Jesus seemed to confirm the fact of his kingship, although immediately he explains, *"'My kingship is not of this world. If my kingship were of this world, my servants would fight, that I might not be handed over to the Jews. But my kingship is not from the world.' Pilate said to him, 'So you are a king?' Jesus answered, 'You say that I am a king.'"* Jesus then gives his own definition of the goal of his ministry on earth. *"For this I was born, and for this I have come into the world, to bear witness to the truth. Everyone who is of the truth hears my voice."* At this point, Pilate mocked Jesus, *"What is truth (aletheia)?"* In Greek, *aletheia* was a compound word, *a* (from) *letheia* (veil), "to pull the veil from," the veil that covered the truth. Greeks and Romans for centuries had sought *aletheia*, to the satisfaction of almost no one. *"After he [Pilate] had said this, he went out to the Jews again and told them, 'I find no crime in him'"* (Jn 18:19-38).

Both John and Mark agree that Pilate's first act after the questioning was to have Jesus scourged, a possible sign that Jesus was to be crucified. But the scourging could be separated from crucifixion and used as punishment by itself. Pilate had the authority to do either or both. Then, *"Pilate went out again to the Jews and said, 'See, I am bringing him out to you, that you may know that I find no crime in him.' So Jesus came out, wearing the crown of thorns and the purple robe."* This paragraph seems to contradict itself. Pilate says he finds no crime in Jesus yet he orders him scourged and has a crown of thorns placed on his head. Both these acts could be part of the ordeal of crucifixion; the crown of thorns probably indicated that Pilate had already passed the death sentence. *"Pilate said to them, 'Behold the man!' When the chief priests and the officers saw him, they cried out, 'Crucify him, crucify him!'"* Then John adds something different from Mark. Pilate began to toy with them, *"Pilate said to them, 'Take him yourselves and crucify him, for I find no crime in him.'"* Pilate knew they did not have the authority to crucify anyone; their high priest Annas had been removed from office because he had claimed it for himself. So the Jews, in their position of subjugation, answered as best they could, *"'We have a law, and by that law he ought to die because he has made himself the Son of God.'"*

When Pilate heard these words, he might have re-considered his original judgment. The Jewish leaders might be correct, that Jesus could be the Son of God. Emperors had assumed this role for themselves. Why not this strange Jewish preacher? *"Pilate entered the praetorium again and said to Jesus, 'Where are you from?' Jesus gave no answer. Pilate said to him, 'You will not speak to me? Do you not know that I have power to release you and power to crucify you?' Jesus answered him, 'You would have no power over me unless it had been given you from above. Therefore he who delivered me to you has the greater sin.' Upon this Pilate sought to release him, but the Jews cried out, 'If you release this man, you are not Caesar's friend. Every one who makes himself a king sets himself against Caesar.' When Pilate heard these words, he brought Jesus out and sat down on the judgment seat at a place called The Pavement, and in Hebrew, Gabbatha."* Again toying with the Jews *"he said to them, 'Behold your King!... Shall I crucify your King?' The chief priests answered, 'We have no king but Caesar.' Then he handed him over to them to be crucified"* (Jn 18:18-19:16). The chief priests of the Temple and Sanhedrin tended to be pro-Rome. Zealots were not. When Rome made a major push against the Zealots in 66CE, they enveloped the whole region in a war to the death. The terrible events of this war resulted in the destruction of the Temple and most of Jerusalem.

The writer Mark undoubtedly relied on one (or more) from the Galilean Twelve for his information of these events. These informants did not recollect a dialogue between Jesus and Pilate. All except Peter had fled and no Gospel reports that Peter was there when Jesus was tried by Pilate. He may not even have stayed in the area once *"the cock crowed."* The writer John probably relied on the memory of one of several Hellenist followers of Jesus (Nicodemus, Joseph of Arimathea, or even Lazarus), who knew the high priest and followed Jesus when he was taken to Pilate, to document what happened there. John concludes his Gospel with the words, *"This is the disciple who is bearing witness to these things and who has written these things and we know that his testimony is true"* (Jn 21:24).

Both Mark's and John's Gospels tell of the release of Barabbas instead of Jesus by Pilate. Both indicate that this was an *"annual custom"* on the part of Pilate. But no other record of such an *"annual custom"* from this time exists. Mark indicated Barabbas was a murderer and insurrectionist, possibly a sicarii; John called him a robber. His name means nothing—translated from the Hebrew it is "son of father."

In Jerusalem: Jesus' Crucifixion (John 19:17-42; Mark 15:21-47; Matthew 27:32-66; Luke 23:26-56)
Danger: The Ending (?)

John 19 and Mark 15 tell several of the same stories about Jesus' sentence and crucifixion while other Gospels differ. Both Mark and John agree that Jesus was scourged. In Mark 15, Jesus' crucifixion began with a scourging by Pilate's soldiers. To beat a victim before he was put on the cross was standard treatment. The beating was brutal. A Roman soldier, applying his full strength, cracked the whip across a prisoner's bare back. The whip could be a multi-strand leather whip like a cat-of-nine-tails with bits of glass and metal embedded into the leather to make it cut more deeply. The victim was a battered, bloody wreck after the scourging. The man applying the whip might have seen his act as merciful. With loss of blood and strength a convicted man would die more quickly on the cross. The cross was not easy, not a piece of golden jewelry around a neck. In mankind's long history of inhumanity to one another, as noted several times earlier, crucifixion was among the most bitter of ways to execute a man.

The soldiers were not done with Jesus when the scourging was over, not with this particular prisoner anyway. Jesus had been tried and scourged in a public place. They now took him inside a building for a little private fun. They called together as many soldiers as were around and put an old discarded Roman officer's scarlet cloak on his shoulders, a mantle of honor and war on the back of a man of humility and peace. They braided a crown of thorns and pressed it against his head, as if it were an emperor's crown or laurel wreath worn by victors in Coliseum games. These Roman grunts might have called to their buddies, "Hey, look at this, let's stick it to him!" Whatever it represented, the bare thorns pressed into Jesus' skull could have caused disorientation or delirium. Then they bowed low, kissed their fingertips toward him, and called him *"King of the Jews."* When tired of their play, they stripped the scarlet robe from him, put his own clothes back on him, and led him away to crucify him (Mk 15:16-20).

"And they pressed into service one passing by, Simon of Cyrene, coming in from the field, the father of Alexander and Rufus, to carry his cross" (Mk 15:21; not in John). Roman law gave them a legal right to impress any Jew into service at any time. It's what a conquering country did to a conquered people, a sign of one's power and the other's subordination. Their power laid heavy hands on Jews to make them do their bidding. Jews hated it. The man they grabbed on this day was named *"Simon..., father of Alexander and Rufus."* Alexander and Rufus were known by name to Christians in Rome (Paul's Letter to the Romans 16:13—Rufus as an informant is a major reason scholars believe Mark wrote his Gospel in Rome). The man who carried Jesus' cross must have become a follower. Simon is remembered both for carrying Jesus' cross and because he was father of Alexander and Rufus. Since Simon of Cyrene was present at the crucifixion, possibly many events of the day came to Mark from accounts given to Rufus and Alexander.

"And they brought Jesus to the place Golgotha which is translated, 'Place of a Skull' (Mk 15:22; Jn 19:17). We do not know Golgotha's exact location. The present Church of the Holy Sepulcher in Jerusalem dates only to 327CE when the

Emperor Constantine ordered that the holy places of Jesus' life be discovered and marked. Golgotha was probably north of the city. The Romans in their 68CE siege of Jerusalem re-arranged the topography of this whole area in building a ramp over the north wall. Today even this north wall has not been located exactly. The name *"Place of a Skull"* might be because the hill resembled a skull or due to the skulls of victims grinning at travelers from a ravine into which dead bodies were dumped. All known for certain is that a hill for crosses was called Golgotha.

"And they offered him wine mixed with myrrh; but he did not take it. And they crucified him" (Mk 15:23-24; not in John). Wine and myrrh would deaden a victim's sensibilities and pain. It was a merciful act in the barbaric procedure of cru-cifixion. Strange, how the Romans mixed some mercy with great brutality. They knew crucifixion was sadistically bru-tal; this was why they did it.

In crucifixion a prisoner was laid on the ground against a rough-hewn crossbeam, the patebulum. His stretched-out arms were fixed to it with ropes or nailed with spikes, some-times both. Then the patebulum and prisoner were rudely dragged to an upright post, often a notch in the stump of a tree cut off 6 to 10 feet high. The crossbeam and prisoner were lifted and roughly dropped into place, stressing the victim's whole body. Death came by a combination of loss of blood from the scourging and nails, strangulation from the victim's inability to keep his head from sinking into his chest which would block the windpipe, and exposure from a body's inability to withstand the various traumatic shocks. An executioner determined how long a victim hung on the cross. To prolong death, he set a peg or platform into the upright to support the prisoner. If he wanted the person to die more quickly, no peg, no platform. Prisoners usually died within 9 to 12 hours, though sometimes they lived for days. Crucifixion was cruel, brutal, and deadly.

"The inscription of the charge against him read, 'The King of the Jews'" (Mk 15:26. Jn 19:19-22). Crucifixion was reserved

for two kinds of criminals, runaway slaves or persons who committed treason such as insurrection against Rome. Above each crucified victim's head was placarded the charge against him. Jesus' charge, *King of the Jews,* was for treason and insurrection. John adds that the inscription *"was written in Hebrew and in Latin and in Greek."* Rome wanted to make certain everyone could read it and everyone in Jerusalem knew at least one of these three languages. Jesus was not *"king of the Jews"* as Rome defined it. Jesus was not about leading an armed insurrection against Rome. He was *"King of the Jews"* in a profound culmination of the line of prophets, kings, priests, and law-givers who came into Jewish life—a prophet telling of God's ways, a priest opening the way to God, a lawgiver setting his people's way of life and death, a king ruling over all. Jesus was executed as *"King of the Jews."* The cross was his enthronement as king.

"They crucified him, and divided his garments among them, casting lots for them, to decide what each should take" (Mk 15:24; see Jn 19:23-24). John's Gospel indicated that four soldiers constituted the execution detail. The soldiers took his garments and made four parts, one for each soldier. But they were stumped by Jesus' seamless tunic—it was not easily divided. So they cast lots for the tunic. This, said John, was to fulfill the scripture, *"They parted my garments among them, and for my clothing they cast lots"* (Psalm 22:18). John's informant provided these small details that Mark did not have.

"And with him they crucified two insurrectionists, one on his right and one on his left" (Mk 15:27; see Jn 19:18). The Romans gave Jesus two insurrectionists to replace his own men, like James and John might have been. But James and John, who asked for choice places in his kingdom, could not yet drink the cup from which Jesus drank. Instead, two rebels shared his "throne."

"And those passing by blasphemed him, wagging their heads and saying, 'Woe, you who would tear down the temple and build it up in three days, save yourself, come down from the cross'" (Mk 15:29; not in John). Jesus did not, of course,

come down from the cross. If he came down from the cross, he would have saved himself. But no one else. He had already chosen against such a course of action. *"Likewise the chief priests ridiculed him, and so did the scribes, saying, 'Others he saved, himself he is not able to save. Christ, king of Israel, come down now from the cross, so that we might see and believe!'"* Even the two rebels crucified with him joined in the chorus, *"And those crucified with him cursed him"* (Mk 15:29-32; not in John).

"And when it was the 6th hour [noon] darkness came upon the earth until the 9th hour" (Mk 15:33; not in John). What darkness was this? An eclipse of the sun or moon? No such record exists. A vapor so thick that it blotted out the sun, or humid hot air, mixed with sand, blowing in from the desert? Was it the darkness Amos spoke of which marked the day when the Lord God came in power? *"On that day, said the Lord, I will cause the sun to go down at noon and I will darken the earth on a clear day"* (Amos 8:9). Or the darkness Isaiah described in which all people sit and wait for their redemption, *"the people who walk in darkness shall see a great light"*? The darkness into which the light of Christ's kingdom was about to break?

"And in the 9th hour Jesus cried in a great voice, 'Eloi, eloi, lama sabachthani,' which is translated, 'My God, my God, why do you abandon me?'" (Mk 15:34; not in John). Was this a cry of distress—Jesus abandoned by humankind now abandoned by God? Friendless, like a man on a deserted island? Some have said so. But these words come from the beginning of Psalm 22. It starts, *"My God, why hast thou forsaken me?"* It moves on to express great trust. *"In thee our fathers trusted, and thou didst deliver them. To thee they cried and were saved."* In his dying hour Jesus Christ did what he did his entire life—he turned to the Word of God, the God of his Word, and found support and strength there. He called to God, because that was the reality left to him. His call was a call of trust. *"All people shall serve God...and proclaim his deliverance to nations yet unborn"* (Ps 22:30-31).

"Someone standing nearby said, 'He calls Elijah.' Someone else ran and dipped a sponge in vinegar and offered it to Jesus, saying, 'Let us see if Elijah will come and take him down'" (Mk 15:35-36; not in John). This latter person apparently wanted to see if he could ease Jesus' obvious pain and suffering but also prolong Jesus' life long enough to see if Elijah would actually come. Mark surely included this incident in his account to show how "average" people misinterpreted who Jesus was while also demonstrating a near-hostile insensitivity to genuine human suffering—the very opposite of what Jesus desired for humankind.

"And Jesus, sending from himself a great shout, breathed his last" (Mk 15:37; not in John). Was this a cry of pain and despair? Or one of victory? Was it like the shout of Moses when he saw the promised land, of David when he restored the Israelite kingdom, or of John the Baptist when he called for repentance? By his death Jesus opened the promised land to all, inaugurated God's kingdom, called everyone in the world to repentance, trans-formation, and mission. Christians believe Jesus' death was not defeat but victory.

"And the veil of the temple ripped in two from top to bottom" (Mk 15:38; not in John). In reporting this event, Mark noted that Jesus' victory was nearing completion. The veil, the curtain separating the Holy of Holies from the rest of the Temple, protected the innermost shrine from contamination. Only the high priest could enter this place and he only once a year after offering sacrifices for his own sins and those of his people. Ripping this curtain showed God, through Jesus' cross, standing before humankind offering divine love to everyone. The mystery is revealed; the veil is not necessary; Truth is found. No more need to rely on a priestly class to discover God. God was on the cross of Jesus Christ.

"And the centurion...seeing that he breathed his last, said, 'Truly this man was the son of God'" (Mk 15:39; not in John). For a Roman soldier to give this title to a condemned and crucified Jew meant a startling change of mind. It meant he saw what was truly divine in the world. Centurions were

committed to believe that the most divine thing on earth was Rome and Caesar's splendor. But on the cross he saw not splendor and might but goodness, courage, self-sacrifice. The veil was indeed ripped down; God stood revealed. The first to recognize it was a pagan soldier who by the cross of Jesus Christ received a new glimpse of what God is really like, sheer goodness, endless love.

John's Gospel overlapped with Mark's on the broad features of the crucifixion but differed on certain details. For instance, at the end John added, *"After this Jesus, knowing that all was now finished, said (to fulfil the scripture), 'I thirst.' A bowl full of vinegar stood there; so they put a sponge full of the vinegar on hyssop and held it to his mouth. When Jesus had received the vinegar, he said, 'It is finished'; and he bowed his head and gave up his spirit"* (Jn 19:28-29). Mark did not have this detail at least in this form.

Several other contrasts between Mark and John seem puzzling.

- In Mark the crucifixion takes place on the third hour (about nine in the morning); in John it took place on the sixth hour (about noon).
- In Mark, Simon of Cyrene carries Jesus' cross to Golgotha; in John, Jesus carried his own cross.
- In Mark the inscription of his charge is *"The King of the Jews"*; in John the inscription is *"Jesus of Nazareth, the King of the Jews."* This, says John, was written in three languages—Hebrew the language of the Jewish religion; Latin, the official language of government; and in Greek, the language of culture. There was great irony in this. The Jewish people possessed the finest religion in the world, the Roman government possessed the most just government in the world, and the Greek culture produced the finest philosophers, poets, and playwrights in the world. In Jesus' crucifixion, the world's finest religion joined hands with the world's most just government and the world's most productive culture to kill a single man, Jesus of Nazareth.

- Mark recognized no spectators friendly to Jesus near the cross but a few were *"looking on only from afar"* (Mk 15:40)—Mary Magdalene, Mary the mother of James the younger and of Joses, Salome, and *"many other women who came up with him to Jerusalem."* The Eleven remaining disciples had all fled. In John's Gospel, standing by Jesus' cross were his mother, his mother's sister, Mary the wife of Clopas, Mary Magdalene, and the Beloved Disciple. Jesus bequeathed the care of his mother to the Beloved Disciple.

- In Mark, only one statement from Jesus on the cross is recorded, Psalm 22; in John, Jesus spoke three times from the cross, *"Woman, behold, your son! ...Behold, your mother!" "I thirst." "It is finished."* The first set of words were those of an official adoption ceremony. *"When Jesus saw his mother and the disciple whom he loved standing nearby, he said to his mother, 'Woman, behold, your son!' Then he said to the disciple, 'Behold, your mother!' From that hour the disciple took her to his own home"* (Jn 19:26-27). Other "words from the cross" are quoted in other Gospels.

- John reported four soldiers in the execution detail; Mark does not report this.

- In Mark, Joseph of Arimathea, *"a respected member of the council, who was also himself looking for the kingdom of God,"* took Jesus' body from the cross. In John, Joseph of Arimathea, *"who was a disciple of Jesus, but secretly, for fear of the Jews,"* took away his body.

John's Gospel used a singular concept in dealing with Jesus' ministerial impact, *"glory"* (and its cognates such as *"glorified"*). Thirty-nine times John employed it, sometimes in passages as short as one line, other times in extended discussions. This concept provides a unique understanding of the meaning of Jesus' ministry. *"Glory"* is first introduced in John's prelude, *"We have beheld his glory, glory as of the only Son from the Father"* (Jn 1:14). Following the meanings of this word in the Oxford English Dictionary (2004), Jesus' relationship to God was one of beauty, splendor, fame, honor, and praise. These depictions of *"glory"* fit well with the four times Mark used the concept (Mk 2:12, 8:38, 10:38, 13:26).

But these meanings are not adequate in John's Gospel when the scene shifts to Jerusalem. *"The hour has come,"* said Jesus, *"for the Son of Humankind to be glorified. Now is my soul troubled. What shall I say? 'Father, save me from this hour?' No, for this purpose I have come to this hour. Father, glorify thy name. Then a voice came from heaven, 'I have glorified it, and I will glorify it again. Now is the judgment of this world, now shall the ruler of this world be cast out. And I, when I am lifted up from the earth, will draw all people to myself'"* (12:31-34). This version of *"Glory"* in John's Gospel means the point at which the God of Splendor enters human life. The point at which God enters most fully into human life is in Jesus' death. The true *"glory of God"* is on the cross's seeming darkness and dreadfulness. This is where God is most clearly shown.

During their last meal together Jesus and his disciples discussed the meaning of *"glory"* (Jn 13:30-17:26). As the meal ended, Judas took the morsel Jesus offered him. *"Immediately,"* says the Gospel, *"Judas went out; and it was night. When he had gone out, Jesus said, 'Now is the Son of Humankind glorified, and in him God is glorified.'"* Jesus is on his way to the cross and his act glorifies God. *"My Father is glorified when you bear much fruit,"* that is, take my sacrificial life of love upon yourselves, *"and so prove to be my disciples. As the Father has loved me, so have I loved you. Abide in my love"* (Jn 15:8-9).

"When Jesus had spoken these words, he went forth with his disciples across the Kidron valley, where there was a garden, which he and his disciples entered" (Jn 18:1). On beyond is the cross, and there the glory of God is perfectly seen. The glory of God is the cross of Jesus Christ.

Chapter 6

Year Three: In Jerusalem, Jesus' Resurrection

(Mark 14:51-52, 16:1-8; Matthew 28:1-20; Luke 24:1-48;
John17:1-26; 20:1-21:19)

Danger to Jesus: Very Low

Danger to Jesus' Followers: Very High

Each of the four Gospels has accounts of Jesus' resurrection from the dead. The accounts differ in many ways. John's Gospel pictures the resurrected Christ as being able to walk through closed doors and inviting Thomas to touch his hands and side. Luke's Gospel portrays Jesus as walking and talking with disciples but when he sits down at a meal with them he disappears. Matthew's Gospel permits women to whom he appears to bow before him and take hold of his feet. Mark's Gospel features an announcement of Jesus' resurrection to the women who came to the tomb rather than an actual appearance of Jesus to those who knew him best.

Figure 5 outlines the diversity in how the Gospels present Jesus Christ's resurrection. Each appearance had a primary location where it took place and both primary and secondary witnesses. Each announced the event and response to the announcement.

As seen in Figure 5, John clearly has the most detailed accounts of appearances after the crucifixion and Luke has the second most. Both these Gospels were probably written for Greek-speaking Gentiles or possibly "Godfearers," Greeks who aligned themselves with Judaism but came largely from a Hellenist culture. Mark offers the fewest details. Both Mark and Matthew directed their Gospels to those who used Hebrew in their synagogues and worship. We suspect these differences occurred, in part, because Gentiles lacked knowledge of Jewish history's long traditions and, being Greeks, were more skeptical and wanted more detailed accounts to justify their beliefs in Jesus as Christ. Those steeped in Hebrew traditions might more readily recognize that Jesus was the Christ. Differences in resurrection and appearances thereafter are significant events in the various accounts and important enough to be explored in detail.

Jesus' Resurrection in the Gospel of Mark (14:51-52, 16:1-8)

In the Garden of Gethsemane *"Jesus' disciples all forsook him, and fled. A young man followed him, with nothing but a linen cloth about his body. They seized him, but he left the linen cloth and ran away naked"* (Mk 14:51-52).

"When the Sabbath was past, Mary Magdalene, and Mary the mother of James, and Salome, bought spices, so that they might go and anoint him. Very early on the first day of the week they went to the tomb when the sun had risen. They were saying to one another, 'Who will roll away the stone for us from the door of the tomb?' Looking up, they saw that the stone was rolled back; it was very large.

"Entering the tomb, they saw a young man sitting on the right side, dressed in a white robe. They were amazed. He said to them, 'Do not be amazed. You seek Jesus of Nazareth, who was crucified. He has risen, he is not here. See the place where they laid him. But go, tell his disciples and Peter that he is go-

(continues on page 176)

Appearances	Mark	Matthew	Luke	John
1)Where?	At the tomb	At the sepulcher	At the tomb	At the tomb
Primary Witness	Young Man	Mary Magdalene,	Mary Magdalene, Joanna, Mary mother of James, other women who had come with him from Galilee	Mary Magdalene saw the stone was taken away and went to Simon Peter, the "*beloved disciple,*" and others. "*They have taken the Lord from the tomb…*" Peter and "*another disciple*" ran to the tomb, saw linen cloths lying there, and believed. The disciples went back home.
Secondary Witnesses	Mary Magdalene, Mary mother of James, Salome	Other Mary		
Announcement	"*Jesus has risen; see the place where they laid him.*" "*Tell his disciples and Peter he goes before you to Galilee*"	"*Jesus has risen;*" "*Tell… disciples;*" "*Go to Galilee*"	"*Son of humankind must be delivered into the hands of sinful men, and be crucified, and on the third day rise.*" Jesus told this to the eleven and to all the rest.	
Response to announcement	They fled from the tomb, said nothing to any one; they were afraid.			
2) Where else?		On the way home from the tomb	On road to Emmaus	Outside the tomb
Primary Witness		Women	Clopas and friend	Mary Magdalene stood weeping, saw two angels sitting in the tomb. Jesus said, "*Woman, why are you weeping?*" "*Because they have taken away my Lord, I*"
Secondary Witnesses		Jesus met them	Jesus told them that Scripture had said Christ should suffer these things and enter into his glory	
Announcement		and said, "*Do not be afraid; go, tell my brethren to go to Galilee, there they*"		

Figure 5   The Resurrection of Jesus Differs from One Gospel to Another.

			will see me."	*do not know where he is."* She saw Jesus but did not know it was him. Jesus said, "*Whom do you seek?*" "*Tell me where you have laid him and I will take him away.*" Jesus said "*Mary.*" She said "*Rab-boni!*" Jesus said "*Do not hold me...; say to my brethren, I am ascending to my Father, my God and your God.*" Mary Magdalene told the disciples, "*I have seen the Lord...*"
		Fell down and worshiped him	Ate meal, recognized him, returned to Jerusalem. Told the eleven who said "*The Lord has risen, has appeared to Simon!*" Then they told what had happened on the road, and how he was known to them in the breaking of the bread.	
3) Where? Primary Witness Secondary Witnesses		Mountain in Galilee Eleven disciples	Jesus stood among them. See hands and feet, handle me, and see; "*a spirit has not flesh and bones as you see that I have.*" "*They*	Evening, doors locked (fearing the Jews). Jesus came, stood among them, said, "*Peace be with you,*" showed them his hands and

Announce- ment Response to announcement		Make disciples, baptize, teach	*gave him a* *piece of broiled* *fish, he took it* *and ate before* *them.*" Repentance and for- giveness; preached in his name to all nations, beginning from Jerusa- lem. You are witnesses of these things.	side. Jesus said, "As Father has sent me, so I send you." He breathed on them, "*Receive the* *Holy Spirit.*" Thomas was not with them. Other disciples told him, "*We have* *seen the Lord.*" He said, "*Un-* *less I ... place* *my hand in his* *side, I will not* *believe.*"
4) Where? Primary Witness Secondary Witnesses Announce- ment Response to announcement			Led them out as far as Bethany, and lifting up his hands he blessed them, parted from them, and was car- ried up into heaven. "*They returned* *to Jerusalem* *with great*	In a house, eight days later, Thomas and disciples behind shut doors. Jesus came, stood among them, "*Peace be* *with you,*" he said. "*Put* *your finger* *here, see my* *hands..., put* *your hand in* *my side; do not* *be faithless,* *but believing.*" Thomas said, "My Lord and my God!"

				joy; were con-tinually in the temple blessing God."	Jesus said, "Have you be-lieved because you have seen me? Blessed are those who have not seen and yet believe."
5) Where					Sea of Tiberias
Primary Witness					Peter, Thomas, Na-thanael of Cana, sons of Zebedee, two other disciples
Secondary Witnesses					
Announce-ment					Jesus stood on the beach, said to "cast nets on right side…" "Be-loved Disciple" said to Peter, "It is the Lord!"
Response to announcement					On the land, they saw a charcoal fire, fish, and bread. Jesus said, "Come and have breakfast." Jesus gave them bread and fish…

ing before you to Galilee. There you will see him, as he told you.' They went out and fled from the tomb; for trembling and astonishment had come upon them; and they said nothing to any one, for they were afraid" (16:1-8).

The Revised Standard Version of the New Testament closes Mark's Gospel with the words, *"For they were afraid."* The translators found this phrase ended the Gospel's oldest manuscripts even if by the second century other endings were given.

Mary Magdalene and other women had followed Jesus and the Twelve from Galilee to Jerusalem. They watched as Jesus was crucified and *"stood afar"* while Joseph of Arimathea took his body from the cross and hastily laid it in a tomb. They determined to bury Jesus properly. On the Sabbath they gathered what they needed and at sunrise on the first day of the week, with fear and trembling, they went to his gravesite—what they were doing could be punished by death. Anyone touching the body of a crucified criminal was liable to the death penalty. They were also anxious about the heavy stone in front of the tomb—how would they roll it away?

Imagine their surprise when they looked up through the dim morning light and found that the stone had been rolled away. Imagine their further surprise when they entered the tomb and found not the dead body of Jesus but *"a young man, dressed in a white robe, sitting on the right side"* of the tomb. The young man spoke to them, *"Don't be alarmed. You are looking for Jesus of Nazareth, who was crucified. He has been raised. He is not here. See the place where they laid him… Go, tell his disciples and Peter that he is going ahead of you to Galilee. There you will see him, just as he told you."* The disciples (Greek, *mathetais*) were to go back to Galilee in order to continue in that region the ministry that Jesus had begun. As Jesus went before them when they came to Jerusalem, now he will go before them again and lead them into the work they are to perform. *"There you will see him,"* the young man said.

The word for *"see," "opsesthe"* in Greek, in this context was first used in this way in Isaiah 6 in the Septuagint (the

Old Testament in Greek), where the prophet said, *"I saw the Lord."* Jeremiah had said, *"The Lord of old appeared to me."* Paul later said, *"Have not I seen the Lord? He appeared to me also."* This word, *"appeared,"* was used for the appearance of God, or his angel, or his glory (Bartsch, 1980). Such appearances were confined to the three great Old Testament epochs of salvation—of Abraham, Isaac, and Jacob; of Moses and Israel in the wilderness; and of David and Solomon. Jesus' appearances to his followers were a fourth set of appearances. Like the earlier ones, these appearances occurred at the beginning of a new time of salvation.

All the disciples had deserted Jesus in the Garden of Gethsemane. In the Garden of the Empty Grave, Jesus begins to mobilize them again so that they can fulfill what they began when he called them to himself. Peter was picked out for special attention. Not only had he deserted his master in Gethsemane, Peter had denied him when Jesus was brought to trial. Peter needs this special invitation if he is to be restored into Jesus' fellowship. A new time of salvation has begun, first for Peter, then for the Twelve, and then for all the world.

At this point fear seized the women and they fled. Mark's Gospel says, *"They said nothing to no one. For they were afraid."* On this strange note, Mark's Gospel ends.

The young man who spoke to the women might be the same young man who was following Jesus and slipped away at Gethsemane (Mk 14:51-52). *Neaniskon,* the Greek word for "young man," is used only twice in Mark, in Gethsemane and at Jesus' tomb. In Gethsemane, arresting soldiers caught hold of him but he slipped out of his linen garment and ran off naked. At Gethsemane, this young man was fearful, silent, and naked. At the Empty Grave his situation was totally reversed. He was poised, confident, and clothed in a white robe. He was seated, not running away and not silent but conveyed a message to the women. He was a changed *neaniskon.*

A clue to this change might have been contained in the man's own words—he was a witness to the risen Christ who had a message for his disciples. Now the *neaniskon* had new control of his life. Mark may have reported this incident because he, or more likely an informant, knew of this young man and how he revealed the resurrection's "before" and "after." At Gethsemane he was Everyman fleeing from life's circumstances but at the Open Grave he is Everyman under the risen Christ's power and influence.

Jesus' Resurrection in the Gospel of Matthew
(28:1-15, 16-20)

"After the Sabbath, toward the dawn of the first day of the week, Mary Magdalene and the other Mary went to see the sepulchre. Behold, there was a great earthquake. An angel of the Lord descended from heaven and came and rolled back the stone and sat upon it. His appearance was like lightning, and his raiment white as snow. For fear of him the guards trembled and became like dead men. But the angel said to the women, 'Do not be afraid; for I know that you seek Jesus who was crucified. He is not here; for he has risen, as he said. Come, see the place where he lay. Then go quickly and tell his disciples that he has risen from the dead, and behold, he is going before you to Galilee. There you will see him. Lo, I have told you.' So they departed quickly from the tomb with fear and great joy and ran to tell his disciples. Behold, Jesus met them and said, 'Rejoice! (Chairete!)' They came up and took hold of his feet and worshiped him. Jesus said to them, 'Do not be afraid. Go and tell the disciples to go to Galilee and there they will see me.'

"While they were going, behold, some of the guard went into the city and told the chief priests all that had taken place. When they had assembled with the elders and taken counsel, they gave a sum of money to the soldiers and said, 'Tell people, His disciples came by night and stole him away while we were asleep. If this comes to the governor's ears, we will satisfy him and keep you out of trouble.' So they took the money and did as they were directed, and this story has been spread among the Jews to this day" (Mt 28:1-15).

This story parallels but does not duplicate Mark's. After his crucifixion on Friday, Jesus was buried quickly, before sundown when Sabbath began. About 32 hours later, the Sabbath had ended at sunset. Still dark, when no virtuous woman ventured out, Mary Magdalene and the other Mary went to Jesus' tomb to fulfill a Jewish custom—to watch a loved one's tomb until the third day after death to ensure that no premature burial occurred. Matthew's Gospel does not say that they went to anoint his body; Matthew does not mention spices or herbs of any sort.

It took unbelievable courage for the women to go to the tomb that dark morning. These two women were not from Jerusalem and might have been uncertain of the way to the tomb. Even if they found the tomb, they might not have been able to find his body. The tomb was a large rock chamber with small tunnels for individual burials opening from a central chamber. They would not have known which opening was used for Jesus' burial. The tomb also was guarded by soldiers and Roman law said that anyone who touched the body of a crucified man could incur the same brutal punishment for themselves. Imagine what must have gone through their minds as they made their way in the dark to a gloomy tomb they could hardly find and a fate they might provoke. No wonder they were *"afraid."*

What they met astonished them. A great earthquake! An angel of the Lord descending from heaven rolling back the stone, sitting on it! His appearance like lightning! His garments white as snow! The panicked guards prostrate on the ground! And the angel spoke to them!

"Do not be afraid!" were the angel's first words, immediately recognizing the women's emotions. The angel acknowledged why the women came, *"You seek Jesus who was crucified."* Then the angel spoke the words we cannot fathom today two thousand years later, *"He is risen."* The angel gave two quick responses to support his statement. *"He said he would rise."* Up to this moment in human history, only God could say what God would do in some future—no human be-

ing could do that. In the past, a voice said to Moses on the mountain, *"God will do what God will do."* Now Jesus fulfills this function of God that had to this moment belonged only to God. Jesus had said that he would rise from the dead and he did. The angel added, *"Come see the place where he lay."* Did they do it? The story does not say so. The women took the word of the angel that it was so.

The angel gave them a command. *"Go, tell his disciples that he is risen and that he will go before you to Galilee."* The disciples were Galileans. They were to return home where they lived and walked with Jesus before. Jesus would meet them in their familiar surroundings, now changed because Jesus who was dead was alive again. And the women departed, still afraid. But their fear was transformed into great joy as they ran to tell the disciples what they had seen and heard.

Then a voice rang out, and a single word was spoken, *"Chairete, Rejoice!"* The women may not have known the meaning of this word but the people who later heard and read the story surely did. It was the happiest word in the Greek language. Five centuries before, 490BCE, Persian armies had landed on Greek soil, intent on capturing the fabled city of Athens. A small Greek army marched out a couple dozen miles from the city to engage this enormously superior horde, the most powerful armed force yet to take the field in any battle. They met on the plains of Marathon. Anxious Athenian citizens—older men, the disabled, women, children, those who had not marched out to meet the enemy— watched from the city walls. A runner appeared, sent by the victorious Athenians to bring news of this incredible and world-changing victory. For more than 25 miles he ran, no doubt sprinting most of the way. Arriving at the city gates, he could gasp out only one word, *"Chairete!* Rejoice!" He fell dead as Athen's answering cry went up—goodbye to despair and glad hello to a new destiny. With this cry, say historians, western civilization was born.

On the morning of his resurrection, according to Matthew, Jesus' *"Chairete!"* announced an even greater victory, a victory over Judas' betrayal, Peter's denial, disciples' desertion, Jewish leaders' complicity, Roman brutality, and death itself. They did not matter now. Jesus was risen from the dead. Through him God accomplished the world's victory over sin and death. In Jesus' loud *"Chairete! Rejoice!"* God's new people were born.

The women at once sensed the victory. They ran forward, prostrated themselves before Jesus as they would before God, took hold of his feet and worshiped him. Jesus repeated the promise of the angel. *"Do not be afraid. Go, tell my brothers to go to Galilee. There they will see me."* And on a mountain in Galilee, they did see him.

"The eleven disciples went to Galilee, to the mountain to which Jesus had directed them. When they saw him they worshiped him; but some doubted. Jesus came and said to them, 'All authority in heaven and on earth has been given to me. Go therefore and make disciples of all nations, baptizing them in the name of the Father and of the Son and of the Holy Spirit, teaching them to observe all that I have commanded you; and lo, I am with you always, to the close of the age'" (Mt 28:16-20). This is the one place in all Scripture where *"Father, Son, and Holy Spirit,"* the Trinity, are mentioned in the same breath. These closing verses of Matthew's Gospel are to be celebrated for what they say in and of themselves.

Meeting the risen Christ in Galilee is clearly the climax of the whole Gospel. The scene is a mountain in Galilee with the remaining eleven disciples. Judas had betrayed Jesus and died, the only disciple, curiously enough, to die with Jesus at the time of Jesus' death. Great events take place on mountains in the Bible—on a mountain Moses received the covenant, Elijah encountered God, Jesus preached the Sermon on the Mount, Jesus was transfigured, and now he appeared to his disciples. Jesus told the disciples they would see him in Galilee on this mountain and this, too, was fulfilled. See him they did.

"They worshiped him." Before this time the disciples stood in awe of Jesus, but only in Matthew's Gospel are we told

"they worshiped him." They now elevated Jesus to the place that only God had in their lives. Worshiping Jesus Christ was their overt expression of the new manner in which they now saw him. In their lives, Jesus stands with God.

"But some doubted." The word "doubted" in Greek, *edistasan*, is a strange word. It is not disbelief, *a-pistis*, belief canceled. *Edistasan* implies wavering, being divided within oneself. Faith is there but imperfect. "Hesitate" is the closest meaning.

"Jesus came and said to them, 'All authority in heaven and on earth has been given to me.'" "Authority," *auctoritas* in Latin, was what people of stature sought. In *The Twelve Caesars*, Michael Grant describes *auctoritas* as "the sum total of qualities in a man that commanded respect for his person and opinion, including his birth, wealth, personal achievement, talent, and virtues" (1975: 68). Jesus had no wealth but his birth has been celebrated in story and song, his personal achievements chronicled, his talents and virtues praised, respect for his person and opinion of the highest order. As has no other, Jesus possesses *auctoritas*.

"Go therefore and make disciples of all the nations." "Nations" (Greek, *ethne*) in Jesus' time did not have today's denotation. Modern nations have borders enclosing a people, laws, and some form of governance. To the Romans, *ethne*, "ethnic," was a class, race, or grouping of people with some cohesion. As long as they did not disturb the Pax Romana by disruptions such as riots, Rome protected such ethnics by granting them "rights" to practice their "ancestral religions" and to their local social identity and cohesion through such associations as eating clubs (Barclay, 1996: 41 ff). Some were granted limited self-rule through a *politeuma*, a grouping within a city that had formalized legal rights of self-government for all to know. Jews in Alexandra had such rights from about 45BCE when Julius Caesar granted them these rights (for helping him to defeat Pompey) until about 40CE when the Emperor Claudius severely limited these rights due to Jewish rioting in Alexandria from 38-40CE (Barclay, 1996: 64

ff). Jesus' direction is clear. *"Go [into all the world] and make disciples of all the ethnics."* No command of Jesus has had more effect in the world than this one. His disciples did go into all the world and made additional disciples, until all the world became aware of Jesus. In all generations, men and women have followed and obeyed him. Most of the world live in civilizations affected by him.

"Baptizing in the name of the Father and of the Son and of the Holy Spirit." But perhaps Jesus did not baptize. John's Gospel says he did and then retracts the statement. *"The Pharisees heard that Jesus was baptizing more disciples than John [the Baptist] (although Jesus himself did not baptize, but only his disciples)"* (Jn 4:2). But Matthew says that Jesus commanded his disciples to baptize to bring new ethnics into his fellowship. Baptisms for individuals and whole families took place through immersion. Dipping and sprinkling came later. Baptism rituals included Matthew's threefold names of *"Father, Son, and Holy Spirit."*

In the entire Bible only Matthew's Gospel uses this threefold credo to describe God. Where the phrase came from is open to speculation. A best guess, in our estimation, posits Egypt as its source. Egyptians customarily thought of God in three-fold terms. In the apocryphal "Gospel to the Egyptians" Jesus is supposed to have said to his disciples, "the same was the Father, the same was the Son, the same was the Holy Spirit" (Kamil, 1987: 36). Whatever its origin, this formulation in Matthew's Gospel was extremely influential in forming the doctrine of Trinity. The closest formulation to it is in John who uses the phrase *"Father, Son, and Counselor (Paraclete)."*

"Teaching them to observe all that I have commanded you." Matthew's Gospel was filled with Jesus' teachings. Up to five distinct sections in the Gospel are devoted to his teachings. His disciples were to continue his teaching at every opportunity.

"I am with you always." Jesus did not withdraw from his disciples. After he appeared to them on the mountain, they

still felt his presence in their teaching and doing what he taught—teaching, healing, seeking justice, extending love. A significant question is, Does his presence continue? To teach, guide, strengthen, direct his church and its people? Matthew asserts he will and experience has taught Christians that he does. The on-going life of the churches consists of its attempts to respond to Christ and to determine Christ's response to it. In making these efforts, Christ is with us even today.

"To the close of the age." What did Matthew mean by the word *"close"*? The context suggests it means "ending of the age." But *"close"* could also mean, "completion of the age," bringing the age to fulfillment. Jesus, when he comes again, will do both. He will end "the present evil age in which we live" and "fulfill the age" by bringing it fully into the peace and love of a righteous God.

This final section is well suited to the stirring development of Matthew's Gospel. He began with the Messiah's royal genealogy, proceeded through Jesus' teaching, healing, and miracles, and ended bowing in worship and awe before the universal savior, Lord of heaven and earth.

Jesus' Resurrection in the Gospel of Luke (24:1-12, 13-35, 36-48)

"On the first day of the week, at early dawn, they [Mary Magdalene, Joanna, and Mary the mother of James, and other women who were with Jesus from Galilee] went to the tomb, taking the spices which they had prepared. They found the stone rolled away from the tomb, but when they went in they did not find the body.

"While they were perplexed about this, behold, two men stood by them in dazzling apparel. They were frightened and bowed their faces to the ground. The men said to them, 'Why do you seek the living among the dead? Remember how he told you, while he was still in Galilee, that the Son of Humankind must be delivered into the hands of sinful men, and be cruci-

fied, and on the third day rise.' They remembered his words, and returning from the tomb they told all this to the eleven and to all the rest. It was Mary Magdalene and Joanna and Mary the mother of James and the other women with them who told this to the apostles, but these words seemed to them an idle tale and they did not believe them" (Lk 24:1-12).

This account reflects those in Mark and Matthew but again differs in details. The women, Mary Magdalene, Joanna, Mary the mother of James, and other unnamed women (except for Mary Magdalene, the names changed from one Gospel to another), took spices to anoint Jesus' body. Unexpectedly, they found the stone rolled away but, entering the tomb, they did not find Jesus' body. Two unidentified men were there, not angels nor one young man (*neaniskon*), but men. They repeated Jesus' words when with his disciples in Galilee, *"Remember how he told you..., that the Son of Humankind must be... crucified, and on the third day rise."* The women told all this to the Eleven and all the rest. But to these weary, frightened, dispirited *apostolous* (not *mathetais*, disciples, as in Matthew and Mark—Luke's was a Gospel of the Apostles' party) called this *"an idle tale"* and did not believe the women. In Luke's experience no one had ever died and risen again. Despite that Jesus said he would rise again, to believe a report like what the women said was not comprehensible in the apostles' milieu.

"That very day two of these men were going to a village named Emmaus, about seven miles from Jerusalem, and were talking with each other about all the things that had happened. While they were talking and discussing together, Jesus himself drew near and went with them. But their eyes were kept from recognizing him.

"Jesus said to them, 'What are you talking about as you walk?' They stood still, looking sad. Then one named Cleopas, answered him, 'Are you the only visitor to Jerusalem who does not know what has happened in these last few days?' He said to them, 'What things?' They said to him, 'Concerning Jesus of Nazareth, who was a prophet mighty in deed and word

before God and all the people, and how our chief priests and rulers delivered him to be condemned to death, and crucified him. But we had hoped that he was the one to redeem Israel. Yes, and besides all this, it is now the third day since this happened. Moreover, some women of our company amazed us. They were at the tomb early in the morning and did not find his body. They came back saying that they had even seen a vision of angels [the story above had said 'men' but 'angels' must have been added to the account early on]. *The angels said that Jesus was alive. Some of those who were with us went to the tomb and found it empty just as the women had said. Him they did not see.'*

"Jesus said to them, 'O foolish men, and slow of heart to believe all that the prophets have spoken! Was it not necessary that the Christ should suffer these things and enter into his glory?' Beginning with Moses and all the prophets, Jesus interpreted to them in all the scriptures the things concerning himself.

"They drew near to the village to which they were going. He appeared to be going farther, but they constrained him, saying, 'Stay with us, for it is toward evening and the day is now far spent.' So he went in to stay with them. When he was at table with them, he took the bread, blessed it, broke it, and gave it to them. Their eyes were opened and they recognized him; and he vanished out of their sight. They said to each other, 'Did not our hearts burn within us while he talked to us on the road, while he opened to us the scriptures?'

"They rose that same hour and returned to Jerusalem. They found the eleven gathered together and those who were with them, who said, 'The Lord has risen indeed, and has appeared to Simon!' Then they told what had happened on the road and how he was known to them in the breaking of the bread" (Lk 24:13-35).

"Two men were going to Emmaus, about seven miles from Jerusalem." Emmaus was a small village that became infamous in 70CE, when the Roman Emperor Vespasian used it as a retirement home for Roman soldiers who had destroyed the Holy

City. For Christians, its fame rests as the site where Christ first broke bread with disciples after his resurrection. These *"two men"* knew Jesus but were not part of the Galilean Eleven. They probably belonged to a group of Judean followers whom Jesus had gathered in his frequent journeys to Jerusalem. Matthew noted that one was named Cleopas; John's Gospel indicated that one of the two was Clopas, Mary's husband. This Mary stood by Jesus' cross (Jn 19:25). She was Jesus' mother's sister, Jesus' aunt, which made Cleopas Jesus' uncle by marriage. The other man is not known by name.

Two full days had passed since Jesus died on a cross in Jerusalem. As they walk, they are joined by a third, and the three talk together. When they arrive in their village, this third man is about to go on, but the two invite him to come in and have an evening meal with them. The stranger broke the bread in their behalf, blessed and gave it to them, and they know that it is Jesus. He vanishes from sight. They rush back to Jerusalem and are met with the news that *"the Lord has risen indeed and has appeared to Simon"* (none of the other accounts in the Synoptic Gospels mentioned Simon). The men tell the others what they had seen and how he was known to them in the breaking of the bread. This in outline is the hauntingly beautiful story of the first Easter eve in the little village of Emmaus.

Cleopas did not recognize Jesus when he joined the two men that evening hour. Disconsolate, Cleopas and his friend had hoped that Jesus would redeem Israel. But the chief priests and rulers had condemned Jesus and crucified him. After the crucifixion, Cleopas and his friend stayed in Jerusalem for two days and even heard a report, from the women, that Jesus' tomb was empty. They also reported a vision of angels who said Jesus was alive. Some men went to the tomb but did not see Jesus. So Cleopas and his friend were going home to Emmaus, their hope in Jesus demolished, their lives mournful.

As they walked, the stranger even asked them, *"Did you not know that Christ should suffer these things and enter into his glory?"* Then he talked with them about Scriptures, beginning with Moses and the prophets, and what Scripture had to say about the Christ. The stranger spoke persuasively, unfolding the meaning of their sacred Scriptures to them. Still Cleopas and his friend did not recognize the stranger.

When they came to Emmaus, the stranger made as if to go on but Cleopas and his friend asked him to have supper with them. *"'Stay with us, for it is toward evening and the day is now far spent.' So he went in to stay with them. When he was at table with them, he took the bread, blessed it, broke it, and gave it to them. Their eyes were opened and they recognized him; and he vanished out of their sight."* When the stranger took the bread, blessed it, broke it, and gave it to them, they finally recognized him.

There was actually more to it. They knew Jesus before and that he said he would rise from the dead. But the terrible vision they had of him writhing on a cross in agony nearly canceled out all he previously said and did. They needed a vision of Christ in his glory at least as compelling as their vision of his death.

Then the women reported they could not find his body in the tomb and that an angel told them he was alive. This report was hard to fathom. No one had died and risen again. They needed to see him to believe such a report.

The breaking of the bread did it. The words used in this story were the exact words Jesus used in the last meal with his disciples. *"He took bread, and blessed, and broke the bread, and gave it to them."* Cleopas and his friend recognized the breaking of the bread and the exact blessing. In extending hospitality to Jesus on this evening in Emmaus, Cleopas and his friend received Jesus' encompassing companionship, the hospitality of the risen Christ.

Food had always been important in Jesus' ministry. Luke indicates that through Jesus God *"has filled the hungry with good things, and the rich he has sent empty away"* (1:53). He had fed 5,000 men. Jesus' favorite picture of life to come was Jesus hosting a great banquet with favored guests who were poor, blind, lame, maimed. Cleopas and his friend knew him as he offered them bread. But then Jesus disappeared.

"They rose that same hour and returned to Jerusalem. They found the eleven gathered together and those who were with them, who said, 'The Lord has risen indeed, and has appeared to Simon!' Then they told what had happened on the road and how he was known to them in the breaking of the bread."

"As they were saying this, Jesus himself stood among them. They were startled and frightened, and supposed they saw a spirit. And he said to them, 'Why are you troubled, and why do questionings rise in your hearts? See my hands and my feet; it is I myself. Handle me and see. A spirit has not flesh and bones as you see that I have.' While they still disbelieved, in joy and wonder he said to them, 'Have you anything here to eat?' They gave him a piece of broiled fish, and he took it and ate before them."

This scene takes place in Jerusalem in the room where Jesus' disciples gathered after his crucifixion. The two men from Emmaus had rushed back into the city and reported to the assembled group that the risen Lord had met them and was known to them in the breaking of the bread. They learn the equally astonishing news that "*the Lord has arisen indeed and has appeared to Simon!*" (Lk 24:34). Doubt and hope are in the vortex of these feelings as the scene begins.

Immediately Jesus himself stood among them. Instead of quieting their doubts and affirming their hopes, his appearance startled and frightened them. They thought that they were seeing a ghost. Recognizing their troubles and questions, Jesus took steps to meet their doubts.

First, he showed them his hands and feet and invited them to handle them. They did not, of course. Seeing his flesh and bones was enough. Then he asked if they had anything to eat. They gave him a piece of broiled fish, like that which he had eaten with them in the feeding of the multitude, and in their presence he ate it. He ate bread with the men of Emmaus. Now he ate fish with the eleven in Jerusalem. As he ate the bread and the fish before them, they knew him.

"Then he said to them, 'These are my words which I spoke to you, while I was still with you, that everything written about me in the law of Moses and the prophets and the psalms must be fulfilled.' Then Jesus opened their minds to understand the scriptures and said to them, 'Thus it is written, that the Christ should suffer and on the third day rise from the dead, and that repentance and forgiveness of sins should be preached in his name to all nations (ethne), beginning from Jerusalem. You are witnesses of these things. Behold, I send the promise of my Father upon you. But stay in the city, until you are clothed with power from on high.'"

They did stay in the city. Luke in the beginning of the Acts of the Apostles says that all the followers in the early Jesus movement were headquartered in Jerusalem (Acts 1:12-14, 2:1-2), not in Galilee as other accounts had indicated. Jesus instructed them to read the Scriptures with an open mind. In Scripture—in the law, prophets, and psalms—they would find those things that are written about him. *"The law of Moses and the prophets and the psalms,"* contrasted with what Sadducees, the Jerusalem authorities, believed. Their Scripture consisted only of the Torah, the Law of Moses, as the Word of God. Pharisees believed that God spoke through all three kinds of writings and the early Jesus movement agreed with the Pharisees on this. Jesus commanded them to preach repentance and forgiveness of sin in his name to all the nations. He said, *"Be my witnesses in your lives, for the promise of my father is upon you, and you will be clothed with power from on high."*

"Then Jesus led them out as far as Bethany. Lifting up his hands he blessed them. While he blessed them, he parted from them and was carried up into heaven. They returned to Jerusalem with great joy and were continually in the temple blessing God" (24:50-53).

Bethany was the home of Mary, Martha, and Lazarus, the village where Jesus had raised Lazarus from the dead and was anointed by Mary before he entered Jerusalem for Passover. There he lifted up his hands to bless his closest followers. At the beginning of Luke's Gospel, Simeon had held the child Jesus in his arms, blessing God for him. Now at the end Jesus blesses his followers—having Jesus' blessing, these formerly terrified men and women could *"return to Jerusalem with great joy and go day after day into the temple to bless God."*

Jesus' Resurrection in the Gospel of John (20:1-18, 19-31, 21:1-19, 17:1-26)

"On the first day of the week Mary Magdalene came to the tomb early, while it was still dark, and saw that the stone had been taken away from the tomb. So she ran and went to Simon Peter and the other disciple (matheten), the one whom Jesus loved, and said to them, 'They have taken the Lord out of the tomb and we do not know where they have laid him.'

"Peter came out with the other disciple...toward the tomb. They both ran but the other disciple outran Peter and reached the tomb first. Stooping to look in, he saw the linen cloths lying there but he did not go in. Then Simon Peter came, following him, went into the tomb. He saw the linen cloths...and the napkin, which had been on his head, not lying with the linen cloths but rolled up in a place by itself. Then the other disciple, who reached the tomb first, also went in and saw and believed; for as yet they did not know the scripture, that he must rise from the dead. Then the disciples (mathetai) went back to their homes.

"But Mary stood weeping outside the tomb and as she wept she stooped to look into the tomb. She saw two angels in white sitting where the body of Jesus had lain, one at the head and one at the feet. They said to her, 'Woman, why are you weeping?' She said to them, 'Because they have taken away my Lord and I do not know where they have laid him.' Saying this, she turned round and saw Jesus standing but she did not know it was Jesus. Jesus said to her, 'Woman, why are you weeping? Whom do you seek?' Supposing him to be the gardener, she said to him, 'Sir, if you have carried him away, tell me where you have laid him and I will take him away.' Jesus said to

her, 'Mary.' She turned and said to him in Hebrew, 'Rabboni!'
(which means Teacher). Jesus said to her, 'Do not hold me, for
I have not yet ascended to the Father; but go to my brethren
(adelphous) and say to them, I am ascending to my Father and
your Father, to my God and your God.' Mary Magdalene went
and said to the disciples (mathetais), 'I have seen the Lord.'
And she told them that he had said these things to her" (Jn
20:1-18).

In John's Gospel only one woman came to the tomb, Mary
Magdalene. She came at approximately the same time that
all the women came, *"on the first day of the week..., early,*
while it was still dark." Possibly others were present, too.
When Mary reported what she saw to Simon and the Beloved Disciple, the plural *"we do not know"* is used (Jn 20:2).

Mary probably came to a horizontal-cave tomb, usually
less than 3 feet high with an entrance at ground level thru
a small doorway so low adults would have to crawl in. The
tomb could be sealed by a boulder rolled against the doorway. Elaborate tombs had wheel-shaped slabs of stone rolled
in a track across the entrance. Some had an antechamber, off
which were burial chambers. Some had 2- to 3-foot niches
cut in the sidewalls, about 2 feet up the wall. The niche had
either a flat slab or trough on which a body could be placed.
A deceased's body was inserted headfirst, filling the niche.
Other tombs had benches, cut into three sides of a chamber's walls, on which to lay a body. Jesus' body was probably
placed in a tomb like one of these.

When Mary Magdalene approached the tomb, no stone
covered it. She, like everyone else on this first Easter Sunday, *"ran"* to report her discovery to Simon Peter and the
other disciple, the one whom Jesus loved. Alarmed, they
ran to the tomb. *"The other disciple"* arrived first but did
not enter the tomb but stooped to see the linen cloths that
had covered Jesus lying there. Peter then came, entered the
tomb, and saw the linen cloths lying where *"the other dis-*
ciple" had seen them. Dead bodies often give off an odor but
such an odor is not reported. Still, being crucified, he must

have died. Perhaps the day's excitement masked any odor. Peter also noticed that the napkin, which had covered Jesus' head, was rolled up *"in a place by itself."* *"The other disciple"* then entered the tomb and, said John's Gospel, *"he saw and believed"* that Jesus had risen from the dead.

Why would the reaction of the two disciples be so different? The gravecloths may provide the clue. *"The beloved disciple"* might have been with Jesus when Lazarus came out of his grave at Jesus' invitation. Perhaps he was the Lazarus that emerged wearing similar gravecloths to those Jesus left behind. This association may be important: Lazarus - gravecloths – risen from the dead; Jesus – gravecloths – risen from the dead.

Then came one of the greatest recognition scenes in all history. Mary Magdalene stood weeping outside the tomb. Looking in, she saw two angels (Mark and Matthew report one; Luke also reports two), who asked her *"Woman, why are you weeping?"* Presuming that Jesus was dead and lying in some unknown tomb, she replied, *"They have taken away my lord and I do not know where they have laid him."* Turning around, through her tears she saw a dim figure behind her. He asked the same question. Mary thought she was addressing the gardener-caretaker of the tomb, so she said, *"Sir, if you have carried him away, tell me where you have laid him and I will take him away."* Then the voice said, *"Mary!"* She knew the voice. *"Rabboni,"* she replied. Mary reached out to touch him, but Jesus pulled away. *"Do not keep holding me"* (the force of verb in Greek is stronger), *"Do not cling to me, for I have not yet ascended to the Father. But go to my brothers (adelphous) and say to them that I am ascending to my Father and your Father, to my God and your God."*

This account has several theological implications. First, Mary Magdalene knew Jesus only after he called her by name. The mere sight of the risen Jesus did not lead Mary to believe. Her faith depended on the personal relationship she had with Jesus Christ. He called her by name and she called him by one of his titles. Since then, some Christians have reported they had similar relationships with Jesus Christ. He calls them by name; they call him by name.

Second, John's Gospel points to three distinct divisions in Jesus' life—the historical Jesus, the person who lived in Judea and Galilee and carried out ministries described for him there; the glorified Christ, living into eternity with his Father and with those whom he loves; and, between the historical Christ and the glorified Christ, is the risen Christ. The risen Christ is simultaneously on earth and glorious; he is seen both by sense-vision and by the vision of faith.

Third, what happened after the resurrection, according to the writer John, has two phases. Before Jesus ascended to the Father, he was seen at least by Mary Magdalene, Peter, the beloved disciple, James, and Thomas. When he ascended to the Father, this first phase of his "resurrected life" ended. He was no more *"seen"* by persons as he was seen earlier. With his ascension, the second phase of Jesus' "resurrected life" began. Now, in his spirit, in the totality of his inner being, Jesus still came to his followers. The resurrected Christ that Christians can know today is not bound by the limitations of space and time. With his ascent to the Father, Christians generally believe the way was opened for Christ to dwell with each and all of his followers at one and the same time.

"*On the evening of that day, the first day of the week, the doors being shut where the disciples were, for fear of the Jews, Jesus came and stood among them and said to them, 'Peace be with you.' When he had said this, he showed them his hands and his side. The disciples (mathetai) were glad when they saw the Lord. Jesus said to them again, 'Peace (eirene) be with you. As the Father has sent me, even so I send you.' When he had said this, he breathed (enephusese) on them, and said to them, 'Receive the Holy Spirit (pneuma agion). If you forgive the sins of any, they are forgiven; if you retain the sins of any, they are retained.'*

"*Thomas, one of the Twelve, called the Twin, was not with them when Jesus came. So the other disciples (mathetai) told him, 'We have seen the Lord.' But he said to them, 'Unless I see in his hands the print of the nails, and place my finger in the mark of the nails, and place my hand in his side, I will not believe.'*

"*Eight days later, his disciples (mathetai) were again in the house and Thomas was with them. The doors were shut but Jesus came and stood among them, and said, 'Peace be with you.' Then he said to Thomas, 'Put your finger here, and see my hands; and put out your hand, and place it in my side; do not be faithless (apistos), but believing (pistos).' Thomas answered him, 'My Lord and my God!' Jesus said to him, 'Have you believed because you have seen me? Blessed are those who have not seen and yet believe (pisteusantes).'*

"*Now Jesus did many other signs in the presence of the disciples (matheton), which are not written in this book; but these are written that you may believe that Jesus is the Christ, the Son of God, and that believing you may have life in his name*" (Jn 20:19-31).

In John's account, Jesus' Galilean followers heard from Mary Magdalene that Jesus was raised from the dead and that she had actually seen him. In the evening, Jesus' Galilean disciples were in a room, perhaps the same room in which they had eaten their last meal with Jesus. They needed to think and pray. And they shut the room's doors for fear that Jesus' enemies might come to arrest them and subject them to the same fate he suffered.

Jesus entered the room, "*Peace (eirene) be with you.*" He showed them his hands and his side, his identifying marks. The resurrected body of Jesus Christ bore the marks of the pain and suffering that he had just undergone. And, says the writer John, "*They were glad when they saw the Lord.*" Jesus' word "*eirene, peace,*" is "*shalom*" in the Old Testament, life at its best, a sense of well-being. *The New Strong's Concordance* (2001: 7965) indicates that *Shalom* means completeness, wholeness, health, peace, welfare, safety, soundness, tranquility, prosperity, perfectness, fullness, rest, harmony, the absence of agitation or discord. "*Eirene*" in Greek connotes "to talk with one another again," usually after a break in a relationship. The relationship between Jesus and the disciples was broken by their desertion and his death. Now it is restored. They are talking with one another again. This is peace.

Add the moment's peace to the joy the disciples felt and we have an instant in time when God's kingdom was fully present for them. Peace and joy were marks of the kingdom to come and the disciples felt both at the moment Jesus rejoined them through the locked door.

Jesus then commissioned the disciples (*matheten*) to carry out his mission. *"As the father has sent me, so I send you."* That his spirit might be with them as they carried out his mission, John said, *"he breathed on them to receive the Holy Spirit (pneuma hagion)."* The word, *pneuma*, can mean wind, breath, spirit; *hagion* is holy. Jesus' act carried his followers back to Genesis and God's creation of the first human being. Holding the clay figure in his hands, says Genesis, God breathed the breath of life into him. When Jesus breathed on his disciples, Jesus bestowed on them the spirit of the new life. Jesus, acting in God's stead, called into being the new creation. *"Receive the Holy Spirit"* (20:22), he says.

"If you forgive the sins of any, they are forgiven; if you retain the sins of any, they are retained," Jesus added. These words are reminiscent of Matthew's *"bind and loose"* (Mt 16:19, 18:18). The disciples now receive the same power that God has and Christ has—to forgive and not to forgive. They are given the right, the awesome power, to bring, or to refuse, persons into Christ's fellowship to be used in accord with Christ's spirit.

Thomas was not with the group when Jesus came into the room. When the other disciples told him they had seen the Lord, Thomas was not ready to accept their testimony. He declared in no uncertain terms, *"Unless I see in his hands the print of the nails, and place my finger in the mark of the nails, and place my hand in his side, I will not believe."* "Will not believe" in Greek, *ou me pisteuso*, contains a double negative, *ou me,* sometimes translated as "by no means," the strongest statement of doubt a person can give. Thomas gave it. Thomas wanted a vision of triumph as vivid as his previous vision of defeat, a vision of resurrection strong enough to blot out his haunting vision of the cross.

"Eight days later, his disciples (mathetai) were again in the house and Thomas was with them. The doors were shut but Jesus came and stood among them, and said, 'Peace be with you all.' Then he spoke to Thomas, 'Put your finger here, and see my hands; and put out your hand, and place it in my side.' Jesus knew Thomas' doubt, down to the exact words that Thomas had spoken to the others. 'Do not be faithless but faithful,' said Jesus." Thomas had no need to reach out his fingers or hand. Jesus was there, transcending any doubt Thomas had. From Thomas' soul came his great confession of faith, *"My Lord, and my God."* Jesus is Lord of Thomas' life. Thomas now sees Jesus as the one who speaks what God would speak, who acts as God would act, who guides as God would guide, who forgives as God forgives.

"Have you believed, Thomas, because you have seen me? Blessed are those who have not seen and yet believe (pisteusantes)." This statement is Jesus' last and greatest beatitude. With an eye on future generations, he pronounced it. Later Christians did not see the Lord in the same way that Mary Magdalene, Peter, James, Thomas, Cleopas, and the others saw him. They believed because they saw the resurrected Christ. Christians now believe the testimony that others have given and what this testimony means for them. *"Blessed are you who have not seen and yet are faithful."*

John closes this chapter with the words, *"These are written that you may believe that Jesus is the Christ, the Son of God, and that believing you might have life in his name"* (Jn 20:31).

These last words in chapter 20 seem to provide a fitting and total conclusion to the Gospel of John. Instead, the writer John continues on.

"After this Jesus revealed himself again to the disciples by the Sea of Tiberias. He revealed himself in this way. Simon Pe-

ter, Thomas called the Twin, Nathanael of Cana in Galilee, the sons of Zebedee, and two others of his disciples (mathetais) were together. Simon Peter said to them, 'I am going fishing.' They said to him, 'We will go with you.' They went out and got into the boat. That night they caught nothing.

"Just as day was breaking, Jesus stood on the beach; yet the disciples did not know that it was Jesus. Jesus said to them, 'Children, have you any fish?' They answered him, 'No.' He said to them, 'Cast the net on the right side of the boat and you will find some.' So they cast it and now they were not able to haul it in, for the quantity of fish.

"The disciple whom Jesus loved said to Peter, 'It is the Lord!' When Simon Peter heard that it was the Lord, he put on his clothes, for he was stripped for work, and sprang into the sea. But the other disciples came in the boat dragging the net full of fish, for they were not far from the land but about a hundred yards off.

"When they got out on land, they saw a charcoal fire there with fish lying on it, and bread. Jesus said to them, 'Bring some of the fish that you have just caught.' So Simon Peter went aboard and hauled the net ashore, full of large fish, a hundred and fifty-three of them; and, although there were so many, the net was not torn. Jesus said to them, 'Come and have breakfast.' None of the disciples dared ask him, 'Who are you?' They knew it was the Lord. Jesus came and took the bread and gave it to them and so with the fish. This was now the third time that Jesus was revealed to the disciples after he was raised from the dead.

"When they had finished breakfast, Jesus said to Simon Peter, 'Simon, son of John, do you love me more than these?' He said to him, 'Yes, Lord; you know that I love you.' He said to him, 'Feed my lambs.' A second time he said to him, 'Simon, son of John, do you love me?' He said to him, 'Yes, Lord; you know that I love you.' He said to him, 'Tend my sheep.' He said to him the third time, 'Simon, son of John, do you love me?' Peter was grieved because he said to him the third time, 'Do you love me?' He said to him, 'Lord, you know everything.

You know that I love you.' Jesus said to him, 'Feed my sheep. Truly, truly, I say to you, when you were young, I girded yourself and walked where you would. When you are old, you will stretch out your hands and another will gird you and carry you where you do not wish to go.' (This he said to show by what death he was to glorify God.) After this he said to him, 'Follow me.'

"Peter turned and saw following them the disciple whom Jesus loved, who had lain close to his breast at the supper and had said, 'Lord, who is it that is going to betray you?' When Peter saw him, he said to Jesus, 'Lord, what about this man?' Jesus said to him, 'If it is my will that he remain until I come, what is that to you? Follow me!' The saying spread abroad among the brethren (adelphous) that this disciple was not to die. Yet Jesus did not say to him that he was not to die but, 'If it is my will that he remain until I come, what is that to you?' This is the disciple who is bearing witness to these things, and who has written these things; and we know that his testimony is true. But there are also many other things which Jesus did. Were every one of them to be written, I suppose that the world itself could not contain the books that would be written" (21:1-25).

Is this last chapter integral to John's Gospel or an addition? Despite that the final words in chapter 20 seem a fitting ending to the Gospel, every ancient copy of John's Gospel included a chapter 21. We believe chapter 21 was originally part of this Gospel.

Jesus' appearance in chapter 21 took place on the shores of the Sea of Galilee. Near here Jesus called his disciples, stilled a storm, taught, and celebrated a meal with 5,000 others. While other resurrection appearances in John's Gospel take place in or around Jerusalem, this appearance is located *"by the Sea of Tiberias,"* the Hellenist name for "the Sea of Galilee."

"Revealed himself" is key to these disciples, *"they knew it was the Lord"* (21:12). This revelation is similar to when he revealed himself to Mary Magdalene and to the Eleven in

the upper room. The writer John wants readers and listeners to know that Jesus revealed himself in his resurrected state, with all this implies for the revelation of the Father himself.

"I am going fishing," said Peter to the others. For the Jesus movement, this incident did not start well. Peter was returning to his familiar vocation and its ways. Despite having seen the resurrected Jesus in Jerusalem, Peter's dealings with Jesus seemed over. Jesus might have been the one to redeem Israel but it did not work out. The others said, *"We will join you."* The Jesus movement was within an eyelash of flickering out.

As day was breaking, Jesus stood on the beach. He called from the shore, *"Have you caught any fish?"* *"No,"* came the answer. *"Cast your net on the right side and you will find some,"* he responded. They cast the net, trolled for a moment, and caught so many fish they were not able to haul the net in. Among those in the boat was Nathanael of Cana. At the beginning of John's Gospel Nathanael had been given a promise, *"Greater things than these you shall see"* (1:50). Now he stood with the disciples by the seashore and with his own eyes saw the risen Christ. Jesus' promise to him had been fulfilled. Two other unnamed disciples were also present. Since *"the disciple whom Jesus loved"* is quickly mentioned in this story, he was probably one of the two. We are not given the slightest clue about who the last disciple was. Is it supposed to be "you or me" as also witnesses to Christ's resurrection?

The beloved disciple was first to recognize the risen Lord. John's Gospel often noted "first" themes associated with the beloved disciple. He was at the final supper resting on Jesus' bosom, the first place, of greatest intimacy, between host and guest. He was first to reach the tomb on resurrection morning and first to *"see and believe."* Here he was first in recognizing the risen Christ on the beach. This Galilean story might have been included because the beloved disciple was at least an informant for, if not the writer of, John's Gospel (as in 21:24). Otherwise, this Gospel has comparatively few Galilean stories.

As soon as Peter recognized who was on the beach, John reports, *"he put on his clothes."* The verb, *diezosato*, can mean to put on clothes or to tuck clothes up and tie them to give one freedom of movement for doing something (Brown, 1979: 1072). The same word was used when Jesus tied a towel around himself at the last meal (Jn 13:4). Possibly Peter put on an *ependuten*, a fisherman's smock, he took off in order to help haul in the catch. Barrett (1978: 483) noted that to offer greetings was a religious act and could not be performed without clothing (greetings were not given in Roman baths where everyone was naked). Peter *"put on his clothes"* to greet his risen Lord in a proper manner.

They hauled in a great catch, 153 fish in all. The word for "haul" or "draw," *helkusai*, was used before in this Gospel when Jesus said, *"If I am lifted up, I will draw all people to me."* At this moment, the disciples hauled in fish. Soon they will be drawing in people.

The number 153 is another enigma. Why such a definite and large number of fish to catch at one time? Possibly an eyewitness counted the fish. But scholars have noted that the numbers 7 and 10 were two Jewish numbers of perfection. The number 153 is the sum of all numbers from 1 to 17. Seventeen also equals 5 loaves of bread plus 12 baskets of food left over from the great supper, the 10 commandments plus 7 gifts of the spirit, 9 choirs of angels plus 8 beatitudes, 153 dots arranged into an equilateral triangle with 17 dots on each side, the number of perfection, or the sum of numbers in the Hebrew letters for "the church of love" (Brown, 1979:1074-1075). St. Jerome noted that Greek zoologists counted 153 species of fish, so the 153 meant that every known type of fish was caught in the post-Easter net, just as the disciples were to catch every kind of man, woman, and child (all *ethne*) in all the world in their evangelistic nets.

Whatever else, the number surely referred to abundance—the abundance of God given to God's people. This reminder occurred frequently in Jesus' ministry. At Cana in the Gospel's beginning Jesus produced an abundance of wine. Jesus fed a multitude with an abundance of food. At the Gospel's ending Jesus produced an abundance of fish. Jesus always brings with him God's abundance. As in John's prologue, *"From his fulness have we all received, grace upon grace"* (Jn 1:16).

On shore, Jesus had built a charcoal fire. When Peter saw it, it possibly reminded him of the charcoal fire by which he warmed himself when in the high priest's Jerusalem courtyard. Three times by that fire Peter denied knowing Jesus. Now, emerging from the water in great haste, he sees before him another charcoal fire. At first Jesus said nothing to Peter about the fire. *"'Come and have breakfast,' he said to them."* Jesus did the same with bread and fish at the feeding of the thousands. In the church's later worship, Eucharistic meals consisted not of bread and cup but of bread and fish. The tiled floor of the fourth century church at Magdala, Mary's hometown just a few miles west of Capernaum, shows the symbols of the Lord's Supper as wine and fish. The earliest church did not have uniformity in its symbolism. Bread and wine, fish and wine, bread and fish—all were used to celebrate Christ's presence.

When all had eaten, Jesus followed up with Peter, addressing him with the same words he used when they first met, *"'Simon, son of John, do you love me more than these?' 'Yes, Lord, you know that I love you.' Jesus said, 'Feed my lambs.'"* Jesus repeated this question twice more. Peter was grieved that Jesus had to say it three times. *"'You know everything, Lord. You know that I love you.' Jesus said, 'Feed my sheep.'"* Peter surely recognized what Jesus was doing. Three times Peter had denied Jesus; three times Jesus restored him. Peter was to be a good shepherd to the church as Jesus was the Good Shepherd for all.

Jesus added one more thing. He invited Peter to martyrdom. *"When you were young, you girded yourself and walked where you would. But when you are old, you will stretch out your hands and another will gird you and carry you where you do not wish to go."* The words carry an image of crucifixion. In being crucified, the victim stretched out his hands to the ugly cross. He would be bound over for the act, his arms and feet fastened to the cross. He would be carried where he did not wish to go. No one sought crucifixion. For some, like Jesus, it could not be avoided. Peter was to be one of these. But for this to happen to Peter, Jesus issued one more challenge. *"Follow me,"* he said.

Chronology: Conclusions

All four Gospels recognize that Jesus' ministry took place in two main regions, near the north shore of the Sea of Galilee and in Judea, a distance of between 90 and 110 miles, depending on the route. Along the Jordan River was the shortest route and it took a minimum of three days' walk, walking quite fast.

Why did the Gospels differ when describing the same event? Jesus apparently attracted several sets of followers in each region who did not recognize one another while Jesus' was alive. The Synoptic Gospels (Mark, Matthew, and Luke), Mark especially, focus on Twelve disciples in Galilee and, later, in Jerusalem. But these Gospels also recognize other followers in Galilee, including women and those who attended the feeding of the 5,000 (and 4,000; Mt 14:21 ff).

The women were mentioned only occasionally in the Synoptic Gospels (more often in Luke and John) but they were extraordinary in Jewish life. Most women were not seen or heard in public unless escorted by a male relative. For women to follow Jesus around in the open, even for short periods, took extraordinary courage by them. That Jesus' traveled from one place to another in "Lower" Galilee with a visible band of disciples set him apart. Except for various officials and other authorities, the vast majority of people in those days stayed close to home with their families or to beaten paths along the Jordan River to and from Jerusalem for traditional Jewish Festivals. Such journeys also set Jewish people apart from most Gentile families during these times.

Jesus' followers in Judea and Jerusalem were separable from those in "rural" Galilee. In Jerusalem and environs, some followers, especially the three siblings, Mary, Martha, and Lazarus, were among Jesus' closest friends. They might have been Hellenists. Others included Nicodemus, Joseph of Arimathea, and Cleopas. Still others were Hebrew *"adelphous, brothers"*(whose core might have been Jesus' blood brothers, the leader being named James), who saw Jesus as continuous with a variety of Hebrew traditions and teachings. Hellenists and Brothers (Brethren), both living in or near Jerusalem, but separately, often disagreed with one another on central issues. The Hellenist Stephen in Acts demonstrated such divisions (Acts 6, 7). We suggest that John's Gospel was based on this Hellenist community and its informants, Mark's on informants associated with the Twelve, Matthew's on informants from the Brothers, and Luke's on Hellenist informants called the Apostles, some from places distant from Jerusalem but who had come to Jerusalem for education, training, and Feasts. Each group experienced a different culture in their backgrounds and therefore saw Jesus from different perspectives.

The above chronology underscores some of the key differences. Part Three, below, presents these and other differences in more detail.

That Jesus, coming from the very small town of Nazareth in Galilee but one close to the thriving Hellenist city of Sepphoris (where he might have worked as it was being re-built after its destruction in 4BCE) but far from Israel's center in Jerusalem, could bridge and meld Hebrew and Hellenist cultures, as seen in this chronology, was truly remarkable. Apparently his followers from the four different backgrounds seldom interacted with one another on personal bases. They could be said to be isolated from one another even if living in near proximity. Jesus' earliest experiences, working alongside his carpenter father on various building projects in Hellenist cities in Galilee, would certainly have made him familiar with much in Hellenist culture—its language, its key concepts, and its way of relating key concepts. Jesus' ability to see how these concepts fit with his traditional Hebrew up-bringing, to integrate the Hellenists' "best" with the Hebrews' "best," according to John's Gospel, was so extraordinary that, as the writer John believed, it could only come from God.

That the four Gospels agreed on so many events in Jesus' life and ministry provides remarkable evidence that Jesus was a real person who was born and who died in a specific time and place. Differences among the Gospels' accounts surely arose because different informants from each party of followers reported slightly different details about the same person and events in his life. We explore details of these differences found among the Gospels in Part Three.

Jesus In The Gospels—
What Each Gospel
Said About Him

While the four Gospels shared much in common with one another, each was distinctive in its individual assessment of the person Jesus. In Part Three we highlight how each Gospel uniquely portrays Jesus of Nazareth, the Christ.

Figure 6 presents an overview of each Gospel's individual portrait of Jesus, the Christ. Each one is consistent with the constituency (party) of people to which the Gospel was directed. Each constituency had differing norms and values. As the four communities searched their memories about Jesus, they recalled different things about him and constructed their pictures in ways that reflected their own socio-economic-geographic-religious situations. Mark's Gos-

Party	Twelve	Brethren	Apostles	Hellenists
Gospel	Mark	Matthew	Luke	John
Main theme	Jesus as the Healing yet Suffering Servant	Jesus as One who was Traditionally Righteous and Just	Jesus as the Caringly Compassionate and Socially Just One	Jesus as One with the Working and Loving God
Composition of the Gospel from Key Informants	The widow and sons of Simon of Cyrene and probably one or more of the original Twelve, members of the Christian community in Rome while this Gospel was being composed	This Gospel emerged from a Hebrew minority in Jerusalem who became, after 70 CE, a Hebrew minority in Alexandria, Egypt	The Gospel was one of two New Testament books written by Luke, a travel companion of Paul, and reflected issues faced by Jewish minorities in smaller Eastern Mediterranean Hellenist cities	Much material in this Gospel probably came from the Hellenist Philip, a member of the original Twelve, who became a Hellenist leader in Judea, and the Beloved Disciple, a Hellenist-Jew in Jerusalem

Figure 6   Thematic Presentation in Each Gospel and their Probable Main Informants.

pel, by most accounts the first one actually written, is our starting point as well as the starting point for Matthew and Luke. John's Gospel emphasizes many traditional Hellenist themes as seen from a Christian perspective. Although the Chronology presented many aspects of these portraits, here we bring them front and center.

Each Gospel's major theme is reflected in the vocabulary it used. Figure 7 presents certain key words in each Gospel, and the number of times each was used.

In Figure 7, the largest number of times a word is used in a specific Gospel tends to reflect a Gospel's major theme. The first bank of words represents those used comparatively more often in Mark. "Immediately" and "enter" show Jesus moving from one place to another with a sense of urgency not found in the other Gospels. As noted in the Chronology, Jesus was probably moving in response to his sense of danger. "Silent" is similar to "tell no one"—Jesus did not want to spread the news of his whereabouts and what he was doing. "Suffer" is used in all the Gospels but disproportionately in Mark compared to the others.

The word "heal" is found in all the Gospels, most often in Luke, 24 times. But "heal" in Mark is misrepresented in this table. In Mark, almost every page, until Jesus went to Jerusalem for his final Passover (chapter 11), has at least one example of Jesus healing someone with an infirmity. But the word "heal" itself is not used as frequently in Mark as it is in Matthew and Luke. For instance, at least four people, probably more, were healed in Mark's chapter one but the word healed was used only once. Mark showed Jesus as "one who healed as well as one who suffered."

All the Gospels see Jesus as a teacher, but Mark comparatively more than the others. Mark uses this term or its cognates 34 times. Luke uses it 38 times but in a much longer Gospel. Matthew uses it 28 times and John 22 times. In his ministry, Jesus was a clearly a teacher and openly recognized as a teacher when people addressed him.

The other Gospels are more consistent than Mark in presenting vocabularies that demonstrate their key themes. Matthew used the word "righteous" or its cognates 19 times, almost twice as often as Luke (10 times) and much more than Mark (3 times) and John (2 times). The word Pharisee, with whom Jesus was often in contention, is used 29 times in Matthew. Matthew, alone, used the phrase "kingdom of heaven" (32 times), the apparent equivalent of the phrase "kingdom of God" which Luke used an equal number of times. Matthew was writing largely to Hebrews who knew that "heaven" and

Word	Mark	Matthew	Luke	John
Number of Words	14,950	23,535	25,569	19,511
In Mark				
Immediately	35	14	12	2
Teach, taught	34	28	38	22
Enter	31	31	41	13
Heal	7	19	24	7
Silent	5	2	6	0
Tell no one	3	2	2	0
Suffer	3	2	5	0
In Matthew				
Righteous	2	19	10	3
Kingdom of Heaven	0	32	0	0
Kingdom of God	14	4	32	2
Son of Man, Humankind	14	30	25	13
Pharisee	12	29	27	20
Fulfill	2	15	9	10
Throne	0	5	3	0
In Luke				
Compassion	2	3	3	0
Woman, Women	8	16	30	22
Forgive	10	16	20	2
Rich	6	5	19	0
Just, Justice	1	10	14	5
Holy Spirit	0	5	14	3
Poor	5	5	11	5
In John				
Father	18	102	56	137
Love, beloved,	8	16	18	57
Loving (agape)	8	12	16	45
(philos)	0	4	2	12
True, Truth	2	2	3	46
Glory, Glorified (and cognates)	4	10	19	39
Eternal Life	2	3	3	30
Work, Working	6	10	4	25
Light	3	18	20	24
Bread	12	14	13	20
Life	8	18	14	17

Figure 7 Number of Times a Given Word is Used in Each Gospel (Revised Standard Version).

"God" were identical and that Hebrews were forbidden to speak the name of Yahweh, God; Luke was writing more to Hellenists who freely used the word "God"— many gods were in their pantheon. Although no other Gospel used the phrase "kingdom of heaven," each one uses "kingdom of God."

Luke's concerns for social justice are reflected in the comparative numbers of times he used the word "just" or "justice" (14 times to Matthew's 10). In connection with "justice," Luke also disproportionately used the words "forgive," "rich," "poor," and "woman" (or "women"), the latter two among the most disadvantaged people in places during his times. Luke also reports that Jesus had great compassion, often expressed in different words, for all disadvantaged people, the blind, the sick, and the infirm but almost no compassion for the rich. In Luke, Jesus is presented as "caringly compassionate and socially just."

John presents Jesus as "one with an active (working) and loving God and Father." His words are not unique but the disproportionate numbers of times he uses such words is astonishing. For instance, he uses the word "father" 137 times, compared to Matthew's 102, Luke's 56, and Mark's 18 times. The word "love" or "beloved" (*agape, philos,* or cognates) John used 57 times compared to 8, 16, and 18, in Mark, Matthew, and Luke. John used the word "true" or "truth," an important Hellenistic concept, 46 times, compared to 3, 2, and 2 in Luke, Matthew, and Mark. The words "work" or "working" as in the *"the Father is working and so am I,"* John used 25 times compared to 4, 10, and 6 in Luke, Matthew, and Mark. All the Gospels refer to a loving God. But John emphasizes more than the others that Jesus is "one with an active, working, and loving God."

These four themes will be expanded upon in considering each of the four Gospels. Our presentation for each Gospel will follow a common format. This format includes:

Social Context of the Gospel
Purpose of the Gospel
Sources of the Gospel
Major Themes in the Gospel

Chapter 7

Jesus in the Gospel of Mark: Jesus, the Healing and Suffering One

Social Context—Suffering in Small Towns in Rural Galilee and in Rome

The Gospel of Mark grew out of two social contexts, one in Galilee during Jesus' ministry and one in Rome during the time the Gospel was being written. Key informants for Mark's Gospel were one or more of Jesus' Eleven Galilean disciples but also Alexander and Rufus, sons of Simon of Cyrene, who were known to be in Rome about the time Mark's Gospel was written.

Galilee was a region where rural and small-town Jews were directly and indirectly dominated by harsh Roman rule. Repressed and powerless, Galilean Jews lived in small rural villages and farming areas. From the relative deprivations in their social and economic conditions, some Galilean Jews rebelled, were hunted down, and killed or crucified by the Romans and Herodians who lived in their urban strongholds of Sepphoris, Tiberias, Caesarea (Maritima), and Caesarea Philippi. Tetrarch Herod Antipas supported by Romans enforced the rules with little recourse for injustices against them. This was especially true in matters of taxation and what we now call civil rights (Horsley, 2011: 134). Galilean Jews apparently had some ways to protest injustices as through regional councils or their synagogues but such protests were often ignored by the Herodians and violent protests were put down ruthlessly by the Romans. Under these conditions, Jews suffered severely both economically and socially. Taxation burdens were so great that many Galilean peasants lost their lands to richer, urban-based landowners who paid the taxes for them but in return confiscated their produce and/or their lands that reduced peasant farmers to sharecroppers (Horsley, 2011: 135).

In Rome in the 50s and 60s, Christians also were suffering a series of persecutions. For a variety of reasons, Jews and Christians could not get along in Rome. According to Roman historian Suetonius the Roman Emperor Claudius exiled many Jewish and Christian leaders in 49CE. Later Emperor Nero blamed Christians for the great fire in 64CE and the persecutions increased to the point that, as the historian Tacitus (116) reported, some were burned on crosses to light Nero's garden. Due to references to the wife and sons of Simon of Cyrene in Paul's letter to the Romans (dated ca 58 CE), we believe the Gospel of Mark was composed near the end of Claudius' reign in 54CE and during Nero's reign into the middle 60sCE .

Mark's Gospel paints a somewhat different picture of Jesus from that in other Gospels. To Mark, along with Galileans and certain Jewish-Christians elsewhere, Jesus was the suffering one. He suffered both physically and spiritually. He struggled to understand his destiny traveling from Capernaum to as far as Tyre and Sidon to avoid Herod Antipas' police. As he traveled, he asked people to *"tell no one"* where he was, where he was going, and what he was doing. Once understanding his destiny, Jesus struggled to accept it as his own. When he accepted it, he struggled with fulfilling it. When he fulfilled it, he struggled during his crucifixion, until he brought to mind a Psalm that spoke exactly to him, *"My God, my God, why hast thou rejected me?"* This Psalm ended with God proclaiming *"his deliverance to a people yet unborn"* (Ps 22:31). When Jesus accepted this final struggle, he emitted a loud cry of victory that echoes down the ages.

Purpose of Mark's Gospel

Mark's Gospel, in contrast to John and Luke, does not state an exact purpose for what is written in it. He refers to a *"reader"* only once (13:14) when referring to otherwise obscure materials from the Old Testament book of Daniel. But the Gospel's purpose can be inferred from its contents. Its opening line is, *"The beginning of the gospel (euaggelion, good news or glad tidings) of Jesus Christ, the Son of God"* (1:1). This is followed by an account of Jesus' baptism by John the Baptist. *"And coming up from the water,"* Jesus *"immediately"* hears a voice from heaven that says, *"Thou are my beloved Son; with thee I am well pleased"* (1:11). Mark's Gospel is then devoted to explain to readers why this is so.

Mark starts with Jesus teaching in a Capernaum synagogue and *"immediately"* he healed a man with *"an unclean spirit"* to the amazement of everyone who saw it (1:23-27). *"And at once his fame spread everywhere throughout the surrounding region of Galilee"* (1:28). Mark's Gospel was written to explain what this unique man did and what happened to him.

Mark's Gospel shows Jesus' ministry as being short, less than one year in duration. Its major substantive themes were of healing, suffering, and trusting. Suffering was a condition of life for many Christians in the Roman Empire, including Christians in Rome as well as in Galilee (even if in different ways), and trust in God in the midst of that suffering was imperative for the person and for the community to survive. Rome would protect religious people if they practiced their "ancestral religion" and did not disrupt the Pax Romana (Barclay, 1996: 64 ff). To Romans, Christians' "ancestral religion" was suspect—Jews in Rome cast aspersions on Christians—and disrupted life there. Christians were pariahs in Rome when Mark's Gospel was being written. Due to such disruptions, both Jews and Christians were exiled from Rome in the 40sCE by the Emperor Claudius, whose edict was not rescinded until about 58CE. Further, they were seriously persecuted before the end of the Emperor Nero's reign (Tacitus, 116). Further, eyewitnesses to Jesus were aging. Consequently, this Gospel was intended to create a document, with its many Old Testament references, that would help unify Christians as they contended for meaningful status in Rome and within the wider Roman Empire.

Sources for Mark's Gospel

Most scholars agree that Mark's Gospel was the first to be written, largely because the Gospels of Matthew and Luke made such extensive use of Mark. These other two Gospels also have information in them that appears to post-date both Mark and the Temple's destruction in 70CE (even if Mark used a key phrase about the Temple, *"not one stone will be left on another";* 13:2). Since the writer Mark fails to identify his Gospel's sources, they must be inferred from other evidence. Most scholars acknowledge that Mark's Gospel was highly likely to have been written in Rome just before or just after 60CE. A key question regarding sources is, Who was in Rome at this time to provide information to Mark as he wrote his Gospel?

A major source of information on this topic comes from Paul in his Letter to the Romans, dated about 58CE, where, near the letter's ending, he sends greetings to a number of acquaintances he knew in Rome. Among the dozen or so he greeted, Paul did not mention any of the Eleven by name. Although earlier he mentioned that Peter and his wife were in Corinth (1 Cor 9:5), he did not include Peter among those he greeted in Rome. Paul did greet a woman named Mary who could have been any one of those named Mary in the Gospels (Rom 16:6). But Mary was also a very common name at the time, as it still is today. Paul also greeted a man named Rufus as well as his mother (Rom 16:13). In his Gospel, Mark mentions a Rufus as a son of *"Simon the Cyrenean, the father of Alexander and Rufus"*(Mk 15:21) who helped carry Jesus' cross to Golgotha. We surmise this Rufus was an eyewitness informant for Mark in writing his Gospel. Since Simon of Cyrene was present at Jesus' crucifixion, quite possibly many events of the day came from his recollections as told to his sons.

Other material in the Gospel may have come from other persons in what was called *"the house church of Philologus"* (Rom 16:15). In Eberts, 2011 (ch 3), we describe this church as made up of Jewish people but, unlike most Brethren churches, it welcomed women into its congregation. Such a practice corresponds with Peter's position after he met with the Roman centurion Cornelius in Caesarea Maritima and became less likely to insist upon upholding Jewish law and customs about circumcision, eating with Gentiles, and women's positions in an assembly. As often happened in oral tradition, stories like these were massaged until a single narrative was agreed upon and delivered to others as authentic. Mark and his colleagues also added Old Testament passages from Isaiah 53 and Psalm 22 to the mix. We speculate that something like this happened in Rome to inspire the writing of Mark's Gospel.

Major Themes in Mark's Gospel

As noted in our discussion of the most common words in each Gospel (Figure 7 above), the major theme in Mark's Gospel is that Jesus was a healing, suffering, and, near the end of his earthly ministry, trusting servant of God. As such he met people's infirmities while struggling to make decisions about his ministry's ultimate outcome in the midst of great danger to his person. Jesus finally decided that, in order to be faithful to his ministry, he had to go to Jerusalem and trust God as he faced whatever consequences might befall him there, including the necessity to suffer severely in his death and triumph in his resurrection.

Mark's Gospel can be outlined as follows:

1. Jesus in Judea before John was arrested—the prologue to the Gospel (*"You are my son..."*; *"the kingdom is fulfilled"*)
2. Jesus in Galilee after John was arrested (considering danger and destiny while healing many; abundance in feeding 5,000; hiding his identity)
3. Jesus in northwestern Galilee, between Bethsaida and the regions of Tyre and Sidon (danger during his decision making, while traveling through a hostile, non-Jewish territory)
4. Jesus' journey from Capernaum to Jerusalem (again healing many, including Simon the leper and a prediction of suffering)
5. Jesus in Jerusalem, which culminated in his crucifixion and resurrection (entry, Gethsemane, "cleansing of the Temple," his suffering before and while enduring the cross).

Jesus in Judea before John Was Arrested: The Gospel's Prologue and Jesus' Titles

"Arche tou euaggelion Iesou Christou uiou tou theou, The beginning of the gospel of Jesus Christ, Son of God" (1:1) are the opening words of Mark's Gospel. These words are, in effect, a brief prologue in setting the stage for the entire Gospel. Mark chose each phrase carefully and each bears considerable meaning for the Gospel.

The name "Jesus" comes from the Hebrew, *Iehoshua* or *Ioshua* (the J is transliterated to I in Greek), meaning "He whose salvation is in Yahweh." After the Jewish exile in Babylon, starting in 576BCE, this name was shortened to *Jeshua*. A Greek ending, "*sus*," instead of the Jewish "*hua*," was added to the original consonant "*J*" or "*Je*" (Yah'weh), so that the name became "*Jesus*." During his lifetime Jesus was called "Jesus of Nazareth" to distinguish him from many other men of the time who bore the same name.

"*Christos, Christ,*" is the equivalent of the Hebrew "*mashi'a, messiah.*" Both words mean "rubbed in, anointed," presumably by oils and salves as in "official" anointing of kings. Since there is no definite article associated with the phrase, "*Jesou Christou,*" a literal interpretation of the phrase would be "Jesus *an* anointed," not "Jesus *the* anointed." Greeks did not use "Christ" as a title while to Jews the word was an honorable designation that reached deep into Israel's history. Part of the inaugural ceremony in consecrating a king (1 Kings 1:39), priest (Exod 30:30) or prophet (1 Kings 19:16) involved pouring sacred oil on a designee's head, thereby setting the person apart for official duties. That Jesus of Nazareth came to be known as *"Christos"* or *"Messiah"* among his followers meant he was recognized as the one who was delegated and empowered by God's Spirit to deliver God's people and establish God's kingdom.

Did Jews expect a "Messiah" to come soon, and, if so, what role was the messiah supposed to play in Jewish life? The questions have no definitive answers. In Jesus' time, "Messiah" had both a political and a religious meaning (Horsley, 2011: 81 ff). A messiah was to drive the Roman armies from Jewish soil and many such messiahs rose up with this expectation. Dodd (1952: 114) cautions that at the beginning of the first century, so far as our information goes, there was no such thing as "the Jewish *doctrine* of Messiah." Dodd along with Josephus saw the term as a vague title, applied to princes of the house of David, to the reigning High Priest, or to various ideal figures in the past or yet to come (see Horsley, 2011: 82). Not until after the fall of the Temple in 70CE, perhaps not until the second century, Dodd maintained, was there any clearly formulated and generally accepted Messianic dogma. In calling Jesus *"the*

Christ," the Christian church was the first to put forward a definitive and coherent doctrine of Messiah unlike the Messianic doctrine that ultimately emerged in Judaism.

The other title given in verse one was *"uiou tou theou, Son of God"* (1:1). This phrase is used only three times in Mark's Gospel, here, when Jesus was recognized as Son of God by *"unclean spirits"* (3:11), and when he was recognized as Son of God by the Roman centurion at his crucifixion (15:39). In contrast, in Mark's Gospel Jesus was recognized fourteen times as "Son of Man," or, more accurately, "Son of Humankind." According to Hay (1964), the "Son of God" designation referred to, among Hellenists, a miracle worker or, among Jews, a redemptive servant. It came to be, says Hay, "a title specifically indicating Jesus' election by God for the passion—Jesus is chosen to suffer humiliation and death in radical obedience to God... Jesus thus becomes the son through historical words and deeds that reveal how total is His sonship." Since the term emphasizes Jesus' total obedience to God more than to any claim about divine intervention in his birth or life, it is more ethical than metaphysical. Jesus' obedience to God was complete—it stands as a model for the obedience all Christians are expected to give to God.

Jesus brought a message of *euaggelion,* "good tidings" or "good news," about God. In English the word used is "gospel," a word coming from an Anglo-Saxon root, "god-spiel," meaning "a tale about God, good news from God." The Hebrew root for *euaggelion* is found even before the Hebrew exodus from Egypt. Isaiah of Babylon used the word to proclaim the new and greater Exodus he saw coming for Judah. The Christian church used it to describe the good news of God in Jesus Christ.

Jesus in Judea before John Was Arrested: John the Baptist, the Messenger

The "good news" begins with a familiar prophecy. *"I am sending my messenger before you..., the voice of one crying in the wilderness, Prepare the way of the Lord"* (1:2-3). These words, from Isaiah 40, were used by Essene men in the Qumran community as the model for their work. They withdrew from Jewish society to establish their own community. The site for their settlement was a deserted area overlooking the Dead Sea. They considered themselves *"a voice crying in the wilderness to prepare the way for the Lord"* (Qumran, 1998).

John the Baptist might have been reared in Qumran. As a man he used their prophecy to proclaim his own message. He *"appeared in the wilderness"* not far from Qumran. The Gospel of John located the Baptizer near *"Bethany across the Jordan"* and at Aenon near Salim, wilderness areas close to important intersections of roads on which people traveled north and south, east and west. There they came to him from Jerusalem and the Judean countryside.

Carl Kraeling (1960) pictured John "deep in the trough of the Jordan valley... preaching his message. Enclosed by precipitous mountains that radiate the sun's heat, the valley was pleasantly warm in winter, but it becomes a veritable inferno when the rains (of spring) are past. Borne by the enervating southern winds, this heat is like a breath from a furnace most of the year, withering and blasting all that is exposed to it."

Like the prophet Elijah in 2 Kings, John the Baptist, with shaggy hair and beard, was *"clothed with camel's hair and had a leather girdle around his waist and ate locusts and wild honey"* (Mk 1:6). Although Mark took little note of the rest of the Baptist's message, Matthew (3:7-10) and Luke (3:7-9) reported that John literally spoke his mind about his people's offenses against an all-powerful and righteous God, asking them to repent their sins lest doom fall on them. People who heard John saw him as a terrifying figure with a terrifying message, dynamic, dramatic, almost demonic in his prophesies. Kraeling further notes, "Not since the days of Malachi had a message of such dire foreboding been proclaimed to the Jewish people."

The Baptist also called on people to be baptized. The baptism was most likely self-administered. Immersion was the usual Jewish rite of cleansing, for women after childbirth and for proselytes after circumcision. John probably followed this method in his own baptizing (Branscomb, 1930).

John called for a *"baptism of metanoeia (repentance, transformation) for the forgiveness of sins"* (Luke 3:3). He demanded that people have a complete change of mind, a new direction of will, an altered purpose in life. They were to turn away from sin, personal and national, and turn toward God. By being baptized, a person declared himself a sinner who deserved punishment at God's hand but who wanted to escape from the fire to come. John's baptism took place in running water, not the still water in which most Jewish baptisms were performed. Running water symbolized the river of fire that God was to send at the end of the age to purge humankind. Baptism was the sign of the cleansing that followed the repentance.

John had another role as well. *"After me comes he who is mightier than I"* (1:7). John was to prepare the way for "one to come," one stronger than John. He would attack the powers of evil and bind and plunder them. In his presence John was humbled. He could not even *"stoop down and untie the thong of his sandals,"* an act that only the humblest slave was expected to perform. The coming one would baptize with *"pneumati hagio, the Holy Spirit"* (1:8).

Jesus in Judea before John Was Arrested: Jesus' Baptism, A Dove from Heaven

Jesus might have gone to Judea deliberately to hear what John the Baptist had to say. Or he might have gone for other reasons and, when hearing about John, listened to him. In either instance, when Jesus was in Judea, he heard John's message and became the Baptist's disciple when he was baptized by John.

John implied in his message that the coming one will cleanse evil through a judgment of fire and reward the good with a purifying spirit, a new breath of life. Jesus gave John's words another meaning. Jesus seemed to believe his baptism would consecrate his role as God's Suffering Servant that would culminate in his death. From his death would come a spirit of commitment and self-sacrifice that would inflame his followers with zeal to continue to incorporate Christ's spirit within themselves—baptism by the Holy Spirit.

Jesus' baptism had an amazing effect. *"When he came up out of the water, immediately he saw the heavens opened (schizomenous) and the Spirit descending upon him like a dove; and a voice came from heaven, 'Thou art my beloved Son; with thee I am well pleased'"* (Mk 1:11). The way Mark presents this incident implies that Jesus alone saw the dove and heard the voice. Mark does not explain how he learned about it but Jesus must have told someone. The Greek word for "opening," *"schizomenous,"* means "ripping something apart," an act more violent than the benign word "opening." Yet something peaceful and meaningful occurred. *"The Spirit descended upon Jesus like a dove from heaven."* This spirit, in Greek *pneuma,* is the same word that later describes the Holy Spirit (*haggios pneuma*).

The dove is a rich Old Testament symbol. It recalls Noah, when, because of their sinfulness, God determined to destroy the earth and all living things in it. God found Noah to be *"a righteous man, blameless in his generation"* (Genesis 6:9). Through Noah, God offered a new start to his creation. By God's direction, Noah built an ark and brought all living things, in pairs, into the ark. Then the floods came and the destruction began. *"God blotted out every living thing that was upon the face of the ground, man and animals and creeping things and birds of the air; they were blotted out from the earth. Only Noah was left and those that were with him in the ark"* (Gen 7:21-23).

Then came the gentle story of the birds. When the rain stopped and flood waters started to recede, Noah sent out a raven, a strong bird which could fly indefinitely. The bird flew around until the waters dried up. But the raven did not return to the ark. So Noah sent out a dove, a docile and gentle creature, to see what he could learn about the earth's condition. *"But the dove found no place to set her foot and she returned to him in the ark... Noah waited another seven days and again he sent forth the dove out of the ark; and the dove came back to him in the evening, and lo, in her mouth a freshly plucked olive leaf; so Noah knew that the waters had subsided from the earth. Then Noah waited another seven days, and sent forth the dove and she did not return to him any more"* (Gen 7:8-13).

The floods brought chaos to the earth's face as if the earth was without form and void when God began his creation. But the dove flew over the waters and in effect reported that God was doing a new thing; God was re-creating the earth. Twice the story used the number "seven." God created the earth and all that was in it in seven days. Now, in twice seven days, God was re-creating the earth, re-establishing his covenant with humankind. The dove was the spirit whereby God reported this news to the waiting Noah and the dove reported that humankind was saved and a new creation had begun. The dove was the first symbol of God's new creation.

The dove was a docile and gentle creature. In the natural science of the day, people did not even recognize that a dove had a beak. Without a beak, it could not tear at food the way a raven, eagle, or vulture did. The dove was, in their thinking, as even today, a creature of peace, an agent of serenity and tranquility. To Jesus the dove also represented a symbol of peace, the coming of a peaceable kingdom.

The dove was an instrument of sacrifice. When richer people came to the Temple to make sacrifices, they brought, or bought, an unblemished lamb for the altar. When poorer people came, all they could afford was a dove for their sacrifices. Jesus' mother was among the poor. For her son's circumcision and her own purification after his birth, she brought with her a pair of turtledoves for her sacrifice. Why choose doves for this? Because the priests found that, when a dove is held by its back in a hand while gently stroking its breast, it will stretch out its neck as if voluntarily to receive the knife that will take its life. The dove was a symbol of sacrifice.

Jesus interpreted the Spirit of God coming on him at baptism like that of a dove's descent. Mark recognized that the dove symbolized Jesus' coming life and ministry. Like Noah's dove, Jesus would inaugurate a new creation, a new hope, a new future for humankind and its world that was out of touch with the destiny God wanted for them. Like the dove of peace, Jesus' task was to bring peace and a peaceable tomorrow to humankind. Jesus voluntarily became the dove of sacrifice—no one takes away my life, he said, I give it for *metanoeia*, redemption, transformation of humankind. In his baptism, Jesus identified with this rich Old Testament symbol, thereby telling the purpose of his life and ministry.

Hearing a *"voice from heaven"* that said, *"Thou art my beloved Son; with thee I am well pleased"* (Mk 1:11), also joined two Old Testament passages, the first from Psalms, the second from Isaiah. Psalm 2 is called a "Royal Psalm," about the coronation of a new king in Israel or Judah. As the crown was placed on the designated-king's head, God says, *"You are my son, today I have begotten you. Ask of me, and I will make the nations your heritage and the ends of the earth your possession"* (Ps 2, 1:7-8). The root word in Greek translated as *"begotten," gennetos*, denotes the ideas of "born," "chosen," "adopted." As noted earlier, the significance of sonship is that the son, the first born son at least, in his father's absence can represent his father in all his dealings with others. He can speak and act in the father's name and bind the father to contracts made in his name. The son has full power of attorney for his father. It begins at a particular time, with the king at his coronation and with Jesus at his baptism. From now on Jesus as the son can speak for God, act for God, and enter into contracts (covenants) that bind God to them. He can do this everywhere and anywhere on earth, for God promises,

"Ask, [my son,] and I will make the nations your heritage and the ends of the earth your possession." Jesus' baptism was the moment he entered on his divine office and began his work as king of all.

The second set of words came from the prophet Isaiah. *"Behold my servant, my slave, whom I uphold,"* says God through the prophet's voice, *"my chosen, in whom my soul delights. I have put my spirit upon him, he will bring forth justice to the nations"* (Is 42:1). *"He was despised and rejected by men, a man of sorrows and acquainted with grief...and we esteemed him not... Surely he has borne our griefs and carried our sorrows... He was wounded for our transgressions, he was bruised for our iniquities. Upon him was the chastisement that made us whole and with his stripes we are healed"* (Is 53:3-5). These words hover around Jesus' scourging and cross. Here at the beginning of his ministry Jesus sees himself in these terms, the servant, the slave, who will suffer for all.

The amazing thing about the event of hearing these words is that these themes, the one concerning the anointed king and the other concerning the servant who suffers, were both in the Old Testament. Until Jesus' baptism, no one had put them together into one person, one event. As the commentator A. B. Taylor, Jr. said, "These two concepts, messianic ruler and suffering servant, had lain side by side in the Hebrew scriptures for centuries, but only in Jesus is it seen that they are united in one individual... To Jesus...we ascribe the bold originality which first made this synthesis" (1960: 301). Jesus did something in his moment of baptism that had not been done before. He saw himself as the sufferer who is king and the king who suffers for his people. This proved to be an astounding insight.

This whole event is attributed to *"a voice from heaven."* *"Heaven"* is a Hebrew circumlocution for *"God."* Hebrews in Jesus' time did not dare speak the sacred word for "God, Yahweh, YHWH" in Hebrew. Instead they substituted the name of God's residence for the name of God. They spoke of *"heaven"* or *"the heavens"* as the voice of God. When God speaks, what language does God use? The Scriptures conveyed God's words. But not in a wooden or literal sense—interpreting this voice from heaven involved a person's totality. Jesus' ear heard this voice when he sat in a synagogue listening to Psalms and Isaiah, his eye saw this voice in the Scriptures, his mind worked it over, his life experiences funneled into this voice, his spirit incorporated it. To discern the fundamental meaning of God's Word in Scripture required of Jesus everything he had within him.

Jesus in Judea before John Was Arrested: Jesus Tested in the Wilderness— Can His Faith in God Be Trusted?

"Immediately the Spirit drove Jesus out into the wilderness. He was in the wilderness forty days, being tempted by Satan. With him [were] the wild beasts; and the angels served him" (1:12-13). The same spirit at his baptism now drove Jesus into the wilderness. The verb, *ekthallei*, "drove," again suggests violence. The spirit "casts" him violently into the wilderness to make him fully face his future ordeals.

"He was in the wilderness forty days." "Wilderness" is the place of testing, the place where God tested Israel for forty years after they came out of Egypt, the place where Elijah fled *"for forty days"* when the forces of Jezebel and Ahab were hunting him. *"Forty days"* was the amount of time Noah was on the ark, wondering if God would save him and his family from the flood. *"Forty days"* was the length of time that Jesus was tempted by Satan in the wilderness.

"Temptation" means that the person being tempted no longer experiences God's presence. Temptation can be that of feeling so strong that one does not need God's help or that one is so weak that not even God can help. Mark does not say what form the temptation took. The verb used indicated that Jesus' temptation was whether to use his powers for his own purposes and not God's. Temptation's powers

must have stayed with him each day of his ministry, for he advised his disciples to pray that God would not lead them into temptation as the spirit of God had hurled Jesus into its midst. The final time temptation used in this Gospel was Jesus' temptation in Gethsemane—temptation or trust, cut off from God or trusting God at all times.

"He was with the wild beasts." Were they there to hurt him or were they a symbol that all creation was to be in harmony with Jesus Christ? Psalm 91 indicated a ministry of safety in the presence of wild animals. These words assured Jesus of divine deliverance from evil and harm. The apocryphal Testament of Naphtali noted, "If you do good, both men and angels shall bless you, the devil shall flee from you, wild beasts shall fear you, and the Lord shall love you" (8:4). Mark noted, *"And the angels served him."*

Jesus in Galilee after John Was Arrested: Preaching, Destiny, Danger, Decision

Shortly after opening his Gospel, Mark inserted another major theme. Mark was dealing with Jesus' destiny and the dangers it brought to him as he worked it out. Danger arose almost immediately. The arrest of John at the hands of Herod Antipas set in motion the events of Jesus' ministry in Galilee.

"After John was arrested, Jesus went into Galilee, preaching the gospel (good news) of God, and saying, 'The time is fulfilled, and the kingdom of God is at hand; repent (transform), and believe in the good news (gospel)'" (Mk 1:14-15). On its surface, this passage seems simple and straight-forward. But, deceptively, it is tightly written. The Baptist's arrest is the critical moment at which Jesus initiated his own ministry. Jesus had been John's disciple in the period after John baptized him. Most likely, the Galileans Simon Peter, Andrew, James, John, and Philip of Bethsaida were also John's disciples. When the Baptist was arrested, they returned to Galilee, to the vocations they had before becoming John's followers. But Jesus had other things in mind for them.

"The time is fulfilled." These words, spoken in Aramaic by Jesus, translated into Greek in Mark's Gospel, set Jesus' ministry in motion. Ancient religions often believed crucial affairs brought pre-determined turning points in history. Such a turning point had now come to the world. The Baptist's call to repentance, *metanoiete,* re- or trans-formation, was the initiating event. The ministry of Jesus of Nazareth with his inner assurance of his relationship to God was its culmination.

"The kingdom of God is at hand." In much Jewish thinking during Jesus' time, God's kingship focused on putting Jewish Law, the Torah, into everyday practice. Dodd in his *Parables of the Kingdom* explained that "God is King of His people Israel, and His kingly rule is effective insofar as Israel is obedient to the divine will as revealed in the Torah. To submit oneself unquestioningly to the Law is 'to take upon oneself the *malkuth,* the kingly rule of heaven.'"

Jesus changed this. His understanding of God's kingly rule focused not on the Torah but on his person, his relationship to God, and the messages he brought. His good news came in four distinct ways. It began with the words, *"the kingship of God is at hand";* then it appeared in deeds—exorcisms, healings, the forgiveness of sins; then in Jesus' lifestyle with its triumph of humanity and human dignity over prejudices in social traditions and customs; finally culminating in his cleansing the Temple, his arrest in the garden, his trial and execution, his death and burial, his rising from the dead to be with his people forever. By Jesus' acts, according to Mark, the kingly rule of God had come.

Perhaps we should say instead that it drew very near. A great deal of discussion centers on the Greek word, *eggiken,* translated as "has come near" in the New Revised Standard Version. Is the kingly rule actually here in Jesus' person or is it still to come at some indeterminate time when Christ is said to return on the clouds of glory? Among others, Dodd (1961) sees "has come near" as meaning that God's kingly rule is not here in its full glory but that it has come so close that we can experience the first effects of its coming. As Jesus healed those who came to him in the first few days of his active ministry, the kingly rule of God came very near. As the demons recognized him and their power over human life was nullified, the kingly rule of God came very near. Jesus went on to suffer and die. In faithfulness to his father the kingly rule of God came near. Forgiveness of sins effected by his death and the hope for life eternal effected by his resurrection brought his kingdom near. If the kingly rule of God is not yet fully here, Christians can experience its impact as day by day they are faithful to the God of Jesus Christ.

"Repent and believe in (be faithful to, trust) the gospel (good news)" (1:15b). The Greek imperative word, *metanoeite*, translated "repent!" seldom occurred in Greek literature. For Greeks *metanoeite* meant to change one's mind or opinion, or to regret a particular act that was done or left undone. In contrast, Hebrew prophets saw sin as the human situation of being utterly disloyal to the God who called and loved his people. *Metanoeite* can be translated "re-order," "re-form," or "trans-form." The new prophets, John the Baptist and Jesus, called for a radical re-direction, *metanoeite*, of people, acknowledging that their old relationship to God had misled them and that a new transforming one must (the –*ite* indicates the imperative form of the verb) be established. Old values were to be jettisoned, a new life initiated.

Metanoeite was followed in Jesus' statement by another imperative, *pisteuete* (the ending –*ete*, again makes a Greek word into an imperative verb), *"be faithful to the gospel, trust in it."* *Pisteuete* is often translated "believe," *"believe the gospel!"* "Believe" in Greek meant substituting one set of concepts for another—a thing of the mind more than of the whole person. To Christians, however, *"Be faithful to!,"* *pisteuete*, comes closer to re-order, to re-organize, one's whole life to show faithfulness to the "good news" of Jesus Christ—in one's family, business, use of money, religion, government, leisure time. By being faithful to God, people will also address the meaning of *metanoeite*.

When asking for these things, Jesus explicitly challenged many groups in his society. The Pharisees thought they were already obeying God's Law, the Torah, in great detail. Jesus wanted them to express the spirit of the Law, not only to follow the multiplicity of details in the Law as individuals but as justice in their society. Jesus challenged the Sadducees in a similar same way. Worship God not in the Temple alone, thoughtlessly following traditional rituals by sacrifices which made the Temple a house of commerce. (Jn 4:24). Jesus challenged the Romans because they had no idea that *all* people were loved by God and should be loved by everyone as God's justice requires. Jesus wanted people to worship God *"in spirit and in truth."*

After Jesus came into Galilee, he called his twelve disciples (Mk 1:16-20). He preached the good news and healed people's ills. For the first six chapters of Mark, these themes were layered into the Gospel. The writer grouped stories of a certain type and listed them. Mark has lengthy sections that tell of Jesus'

- Many healings (1:23-2:12, 3:1-5),
- Controversies between Jesus and his opponents (2:13-28,3:6-35),
- Parables about the kingdom of the heavens (4:1-34),
- Power over forces of nature (the sea), over demons, over illness, over death itself (4:35-5:43).

Mark also introduced another key word, *eutheus*, "immediately," from the start, in his first chapter. Mark used this word 35 times (e.g.1:10, 12, 17-23; 3:6; 4:5-6; 5:29; 6:25; 14:72). *"When Jesus came up out of the water (of baptism), immediately he saw the heavens opened"* (1:10). *"The Spirit immediately drove him out into the wilderness"* (1:12). *"And immediately they [Simon and Andrew] left their nets and followed him…. Immediately he called them [James the son of Zebedee and John his brother]; and they left their father Zebedee in the boat with the hired servants, and followed him. They went into Capernaum; and immediately on the Sabbath he entered the synagogue and taught. And immediately there was in their synagogue a man with an unclean spirit"* (1:17-23).

This speed of events continues throughout Mark's Gospel. After one healing by Jesus, *"the Pharisees went out and immediately held counsel with the Herodians against him, how to destroy him"* (3:6). In Jesus' parable of the seed and the soil, Jesus uses the word, *"Other seed fell on rocky ground, where it had not much soil, and immediately it sprang up since it had no depth of soil; and when the sun rose it was scorched and, since it had no root, it withered away"* (4:5-6). When the woman with the hemorrhage touched Jesus' garment, *"Immediately the hemorrhage ceased; and she felt in her body that she was healed of her disease"* (5:29). When the daughter of Herodias danced before the king and his courtiers, the king asked what she wanted for her performance, *"'even half of my kingdom,' he said… She came in immediately with haste to the king, and asked, saying, 'I want you to give me at once the head of John the Baptist on a platter'"* (6:25).

The word *eutheus* continued throughout the Gospel until it describes Peter's denial, *"And immediately the cock crowed a second time"* (14:72). This Gospel continues with all possible speed; all we can do is hang on breathlessly to its story.

Jesus in Galilee after John Was Arrested: Danger Intensified

John the Baptist surely saw himself as a prophet for his time. One feature of a prophet was to call people's attention to nasty things, injustices, done by their leaders. About a thousand years before the Baptizer appeared, the prophet Nathan called the people's attention to the affair between King David, a married woman named Bathsheba, and her husband Uriah the Hittite. Nathan asked for a judgment in a story about a rich man demanding of a poor man that the poor man's only ewe lamb be cooked for the rich man's dinner and whether the rich man was within his rights. David indicated he was not and actually deserved to die. Nathan concluded, with the accusation while pointing to King David, *"Thou art the man"* (2 Samuel 11:2-12:25). David understood this meaning. The Baptizer did something very similar, denouncing the intricate affair whereby Tetrarch Herod Antipas, after an affair with Herodias while she was still married to his brother Philip, then divorced his wife to marry his brother's wife after engineering their divorce. Then Herod Antipas took offense at the Baptist's denunciation. This was a main reason the Baptist was arrested and later executed.

Mark's main interest about the Baptist was less in what happened to the Baptist himself and more on details of Jesus' ministry in Galilee from the time of the Baptist's arrest until he was executed by Herod Antipas. When Jesus went to Galilee after the Baptist was arrested, he immediately went to Capernaum where he called four fishermen to be his disciples—Simon Peter, Andrew, James, and John, who might previously had been the Baptist's disciples (Mk 1:16-20). He immediately began a series of astonishing healings, including a man with an unclean spirit, Simon Peter's mother-in-law, and others who were ill with various diseases and demons ("demons" seem to refer to what we now call "mental illness"). He left Capernaum and went throughout Galilee, preaching in synagogues, healing the ill, and casting out demons (1:40-45).

With all the fame and publicity caused by these acts, Jesus withdrew with his disciples to the Sea of Galilee. A great multitude of people, from all over—Galilee, Judea, Jerusalem, Idumea, Tyre, Sidon, and from beyond the Jordan—followed him (3:8). Jesus went up on the mountain, where he appointed Twelve to be with him and sent them out to preach and have authority to cast out demons. *"Then he went home; and the crowd came together again, so that they could not even eat"* (3:13-20).

Scribes and Pharisees came down from Jerusalem to investigate his ministry (3:22-30). Standing by the sea to preach, Jesus attracted a very large crowd. He had to get into a boat to speak to them (4:1). When evening came, he said to his disciples, *"Let us go across to the other side."* Leaving the crowd, Jesus and his disciples got into a boat and left. But other boats followed them. When a great storm arose, Jesus calmed the sea for them (3:35-41).

Jesus was now approaching the zenith of his healing ministry. He went to the country of the Gerasenes and healed a powerful man who had multiple mental problems, *"unclean spirits"* Mark's Gospel calls them, a *"legion."* The depth of the man's illnesses challenged Jesus; he went a long way from Galilee to find him. When Jesus arrived, the unclean spirits begged Jesus not to expel them from the country but to send them into a nearby herd of two thousand pigs, which Jesus did. The pigs *"immediately"* rushed down a steep bank and drowned in the sea. Possibly the young man's disturbances during his healing startled the pigs so that, despite pleas from their Gentile herdsmen, they fled. (We can imagine Jews chortling when they heard this story; pigs were unclean animals in their thinking, and the pigs got exactly what they deserved!) After this healing, the young man, who previously had torn his garments in his rage and broken the bonds with which he had been shackled, sat quietly, fully dressed, and asked Jesus what he should do next to further Jesus' ministry (5:1-20).

When Jesus crossed the sea again, another great crowd gathered around the famous Jesus. A synagogue's ruler, Jairus, sought Jesus to heal his 12-year old daughter who was very near death (5:21). As Jesus went with him, a woman, who had a flow of blood for twelve years, touched his garment. Immediately her hemorrhage ceased and the woman believed she was healed. Jesus felt power go out of him, looked around, and asked, *"'Who touched my garments?' The woman confessed and Jesus said, 'Daughter, your faith has made you well. Go in peace and be healed of your disease.'"* Word then came to the synagogue's ruler that his little girl had died. Jesus went to the child, took her hand, and the girl got up immediately and walked. All present were amazed (5:22-43). Building on these successes, Jesus sent out the

Twelve to expand his work. They were successful, casting out many demons and, by anointing with oil, many sick people were healed (6:7-13). *"The apostles returned to Jesus and told him all they had done and taught"* (6:30), a fitting climax to a powerful ministry.

After receiving word of the Baptist's death, Jesus decided to go with his disciples to a *"lonely place"* where they could rest and pray. The crowd that had been with Jesus earlier had a good idea of where he was going, so they preceded him to this deserted spot. The crowd was composed of five thousand men (6:44). Although John's Gospel also recorded the event (Jn 6:1-14), Mark's account is significantly different from John's. In Mark's Gospel, the event was extraordinary. It was a Lord's Supper before the Last Supper.

Walter Brueggemann (1999: 346-347) brilliantly catches the sense of the event. "The feeding of the multitudes, recorded in Mark's Gospel, is an example of the new world coming into being through God. When the disciples, charged with feeding the hungry crowd, found a child with five loaves and two fishes, Jesus *"took, blessed, broke, and gave the bread"* (to the people). These are the four decisive verbs of the sacramental experience. Jesus conducted a Eucharist, a gratitude. He demonstrated that the world is filled with abundance and freighted with generosity. If bread is broken and shared, there is enough for all. Jesus is engaged in the sacramental, at the time subversive, re-ordering of public reality.

"The profane is the opposite of the sacramental. 'Profane' means flat, empty, one-dimensional, exhausted. Market ideology wants us to believe that the world is profane—life consists of buying and selling, weighing, measuring and trading, and then finally sinking into death and nothingness. But Jesus presents an entirely different kind of economy, one infused with the mystery of abundance and a cruciform kind of generosity. Five thousand are fed and twelve baskets of food are left over—one for every tribe of Israel. Jesus transforms the economy by blessing it and breaking it beyond self-interest. From broken Friday bread comes Sunday abundance. Here, people do not grasp, hoard, resent, or act self-ishly. They watch as the juices of heaven multiply the bread of earth."

In telling these stories, Mark adds many features to his original picture of Jesus. The Jesus he knew was a teacher (see Fig 7, above). Thirty-four times in his Gospel Mark uses the word "teach," "taught," or its equivalents. His Jesus was also a healer, raising some from the dead. He forgave people's sins. He was a leader of men and women. Until his ministry ended, his disciples, and also the women who followed him, willingly went with him wherever he went. He called himself the Son of Humankind. He was a martyr to his cause. He was raised from the dead by his God. Teacher, healer, forgiver, one who raised others from the dead, leader, Son of Humankind, martyr, risen Christ. To Mark Jesus was all these things.

Jesus in Northwestern Galilee, between Bethsaida and Tyre and Sidon, after John the Baptist was Executed

Having commissioned his disciples to go, preach, teach, and heal, Jesus learned bad news. King Herod Antipas had executed John the Baptist. This act set in motion a critical part of Mark's Gospel. Now Jesus knew what Herod Antipas would do to prominent people who criticized him too much. He sensed a real and present danger to himself. Faced with this new reality from Herod Antipas, Jesus withdrew into the territory of the more tolerant Herod Philip, the area called the Decapolis, east of Galilee, then he returned to Bethsaida and went north and west to the regions of Tyre and Sidon. He went there intentionally; these regions were not ruled by Herod Antipas who had executed John the Baptist.

Jesus did not want anyone to know where he was going. Jesus had many decisions to make. Mainly Jesus had to decide God's intentions for the remainder of his ministry. Slowly Jesus began to see clearly God's destiny for him. But he not only had to see it he had to accept such a destiny. His struggle took time to work out. When he moved out in a boat (6:32), he was interrupted by a hungry crowd. He responded by feeding them (6:32-45). Then they crossed the sea and landed at Gennesaret. Immediately people recognized him and everyone started to bring sick people on their pallets to any place where they heard he was (6:53-56). He had a long argument with local Pharisees over the matter of kosher food and eating things that were not kosher (7:1-23).

Still moving on quietly, secretly even, he was accosted by a Syro-Phoenician woman and healed her daughter (7:30 ff). Continuing farther from his home base of Capernaum, he went into the Decapolis region where he privately healed a deaf man (7:32-37). There another hungry crowd confronted him and he fed them too (8:1-9). Then he and his disciples went to Dalmanutha (8:10; still not located by scholars), then to Bethsaida and north to the region of Caesarea Philippi, far from Capernaum, his home base, and from Nazareth, his boyhood home. He then went back to Bethsaida, then north again to the villages of Caesarea Philippi. Jesus was clearly trying to escape notice. Mark says, *"After he healed the deaf man he took him aside privately and charged him to tell no one"* (7:33-37). *"He sent the crowd he had fed away immediately"* (8:10). He healed a blind man, saying to him, *"Do not even enter the village"* (8:26). In a discussion with his disciples, Peter announced that Jesus was indeed the Christ and Jesus *"charged them to tell no one about him"* (8:30). He was transfigured before Peter, James, and John, and once again *"he charged them to tell no one what they had seen"* (9:9).

In Caesarea Philippi, danger and destiny met in Jesus' life. Destiny won. On this trip he determined that he, the Son of Humankind, must *"suffer (pathein) many things,"* be rejected by the elders, chief priests, and scribes, be killed, and *"after three days rise again."* The Greek word, *pathein*, is cognate with the Greek (and English) *pathos*, "deeply hurt feelings as in a calamity." This was God's destiny for him and he accepted it. The forces of religion and government had done away with John the Baptist. Jesus's destiny would be similar. What was new was that Jesus announced he would *"rise again"* (8:31). His disciples did not assimilate this pronouncement. When Jesus died, they did not stand around his tomb waiting for him to *"rise again."* Instead, they fled.

"Jesus called to him the multitude with his disciples, and said to them, 'If any man would come after me, let him deny himself and take up his cross and follow me'" (8:34). Why did Jesus focus on crucifixion? In Jesus' generation, it was a common means of execution for what the Roman Empire considered treason in its various forms. Jesus had surely witnessed such executions. But Jesus was calling his followers to *"take up your cross and follow me."* Who not in desperation would possibly do this? Many people in Jesus' time, indebted peasants, the poor and disabled in Galilee and those being persecuted in Rome (where Mark was probably written), were, in reality, desperate.

Jesus' Journey from Capernaum to Jerusalem: Bartimaeus in Jericho

After struggling with discovering his destiny, Jesus returned from Caesarea Philippi to his home base in Capernaum. He gathered the Twelve and led them down the "Jordan Way" to Jerusalem by following the Jordan River as it flowed from the Sea of Galilee to Jericho. In Jericho the last of Jesus' healings took place (10:46-52).

The streets of Jericho were narrow, twisting, and filled with people on the morning Jesus arrived. Jesus, his disciples, and the large multitude of people accompanying them had to shoulder their way through the crowds. As also noted in the Chronology earlier, when they were leaving the city, Bartimaeus, a blind beggar, was sitting by the roadside. Hearing the name, *"Jesus of Nazareth"* above the din, he also heard *"Teacher," "Christ," "Son of David."* Bartimaeus cried out, *"Jesus, Son of David, have mercy on me!"* (10:47). Some in the crowd rebuked him. Why should Jesus pay attention to him? He was a nobody, a worthless beggar straddling a street filled with beggars. But Bartimaeus called again, *"Jesus, Son of David, have mercy on me."* Through the clamor, Jesus heard his call and stopped. *"Call him,"* Jesus said. Bartimaeus threw off his garment, probably all he owned, the sum of his possessions, got up and went to Jesus. A rich man who approached Jesus just days before could not do this—he had too many possessions to throw them aside and follow Jesus. Not Bartimaeus.

"What do you want me to do for you?" Jesus asked him. Bartimaeus said, *"Let me receive my sight."* Jesus said to him, *"Go your way. Your faith has made you well."* Jesus made no spittle of clay nor laid his hands on the man. He simply said, *"Go your way."* But Bartimaeus did not go his way. He went Jesus' way. He followed Jesus to Jerusalem. Blind Bartimaeus was freed, liberated, became a disciple, and followed Jesus.

This final healing incident is significant in at least three ways. First, Jesus wanted people to see his power—he wanted blind people everywhere to "see" what his healing ministry could do. Second, the incident took place in Jericho, perhaps the oldest city in the known world and the first city the Israelites conquered when they moved into *"the Promised Land"* (Joshua 6:20). Now God's new promise through Jesus Christ was about to be fulfilled. This history would not be lost on those reading Mark's Gospel. And, third, once Bartimaeus could see, he followed Jesus because he could see. In none of the other healings in Mark's Gospel did those healed follow him.

Jesus in Jerusalem: His Last Supper, Crucifixion, and Resurrection

When Jesus and the multitude left Jericho, they climbed the Mount of Olives, the large hill directly east of Jerusalem. People approaching Jerusalem from the Jordan Valley, Jericho, and Bethany would come up the far side of the Mount and from its peak looking west would see a marvelous sight—

Judaism's grand Temple gleaming atop Mount Zion with Jerusalem gathered around it. From the Mount of Olives, King David had also viewed Jerusalem and had vowed to make it his capital. On the Mount of Olives a Jewish Messiah was someday to appear.

Bethpage was a small village just over the mountain from Bethany on the Jerusalem side. Its significance was that Bethpage, unlike Bethany, was considered part of Jerusalem. According to Jewish law, a Jew may not work on the Sabbath. According to the Talmud, this forbade a Jew from carrying anything into the city on the Sabbath from outside the enclosed area of the city. Since Bethpage was enclosed within Jerusalem, Jesus could legally go there to pick up an animal on which to ride into the city.

Jesus rode into the city on a donkey to people's cheers (Mk 11:7-10). He went back to Bethany, to the house of Simon the leper, and there an unnamed woman anointed him with costly pure ointment called *"nard"* (14:3-9). Then Judas, seeing that Jesus accepted being anointed, went to the chief priests to betray him (14:10-11). While this was happening, Jesus remained in the city teaching and preaching, returning each night to a place that he and the Twelve had chosen as a campsite when visiting the Holy City for the Passover celebration. The place was called "The Garden of Gethsemane."

On the first night of Passover, according to Mark's Gospel, Jesus and the Twelve went into the city to a predetermined room to eat the Passover meal. When the meal was ended, *"having sung a hymn, they went out to the Mount of Olives"* (14:26). The customary hymn concluding the Passover meal was the last few verses of 118 Psalm.

"The Lord is my strength and my song; he has become my salvation.

This is the day which the Lord has made; let us rejoice and be glad in it.

O give thanks to the Lord, for he is good; His mercy endures forever."

Then Jesus and his disciples crossed the Kidron Valley that cut between the hills and proceeded up the slope of the Mount of Olives. As they were traveling, Jesus said to them,

"You shall all fall away because it is written, 'Smite down the shepherd and the sheep will be scattered...' Peter said to him, 'If all fall away, but not I.' Jesus said to him, 'Truly I say to you that this day, in this night, before twice the cock crows, thrice you will deny me.' With intense earnestness Peter said, 'If it is necessary that I die with you, I will not deny.' All said the same. And they came into a garden, the name of which was Gethsemane" (14:27-32).

The name *"Gethsemane"* means "Olive Press." It was most likely a thick grove of olive trees on a hillside of the Kidron river. Here Jesus and his disciples camped out while in Jerusalem. As soon as they arrived at the site that night, the disciples fell asleep. They always slept under these covering branches, and this night they also did what was natural to them. It had already been a tiring day for them.

"Jesus said to his disciples, 'Sit here while I pray.' He took with him Peter and James and John, and he began to be alarmed and distressed. He said to them, 'Circled with grief is my soul unto death. Remain here and watch.' Going on a little he fell upon the earth and he prayed that if it be possible let this hour depart from him, and he said, 'Abba, Father, all things are possible to you; take this cup from me. But not what I will but what you will'" (14:32-36, our translation).

"Again going out he prayed saying the same word. Again coming he found them sleeping, for their eyes were weighted down, and they did not know what to answer him. He came a third time and said to them, 'Sleep hereafter and rest. It is enough. Comes the hour, behold, betrayed is the Son of Humankind into the hands of sinners. Rise, let us be going'" (14:37-42).

The hour had come. While Jesus prayed and the disciples slept, the hour came. Judas did his work. Soldiers and a mob advanced on the hill. Yet Jesus met the hour courageously, *"Rise, let us be going,"* he said. He did not try to escape from the garden by flinging himself over the hill into oblivion. He went openly and boldly to meet his tormentors and do battle on the cross for humanity's soul. Jesus' vigil ends in action, as did every vigil, every prayerful struggle he had with God.

The culmination of Mark's Gospel comes when *"there was darkness on all the earth. And in the 9th hour Jesus cried in a great voice, 'Eloi, eloi, lama sabachthani,' which is translated, 'My God, my God, for what do you abandon me?'"*

Was this cry of Jesus one of dereliction, as some say it was? Was Jesus, abandoned by humankind, now abandoned by God? On the surface these words imply it. But these words mean far more than that. They come from the opening lines of 22 Psalm. *"My God, why hast thou forsaken me?"* All Jewish people knew this Psalm, and they knew that it concluded with an expression of greatest trust, *"In thee our fathers trusted, and thou didst deliver them. To thee they cried and were saved; ...all people shall serve God and proclaim his deliverance to nations yet unborn."*

In his dying hour Jesus Christ did what he had done his entire life. He turned to God's Word, the God of his Word, and in them he found the answer to the pressing question with which he had been struggling during the past months. God was trustworthy, he knew that now, and Jesus trusted his life and destiny to this trustworthy God. As late as his prayer in Gethsemane he had said, *"Father, remove this cup from me."* Now he declared that his life mission was fulfilled. *"All people shall serve God and proclaim his deliverance to nations yet unborn."* Jesus of Nazareth had served his suffering people whenever he was called upon to do it. Now he suffered with them at the hands of those—Sanhedrin, Temple, Herod, Pilate, the Roman government—who had oppressed his people. Even these enemies, together, could not thwart the work that God had entrusted to him. Through his cross, *"All people shall serve God and proclaim his deliverance to nations yet unborn."* This was Mark's Jesus—the serving and suffering one, the servant who suffered and, through his suffering, healed. In this trusting spirit Jesus lived, and died, and lives again.

Chapter 8

Jesus in the Gospel of Matthew: Jesus, the Righteous and Just One

Our characterization of Matthew's Gospel focuses on "Jesus, the Just and Righteous One." Figure 7, above, which compares the numbers of times certain words appear in the four Gospels, corroborates this characterization. Matthew's Gospel used the word *righteous* or *righteousness* 19 times, almost twice as often as Luke (10 times). Mark used it twice and John three times. Another word used more often than righteous or righteousness in Matthew is the word *"Pharisee"* (used 29 times in Matthew, 27 times in Luke, 20 in John, and 12 in Mark). Pharisees were much concerned to achieve *righteousness* in their daily lives, and advocated following Torah Law both in its written and interpreted forms in order to do this. In Matthew's Gospel, Jesus often contested with Pharisees on the meaning of Torah Law and its righteousness. Jesus' version of righteousness connected it to a spiritual righteousness in God's kingdom (another word used slightly more often in Matthew than in the other Gospels; see Fig 7). *"Seek first his kingdom and his righteousness"* (Mt 6:33).

Matthew repeatedly reported on the connection between the law and Jesus' teachings. *"Think not that I have come to abolish the law and the prophets"* Matthew reports that Jesus said. *"I have come not to abolish them but to fulfil them. For truly, I say to you, till heaven and earth pass away, not an iota, not a dot, will pass from the law until all is accomplished. Whoever then relaxes one of the least of these commandments and teaches men so, shall be called least in the kingdom of heaven; but he who does them and teaches them shall be called great in the kingdom of heaven. For I tell you, unless your righteousness exceeds that of the scribes and Pharisees, you will never enter the kingdom of heaven"* (5:17-20). This statement is a very strong endorsement for keeping the Law. Pharisees wanted all Jews to keep the law in great detail. More than in other Gospels, Matthew saw a connection between keeping the Law in even more detail than the Pharisees as part of righteousness and God's kingdom. Jesus emphasized this connection in his series of statements (beatitudes and woes) that begin *"You have heard that is was said… but I say to you…"* (Mt 5:21-48). A key among the "woes" is *"Woe to you, scribes and Pharisees, hypocrites! for you tithe mint and dill and cummin and have neglected the weightier matters of the law, justice and mercy and faith; these you ought to have done, without neglecting the others"* (Mt 23:23). Righteousness is also to work for and demonstrate *"justice and mercy and faith."*

Social Context of Matthew's Gospel

A possible reason righteousness and the contests with Pharisees over its meaning were so prominent in Matthew's Gospel may be because Pharisees were close to, if not actually in, the Brethren Party that produced Matthew's Gospel (Acts 15:5 ff). Oral traditions for Matthew's Gospel probably started in Jerusalem with a group of Hebrew Jews that later became the party of the Brothers (or Brethren). James, probably Jesus' blood brother, was its major leader (Acts 12:17; Eberts, 2009, ch 3). The Acts shows James' beliefs as quite similar to Pharisees' beliefs on the importance of Torah Law for all Jews (Acts 1:5 ff; 15:1 ff). Although Acts does not relate these issues directly to Pharisees, Matthew's Gospel shows clearly that Pharisees' issues were mainly "how to be righteous individuals" and "how to be a righteous community." Matthew's Gospel emphasizes Jesus' concerns over the nature of such righteousness.

Jerusalem certainly had a unique social context because it was the only mideastern city with about 40,000 residents that had a very large Jewish majority. Although the Romans held ultimate authority, the Jewish government, the Sanhedrin, was locally dominant. Roman policy toward subject people often tried to establish legal local governments composed largely of local elites acceptable to Rome and to let them run their own political affairs as long as they would pay monetary and political tribute to Rome by providing soldiers to Rome as needed and not to undertake any political involvement with foreign entities without Rome's consent (Grant, 1975).

In Jerusalem, the Sanhedrin, collaborated with the Herodians and Romans in maintaining law and order and in collecting various taxes, including Roman taxes. The Sanhedrin made some laws, administered others, meted out certain forms of punishment, and recommended mortal punishments to the Romans. Its 71 self-coopting members included elders, Temple priests, Sadducees, Levites, scribes, rabbis, and a few Pharisees. The High Priest was its presiding officer. Essenes and Zealots were not members of the Sanhedrin but were mentioned by the military general and historian Josephus, who was originally a Pharisee (Pharisee, 2012). Zealots and Sicarii were seeking to overthrow the existing regimes, including the Sanhedrin, by using violence. Further, extrapolating from the beginning of Acts, relatively large numbers of Hellenist Jews, though a minority, were also present in Jerusalem. Hellenist Jews differed in their theology and ethics from Hebrew Jews (Acts chs 6-7). They gave less recognition to the Temple's legitimacy than most Hebrew Jews while recognizing that Jerusalem was the de facto center of Jewish religious life. Many Hellenist and Hebrew Jews in the diasporas also sent their sons to Jerusalem for religious training. These latter became the base of the Apostles' party. The Brothers, shunned by their fellow Jews, became among the poor. Jerusalem's religious politics was tumultuous.

In this complex of groupings and their issues, the Pharisees were perhaps the largest status group and challenged other Jewish groups in Jerusalem on the meaning of righteousness within Judaism (Zeitlin, 1988: 15-16, 20). Jesus and his followers repeatedly engaged with Pharisees on key interpretations and other issues within the overall conflicts among Jerusalem's status groups. Extrapolating from Acts (chs 5-8), Hebrew-Hellenist conflicts were also just below the surface. The stoning of Stephen was a proximate result which then led to the banning of Christians from Jerusalem.

The shunning and banning had disastrous results on the Brethren-Christian party in Jerusalem. The banning left the Brethren, in effect, excommunicated from all aspects of Jewish life in Jerusalem so that Brethren in Jerusalem became quite poor and needed support from Christian congregations throughout the eastern Mediterranean region for, literally, their collective life. Paul and Barnabas, among others, were much concerned with "collections" to support their fellow Brethren-Christians in Jerusalem (Acts 11:29-30, passim). The Brethren might have stayed in Jerusalem because they believed Jesus Christ was continuous with, the fulfillment of, Hebrew traditions in seeking righteousness for Hebrew people.

James' execution, probably around 63CE, and the destruction of the Temple and Jerusalem in 70CE had disastrous results for the Brothers in Jerusalem. Many were killed while others became refugees, moving to various Eastern Mediterranean cities, among them, Pella, Antioch, and Alexandria (see Eberts, 2011, ch 1). A remnant of the Brothers (Brethren) had to reconsider many issues that James, for instance in Acts 15, had espoused. We believe that Christ as heavenly judge, when he equated the righteous with serving *"the least of these, my brethren"* (Mt 25:31-46), was one such reconsideration from earlier depictions in Acts 15.

Exactly where Matthew's Gospel was written is disputed but most scholars have it coming from Antioch (Gospel of Matthew, 2012a). Yet an early draft in Hebrew, the Gospel of Mattiyu (or MattitYahu), was said to have surfaced in Egypt (Eusebius, 2012) and from evidence internal to the Gospel, as we shall see below, we believe that Egypt was where the Gospel was written.

The social context in Jerusalem from which the party of the Brethren emerged was contentious in many ways—between Jews and Romans; between Hebrew Jews and Hellenist Jews; between Pharisees and Sadducees; between Zealots and everyone else; between Jesus and the others. Matthew's Gospel reflects nearly all these conflicts but saw the contentiousness of Jesus with the Pharisees on the issue of what it meant to be righteous and just as the most critical.

Purpose of Matthew's Gospel

As with Mark's Gospel, Matthew does not provide a particular purpose for his Gospel. From its context, we surmise that Matthew, like Luke, wanted to provide *"an orderly account"* (Luke 1:3) of Jesus' life for Jesus' followers in the Brothers' party which fit with one of his major themes, of Christian righteousness and justice.

Internal Organization of Matthew's Gospel

Scholars have determined that the internal organization of Matthew's Gospel is akin to the five books of the Law of Moses (Gospel of Matthew, 2012b). Although it may or may not have been the author's intention to use an outline of ancient writings as an aid in understanding his document, five major sections can be found, "books" inside this one book.

The Book of Discipleship, chapters 3 through 7
The Book of Apostleship, chapters 8 through 10
The Book of the Mystery of the Kingdom of Heaven,
    chapters 11 through 13
The Book of the Church, chapters 14 through 18
The Book of the Future, chapters 19 through 25

Why was Matthew organized in this way? It may be in imitation of the Torah's five books. These books nurtured Jewish people from birth by teaching the stories of Israel's life. When Hebrews became adults, they could identify with men and women from the Israelites' past. Matthew does the same thing for people in his congregations. What does it mean to be a disciple of our Christ? Read chapters 3 through 7. Want to know how to extend Jesus' message to others? Read chapters 8 through 10. Want to know about the mystery of the Kingdom of the heavens? Read chapters 11 through 13. Want to know how to organize your congregation? Read chapters 14 through 18. Want to know what the future holds? Try chapters 19 through 25. Like the Jewish people of old who lived their life in accordance with their Scriptures, Christians in this early Jesus party were to incorporate the words of Jesus Christ into the very fiber of their being.

Another important reason for the material's organization was that Jewish people considered Torah, the first five books of the Hebrew Bible, to be both law and teaching. The complete Torah was read in the synagogues at least once a year. Genesis would normally be read over twelve Sabbaths, the Book of Exodus over eleven Sabbaths, Leviticus for eight Sabbaths, the Book of Numbers for ten, and the Book of Deuteronomy for twelve. To fulfill this reading, approximately five chapters of each book would be read every Sabbath. Torah was written on large, heavy scrolls, not easily handled. It was easiest to read the Torah in order, beginning each Sabbath at the point where the reading had ended the previous Sabbath. This process was "required reading" in every synagogue service (see Spong, 1996: 60 ff).

Samuel Terrien (1985: 3) describes why this was important to Hebrew people. He insists that Torah was no mere book of laws; it had a more comprehensive purpose than this. Torah, he says, first meant "nurture thru narrative and lore," then it meant "teaching," and, finally, "law." In other words, Torah was the main tool for communicating the culture of the Hebrew people to coming Hebrew generations. It incorporated all things necessary for the proper continuation of Hebrew life: nurture, teaching, and law.

For 21st century people, this may be hard to understand. Today we tend to draw a firm line between "nurture," "teaching," and "law." For us nurture belongs to the family, teaching to the schools, and law to the legislatures and courts. It was not so in Judaism in the first century—all this was covered by the proper use of the Torah. Nor was it true in the early Jesus movement. Jesus in his resurrection said *"Go into all the world and make disciples of all the ethnics. Teach them all that I have commanded you, and I will be with you to the end of the age."* First nurture—*"Make disciples of all the ethnics."* Then teaching—*"Teach them all that I have said to you."* Then law—*"all that I have commanded you."* Do these things with your lives in your new communities. Matthew's extended organization of the words and acts of Jesus is the Torah equivalent in the early church. *"If you teach what I have commanded you, then I am indeed with you to the close of the age."*

Sources for Matthew's Gospel

Again, as in Mark's Gospel, sources for Matthew's Gospel are not explicitly reported. Since Matthew follows the general outline of Mark's Gospel, Matthew surely had this Gospel in front of him as he wrote his Gospel (or dictated it to an unknown scribe). Figure 8, columns two and four, below, demonstrates Matthew's extensive use of Mark's Gospel. Scholars also tend to agree that the material shared by Matthew and Luke came from unknown sources they call Quelle, or

Matthew's Own	Shared With Mark	Shared With Luke (Quelle)	Shared With Mark And Luke
1:1-17- 2:23	3:7-12	3:4-6	1:1-16
3:14-15	4:3-11, 23	4:18-22	3:1-3, 16-17
5:17, 19-23	5:1-4, 6,	6:14	4:1-2, 12a, 17
5:27-31, 33-38	5:11-16, 18	12:31, 48-49	4:23-25
6:1-8, 15-16	5:24-26, 32	13:53-58	5:13
6:24	5:39-48	14:3-27, 32-36	7:28-29
7:6, 28	6:9-13, 19-34	15:1-11, 15-22	8:1-4, 14-17
8:12	7:1-5, 7-27	15:25-39	8:23-34
9:23, 32-34	8:5-13, 18-22	16:7-10	9:1-14, 18-20
10:17-25	9:15-16, 22, 35	17:14	9:22-31
10:41-11:1	9:37-38	18:8-9, 21-22	9:35-10:8,
11:20, 28	10:9-15, 19-20	19:1-9	10:13-16
12:5-7, 17-21	10:26-40	21:10, 15	12:1-4, 8, 9-16
12:36	11:2-19, 21-27	21:18-22	12:24-26, 29-30
13:12, 14-15	12:22-23, 27-28	22:34	12:32, 46-47, 50
13:24-30, 35-52	12:30, 32-35,	23:20-22	13:1-13, 18-23
14:28-31	12:38-45	24:17-18, 23-25	13:31-32, 54-58
15:12-14, 23-24	13:16-17, 33-34	26:6-16, 21-22	14:1-2
16:11-12, 17-19	16:3	26:31-32, 37-38	16:1-2, 4-6, 8
17:6-8, 13	17:9-12, 19-20	26:42-46, 56	16:13-16, 20-28
17:24-27	18:10-15, 22	26:59-62	17:1-5, 9, 14-18
18:4, 7, 16-21	19:28	27:13-15, 17-18	17:22-23
18:23-35	21:17, 21	27:27-31, 46-49	18:1-3, 5-7
19:10-12	22:1-10		19:13-15, 16-27
20:1-16, 22	23:4, 6-7, 12-13		19:29-35
21:4-5, 11	23:23, 25-27, 29,		20:17-19, 23-28
21:14-16, 28-32	23:32-39		20:29-34
23:2-5, 11	24:26-28, 37-51		21:1-3, 6-10
23:16-21, 28,	25:1-13, 15-16		21:12-13, 15, 17
23:30-31	25:19-22, 24-30		21:23-27, 33-46
24:10-12	26:25, 52-54		22:15-46
25:1-13, 17-18	27:12, 55		23:1, 11, 15
25:23, 31-46			24:1-9, 13-22
27:3-10, 19			24:29-36, 39
27:24-25, 52-53			25:13-15, 42
27:62-66			26:1-5, 17-20
28:2-4, 9-20			26:24, 26-30
			26:33-36, 39-41
			26:47-51, 55
			26:57-58, 63-75
			27:1-2, 11, 16

Source: Gospel Parallels, 1949, Edited by Translators, Revised Standard Version. It is unclear whether Luke got the idea of lineage from Matthew or Matthew from Luke—much depends on which was written first; we suspect Luke was first. All references in Figure 8 (e.g. 1:1-17- 2:23; 28:1, 5-8) are to Matthew's Gospel.

Figure 8 Sources of Material in the Gospel of Matthew.*

simply Q, which means, in German, "source" or "document" (Q, 2012). Material from Q is found in Figure 8, column three. Such a wide variety of stories in Q probably indicates it was not a single written source of "sayings" but multiple sources. Q's stories include some teachings from John the Baptist (Mt 3:7-12), the centurion and his paralyzed servant (8:5-13), and Jesus' charge to his disciples to *"go...to all nations"* (28:16-20). Matthew also added stories or sayings of his own, not told in other Gospels or Quelle (Figure 8, column one), about John the Baptist (3:14-15), parables (of the weeds and net, 13:35-52), and a resurrection story (guards told to lie that Jesus' body was stolen, 28:9-15). Such an array of stories suggests that Matthew's sources, too, were extensive even if not identified. Our best guess is that these sources included people within the Brothers' community, some perhaps from original members of Jesus' Eleven, others from Galilee, and others from the Jerusalem-based Brothers. They probably included eyewitness accounts, oral reports, and some written documents, as Mark's Gospel might have been and Q was assumed to be.

Figure 8 also shows what a colossal editing job Matthew accomplished. As column one shows, long narratives and single sentences were interspersed with other long narratives from various sources. Since people's "oral memories" of stories in non-literate societies (as in less-industrialized societies even today) and in Jesus' time were extensive, oral traditions were major ways to keep current. Matthew undoubtedly was an expert in remembering these stories so that he could relatively easily intersperse comments from others' stories. Still, to keep all these things in mind as he was writing his Gospel is truly remarkable.

A clue to Matthew's thinking is in his very first story. Unlike Jesus' genealogy in Luke which begins with God, then Adam and his successors, Matthew's genealogy begins with Abraham, the recognized father of all Jews, then recapitulates Jewish history by citing Abraham as the father of Isaac, Isaac the father of Jacob, Jacob the father of Judah and his brothers, and so on, finally tracing Jesus' lineage through David, whom Matthew calls the son of Abraham. Matthew neatly schematized this genealogy into fourteen generations from Abraham to David, fourteen generations from David to the deportation to Babylon, and fourteen generations from then until Jesus (1:1-17). Seven was a sacred number to the Jews and twice seven was even more sacred.

Use of Hebrew Scripture in Matthew's Gospel— To Fulfill Hebrew History

Matthew's Gospel features words and themes of Jewish Scripture, the Old Testament, as giving structure to Jesus' life. Matthew used the word "fulfil" fifteen times, more than any other Gospel (see Fig 7, above). Such usage recognizes the continuity of Jesus with Hebrew history which would be important for a Christ-following community in Jerusalem when so many highly regarded groups there opposed them. For many years scholars noted that Matthew's account of Jesus' birth consisted of five quotations from the Hebrew Bible. The first described Jesus' birth by Mary and her husband Joseph, who, when he discovered she was pregnant, *"resolved to divorce her quietly"* (Mt 1:19). But *"an angel of the Lord"* came to him asking him not to divorce her. *"She will bear a son, and you shall call his name Jesus, for he will save his people from their sins."* Then Matthew adds, *"All this took place to fulfil what the Lord had spoken by the prophet, 'Behold, a virgin shall conceive and bear a son, and his name shall be called Emmanuel' (which means, 'God with us'; Isaiah 7:14)."*

The second story concerned the wise men. They made their way to King Herod in Jerusalem and asked where the child was to be born. Herod's scholars told them, *"In Bethlehem of Judea; for so it is written by the prophet: 'And you, O Bethlehem, in the land of Judah, are by no means least among the rulers of Judah; for from you shall come a ruler who will govern my people Israel' (Micah 5:2)."*

A third story from Old Testament Scriptures occurred when Herod asked the magi to report to him once they found the child. Knowing Herod's craftiness, *"they decided not to return to Jerusalem and the royal court but went to their own country by another way. When Herod saw that he had been tricked by the wise men, he was in a furious rage. He sent and killed all the male children in Bethlehem and in all that region who were two years old or under, according to the time which he had ascertained from the wise men. This,"* said Matthew, *"fulfilled what was spoken by the prophet Jeremiah (31:15), 'A voice was heard in Ramah, wailing and loud lamentation, Rachel weeping for her children'"* (Mt 2:16-18).

The fourth story concerns the flight of Joseph's family into Egypt. Herod was determined to kill the child. In response, Joseph gathered his family and took them to Egypt for refuge. When Herod died, Joseph brought his family back to Judea and then to Nazareth of Galilee. *"This was to fulfil,"* said Matthew, *"what the Lord had spoken by the prophet, 'Out of Egypt have I called my son'"* (Hosea 11:1; Mt 2:15).

The fifth story concerns Joseph's return to Galilee. *"He went and dwelt in a city called Nazareth, that what was spoken by the prophets might be fulfilled, 'He shall be called a Nazarene'"* (Is 11:1; Mt 2:23).

An addendum to these stories turns up in Matthew's fourth chapter. Leaving Nazareth, Jesus went to dwell in Capernaum by the Sea of Galilee, in the territory of Zebulun and Naphtali, that, according to Matthew, what was spoken by the prophet Isaiah might be fulfilled. *"The land of Zebulun and the land of Naphtali, toward the sea, across the Jordan, Galilee of the Gentiles—the people who sat in darkness have seen a great light, and for those who sat in the region and shadow of death light has dawned"* (Mt 4:13-16).

Matthew's story of Jesus' temptation is also built on passages from the Hebrew Bible. *"The tempter came and said to Jesus, 'If you are the Son of God, command these stones to become loaves of bread.' Jesus answered, 'It is written, Man shall not live by bread alone, but by every word that proceeds from the mouth of God' (Deut 8:3).*

"*Then the devil took him to the holy city, and set him on the pinnacle of the temple, and said to him, 'If you are the Son of God, throw yourself down; for it is written, 'He will give his angels charge of you' (Psalms 91:11-12), and 'On their hands they will bear you up, lest you strike your foot against a stone.' Jesus said to him, 'Again it is written, 'You shall not tempt the Lord your God' (Deut 6:16; Mt 4:5-7).*

"*Again, the devil took Jesus to a very high mountain, and showed him all the kingdoms of the world and the glory of them; and he said to him, 'All these I will give you, if you will fall down and worship me.' Jesus said to him, 'Begone, Satan! For it is written, 'You shall worship the Lord your God and him only shall you serve'" (Deut 6:13; Mt 4:8-10).*

Matthew even saw Jesus' healings as fulfilling Jewish Scripture. "*They brought to him many who were possessed with demons; and he cast out the spirits with a word and healed all who were sick. This was to fulfil what was spoken by the prophet Isaiah, 'He took our infirmities and bore our diseases'" (Is 53:4; Mt 8:16-17).*

Matthew quoted Scripture to counter the Pharisees' charge when they perceived that Jesus' followers broke the law of Sabbath. On one Sabbath, as Jesus and the Twelve went through the grainfields, his disciples were hungry and began to pluck heads of grain to eat. Jesus said to the Pharisees, "*Have you not read what David did, when he was hungry, and those who were with him, how he entered the house of God and ate the bread of the Presence, which it was not lawful for him to eat nor for those who were with him, but only for the priests? (1 Samuel 21:1-6). Or have you not read in the law how on the Sabbath the priests in the temple profane the Sabbath and are guiltless? (Numbers 28:9-10). I tell you, something greater than the temple is here. For the Son of Humankind is lord of the Sabbath*" (Mt 12:2-8).

Because, on this and other occasions, Jesus baffled, "bested," the Pharisees over what they considered their greatest strengths, the Pharisees *"took counsel against him, how to destroy him. Jesus, aware of this, withdrew from there. Many followed him and he healed them all and ordered them not to make him known. This was to fulfil what was spoken by the prophet Isaiah, 'Behold, my servant whom I have chosen, my beloved with whom my soul is well pleased. I will put my Spirit upon him, and he shall proclaim justice to the Gentiles. He will not wrangle or cry aloud…till he brings justice to victory; and in his name will the Gentiles hope'"* (Is 42:1-4; Mt 12:14-21).

People questioned why Jesus so often spoke in parables and he replied, *"This is why I speak to them in parables, because seeing they do not see and hearing they do not hear nor do they understand. With them indeed is fulfilled the prophecy of Isaiah which says, 'You shall indeed hear but never understand and you shall indeed see but never perceive. For this people's heart has grown dull, their ears are heavy of hearing, and their eyes they have closed, lest they should perceive with their eyes and hear with their ears and understand with their heart and turn for me to heal them'"* (Is 6:9-10; Mt 13:13-15).

Even his disciples' desertion in the face of the cross was to fulfill Scripture. *"Then Jesus said to them, 'You will all fall away because of me this night; for it is written, 'I will strike the shepherd and the sheep of the flock will be scattered'"* (Zechariah 13:7; Mt 26:31).

All the above demonstrate that Jesus fulfilled what had been told beforehand. In a unique way, many Jewish people built their lives around strict adherence to traditional Jewish writings and Matthew casts Jesus' life as in this tradition.

But in Matthew Jesus also took upon himself the right to interpret Jewish Scripture in ways that fit his ministry. A passage from the Sermon on the Mount contains a statement that refers to Jewish Scriptures but to understand them Jesus maintained that these Scriptures needed further assessment. *"Truly, I say to you, till heaven and earth pass away, not an iota, not a dot, will pass from the law until all is accomplished. Think not that I have come to abolish the law and the prophets. I have come not to abolish them but to fulfil them. Whoever relaxes one of the least of these commandments and teaches men so, shall be called least in the kingdom of heaven. But he who does them and teaches them shall be called great in the kingdom of heaven."* But then he adds, *"I tell you, unless your righteousness exceeds that of the scribes and Pharisees, you will never enter the kingdom of heaven"* (Mt 5:17-20).

Such statements show that Jesus meant to replace certain interpretations and even commands used in Jewish synagogues. Jesus offered five such examples in a series.

... "You have heard that it was said to the men of old, 'You shall not kill and whoever kills shall be liable to judgment.' But I say to you that every one who is angry with his brother shall be liable to judgment, whoever insults his brother shall be liable to the council, and whoever says, 'You fool!' shall be liable to the hell of fire.

... "You have heard that it was said, 'You shall not commit adultery.' But I say to you that every one who looks at a woman lustfully has already committed adultery with her in his heart. It was also said, 'Whoever divorces his wife, let him give her a certificate of divorce.' But I say to you that every one who divorces his wife, except on the ground of unchastity, makes her an adulteress and whoever marries a divorced woman commits adultery.

... "Again you have heard that it was said to the men of old, 'You shall not swear falsely but shall perform to the Lord what you have sworn.' But I say to you, Do not swear at all, either by heaven, for it is the throne of God, or by the earth... And do not swear by your head, for you cannot make one hair white or black. Let what you say be simply 'Yes' or 'No'; anything more than this comes from evil.

... "You have heard that it was said, 'An eye for an eye and a tooth for a tooth.' But I say to you, Do not resist one who is evil. But if any one strikes you on the right cheek, turn to him the other also; and if any one would sue you and take your coat, let him have your cloak as well; and if any one forces you

to go one mile, go with him two miles. Give to him who begs from you and do not refuse him who would borrow from you.

... "You have heard that it was said, 'You shall love your neighbor and hate your enemy.' But I say to you, Love your enemies and pray for those who persecute you so that you may be sons of your Father who is in heaven; for he makes his sun rise on the evil and on the good and sends rain on the just and on the unjust" (5:21-45).

These assertions seem to change Torah Laws. Jesus' freedom to set independent interpretations certainly came to Pharisees' and scribes' attentions in Jerusalem. So they sent a delegation from Jerusalem that said to Jesus, *"'Why do your disciples transgress the tradition of the elders? For they do not wash their hands when they eat.' Jesus answered, 'Why do you transgress the commandment of God for the sake of your tradition? For God commanded, 'Honor your father and your mother' (Exodus 20:12, Deut 5:16), and, 'He who speaks evil of father or mother, let him surely die' (Ex 21:17, Leviticus 20:9). But you say 'If any one tells his father or his mother what you would have gained from me is given to God, he need not honor his father.' So, for the sake of your tradition, you have made void the word of God. You hypocrites! Well did Isaiah prophesy of you, when he said, 'This people honors me with their lips, but their heart is far from me; in vain do they worship me, teaching as doctrines the precepts of men' (Is 29:13). Jesus called the people to him and said to them, 'Hear and understand: not what goes into the mouth defiles a man, but what comes out of the mouth, this defiles a man'"* (Mt 15:1-11).

But the Pharisees were not done with Jesus. *"They came up to him again..., asking, 'Is it lawful to divorce one's wife for any cause?' Jesus answered, 'Have you not read that he who made them from the beginning made them male and female, and said, 'For this reason a man shall leave his father and mother and be joined to his wife and the two shall become one flesh? ... What therefore God has joined together, let not man put asunder' (Genesis 1:27, 2:24). They said to him, 'Why then did Moses command one to give a certificate of divorce and to put her away?' (Deut 24:1-4). He said to them, 'For your hardness of heart Moses allowed you to divorce your wives but from the beginning it was not so. I say to you, whoever divorces his wife, except for unchastity, and marries another, commits adultery'"* (Mt 19:3-8; see 5:32).

At one point, Jesus reduced the commandments to a reasonable whole. *"One came to him, saying, 'Teacher, what good deed must I do to have eternal life?' Jesus said to him..., 'One there is who is good. If you would enter eternal life, keep the commandments.' He said to him, 'Which?' Jesus said, 'You shall not kill, You shall not commit adultery, You shall not steal, You shall not bear false witness, Honor your father and mother, and, You shall love your neighbor as yourself.' Jesus added, 'If you would be perfect, go, sell what you possess and give to the poor, and you will have treasure in heaven. And come, follow me.'"* (Mt 19:16-21). Mark, telling the same story, added that the man went away in despair for *"he had great possessions"* (Mk 10:17-22).

The Sadducees, who did not believe in resurrection, also challenged him. They told him an absurd story (it was meant to be absurd) *"about a woman who had married seven brothers in succession and they all died. Asked the Sadducees, 'Whose wife will she be in the resurrection?' Jesus turned to the Scripture for his answer. 'As for the resurrection of the dead, have you not read what was said to you by God, 'I am the God of Abraham, and the God of Isaac, and the God of Jacob? (Ex 3:6). He is not God of the dead, but of the living'"* (Mt 22:31-32).

Matthew also recorded another of Jesus' statements on the Law, a gracious statement reflecting the milieu from which it came (11:28-30). Many Jewish people considered themselves yoked to the Torah. Jesus took their image but changed it. Two oxen are yoked together, an experienced ox and a young one, he told them. The older one was trained to work in a team but the younger was not. As they worked in a field, the young ox bucked, lunged, and pulled away from the task, so that the yoke cut into the necks of both oxen, making the task burdensome for both. About this situation Jesus said, *"Come to me, all who labor and are heavy laden and I will give you rest. Take my yoke upon you and learn from me; for I am gentle and lowly in heart and you will find rest for your souls. For my yoke is easy, and my burden is light."* Jesus saw the Law as a burdensome yoke; people who struggled under it labored and were heavy laden. But Jesus' *"yoke is easy and his burden is light."* Why? *"Because I am gentle and lowly in heart."*

In all these cases, Jesus offended major Jewish parties (the higher status groups) in Jerusalem—Pharisees, Sadducees, Scribes. Matthew portrays Jesus as "coming out ahead" in his verbal contests with Pharisees over what they considered their greatest strengths, so the Pharisees *"took counsel against him, how to destroy him."* Later, the Sadducees did the same. These two groups were the most well-organized and powerful Jewish parties in Jerusalem. Even if, on his entry into Jerusalem for what was to be his final Passover, *"most of the crowd spread their garments on the road and others cut branches from the trees and spread them on the road and the crowds that went before him and after him sang 'Hosanna to the Son of David! Blessed is he that comes in the name of the Lord!'"* (21:8-9) and even if *"all the city was stirred,"* many seemed perplexed at this spectacle. Jesus may have been the favorite of certain crowds but in the end his conflicts with key organized Jewish parties, allied with the powerful Herodians and Romans, were fatal. The major Jewish parties in Jerusalem, not the people, had their way with Jesus. Later, the Brethren, were thrown out of Jewish life by those who remained faithful to these Jewish parties. In effect the Brethren were shunned, excommunicated, by faithful Jews. They became known as "the poor" who, to survive, needed aid from fellow congregations throughout the Roman Empire (Acts 11:29-30, passim).

Matthew's Account of Jesus' Relationships with Gentiles

Gentiles were not the Jews', or Matthew's, favorites. Nine of the eleven times Matthew mentioned Gentiles, the references carried negative connotations about them. For instance, Matthew recorded that, when Jesus sent out the Twelve, he charged them to, *"Go nowhere among the Gentiles, and enter no town of the Samaritans [the vast majority of whom were Gentiles], but go rather to the lost sheep of the house of Israel"* (10:5-6). No other Gospel has this passage. Moreover, Jesus in effect compared the chief priests and scribes to the Gentiles (Greeks and Romans) due to their collaboration when he told his disciples *"Behold, we are going up to Jerusalem; and the Son of humankind will be delivered to the chief priests and scribes, and they will condemn him to death, and deliver him to the Gentiles to be mocked and scourged and crucified, and he will be raised on the third day"* (Mt 20:18-19).

Matthew also reported, along with Mark (7:25-30), when, near Tyre and Sidon, Jesus was confronted by a woman, *"a Canaanite woman"* (Mark calls her *"a Greek, Syro-Phoenician by birth"*), a Gentile. She begged Jesus to have mercy on her daughter who was severely possessed by a demon. This woman was desperate. Otherwise she, a Gentile, would never approach Jesus, a Jew, to heal her daughter. Nor in any culture at the time was it appropriate for a woman to address a man she did not know and certainly not on an open street as this woman did. But here, in her desperation to seek her daughter's health, this Gentile woman willingly broke down both human barriers.

Matthew enhanced the story compared to Mark. He reported that Jesus at first was reluctant to respond to her desperate plea, *"Have mercy on me, O Lord, Son of David. My daughter is severely possessed by a demon."* Jesus' disciples begged him to *"send her away, for she is crying after us."* Jesus then answered her, *"I was sent only to the lost sheep of the house of Israel."* But *"she knelt before him, saying, 'Lord, help me.' He answered her, 'It is not fair to take the children's bread and throw it to the dogs.' She said, 'Yes, Lord, yet even the dogs eat the crumbs that fall from their masters' table.' She had bested him in argument so he answered her, 'O woman, great is your faith! Be it done for you as you desire.' And her daughter was healed instantly"* (Mt 15:21-28).

Matthew was simply asserting that Jesus, like the Brethren from which this Gospel stemmed, was thoroughly Jewish. Jesus fulfilled what had been presented previously as central in Old Testament Scriptural traditions.

Major Theme: Jesus as the Righteous and Just One

"Righteousness" was a significant Jewish concept. The Biblical definition of righteousness focused on the inherent rightness of God. God is righteous because He is right, therefore God can only act righteously. The Hebrew word for righteousness, *tzedek,* appears more than five hundred times in the Hebrew Bible. It denoted righteousness, just, integrity, equity, straightness. The root of *tseh'-dek* is *tsaw-dak'* which points to an upright, just, straight, innocent, true, sincere person or society.

The 8th centuryBCE prophet Amos called the Hebrew people to righteousness. He used both *mishpat,* justice, and *tzedek,* righteousness, in the same sentence. He saw his society as unjust, serving primarily rich people while neglecting its widows, orphans, poor, and small, indebted farmers. *"Let justice (mishpat) roll down as the waters, and righteousness (tzedek) as a mighty stream,"* he said (5:24). *Mishpat* and *tzedek* could also be verbs—"do justice," "do the right thing." The prophet Micah summed it up as, *"What does the Lord require of us but to do justly, to love mercy, and to walk humbly with our God"* (6:8). In these earlier times, righteousness focused on ethical conduct in and by society. Righteousness became almost a legal term (Lev 19:36; Deut 25:1; Psalm 1:6; Proverbs 8:20). When the guilty were judged, the guiltless were deemed righteous. God's faithfulness to His covenant was a large part of His righteousness (Neh 9:7-8). In God's role as savior, God is a *"righteous savior"* (Is 61) and *"deliverer"* (Is

46:12-13). The righteous trusted that they will be vindicated by the Lord God (Ps 37:12-13).

Abraham was described as righteous as was Moses and David. After David, the character of Job emerged as a chief example of righteousness. Job was introduced as a person *"perfect in righteousness."* This does not mean he was sinless. *"Perfect"* in this sense meant (as in the end of the Sermon on the Mount, Mt 5:48) that Job's righteousness permeated all life's relationships as his working principle. Righteousness was a matter of relationships, with God, the world, other people, and one's self. In one instance the word meant "being right"; in another it meant "doing right"; in still another it meant "putting right." Job qualified as a righteous person on each count, so much so that he was commended by God as *"wholly righteous."*

The Greek words for righteousness, *dikaios* and *dikaiosune,* appear more than two hundred times in the New Testament. Their root, the Greek word *dikai,* means "justice." Seeking *dikai,* according to Plato and Aristotle, was a major aim of Greek life. William Tyndale in his early translation of the New Testament was probably the first person to use the word righteous in the English language. He modeled the word after an earlier old English word, *rihtwis,* which would have yielded the modern English "rightways."

Key issues in Jerusalem's Judaism during Jesus' ministry, as in previous Jewish history according to Matthew, were over "how to be righteous as individuals" as well as "how to be a righteous community." In a context dominated by the Sanhedrin, Pharisees, scribes, and priests, Jerusalem's Jews fell into several contentious groupings over the meaning of righteousness. In essence, Pharisees thought righteousness happened when each person kept details of Torah Law. Sadducees thought righteousness came through priests caring for and sacrificing for all Jews in the Temple and for righteous rulings in the Sanhedrin. Essenes thought it was for healthy men to live in a righteous and loving community separate from the rest of society. Zealots thought righteousness would come only when the political and religious systems were together thoroughly Jewish from top to bottom, without any Roman or Herodian influence or interference. As today, most people were probably much less ideological—they simply wanted to make their way in a kind and fair world with as few disruptions as possible.

Into the mix of these Jewish parties in Jerusalem, came first Jesus and, then, the Hebrew-Christian Brethren party. They had a different vision of righteousness. They were deeply concerned with what it meant to be righteous and initially turned to the Torah for answers. Their Gospel of Matthew showcased these concerns by using or recasting Jesus' statements on righteousness.

A first statement came at Jesus' baptism. An enduring question was why did the exemplary person, Jesus of Nazareth, need to be baptized by John's baptism of repentance for forgiveness of sins? After puzzling the Jesus movement for years, Matthew found what to him (and the Brethren but not the other Gospel writers and their parties) was a satisfactory answer. When Jesus appeared before John to be baptized, Matthew said, *"John would have prevented him, saying, 'I need to be baptized by you and do you come to me?' Jesus answered him, 'Let it be so now; for thus it is fitting for us to fulfil all righteousness.' Then John consented"* (3:14-15). *"To fulfil all righteousness"* means that Jesus embodied righteousness. What Jesus said and did is what it meant to be righteous. No longer would Christians turn to Abraham, Moses, David, or Job as examples of the righteous man. In his person, Jesus *"fulfills all righteousness."* He embodies what is meant by the righteous man. Such a stance by Matthew and the Brethren party in the Jesus movement certainly put them at odds with other Jewish groups in Jerusalem who had different ideas about righteousness.

Twice in the aptly named Sermon on the Mount, Jesus introduced the concept of righteousness. *"Blessed are those who are persecuted for righteousness' sake, for theirs is the kingdom of heaven"* (5:10). Jesus added, *"Do not be anxious, saying, 'What shall we eat?' or 'What shall we drink?' or 'What shall we wear?' …But seek first his kingdom and his righteousness and all these things shall be yours as well"* (6:31-33). This equates the search for the kingdom with righteousness, with pursuing a just cause. Commit to a just cause and God will provide what is needed for living.

Jesus' final parable sums up his meaning of righteousness. *"'I was hungry and you gave me food, I was thirsty and you gave me drink, I was a stranger and you welcomed me, I was naked and you clothed me, I was sick and you visited me, I was in prison and you came to me,' said the king. Then the righteous will answer him, 'Lord, when did we see thee hungry and feed thee, or thirsty and give thee drink? When did we see thee a stranger and welcome thee, or naked and clothe thee? When did we see thee sick or in prison and visit thee?' The King will answer them, 'Truly, I say to you, as you did it to one of the least of these, my brethren, you did it to me'"* (25:35-40). Matthew alone has "King Jesus" narrate this parable to let his followers know finally and completely what righteousness is—meeting the needs of *"the least of these."*

Matthew's Gospel and Rabbinic Judaism

Matthew's concerns with church and congregational organization (chs 14 through 18 with hints elsewhere) focused on questions of worship, theology, ethics, and leadership not found in other Gospels. This interest paralleled a similar movement within Judaism at the time. When the war over Jerusalem between Zealots and Romans ended with Jerusalem's destruction in 70CE, rabbinic leaders settled near Jamnia (called in Hebrew 'Yavneh') near present-day Tel Aviv on the Mediterranean coast. They sought to organize the oral tradition of Judaism into meaningful patterns and to codify Jewish laws and Scriptures focusing largely on families and synagogues rather than the now-destroyed Temple. Matthew showed a similar interest.

Scholars tend to agree that Matthew was writing his Gospel for Christian congregations composed largely of Hebrew people, interpreting Christ to people deeply nurtured in the Old Testament and the five books of Torah Law. This Gospel also showed knowledge of the Jerusalem catastrophe in 70CE and subsequent organizational problems faced by Christian churches after this event. Most likely, this book was composed in the late seventies or early eighties of the first centuryCE by refugees from the Brethren's Jerusalem survivors who went to major cities in the eastern Mediterranean, including Damascus, Antioch, Ephesus, and Alexandria.

Since we believe Matthew's Gospel was most likely written in Alexandria in Egypt and directed largely to a part of the Christian community developing there, it certainly reflected a struggle over introducing the Christian faith into a city, such as Alexandria, that centered on an extensive existing Hellenist-influenced synagogue system. To win this battle, Christians had to establish Jesus' supremacy over Moses, work out how the Gospel related to Torah, affirm Jesus' teaching ministry in a city with the world's first university and its intellectual traditions, and demonstrate the authenticity of Jesus' resurrection. Such theological issues were important in these synagogues as they converted from Jewish to Christian orientations.

In Egypt, Jewish people's history also had to be acknowledged. It had been a place both of Jewish oppression under the ancient Pharaohs and of refuge for Jews during Maccabean and later times. As seen earlier, Matthew's Gospel chose to affirm the latter part of this history, of Jesus in Egypt, rather than the former. All this was played out against the foreground of the bitter struggle in the Jewish sector in Alexandria during a time of Jewish revolt in Judea and Galilee, when Jew fought Jew over the question of actively participating with their homeland comrades in this Hebrew-Roman struggle as Roman power in Alexandria brutally repressed those who supported Jewish rebels. Matthew's Gospel reflects these questions and conflicts.

Matthew, Jewishness, and Egypt

Matthew affirmed a kind of Jewishness that emerged from an intertwined Jewish and Egyptian milieu. Alexandria had been a viable, Hellenistic center for Judaism for several centuries before Jesus was born. Migrations into and out of Egypt, often mediated through dreams (Greek, *ovar*), were important in both Hebrew and Egyptian cultures. Dreams figure significantly in Matthew's Gospel whereas the other Gospels do not even use the word "dream," no less the important stories based on dreams.

The story of Jesus' birth spoke both to a Jewish presence in Egypt and also how dreams played a significant role in relating Hebrews with Egypt. In Matthew's Gospel, Mary's husband Joseph has a character similar to that of Joseph, the son of Jacob, who was *"sold into slavery by his brothers"* but rose to a high place in Egypt's government, just below the pharaoh. Genesis describes Joseph as a man of great integrity who could interpret dreams (40:8-50:26). This was the ability that secured his place in government. Mary's husband, Joseph, had a similar character. He was a just man, unwilling to put Mary to shame even though she had a pregnancy in which he had no part before they married. An angel appeared to him "*in a dream*" and said, *"Joseph, son of David, do not fear to take Mary your wife, for that which is conceived in her is of the Holy Spirit. She will bear a son, and you shall call his name Jesus, for he will save his people from their sins"* (1:18-21). Joseph obeyed the dream, as the earlier Joseph had done, and Jesus became his son.

A second incident about Egypt and dreams is Jesus' family's flight to Egypt. The magi found that Jesus had indeed been born in Bethlehem. But knowing something of King Herod's duplicitous character, they did not return to Jerusalem to tell him where he was and what had happened. Instead, warned by a dream, they departed to their homeland *"by another way."* When Herod learned this, he was furious. Then *"an angel of the Lord appeared to Joseph in a dream and said, 'Rise, take the child and his mother, and flee to Egypt, and remain there till I tell you. For Herod is about to search for the child, to destroy him.' Joseph rose, took the child and his mother by night, departed to Egypt, and remained there until Herod's death"* (2:12-15).

In the decades following Jesus' birth, when war and threats of war emerged in Galilee and Judea in the first centuryCE, many Christ-observant Jews joined their families and co-religionists in Egypt. These passages from Jesus' birth story gave them permission and opened a way for them to do this.

In Matthew's crucifixion story, even Pilate's wife is credited with an important dream. When the governor was sitting on the judgment seat, his wife sent word to him, *"Have nothing to do with that righteous man, for I have suffered much over him today in a dream"* (27:19).

Another Egypt story, built on a phrase in the Sermon on the Mount, has puzzled many New Testament students since they first read it, *"Blessed are the poor in spirit, for theirs is the kingdom of heaven"* (5:3). Kamil (1987: 17) noted this exact phrase was cut into monuments located at the workers' community of Deir el-Medina, the workers' community responsible for preparing pharaohs' tombs. Another such inscription is at the temple of Seti I at Abydos, where the pharaoh is shown bending slightly at the waist before the deity. Even the all-powerful pharaoh was *"poor in spirit."*

Another controversy surrounded the phrase *"in the name of the Father and of the Son and of the Holy Spirit"* (Mt 28:19). Nowhere else in the New Testament is there reference to this trinity. John's Gospel, certainly influenced by Philo of Egypt, came close to saying it when he said, *"Father and Son and the paraclete (Counselor)"* (Jn 14:26). Matthew's phrase on the trinity became a battleground at the Council of Nicea in the fourth centuryCE. Why did Matthew use it? Kamil (1987) and others posit that the phrase was inserted because Matthew was strongly influenced by Egypt. Egyptians often referred to trios of gods—Isis, Osiris, and Horus;

Satis, Anuket, and Khnum; Amun, Mut, and Mentu; Hathor, Menkaure, and Bat. *"Father, Son, and Holy Spirit"* fit with such triads.

That Egypt and Egyptian thinking played important roles in Matthew's Gospel suggests an Egyptian milieu for its author. The destruction of Jerusalem and its Temple in 70CE resulted in another Jewish diaspora to many places in the eastern Mediterranean, including Egypt (Josephus, 94). In Alexandria, Jews were protected to some extent by its *politeuma*, a Jewish government within a city governed and administered from Rome, given to Alexandria's Jews by Julius Caesar in 45BCE when Jews militarily helped him to defeat Pompey. This *politeuma* for Jews in Alexandria was renewed by later Caesars (even if changed somewhat by Claudius in 40CE). Matthew's Gospel could be considered as directed to the Hebrew-Christian community of war refugees that developed in this city after 70CE. It reflected conditions in the church there. An early (but undated) version of this Gospel written in Hebrew was also attributed to having come from Egypt by an early second-century scholar, Pamphilus of Caesarea Maritima, who had lived both in Alexandria and Antioch. The Hebrew version of the Gospel was referred to as the Gospel of MattitYahu (Eusebius, 2012). In contrast to most scholars, we believe Matthew's Gospel was most likely written in Alexandria.

Matthew's Passion Stories

The body of Matthew's text includes two additional sections, the passion story followed by accounts of Jesus' resurrection.

The passion story has much in common with similar narratives in Mark and Luke. It announced that the Passover was coming and the Son of Humankind will be handed over to be crucified (26:2). It tells of the conspiracy to arrest Jesus by stealth and then execute him. The conspirators, chief priests and elders, wanted to wait to carry out their plot until after Passover. But at Bethany Jesus let himself be anointed by an unnamed woman, making Jesus in fact what had been hinted at before—he was the *"Messiah,"* the anointed one, the Christ. After the anointing, Judas went to the chief priests with a plan to betray Jesus.

Then followed Jesus' last supper with his disciples, Jesus praying in Gethsemane, his arrest, the hearing before the chief priest Caiaphas, Peter's three-fold denial, Judas' failure to repent his crime, Peter's repentance, Jesus' trial before Pilate, Pilate's attempt to release Jesus, the charge, *"This is Jesus, the King of the Jews"* in three languages, the sentencing, and the crucifixion.

On the cross, Jesus cried out, *"My God, my God, why hast thou forsaken me!"* then, with another loud cry, breathed his last. At this moment, Matthew (and Mark) reported, the Temple's curtain was torn in two (Mt 27:51; Mk 15:38). A centurion on the cross detail gave the first confession to come from a Gentile, a Roman, *"Truly this man was a Son of God."* Joseph of Arimathea, a disciple, took Jesus' body from the cross, and placed it in his own new tomb. Because Jesus said he would rise again, Matthew alone reported that Pharisees requested Pilate to place a guard over the tomb, which Pilate did (Mt 27:62-66).

Women who witnessed his burial *"from afar"* (27:55, Mk 15:40, Lk 23:49) went to the tomb before dawn two days later and were met by an angel (or one or two "young men"), who invited them to see the place where Jesus was laid. The women were charged to tell the disciples that Jesus had been raised from the dead and was going before them to Galilee. Then Jesus met the women on their way and reinforced the message, *"Tell my brothers to go to Galilee. There they will see me."* The eleven disciples went to Galilee, to the mountain where Jesus had directed them. There Jesus delivered what we know as the Great Commission, *"Go into all the world and make disciples of all the nations (ethne). Baptize them and teach them. And I will be with you to the end of the age"*(Mt 28:16-20).

The Brethren Party and Its Gospel

Because nearly half of all known churches in the first half of the first centuryCE were Brethren in their orientations (our 2011 book: ch 1, Table 1), the Gospel of Matthew was probably the most influential among the four Gospels in the early Jesus movement. This fact probably explains why first century notables put it first in the New Testament. Its five sections, for discipleship, apostleship, church leadership, the mystery of the kingdom of heaven, and of the future ("books" within the book, noted earlier) made it formidable both in bringing so many sources together and also as a handbook for church leaders in dealing with complex issues of the present and future from a Christian perspective.

Distinguishing Christian righteousness from that practiced by contemporary Jews, as well as Gentiles, evident throughout the work, made the book especially important, indeed essential, for Christians as they struggled to find their roles in the first century Roman Empire. Righteousness, in its many facets as Jesus defined it according to Matthew, had a huge impact on both individuals and their communities. Matthew's final conclusion on righteousness as serving the *"least of these my brethren"* gave a concise and essential shorthand for Christian lives. This formulation certainly provided early Christians both a vision to take care of their own in their communities and the courage *"to pray for those who persecute you [and their many enemies who hated them]"* in these very same communities. On these bases alone, Matthew's Gospel certainly deserved the place early church fathers gave it.

Chapter 9

Jesus in the Gospel of Luke: Jesus, the Caring, Compassionate, and Just One

Urban Social Context— Urban Greeks in Smaller Eastern Mediterranean Cities Outside Jerusalem

The Apostles (*Apostolous*, the "sent"), young Diaspora Jews who became Christians, came from urban milieus different from either Galilean or Judean Jews or Judean Hellenists. Their hometowns tended to be smaller Hellenist cities and towns in Hellenist-dominated regions of the Roman Empire scattered throughout the eastern Mediterranean. Of the Apostles' two main leaders, Barnabas was from Cyprus and Paul was from Tarsus (Acts 9:26-27). Luke was from an unknown place in northern Asia Minor and considered himself a friend of Paul's (Acts 16:10 ff, 20:5 ff, 21:1 ff). Timothy, *"whose mother was Jewish and father was Greek,"* was from the area of Derbe and Lystra, small places in Asia Minor (Acts 16:1). The backgrounds, experiences, and viewpoints of these men, these Apostles, tended to align with one another.

In smaller cities and towns, Jews and Christians were definite minorities in a dominant Hellenist culture. Rome officially did not permit people to associate in recognizable "formal" organizations except to enhance their "ancestral religious practices" or their social affiliations (Josephus, 94, 14: 214-215; Barclay, 1996: 64 ff; Kloppenborg, 1996: ch 2). In 45BCE, because of their good deeds for Julius Caesar when they fought against Caesar's enemy Pompey, Julius Caesar gave Jews in Alexandria official dispensation to associate in their synagogues, be exempt from paying certain taxes and from serving in the military, and, within the limits of Roman law, make their own laws for their community (Barclay, 1996: 64 ff). These Jews were granted a *politeuma*, a form of government within a more inclusive government (Neusner, 1975; Barclay, 1996: 64 ff).

In most cities, Christian communities in their *ekklesia* (small "assemblies set apart for special purposes") initially had few protections comparable to the Jews' protection. Rome did not recognize "new" religions for protection if they did not have "ancient roots." Roman officials sometimes denied that Christians had such "ancient roots." Many Diaspora Jews saw Christians coming into their synagogues to convert their members to Christianity, thus they had no incentive to support Christian claims of ancient roots. This situation, along with certain theological differences, also worked against Jewish and Christian cohesion in these urban settings. To demonstrate such ancient roots may be why Gospel writers were so careful to include many references to Old Testament Scriptures in their Gospels. Other types of associations (*phyle, hetairia, kollegion, synedrion, synodos,* etc.), which did not have "ancient" roots, were legally prohibited, even if local officials did not universally enforce these prohibitions (Kloppenborg, 1996: ch 2; Ascough, 2003: ch 1).

Many "voluntary associations" including merchant, craft, trade guilds, ethnic associations, and religious organizations associated with the many Greek and Roman gods were found in larger cities in the Roman world. But associations to extend business or political aims were strictly prohibited under the Empire. Even "teaching" within such associations was heavily scrutinized by Roman officials (Kloppenborg, 1996: 16 ff). Many religious associations, as well as Christians, emphasized equality of men, women, slaves, free men, and even ethnic mixing (Kloppenborg, 1996: 16 ff). Some mystery religions were trans-local, as were Jewish synagogues and Christian *ekklesiai*. But these were exceptions. Rome had outlawed "new religions'" entrance into Roman territories so that Roman officials were suspicious of all trans-local associations, especially of "new Eastern religions," such as the early Jesus movement was deemed to be. Luke's emphases that rich people would find difficulty in entering God's kingdom would also make Christians suspect by Roman and local elites.

"Eating clubs," however, were permitted and even encouraged and many "eating clubs" were available to advance "social life" (Kloppenborg, 1996: 16 ff; see 1 Cor, ch 8). Perhaps this was a legitimate way, and a reason why, Christians so frequently engaged in "fellowship meals" (see 1 Cor 11:20 ff and Crosson, 1998:433-441 on Christian "communal" traditions). Such clubs would encourage people to form "social bonds" and common viewpoints toward their circumstances (Flora and Flora, 2003). These "bonds" worked to Christians' advantages and disadvantages. They would enable Christians to give mutual support to one another. Yet they would also give non-Christians, especially those with more status and power than Christians, a way to become suspicious of Christians, with or without good evidence (see Tacitus, 116, 2013, who claimed Christians, as part of their rituals, "ate the body and blood of someone named 'Chrestos,'" hence accused Christians of cannibalism).

Under these circumstances, many Christians would experience prejudice and discrimination (Barclay, 1996, passim). Judaeo-Christian traditions and Jesus' teachings often set Christians in tense cooperative-competitive relationships with others in the dominant Hellenist-Roman culture. Within such a context, the Apostles' Gospel of Luke was consistent with Jesus' example and Paul's understanding that Christians' *ekklesiai* were intended to be inclusive of Jews, Greeks, slaves, freedmen, men, and women (Gal 3:28). Luke's Gospel also showed concerns with what Rome's leaders would consider radical ideas of extending social justice to disadvantaged people in helping them become part of communities in these cities and towns rather than pariahs in them. For people in this socio-religious context, Luke's Gospel was written.

Themes of Luke's Gospel: Caring Compassion and Social Justice

Two phrases, "caring compassion" and "social justice," summarize Luke's portrait of Jesus in the Apostle's party of the Jesus movement. Luke used the word translated "compassionate" in summarizing the "Sermon on the Plain"—*"Be compassionate (oiktirmones) even as your Father is compassionate"* (6:36; see Borg, 1994, ch 2). Many examples in Jesus' life also point to concerns with social justice, as we will see below.

Oiktirmones was a seldom-used, difficult to translate Greek word that came at the climax of Luke's Sermon on the Plain. In the New Testament, it was used only here and in the Letter of James (5:11). The Greek-English Lexicon by Arndt and Gingrich (1979), gives its meaning as "compassion, heartfelt compassion, pity, mercy." "Mercy" and "compassion" had long histories in the Jewish Bible via the Hebrew word *"hesed."* Translating this word was so difficult that scholars of the Revised Standard Version of the Bible left it as the very last word to be translated. They could find no English equivalent. Finally they settled on "steadfast love," knowing that even this was unsatisfactory.

Breaking the compound word, *oiktirmones*, into its three components, *oik* in various forms refers to "family" or "household," *tir* probably stems from *etairos* meaning "companion" or "friend," and *mone* means "staying with," "abode," or perhaps the root *monos* meaning "alone," "isolated," or "only." Putting these roots together gives the notion of "making a lonely person a friend and bringing this person into a family or household." Another definition could be "staying with or reaching out to a lonely person to make this person a family member." Such a meaning does not translate easily into one word. But it does provide "flesh" to a word like *agape*, love, which was frequently used among Jesus' followers. It also fits with the "reaching out" implied in H. Richard Niebuhr's definition of love as joy in the presence of an "other," gratitude that an "other" accepts a self, respect for the otherness of an "other," and loyalty to this "other" (Niebuhr, et al, 1956: 34 ff). *Oiktirmones* is not an emotion within a person, but is reaching out to others with caring compassion.

The Hebrew word *hesed* appears throughout the Old Testament. The Exodus version of the Ten Commandments used the word. *"I the Lord your God am a jealous God, visiting the iniquity of the fathers upon the third and fourth generation of those that hate me but showing steadfast love (hesed, caring compassion) to the thousands of those who love me and keep my commandments"* (Ex 20:6). The passage overall was harsh; the Hebrews' God demanded that they worship Him alone. Israelites who did not love God hated him. The Old Testament presented no middle ground. But those who loved God kept His commandments and God showed them steadfast love, *hesed, oiktirmones,* caring compassion, throughout generations to come. God is caring and compassionate, treating his people with all the mercy in His heart.

Commandments in Exodus 23 also built on the meaning of *hesed. "You shall not utter a false report. You shall not pervert the justice due to the poor. You shall take no bribe, for a bribe blinds the officials and subverts the cause of those who are in the right. You shall not oppress a stranger; you know the heart of a stranger, for you were strangers in the land of Egypt. For six years you shall sow the land and gather in its yield; in the seventh year you shall let it rest and be fallow, that the poor of your people may eat; and what they leave the wild beasts may eat. You shall do likewise with your vineyard and with your olive orchard"* (23:1-11). No false reports, bribes, oppression of others; show justice, caring compassion to the poor, feed the hungry. This is what Old Testament Law says about *hesed*, "be merciful, be caringly compassionate."

The Psalmist put *hesed* at the heart of his melodies. *"I will sing of thy steadfast love (hesed) forever; for thy steadfast love was established forever, thy faithfulness is firm as the heavens"* (89:1-2). The prophets declared it. Amos proclaimed, *"I hate, I despise your feasts. I take no delight in your solemn assemblies. But let justice roll down like the waters and righteousness like an ever-flowing stream"* (5:21, 24). Micah proclaimed, *"What does the Lord require of you but to do justice, love kindness, and to walk humbly before your God"* (6:8). Terrien (1985) in his translation of Mary's Magnificat calls it "womblike compassion," the compassion a woman has for her unborn child. Jesus put it at the center of his life and ministry. *"Be merciful (hesed), even as your Father is merciful,"* says a key verse in Luke's "Sermon on the Plain" (Lk 6:36). God is *hesed, oiktirmones*, caring, compassionate; therefore be like God.

Purpose of Luke's Gospel

Luke sets out the purpose of his Gospel at its very beginning. *"Inasmuch as many have undertaken to compile a narrative of the things which have been accomplished among us,"* wrote Luke, *"just as they were delivered to us by those who from the beginning were eyewitnesses and ministers of the word, it seemed good to me also, having followed all things closely for some time past, to write an orderly account for you, most excellent Theophilus (lover of God), that you may know the truth concerning the things of which you have been informed"* (1:1-4). Theophilus could have been a generalized "God-lover" who wanted *"a narrative…an orderly account"* about Jesus' life and actions, *"the truth concerning the things of which you have been informed."*

Sources of Luke's Gospel

A compelling question over Luke's Gospel is about his sources of information, *"eyewitnesses and ministers of the word"* who *"delivered to us"* those *"things that have been accomplished among us."* A major source was Mark's Gospel. Luke straightforwardly followed Mark's outline. Yet Luke omitted, for example, Jesus' desire not to be known which figured prominently in Mark. Although many of Luke's stories can be traced to Mark, Luke did not reorganize the material in ways comparable to Matthew's five books of teachings. "Mary's song" was probably part of Brethren worship and liturgies which Luke incorporated. The "angels' songs" to the shepherds were also early church liturgies, whether Brethren or Hellenist is hard to determine. The "beatitudes," instead of being pious aphorisms as in Matthew, described woeful conditions among Galilean peasants' lives and bore a prophet's sense of what God intended to do about them.

The beginning of the Acts of the Apostles, Luke's companion to his Gospel, sets limits on what he intended in his Gospel, namely, to *"deal with all that Jesus began to do and teach, until the day when he was taken up"* (Acts 1:1). Luke turned accounts from many authentic eye-witnesses into an orderly account of Jesus' teachings and actions between his first public appearance and his resurrection. Since Luke was a longtime companion of Paul, Barnabas, and other Apostles (Acts 16:10 ff, 20:5 ff, 21:1 ff), he undoubtedly learned a great deal about Jesus from them and from the Apostles' assemblies, *ekklesiai*, and communities.

John the Baptist's followers provided other information from oral, literary, and liturgical traditions. Luke's Gospel contains precise dating of the beginning of the Baptist's ministry (Lk 3:1-2). Accounts of John's birth to Elizabeth and Zechariah (1:5-25, 39-45) surely came from oral traditions in the Baptist's movement. In Luke's contemporary world such traditions accompanied outstanding men without distinguishing between literary writings, oral traditions, and worship of the man central to them.

Luke clearly drew on many sources—oral traditions that had come to him, Mark's Gospel, perhaps a draft of Matthew's Gospel, traditions in the Baptist's movement, teachings from the Quelle, and material from his own sources. Figure 9 indicates where Luke found most of his material.

One of Luke's own stories was unique among the Gospels. When Jesus was twelve years old, for the first time his parents took him to Jerusalem for Passover. When the feast ended and they were returning home, they could not find him among family and friends. They went back to Jerusalem to look for him. After three days they found Jesus sit-

Luke's Own	Shared With Matthew (Or Quelle)	Shared With Mark	Shared With Matthew And Mark	Traditions From John The Baptist
1:1-4	6:20-49	4:31-44	5:7-39	1:5-25
1:26-56	7:11-8:3	5:11-29	6:1-19	1:57-80
2:1-52	9:57-62	8:19-56	8:8-18	3:1-20
3:21-4:30	18:15-30	9:1-6	9:7-10:36	
5:1-10		21:1-4	18:31-43	
5:12-16			19:29-38	
9:1-18:14			19:45-48	
19:1-28			20:1-47	
19:39-44			21:5-19	
20:20-24			21:23, 25-33	
21:24-38			22:1-23:56	
24:21-12				
24:13-53				

Figure 9   Sources of Material in the Gospel of Luke.

ting among, listening to, and asking questions of teachers in the Temple. When Mary and Joseph saw him they were astonished. His mother said, *"Son, why have you treated us so? Behold, your father and I have been looking for you anxiously."* Jesus responded, *"How is it that you sought me? Did you not know that I must be in my Father's house?"* But he obediently went back with them to Nazareth and *"his mother kept all these things in her heart. And Jesus increased in wisdom and in stature and in favor with God and man"* (2:41-52). Luke alone reported this unique story of Jesus' childhood. Luke alone knew its source.

Luke's genealogy also differs markedly from Matthew's. Matthew traced Jesus' lineage through Israelite parentage. In contrast Luke traced Jesus' lineage back to Adam and to God, *"Being the son (as was supposed) of Joseph, the son of Heli,...the son of Enos, the son of Seth, the son of Adam, the son of God"* (3:23-38). In doing this, Luke gave his Gospel a universal outlook, likely to appeal to Hellenists and Gentiles, the Apostles' party's "target" audiences.

From his sources Luke indicated Jesus was about thirty years old when he began his ministry (3:23). Luke put Jesus in Galilee but does not recount the Baptist's arrest, the event that drove Mark's Gospel. Luke alone told of Jesus' return to Nazareth and his sermon there. This important event described Jesus' ministry as taking its program from the prophet Isaiah (Lk 4:16-30).

Only then, for the first time, did Luke's Gospel start to parallel Mark's. Luke brought Jesus into Capernaum, told of Jesus healing the sick, casting out demons, then going into a deserted place to pray. In each story Luke seemed to be editing material before him (see Lk 4:31-44; 5:17-39). Luke continued to parallel Mark when Jesus called the Twelve, his disciples plucked grain on the Sabbath, and Jesus cured the man with the withered hand (6:1-20).

The story of a mighty catch of fish (Lk 5:1-11) seems suspiciously similar to one in the resurrection stories in John when Jesus instructed the disciples to cast their net on the *"other side"* of the boat and he instructed Simon Peter to feed his sheep (Jn 21:1-19). Did both Gospels use the same source for this story? Parts of Matthew's "Sermon on the Mount" found their way into other places in Luke's Gospel, on salt (Lk 14:34-35), the lamp on a stand (8:16 and 11:33), going before a judge (12:57-59), concerning divorce (16:38), laying up treasure in heaven (12:33-34), the eye as the lamp of the body (11:34-36), serving two masters (16:13), the powerful statement on anxiety (12:22-32), and entering by the narrow gate (13:23-24). The matters of asking, knocking, seeking, and *"requesting son"* are dealt with seriatim (11:9-13).

Two other contrasts are clear. Luke was not interested in disciples' practices of piety (listed in Matthew as giving alms, fasting, and prayer) but may not have known about them except as these questions were raised by Jesus' opponents. Luke also did not include the Lord's prayer early on or Matthew's re-interpretation of the law concerning murder, adultery, and oaths. Matthew included these issues probably because they were matters discussed and decided in local congregations that Matthew knew about and Luke did not. Matthew's re-interpretation of the law was necessary in a setting that included other Jewish people but such issues mattered less to Luke's Hellenist Greek-Gentile-Christian audiences.

Also unique in Luke was Jesus' long journey through Samaria to Jerusalem (Lk 9:51-18:14). On this trip he spoke of the parables of the Good Samaritan (10:29-37), of the barren fig tree, the mustard seed, the leaven (13:6-21), the great supper (14:15-24), the lost sheep, the lost coin, the lost son (15:3-32), the rich man and the poor man Lazarus (16:19-31), and the Pharisee and publican (18:9-14). On the way Jesus taught his disciples how to pray (the abbreviated Lord's prayer, 11:1-4), about the unpardonable sin (12:10), lamented over Jerusalem (13:34-35), met the rich young ruler (18:18-23), entered Jerusalem (19:29-38), and cleansed the Temple (19:45-46). He went on to his death and resurrection.

Two unique resurrection stories are recounted in Luke's Gospel, the story of the meal with the two followers from Emmaus and his command that his followers *"remain in the city of Jerusalem"* (the Apostles' party initially had most, if not all, of its followers in Jerusalem) along with his promise to give them power from on high. *"Then he led them out as far as Bethany and lifting up his hands he blessed them. While he blessed them, he parted from them and was carried up into heaven. And they returned to Jerusalem with great joy and were continually in the temple blessing God"* (24:50-53). Matthew and John have no ascension story. Mark has no location for the ascension other than it happened in the presence of the Eleven (Mk 16:14, 19). Despite being considered a Synoptic Gospel, Luke contains much unique material that seemed relevant and important to his Greek-Gentile-Christian audience.

John the Baptist's Ministry, Precursor to Jesus' Ministry

Compared to Matthew and Mark, Luke looked more intensely at the Baptist's ministry, drawing several implications from it for Jesus' ministry.

One implication is in John the Baptist's birth to a priest named Zechariah and his wife Elizabeth. John was born "miraculously" because Elizabeth was beyond childbearing age. Word of his birth came to Zechariah while he was serving as a priest in the Temple. An angel standing on the right side of the altar of incense appeared and said, *"Do not be afraid, Zechariah, for your prayer is heard and your wife Elizabeth will bear you a son and you shall call his name John. He will go before him in the spirit and power of Elijah to turn the hearts of the fathers to the children and the disobedient to the wisdom of the just to make ready for the Lord a people prepared."*

Luke attributed a song to Zechariah that reputedly contained the first words to come from Zechariah's mouth after he saw the vision of God's messenger in the Temple, doubted

God's word, and was struck dumb. Only after the child was born could he sing again. *"Blessed be the Lord God of Israel for he has visited and redeemed his people and raised up a horn of salvation for us in the house of his servant David...to perform the mercy promised to our fathers and to remember his holy covenant, the oath which he swore to our father Abraham, to grant us that we, being delivered from the hand of our enemies, might serve him without fear, in holiness and righteousness before him all the days of our life. And you, child, will...go before the Lord to prepare his ways, to give knowledge of salvation to his people in the forgiveness of their sins, through the tender mercy of our God, when the day shall dawn upon us from on high to give light to those who sit in darkness and in the shadow of death, to guide our feet into the way of peace"* (1:68-79).

The song's first part faithfully recites what God has done in the past, for visiting and redeeming his people, *"to turn... the disobedient to the wisdom of the just"* (1:17, 68-75). By his prophets God promised to save his people from their enemies, to grant mercy to the people, and to remember his holy covenant with them. The song related this covenant to Abraham, a universal prophet, rather than to Moses, a Hebrew prophet. God promised Abraham that *"in thee . . . all the families of the earth shall seek one another's welfare"* (Gen 12:1-5; Terrien's translation, 1985: 155). By seeking one another's well-being instead of their own gains, all people on earth shall live without fear of one another, serve God in holiness and righteousness all the days of their lives, and find peace. This message applied to all, whether Greek, other Gentile, or Hebrew. The song says that *"the horn [the means] of salvation"* shall come from the house of David.

The second part, addressed to the child John (the name means "God has been gracious") gave him a detailed job description as God's prophet.

- He will go before the people to prepare the ways of the Lord

- He will give knowledge of salvation to the people
- He will offer forgiveness of sins through God's tender mercy
- When God brings the new day to give light to those who sit in darkness, in the shadow of death, he will guide people's feet to the way of peace.

"Peace," eirenes in Greek (as in Irene), is an important concept in Luke's Gospel. Promised here and in the angel's song at Jesus' birth, Jesus' birth brought peace to the aged Simeon and in his maturity Jesus brought peace to a woman *"who had a flow of blood for 12 years"* (Mk 5:25). Jesus died, so Luke believed, to bring peace to Jerusalem. In his resurrection, Jesus said to his disciples, *"Peace be with you."* This *"peace"* is the "shalom of God." God brings well-being to all people. Luke believed that in Jesus this peace had come.

Luke carefully noted the year of the Baptist's appearance in the wilderness. *"It was the fifteenth year of the reign of Tiberius Caesar, Pontius Pilate was governor of Judea, Herod was tetrarch of Galilee, his brother Philip was tetrarch of the region of Ituraea and Trachonitis, Lysanias was tetrarch of Abilene in the high priesthood of Annas and Caiaphas"* (3:1-2). This would make John the Baptist appear in the year 29CE.

Luke gives a more complete view of the Baptist's ministry than either Matthew or Mark. Luke saw the Baptist as an Old Testament prophet, *"You brood of vipers!"* John said. *"Who warned you to flee from the wrath to come? Bear fruits that befit repentance (metanoeia) and do not begin to say to yourselves, 'We have Abraham as our father.' I tell you, God is able from these stones to raise up children to Abraham. Even now the axe is laid to the root of the trees. Every tree therefore that does not bear good fruit is cut down and thrown into the fire. His winnowing fork is in his hand to clear his threshing floor and to gather the wheat into his granary but the chaff he will burn with unquenchable fire"* (Lk 3:7-9, 17).

Luke reported that John taught the crowds like one of the prophets. The multitudes asked him, *"'What shall we do?'*

John answered, 'He who has two coats, let him share with him who has none; and he who has food, let him do likewise.'" When tax collectors came to be baptized saying, *"Teacher, what shall we do?"* John said, *"Collect no more than is appointed you."* To soldiers asking the same question, John said, *"Rob no one by violence or by false accusation and be content with your wages"* (3:11-14).

Most importantly for Jesus' ministry, the Baptizer John announced the coming of the Messiah. *"I baptize you with water. He who is mightier than I is coming, the thong of whose sandals I am not worthy to untie. He will baptize you with the Holy Spirit and with fire"* (3:16).

John reproached the tetrarch Herod Antipas for *"all the evil things he has done"* (Lk 3:19) including divorcing his wife, Phasaelis, the daughter of King Aretus IV of Nabatea, who, in retaliation for his daughter shamefully being returned to him, started a war with the Jews (Herod Antipas, 2012). Antipas then married Herodias, the former wife of his brother Philip. For these things, Antipas *"shut up John in prison"* (3:20).

Luke reported that Jesus later told his followers of his high regard for John. *"What did you go out into the wilderness to behold? A reed shaken by the wind? What then did you go out to see? A man clothed in soft clothing? ... A prophet? Yes, I tell you, and more than a prophet. This is he of whom it is written, 'Behold, I send my messenger before thy face, who shall prepare thy way before thee.' I tell you, among those born of women none is greater than John"* (7:24-28).

Later, Luke's Gospel reported that John represented the end of an old age and the beginning of a new age. *"The law and the prophets were until John. Since then the good news of the kingdom of God is preached and every one enters it violently"* (16:16). The Greek word for "violently" is *diazetai*, meaning "disjoined, breaking." Another translation, then, might be, *"and every one enters it with a thorough break from the past."* The break happened in John. He was the transition to Jesus who brought in a new future. No one had as much influence on Jesus' ministry as did John the Baptist. John's sense of social justice foretold Jesus'.

Themes in Luke's Gospel: Jesus' Compassionate and Caring Social Justice

In Luke, Jesus' ways of treating people, what we call his social justice policies, were built on the principle of a non-violent, peaceful prophetic campaign with a hallmark of caring, compassion, respect, and human dignity (what today is called social justice) for all persons, especially the disadvantaged in their communities. More than any other Gospel, Luke includes at least six long sections that introduce these policies.

Social Justice in the Annunciation of Jesus' Birth

Mary's song, labeled "The Magnificat," talks of God's justice and mercy. The song was written first in Hebrew, then translated into Greek (Lk 1:47-55). Samuel Terrien (1985: 146-153), explores the Hebrew ideas behind the Greek words. He begins by providing a new translation of the song, parts of which we will comment on.

"My whole being celebrates the grandeur of the Lord." To translate this sentence as "magnifies the Lord," said Terrien (1985), gives the wrong impression. A human being cannot make God great. The Hebrew word refers to "celebrating." Mary celebrates, praising God with her flesh leaping with new life, her womb quickened with the child. In her whole being Mary fleshes out God's greatness.

"My spirit thrills in God my salvation." The verb, *egalliase*, "exults, thrills" implies a shriek of delight, a primal scream, the shriek at the nearness of God's presence. It connotes the whirl of a dance or sexual ecstasy.

"God has looked upon the lowliness of his woman-slave. Behold! On this account, all generations shall proclaim my hap-

piness." The Hebrew verb for "proclaim" comes from a root that means "to go forward, to race toward a goal, to lead the way, purposefulness." "Happiness" in Hebrew is never individualistic—it spreads and catches on in a community. A person is not happy alone but when sharing happiness with others.

"Because God has done great things (megaleia) for me, the woman-slave," "Megaleia" refers to God's huge interventions in history, through deliverance from Egypt, giving the covenant, bringing Judah home from exile, disclosing Israel's mission to humankind. Mary's song updates these events. God has done great things for me, the woman-slave. Christians, too, for whom the Gospel was written were aware of these *"great things."* They said, God has drawn near, has revealed his love toward humankind, has saved humankind from sin and despair, and has filled hearts with joy, hope, and assurance of eternal life.

"And his womb-like compassion (eleous, not *oiktirmones) shall be from generation to generation toward those who fear him."* Terrien gives a new translation to the nearly untranslatable word for "mercy," *eleous,* a word Terrien also translates as *"womb-like compassion,"* Another dictionary translates *eleous* by adding the word "piteous" to mercy and compassion. This word then suggests that God the father has a mother's regard for her child. She bears the child and nurtures it. She treasures what the child does. She rejoices in the child's successes and weeps at the tragedies that befall her child. God treats all humankind in this manner, says Terrien in this daring translation.

"God has dispersed the proud into the imagination of their hearts, deposed the potentates from their thrones, and exalted the humble. He has filled the hungry with good things, and the rich he has dismissed empty-handed." This passage in Luke's first chapter, at Jesus' birth, introduces into the early Jesus movement the prophets' passion for what we now call "social justice." It theologically critiques, negatively, any political system that favors the rich at the expense of the poor. In

sixth-centuryBCE tradition, Luke asserts from the beginning that wealth accumulated by the proud for the proud alone is for naught.

Mary's song then picks up a main theme from Isaiah of Babylon (the name given to chapters 40 to 53 in Isaiah; Isaiah with his people prior to 540BCE was in exile in Babylon). In this song *"the man-slave,"* Israel, now becomes Jesus, the slave-boy of God. "Placed in the mouth of Mary, the mother of Jesus," says Terrien, "the motif of the suffering servant unites Judaism and Christianity. God suffers on Calvary and through all the holocausts, Christian as well as Jewish, in the course of the ages (we add Muslim, Buddhist, Hindu, Shinto, animist, etc. as well). The church is the company of those who suffer and still hope for a better world."

Another statement rounds out the account of Mary's Song. Walter Brueggemann supplied it. We need to remember, he wrote, how completely "Jesus enacted his mother's song. Everywhere he went he broke the vicious cycles of poverty, bondage, fear, death; he healed, transformed, empowered, brought new life. Jesus' example gives us the mandate to transform our public life" (1999: 345).

Social Justice in the Location of Jesus' Birth: "A greater than Caesar is here"

Social justice was also set in Luke's announcement of Jesus' birth. In Luke's Gospel this story breathes an atmosphere of reverence and grace. As with much of every Gospel, most likely the story was originally spoken in an oral tradition, then written in Aramaic, the native language in and around Jerusalem and the language Jesus spoke. Someone soon translated the story into Greek so Greek-speakers in the Jesus movement could hear it as well.

"In those days a decree went out from Emperor Augustus that all the world should be registered" (2:1). *"Emperor Augustus"* was born September 23, 63BCE and lived until August 19, 14CE. His given name was Octavian. He was son of a senator

and a nephew of Julius Caesar. Through a series of wars, Octavian welded the various regions of the Roman world into one Empire. His wars eventually brought relative peace and prosperity to the Empire, the famous "Pax Romana," Roman Peace. In 9BCE an altar was dedicated to Augustus's peace. In 17BCE the new golden age was celebrated by secular games and heralded by poets and statesmen alike, ancient monuments, like the one in the town of Priene in the Roman province of Asia, even gave him the title "savior." In 27BCE, the Roman Senate declared him Rome's first emperor, giving him the name "Augustus, the Exalted One." Augustus was emperor when Jesus was born, but his adopted son, Tiberius, was emperor when John the Baptist and Jesus began their ministries.

"All the world should be registered. This was the first registration and was taken while Quirinius was governor of Syria." Scholars used to say that the enrollment under Quirinius took place about 6CE and that Luke was incorrect to associate this enrollment with Jesus' birth. But recent scholarship has shifted in Luke's favor when an Egyptian papyrus in the British Museum was re-translated. The re-translation recognized that in 103-104CE a census in Egypt was apparently taken on a kinship basis. A proclamation in it declared that all who were residing elsewhere should return to their family homes (Wright, 1961: 235). Information culled from other sources indicated that such registration periods took place every twelve to fourteen years and were often strongly resisted so that many such censuses took years to complete. Thorley noted that Luke's text could refer to either of two enrollments at this time (1979: 81). The second census took place around 6CE but the "first registration" probably took place a dozen years earlier, around 6BCE. This latter date matches the approximate date of Jesus' birth.

"All went to their own towns to be registered. Joseph also went from the town of Nazareth in Galilee to Judea, to the city of David called Bethlehem, because he was descended from the house and family of David. He went to be registered with Mary, to whom

he was engaged and who was expecting a child." Bethlehem meant "House of Bread," taking its name from the fairly fertile Judean area where it was located. Most Judean regions are hilly and barren, just like areas of Sinai, Moab, and the Negev. But wheat, figs, and olives grew and still grow in Bethlehem setting it apart from nearby areas. Bethlehem was also the home of David, the greatest of Israel's kings.

In the Mideast, "to be engaged" spoke of a formal service prior to marriage. To break an engagement was equivalent to a divorce. The couple did not live together during this time but was bound by sacred oath to continue the engagement into marriage. For Mary, pregnancy during the engagement was, to say the least, unusual. Matthew's Gospel raised Joseph's perplexity over the issue and whether Joseph should divorce her. He decided not to take this step. When the child was born, he named it. When a father named a child, he accepted the child as his own.

"While they were there, the time came for her to deliver her child. And she gave birth to her firstborn son and wrapped him in bands of cloth and laid him in a manger because there was no place for them in the inn." The "inn" was probably not really an inn. An article in *Jerusalem Perspective* (6, 1991: 8) said that in Jesus' time a typical inn had one room with no allowance for separating men from women. Mideastern inns were known for their hospitality but also for abuses that took place in them, especially robbery.

The Greek word, *kataluma,* mistranslated "inn," means "a guest chamber." The same word is used for the place where, decades later, Jesus held his last supper with his disciples in Jerusalem. A *kataluma* was an "add-on" room usually constructed on a Palestinian house's flat roof. Because no space was available in the *kataluma,* Mary gave birth to Jesus on the ground floor. The ground floor was shared by a house's other inhabitants, with their donkeys, sheep, and goats. A manger, probably made of hardened clay or rocks, was built into the house's first floor. The infant Jesus was placed temporarily in such a manger. The manger may have been mentioned in Luke's story because of a prophecy in Isaiah, *"The ox knows its owner and the donkey its owner's manger but Israel does not know, my people do not understand"* (Is 1:3). Placing Jesus in a manger is another indication that those to whom he came did not know who he was.

"In that region there were shepherds living in the fields, keeping watch over their flock by night." Usually in August and September when lambs were being born, shepherds lived with their sheep in the fields. Scholars have given different interpretations of a shepherd's vocation. Bishop said shepherds were vital, and honored, in Palestine (1964: 401-413). But Temme viewed shepherds among society's outcasts (1991: 376-378). If outcasts, their presence at Jesus' birth would be the equivalent of associating with sinners. Whether to honored members of society or to outcasts, Jesus' birth was proclaimed to humble people. David, of course, was also a shepherd boy in Bethlehem. Shepherds' presence at Jesus' birth reminded everyone that Jesus was a son of David. Shepherds were watching over their flocks on the night David's heir was born in David's city.

"Then an angel of the Lord stood before them and the glory of the Lord shone around them and they were terrified. But the angel said to them, 'Do not be afraid; for see—I am bringing you good news of great joy for all the people: to you is born this day in the city of David a Savior, who is the Messiah, the Lord. This will be a sign for you: you will find a child wrapped in bands of cloth and lying in a manger'" (Lk 2:10-12).

"Euaggelizomai humin charan megalan...soter" (*"I bring good news to you of joy great...a savior"*) were among the most repeated words in the early Jesus movement. *Charan* ("ch" is the letter Chi, or X, in Greek) is the noun connected with the imperative verb, *chairete*. These words echo the *"chairete"* of the Athenian victory over the Persians. It was also used at Jesus' resurrection. The words echo, too, the portrayal of Emperor Augustus' reign when he was praised by his poets and playwrights and called "savior." Now one greater than Augustus is born, greater than the Emperor of the whole world. In the

four Gospels, the "angel's song" of Luke contains the only use of the title *soter*, *"savior,"* applied to Jesus.

The word *kurios*, *"Lord,"* is used in both the New and Old Testaments to describe God himself. In Roman and Hebrew worlds, the Lord was also the chief, the *kurios*, the *pater familias* in Latin, of an extended household that included all relatives, servants, and slaves. In the New Testament from this time, on all things said about God as Lord are now transferred to Jesus Christ as *kurios*, Lord of humankind.

The shepherds were given a strange sign. The cry of a baby, the age-worn trough of stone, the bands of cloth, swaddling clothes to wrap him—no one would expect to find a *soter*, deliverer, here. But then, no one expected to find a deliverer covered with a linen shroud deposited in a rock-hewn tomb where Luke placed him at the end of his Gospel. The person who emerges from the stone manger also rises from a stony tomb to deliver God's people, as the hymnist said, "from sin and error pining."

"And suddenly there was with the angel a multitude of the heavenly host, praising God and saying, 'Glory to God in the highest heaven and on earth peace among those whom he favors!'" (2:8-9). Glory and peace accompany God when He visits His people. These words promised that they will accompany those who follow Christ and find God's peace in him. Christ will fill his people with God's gracious goodwill.

Where is the social justice in this story? It is everywhere.

- Jesus' birth was not a local occurrence but had worldwide significance.
- Emperor Augustus was said to bring peace and justice to the world; poets and playwrights saluted Augustus' reign. Jesus' birth would result in *"Good news of great joy for all people."*
- The emperor was called "savior." Now a greater than Augustus is born, one greater even than the Emperor

of the entire world. Jesus, not Augustus, is the world's *"soter."*

- Augustus' "golden age" gives way to Jesus' "golden age." Augustus brought a Roman version of peace and order built on war and domination. Without violence and without dominance over the poor and helpless, Jesus brings God's peace and God's justice.
- He who would feed the poor and care for the starving was born in Bethlehem, which meant "House of Bread."
- The birth took place in utter poverty and was announced first to the poor and outcasts.
- One greater than David is born in David's city.
- This child will be called Messiah, *christos*, the anointed, and, *kurios*, Lord.
- God' glory and God's peace will accompany him wherever he goes.

Luke's themes speak of Jesus' commitment to the poor, homeless, and vulnerable. Who was more vulnerable than Mary, a poor teenager, not yet married, pregnant with her first child? Or the widow Anna who was reduced to living in the Temple itself because she had no one to care for her? Or the old man, Simeon? He greeted the child, *"Lord, now let thy servant depart in peace, according to thy word; for mine eyes have seen thy salvation, a light for revelation to the Gentiles, and for glory to thy people Israel"* (Lk 2:29-32). The word *ethne*, is translated here as *"Gentiles."* More accurately it could be translated, "all ethnics" or "all people." By including the word *"Gentiles"* (*ethne*), Luke's birth story contrasts significantly with the birth story in Matthew's Gospel and speaks directly to a Greek-Gentile constituency, the Apostles' constituency.

Social Justice in Nazareth's Synagogue

Early on, Luke (as well as Mark) put Jesus in his hometown synagogue (Lk 4:14, 21). Being about eight miles from

Sepphoris, the region's main city of 8,000 to 10,000 people, and about five or six miles from Cana's home to Mary's relatives, Nazareth's population was about 400 people in Jesus' lifetime. Sepphoris, an inland city, was the capital of Galilee until Herod Antipas built Tiberias on the Sea of Galilee (see Fig 1, Map). When Jesus lived in Nazareth, Sepphoris was being re-built as a sophisticated, Greek-speaking Hellenist city with colonnaded paved streets, multi-storied buildings, and water installations with cisterns under the streets. Galilee was ruled and taxed from Sepphoris (Horsley, 1996: 108-111). Its reach extended into Nazareth and other of the approximately 204 villages in this part of Galilee. Strangely, the important city of Sepphoris, which controlled the destinies of so many Galileans, is not mentioned even once in the New Testament.

Synagogues were more than places of worship in Galilee's small villages. They may have been in structures designed to be synagogues or in a home or other kind of multi-purpose building (Galilee, 2013). They were also marketplaces for buying and selling goods, meeting places for commercial and political discussions and activities, and provided some governmental functions. As long as taxes were paid, Galilee's villages were not closely scrutinized by Roman authorities. Galilee's synagogues, then, could become places from which even revolts against Roman authorities could be surreptitiously plotted. Duties of a synagogue's attendant, called a *Hazzan*, ranged from teaching children, to taking a Scripture roll from the ark, and to returning it there (Bible Knowledge Accelerator, 1995-96; Gilmour, 1952).

Luke reports that Jesus went to the synagogue *"as his custom was."* This phrase is used only twice in the Gospels, here and when Jesus went to the Garden of Gethsemane. Both times it related to Jesus praying. Jesus regularly went to the synagogue, a center of religious worship and political activities, where he learned in depth about both sets of duties.

Worship in Palestinian synagogues consisted of recitations from the *Shema* (*"Hear, O Israel, the Lord our God, the Lord is one"*), a prayer, a fixed reading from the Law, and a free reading from the Prophets. The Torah—the Law, the Five Books of Moses—was read in its entirety in a period of 3 years (Gilmour, 1952: 90). Since the synagogue had no officiating officer, an invitation to read and preach could be extended to any member of the congregation or even any visitor (such as, later, Paul in Acts 13:14 ff).

Jesus chose as his "free reading from the Prophets" a passage from Isaiah (61:1 ff). Being deep in the scroll, this passage was not easy to find, recognized only as the scroll unrolled. Finding such a reading implies that Jesus, like many adult Jews, could read the text in Hebrew. Jesus, then, was literate in reading Hebrew, probably in Aramaic, and perhaps some Greek since he lived so close to Sepphoris, a Greek-speaking city where, being carpenters, he and his father might have worked as the city was being re-built. The Greek he learned would have been commoners' (*koine*) Greek.

From the Isaiah passage Jesus saw a job description for his own mission, *"to preach good news to the poor, to proclaim release to the captives and recovering of sight to the blind, to set at liberty those who are oppressed, to proclaim the acceptable year of the Lord" (Isaiah 61:1-2;* Lk 4:18-19). God's saving will for his people became the theological basis for Jesus' proclamation of good news to the poor. In Isaiah the *"poor"* and *"captives"* included both enslaved captives of Hebrews and fellow Israelites reduced to slavery through debt (Deut 15:1-2). The latter were to be released after seven years (which may not have happened). The command to let the land lay fallow every seventh year likewise served the poor (Ex 23:10-11). Already in the Ten Commandments, the prohibition of theft proscribed kidnapping and selling fellow Israelites into slavery. The command of Sabbath rest pertained to both slaves and free persons—the first commandment implied the liberation of all Israelites. Jesus' ministry was to be one of justice and redress in behalf of those most hurt by his society, the poor, the captive, the blind, the slave, and the oppressed.

Luke's Gospel brings together salvation and service. In this Gospel, disadvantaged individuals were to receive service from others. Luke also calls for re-dressing, what we would call "re-structuring," Jesus' current society in ways that would not force people into being disadvantaged and oppressed. Jesus was eager that these conditions become more humane and society become more caring, more compassionate. The needs of human beings were matched by the need for people in society to act compassionately and caringly in a culture that favored the rich, men, and slave-owners over all others.

Martin Luther King, Jr., preached on and updated Isaiah's prophecy on *"the year of the Lord"* (Lischer, 1995: 235-236).

> "The acceptable year of the Lord is any year
>   when men and women decide to do right.
> The acceptable year of the Lord is any year
>   when people will stop throwing away the precious
>   lives that God has given them in riotous living.
> The acceptable year of the Lord is that year
>   when people in Alabama will stop killing
>   civil rights' workers.
> The acceptable year of the Lord is that year
>   when every knee shall bow and every tongue confess
>   the name of Jesus, and everywhere
>   people will cry, Hallelujah, Hallelujah!"

Jesus said to the people, *"Today this scripture has been fulfilled in your hearing,"* "Today, in my ministry, the kingdom of God is active among you in a new way. God will bring good news to the poor, God will release the captives, God will restore sight to the blind, God will set at liberty those who are oppressed. God has set me to this task, and I accept it, come what may."

Social Justice in Jesus' Relation to John the Baptist

Jesus revealed his priorities for healing when his healing power came to the attention of John the Baptist. *"John [the Baptist], calling to him two of his disciples, sent them to the*

Lord, saying, 'Are you he who is to come, or shall we look for another?'...In that hour Jesus cured many of diseases and plagues and evil spirits, and on many that were blind he bestowed sight. He answered them, 'Go and tell John what you have seen and heard: the blind receive their sight, the lame walk, lepers are cleansed, and the deaf hear, the dead are raised up, the poor have good news preached to them. Blessed is he who takes no offense at me'" (Lk 7:18-23).

At first glance, Jesus' words seem only to summarize the kind of healing that he performed. But another look shows Jesus' systematic purpose in his healings. Since John the Baptist's parents were old (his father said, *"I am an old man, and my wife is advanced in years,"* 1:18), when John the Baptist was a boy, he might have been raised in the Essenes' Qumran community, not far from the spot where John carried out his ministry, preaching and baptizing. This celibate community continued to grow and thrive both because many pious men were attracted to its communal life but also because this community took in and raised orphans. If John were an orphan, he may have been raised according to Qumran rules. Beyond such speculation, we know that the Baptist was much influenced by Qumran. John preached in an area not far from it and his message was derived from its most important Scripture, Isaiah 40:3. John quoted these words as a preface to his preaching, *"Behold, I send my messenger before thy face, who shall prepare thy way. The voice of one crying in the wilderness: Prepare the way of the Lord, make his paths straight!"* (3:4). Jesus may have had in mind the influence of this community over John when he said, *"Tell John what you have heard and seen."*

Both Jesus and John knew of Qumran's exclusionary policies (Dead Sea Scrolls, 1998). Its regulatory code said that no one who was blind, lame, deaf, or a leper could be members. The lame were excluded because they might trip over the community's sacred artifacts, the blind because they could not read for themselves the community's sacred books, the deaf because they could not hear the angels sing, and lepers because their disease could contaminate both the community's men and grounds. These were exactly the diseases Jesus set himself to eliminate, *"the blind receive their sight, lame walk, lepers are cleansed, the deaf hear."* Jesus intended to heal the diseases that kept men and women from the communities of every man and woman. He was preparing them to fill their rightful places in God's caring communities.

Social Justice in the Sermon on the Plain

The opening of the "Sermon on the Plain" is a prophetic statement in which Jesus describes what God is doing in the world. These statements became Jesus' program for dealing with these issues (6:20-26).

> *Blessed are you poor, for yours is the kingdom of God.*
> *Blessed are you that hunger now, for you shall be satisfied.*
> *Blessed are you that weep now, for you shall laugh.*
> *Blessed are you when men hate you, and when they exclude you and revile you, and cast out your name as evil, on account of the Son of Humankind!*
> *Rejoice in that day, and leap for joy, for behold, your reward is great in heaven; for so their fathers did to the prophets.*
> *Woe to you that are rich, for you have received your consolation.*
> *Woe to you that are full now, for you shall hunger.*
> *Woe to you that laugh now, for you shall mourn and weep.*
> *Woe to you, when all men speak well of you, for so their fathers did to the false prophets.*

Luke saw Jesus describing the life conditions under which most men and women lived in his time—poor, hungry, often weeping. Luke said these conditions will change by God's work in Jesus' ministry. Further, said Luke, only a prophet can pronounce *"blessings"* and *"woes."* In doing this Jesus was acting as the quintessential prophet.

Social Justice in Jesus' Trials before his Death Sentence: Jesus' Enemies Understanding of Him

The only statement in Luke's Gospel that described Jesus' ministry from the viewpoint of those who opposed him came during Jesus' trial. Luke provided what was probably the exact charge against him, *"We found this man perverting our nation and forbidding us to give tribute to Caesar and saying that he himself is Christ a king"* (23:2). These three charges pitted Jesus against both Jewish and Roman policies. The charge from the Jews was *"perverting our nation."* The charge from the Romans was *"forbidding us to give tribute to Caesar."* Both joined in charging him with *"saying that he himself is Christ a king."* Each charge was considered treason for which the penalty was death.

These charges were valid. Although Jesus did not seek the title *"Christ,"* both his followers and opponents forced it on him. His anointing by Lazarus' sister, Mary (in John's Gospel), or an "unknown" woman (in Mark and Matthew) in Bethany, supported this charge. Jesus did not explicitly claim to be king but was widely known as a Son of David. Luke recognized this by recording that his birth took place in King David's city. At least implicitly Jesus spoke of his facilitating role in bringing about *"the kingdom of God."* The charge of *"forbidding tribute to Rome"* was based on his admonition, *"Render unto Caesar the things that are Caesar's and to God the things that are God's"* (20:25). Though he paid taxes with borrowed money (Mt. 17:24-27), suspicions against him were widespread. The charge of *"perverting the nation,"* stemmed from his attack on the Temple, a national shrine, as his first public act of ministry. This action loomed large to both Jewish and Roman authorities. Without question, Jesus wanted a structurally re-formed Judaism that would initiate caringly compassionate (*oiktirmones*) changes in Jewish and Roman imperial practices (on such "structures," see Crosson, 1998: 342 f). Although Luke alone noted this charge, by describing Jesus' pursuit of social justice in such detail, his Gospel supported it. Jewish authorities saw Jesus as a threat and clearly wanted him removed from the scene. Pilate was a willing accomplice; his reluctance feigned.

Implementing his Inclusive Social Justice Policies in Ministering to the Vulnerable, His Priorities in Healing— Women, the Poor, Slaves, Children, Samaritans, Captives

A major reason to support Luke as the Apostles' Gospel is that its companion volume, The Acts of the Apostles, features Paul as the apostle par excellence. Values affirmed in the Apostles' party of Acts and Paul were also affirmed in Luke's Gospel. The Apostles' charter treated all equally— *"neither Jew nor Greek; slave nor free; male and female; you are all one in Jesus Christ"* (Galatians 3:27-28); *"And all who believed were together and had all things in common"* (Acts 2:44). In an otherwise male- and wealth-dominated society, the Apostles worked to establish communities in which men had no priority over women, nor rich over poor, nor free over slaves. Celebrating the Lord's Supper in their *ekklesiai* featured men and women sitting together around a table along with Gentiles, Jews, free persons, and slaves. The Gospel of Luke mirrors this value of inclusiveness (see also *"Blessed are you when men…exclude you"*; Lk 6:22).

In Luke, Jesus told at least a dozen stories that focused on women, especially widows, among the most vulnerable women. When Jesus was an infant, the widow Anna, the daughter of Phanuel of the tribe of Asher and a prophetess, heard of his birth. *"She was of a great age, having lived with her husband seven years from her virginity, and as a widow till she was eighty-four. She did not depart from the temple but worshiped with fasting and prayer night and day. Coming up at the very hour that Jesus' parents brought him into the temple, she gave thanks to God and spoke of him to all who were looking for the redemption of Jerusalem"* (2:36-38).

A widow was also central in a Jesus parable. Luke said, *"In a certain city there was a judge who neither feared God nor regarded man. And there was a widow in that city who kept coming to him and saying, 'Vindicate me against my adversary.' For a while he refused. Afterward he said to himself, 'Though I neither fear God nor regard man, yet because this widow bothers me, I will vindicate her or she will wear me out by her continual coming.'"* Jesus said, *"Hear what the unrighteous judge says. And will not God vindicate his elect, who cry to him day and night? Will he delay long over them?"* (18:1-8).

Much of Jesus' healing involved women. Simon's mother-in-law was ill with a high fever. People sought him for her, he stood over her, and rebuked the fever (4:38-39). Another time, Jairus, a ruler of the synagogue had an only daughter, about twelve years old who was dying. He sought Jesus but, while they were speaking, word came to them that the girl had died. *"Jesus said, 'Do not fear. Only believe. She shall be well.' Coming to the house, Jesus took her by the hand and said, 'Child, arise.' Her spirit returned, and she got up at once. Jesus directed that something should be given her to eat"* (4:48-55).

Yet another woman had a flow of blood for twelve years and could not be healed by anyone. She came up behind Jesus, touched his garment, and immediately her flow of blood ceased. Jesus said, *"'Who was it that touched me?' When all denied it…, Jesus said, 'Someone touched me for I perceive that power has gone forth from me.' When the woman…,trembling and falling down before him, declared in the presence of all the people why she had touched him and how she had been immediately healed, Jesus said to her, 'Daughter, your faith has made you well; go in peace'"* (4:43-48). Instead of being called "woman," Jesus now addressed her by the tender name *"Daughter."*

In another instance, Jesus was teaching in a synagogue on the Sabbath when he came upon a bent-over woman who had not been able to fully straighten out for about eighteen years. When Jesus saw her, he called her and said, *"'Woman, you are freed from your infirmity.' He laid his hands upon her, and immediately she was made straight, and she praised God"* (13:10-13). Jesus cast out *"seven demons"* from Mary Magdalene and healed the infirmities of *"Joanna the wife of Chuzas, Herod's steward, and Susanna, and many others"* (8:2).

Jesus was concerned about life conditions faced by widows. Near the city gates of Nain, a man who had died was being carried out, *"the only son of his mother and she was a widow. When the Lord saw her, he had compassion on her and said to her, 'Do not weep.' He touched the bier, and the bearers stood still. He said, 'Young man, I say to you, arise.' The dead man sat up, and began to speak and he gave him to his mother"* (7:11-15). This is a second instance of raising people from the dead—Lazarus will be a third.

Again, when a Pharisee *"asked Jesus to eat with him,"* Jesus went into the Pharisee's house and sat down at the table. A woman of the city, *"a sinner,"* Jesus learned, was there and brought a flask of ointment, *"and standing behind him at his feet, weeping, she began to wet his feet with her tears, wiped them with the hair of her head, kissed his feet, and anointed them with the ointment."* When the Pharisee saw this, *"he said to himself, 'If this man were a prophet, he would have known who and what sort of woman this is who is touching him, for she is a sinner.' Jesus answered him,.... 'A certain creditor had two debtors. One owed five hundred denarii, and the other fifty. When they could not pay, he forgave them both. Now which of them will love him more?' [The Pharisee] answered, 'The one, I suppose, to whom he forgave more.' Jesus said to him, 'You have judged rightly.' He said to her, 'Your sins are forgiven. Your faith has saved you. Go in peace'"* (7:36-50).

Yet another time he said this, *"'When you give a feast, invite the poor, the maimed, the lame, the blind.' He told them a story. 'A man once gave a great banquet and invited many. At the time for the banquet he sent his servant to say to those who had been invited, 'Come, for all is now ready.' But they all alike began to make excuses. The first said to him, 'I have bought a field and I must go out and see it...' Another said, 'I have bought five yoke of oxen and I go to examine them...' Another said, 'I have married a wife and therefore I cannot come.' The servant reported this to his master. Then the householder in anger said to his servant, 'Go out quickly to the streets and lanes of the city and bring in the poor and maimed and blind and lame.' The servant said, 'Sir, what you commanded has been done and still there is room.' The master said to the servant, 'Go out to the highways and hedges and compel people to come in, that my house may be filled. For I tell you, none of those men who were invited shall taste my banquet'" (14:13-24).*

Another story about rich and poor had a similar message. *"There was a rich man, who was clothed in purple and fine linen and who feasted sumptuously every day. At his gate lay a poor man named Lazarus, full of sores, who desired to be fed with what fell from the rich man's table. The dogs came and licked his sores. The poor man died and was carried by the angels to Abraham's bosom. The rich man also died and was buried. In Hades, being in torment, he lifted up his eyes, and saw Abraham far off and Lazarus in his bosom. The rich man called out, 'Father Abraham, have mercy on me and send Lazarus to dip the end of his finger in water and cool my tongue. For I am in anguish in this flame.' But Abraham said, 'Son, remember that you in your lifetime received your good things and Lazarus in like manner evil things. Now he is comforted here and you are in anguish. Besides all this, between us and you a great chasm has been fixed, in order that those who would pass from here to you may not be able and none may cross from there to us.' The rich man said, 'Then I beg you, father, to send him to my father's house, for I have five brothers, so that he may warn them, lest they also come into this place of torment.' But Abraham said, 'They have Moses and the prophets. Let them hear them.' He said, 'No, father Abraham, but if someone goes to them from the dead, they will repent.' He said to him, 'If they do not hear Moses and the prophets, neither will they be convinced if someone should rise from the dead'" (16:19-31).*

The "Good Samaritan," whose ethnic background was held in contempt by Jews, is another such story. After a priest and Levite saw a wounded man beaten by thieves and *"passed by on the other side"* of the road, *"a Samaritan, as he journeyed, came to where the wounded man was. When he saw him, he had compassion (esplagchnisthe), he was moved with pity,"* went to him, and tended his wounds. *"Then he set him on his own beast and brought him to an inn and took care of him. The next day he took out two denarii and gave them to the innkeeper, saying, 'Take care of him. Whatever more you spend, I will repay you when I come back.' Which of these three, do you think, proved neighbor to the man who fell among the robbers?' His hearers said, 'The one who showed mercy on him.' Jesus said to him, 'Go and do likewise'"* (10:33-37).

Jesus had compassion on slaves. *"A centurion had a slave who was dear to him, who was sick and at the point of death."* Hearing of Jesus, the centurion asked elders of the Jews to ask Jesus to heal his slave. When they came to Jesus, they told him, *"'He is worthy to have you do this for him, for he loves our nation and he built us our synagogue.' Jesus went with them."* Then the centurion had second thoughts and sent friends to tell Jesus, *"Lord, do not trouble yourself, for I am not worthy to have you come under my roof. I did not presume to come to you. But say the word and let my servant be healed. For I am a man set under authority, with soldiers under me, and I say to one, 'Go,' and he goes; and to another, 'Come,' and he comes; and to my slave, 'Do this,' and he does it.' When Jesus heard this he marveled at him and turned and said to the multitude that followed him, 'I tell you, not even in Israel have I found such faith.' When those who had been sent returned to the house, they found the slave well"* (7:2-10).

Another incident serves as a bridge between Jesus' concern for women in his society and his predilections toward poor people. As he and his disciples sat in the Temple one day, *"Jesus looked up and saw the rich putting their gifts into the treasury. He also saw a poor widow put in two copper coins. He said, 'Truly I tell you, this poor widow has put in more than all of them. They all contributed out of their abundance but she out of her poverty put in all the living that she had'"* (21:1-4; see Mk 12:41-44). The Temple had asked her to give up everything she had. How was she to buy bread to eat? What right had Temple authorities to reduce her to extreme poverty? The God of abundance would not be pleased by the Temple's part in her hardships.

This story recognizes how Jesus distinguished serving people as individuals and serving people through changing a policy at the highest level, which would, in today's terms, be a *structural* policy response to people's predicaments (for a systematic approach to "structures" in the social policy sciences, see Eberts and Sismondo, 1978). In this incident Jesus implies that the Temple should not ask the very poor to contribute large percentages of their meager incomes to the Temple. The Temple priests should change their policies so that such an injustice does not occur. In today's world people are sensitive to how social and economic structural policies by political, economic, and industrial leaders affect social-justice relations among people, the *ethne* (see, for example, *The New York Times*' editorial pages on almost any day). Jesus was aware how Herodian and priestly policies negatively affected people's relations with one another and wanted them to change—each Gospel reports Jesus *"cleansing the Temple"* as a major incident where he was saying, in effect "a structural policy change is necessary" to bring a Temple into alignment with what God wants in this world. This story of *"a poor widow"* is another example.

Near his Gospel's ending (23:33-43), Luke described a great caringly compassionate act by Jesus directed at an individual. Of the three crosses standing on a hillside outside Jerusalem's city wall, two were labeled *"criminals,"* in Greek, *kakourgon*. These "criminals" were not robbers or pickpockets but thought of themselves as patriots. In reality they were guerilla fighters, probably sicarii, intent on defeating the Roman Empire. They or their friends might have stabbed or garroted a Roman legionnaire or Jewish collaborator caught off-guard in a deserted Jerusalem alley. Their successors thirty or so years later battled the Romans in a war that resulted, by 70CE, in the utter destruction of Jerusalem and its Temple.

Picking up a refrain from Jewish rulers and the crowd scoffing at Jesus, one murderer kept reviling Jesus, *"If you are the Christ, save yourself and us."* He had never met Jesus before, did not know who Jesus was, or what he stood for. But he mimicked others around him and rejected Jesus.

The man hanging on the other side of Jesus heard what his compatriot said and rebuked him. *"Do you not fear God, since we are under the same condemnation that Jesus is?"* He turned to Jesus and said, *"Jesus, remember me when you come into your kingdom."* Jesus replied, *"Truly, I say to you, today you shall be with me in Paradise."* With his answer to this man, Jesus spoke to an existential question that confronts every human being.

In Jesus' day, Paradise was a great walled garden in Persia belonging to the Persian king, who stocked the garden with fish to be caught and animals to be hunted. A stream of water ran through it, fruit and flowering trees were there, welcome shade from the day's heat, and abundant food to eat, transforming the desert around it. The only ones who could go into this Paradise were personal friends whom the king invited.

The crucified man beside Jesus would not have been counted among the king's personal friends. He had been hunted down by Rome's soldiers, no friend of any king. He lived his life furtively, eking out a bare existence. To this man Jesus made a remarkable statement. *"Today you shall be with me in Paradise,"* in the beautiful garden, his situation all turned around, human needs met, a friend of the king himself. This is the only recorded time in his ministry that Jesus used the word, *"Paradise."* He might have held this word in reserve his whole life until he could speak it to the one person who needed it most, one whose situation it most perfectly fit. To the end of his life, Jesus continued to minister to the wounded, vulnerable, and those rejected by their society.

But Luke recorded an even greater act of incomparable compassion and caring. On his cross Jesus fought a great battle. In this battle, the powers of evil raged against him. Betrayal put him there after the priests propositioned Judas with *"thirty pieces of silver for you, if you tell us where we can arrest him."* Judas did; the soldiers came. A friend's betrayal was the proximate cause that put Jesus on the cross. Desertion was another. His disciples, present when Jesus was arrested in the Garden, deserted him, fled. They might have testified in his favor but chose not to get involved. The sin of desertion put him on this cross. Denial also played a part. Simon Peter stood in the high priest's courtyard when someone said, *"You are a follower of that man."* Peter, everyman at this point, denied it, not once but three times.

Pride also played a part. Jewish priests were proud of their Temple and their religion. Jesus challenged both. Jesus said that the Temple would be destroyed, their law did not bring salvation, and their Sabbath was made for humanity, not humanity for the Sabbath. Each accusation cut into Jewish authorities' cherished beliefs. They plotted to kill him for it. Pride of self, pride of religion, pride of nation put Jesus on the cross.

Indifference played its part, too. *"People stood by watching."* No one lifted a finger to aid him in any way. No one ran to the Sanhedrin or to Pilate to say, "You can't do this dastardly thing." Instead, they stood and watched, not wanting to get involved. Violence played a part. Arrogance of power always produces violence. Rome looked on itself as the world's greatest power. This Galilean Jesus was in their way. Dispatch him. They fastened a crown of thorns on his head, then nailed him to a cross. Jesus' weakened body fought on, but could not sustain him against his bloody wounds. He tried to breathe but his neck muscles could not hold his head upright. As it lowered, he gasped for air, asphyxiation.

The shock of hanging bloody and naked with outstretched arms drove life from his frail body.

Betrayal, denial, desertion, pride, indifference, arrogance, violence—each evil power had a hand in putting Jesus on the cross. Yet in facing this onslaught, Jesus said, *"Father, forgive them, they know not what they do."* His forgiveness was more powerful than all this evil. His forgiveness breaks the power of every sin. He said, *"Father, into thy hands I commit my spirit."* Pain, loneliness, death could not conquer his faithfulness, his loyalty, to his father; his loyalty was more powerful than these. He said, *"I will love you to the end."* His love stood beyond all those things done to him. He loved to the end of his earthly life. His love goes beyond any conceivable end of life. No evil could prevail against his forgiveness, faithfulness, loyalty, love. When the fog and dust of his battle lifted, the victim of sins clearly became the victor over sin. The compassionate and caring God and the caring and compassionate Jesus are central to Luke's understanding of the good news in his Gospel.

In Sum

Luke's Gospel was written for people, many of them Greek but also former Hellenist- or even Hebrew-Jews, poor, of various *ethne*, or otherwise disadvantaged, living in cities. They were also members of an *ekklesia* but who were feeling discrimination and prejudice while committed to a charismatic leader, Jesus of Nazareth. Luke described Jesus as having what he considered divine qualities and commitment to caring compassion and social justice for his followers. The other Gospels were not as outspoken on these issues.

Chapter 10

Jesus in the Gospel Of John: One with a Living, Working, and Loving God

Urban Context—Urban Hellenist Jews

In the larger cities of the Jewish Diaspora, Jews accommodated with, even became wealthy through, Hellenist culture. Especially in Alexandria, the ancient world's seat of learning where the world's first university, the Museum, had been established and where the Septuagint had been translated, Jewish people and their leaders came into routine contact with key Hellenist philosophical and ethical issues. In this Greek-Hellenist atmosphere Jews organized themselves to deal with the pagan world through their synagogues and introduced into their liturgies and presentations certain concepts that were primarily from the Hellenist world.

Hebrew and Hellenist cultures were separable in critical ways. Hellenism was committed to "philosophical, ethical, and rational concepts per se" in contrast to Hebrews' commitments to "a history of collective accountability by God's 'chosen' people." Non-Jewish Hellenists, proud of their heritage and culture, found Hebrew formulations largely incomprehensible.

Hellenism's focus on concepts began to blossom with philosophers and tragedians in urban Athens about 450BCE. Hellenist concepts used fluently and cogently were those of Homer, Plato, Aristotle, and other Greek philosophers and playwrights. Alexander the Great was so certain these concepts were critical for all the world's people that he became determined to spread them throughout the known world (334-323BCE). Hellenist culture continued as the culture of most people even after Romans supplanted the heirs of Alexander's Greek generals to become politically dominant in the Mideast.

Hebrews' culture of loyalty as a people of God began in earnest with Moses sometime between 1450 and 1250BCE and blossomed in the following half-dozen centuries. Hellenist Jews and Hellenist Christians, more than other Judaeo-Christians, tended to live in the two separable but intersecting worlds of Hellenism and Judaism.

Many Hellenist Jews had lived in Jerusalem prior to Jesus' ministry. Speaking Greek and using the Septuagint in their worship services, Hellenist Jews were also deeply committed to Hebrew traditions. When converted to the Christian faith, these Hellenist Jews formed the core of a Hellenist-Jewish-Christian party within the early Jesus movement in Jerusalem. But they were expelled from Jerusalem after the lethal struggle that resulted from Stephen's speech (Acts 8:1). Leaders in the Hellenist party of the early Jesus movement—Philip with his four daughters, Jesus' mother, and the "beloved disciple"—eventually settled in Ephesus. We surmise that John's Gospel came from and was largely directed toward this large Hellenist-Jewish-Christian minority in larger Mideastern cities such as Ephesus, Alexandria, and, later, Corinth.

As Luke in Acts (13:14-16) indicated, services in synagogues and churches often included open discussions of ideas as Jews and Christians worked to deal effectively with their various life situations. John's Gospel uses concepts from this milieu to come to terms with these two cultures. This Gospel re-interprets its Jewish traditions into Hellenist ideas such as *"Word"* (*logos*, rationale) and *"light, life, love, grace, truth"* (see Fig 7, above). The Gospel described Jesus' relationship to God through both its Judaism and its Hellenism. Jesus stated his being "one with a living and loving God" by using the same *"I am...(ego eimi...)"* concept to describe himself to others that God had used when describing himself to Moses, *"God said to Moses, 'I am who I am (ego eimi ho on, I am he who is)'"* (Exodus 3:14 in Septuagint). In the preamble to the commandments in the Torah, God had spoken in a similar fashion, *"I am the Lord your God."* Jesus used this self-identification of God when he introduced himself to his contemporaries. *"I am,"* said Jesus, *"the bread of life..., the resurrection and the life..., the life eternal."* Differences in these two cultures led the writer John to present Jesus as God incarnate to Hellenist Christians by using Hellenist explanations, commentaries, and interpretations in his Gospel.

Purpose of John's Gospel

John's Gospel stated its purpose in its two conclusions. The first says, *"These are written that you may believe that Jesus is the Christ (the anointed), the Son of God, and that believing you may have life in his name"* (20:30-31). *"Son of God"* is only one designation the writer John recorded for Jesus. At another point, John recorded Jesus as making the dramatic and daring statement, *"I and the father are one"* (10:30).

In the conclusion's second part, the Gospel identifies its writer. *"This [referring to the Beloved Disciple] is the disciple who is bearing witness to these things and who has written these things; and we know that his testimony is true."* He also recognizes the selectivity of what he has written. *"There are also many other things which Jesus did; were every one of them to be written, I suppose that the world itself could not contain the books that would be written"* (Jn 21:24 –25).

Sources of John's Gospel

John acknowledged that in composing his Gospel he was choosing from a wide variety of sources, both written and oral (Jn 21:24 –25). His choices were undoubtedly those in support of his thesis that Jesus was God's only begotten Son who was one with the Father.

"The Beloved disciple, ...the disciple whom Jesus loved," was the chief source for the unique information in John's Gospel. He was a shadowy but omnipresent figure in the events surrounding Jesus' crucifixion and resurrection. He attended the last meal with Jesus and his disciples, lying in the honored place *"on Jesus' breast."* At the cross, Jesus gave his mother, *"the Mother of Jesus,"* into his care and as his legacy. *The beloved disciple* anticipated and moved Jesus' mother to Ephesus before the events of 66-70CE. He accompanied Peter to Jesus' tomb and properly interpreted Jesus' resurrection. He appears to have been an impressive figure who lived in Judea and had access to important persons and places in Jerusalem. All this gave him credibility as a source for the Gospel's Jerusalem material. Being in Ephesus with Jesus' mother, we assume the *beloved disciple* was a key informant for, and perhaps the author of, John's Gospel.

The Gospel's language is *koinai*, or *koine*, Greek, spoken by ordinary people at this time. *Koine* Greek had a smaller vocabulary and less rigid grammar than classical Greek. The Gospel's outline includes a prologue (a stylistic device not used in the other Gospels) followed by a series of events. The format for these events is another stylistic device. It starts by describing certain conditions, moves into a dialogue between Jesus and key actors in the event, and then into a monologue by Jesus explaining the meaning of what was previously said and done. The Gospel's climax describes Jesus' final meal in Jerusalem with his disciples and the familiar dialogue and monologue explaining things said during the meal. The Gospel concludes with Jesus' death and resurrection and then the brief epilogue that states the Gospel's overall purpose.

Use of Scripture in John's Gospel

Use of Scripture looms large in John's Gospel both in the public period of Jesus' ministry and in events during his last week and crucifixion.

Translations

Since John was writing primarily to Hellenist congregations, he considered it necessary to translate Hebrew names and terms into Greek for his Gospel to be understood. *Rabbi* (1:38), *Messiah* (1:41), *Cephas* (1:42), *Siloam* (9:7), *Gabbatha* (19:13), *Golgotha* (19:17), *Rabboni* (20:16) are such words. In John the Hebrew name is given, followed immediately by its Greek translation. *"Rabbi means teacher"; "Messiah means Christ"; "Cephas is Peter"; "Siloam means Sent"; "Gabbatha means The Pavement"* (where Pilate issued judgments); and *"Golgotha means the Place of a Skull"* (where offenders were crucified). John makes these translations for his Greek-speaking readers.

Hebrew Scriptures in Jesus' Public Ministry

In describing events in Jesus' public ministry, John was concerned to demonstrate both the continuity between what Jesus said or did with its Old Testament precedents as well as the manner in which Jesus challenged traditional Hebrew interpretations in favor of new understandings about what God was doing in these Scriptures. As such, the writer John offered roughly two dozen references to Hebrew Scriptures.

A few brief examples are presented here, several previously mentioned in the Chronology. Special attention is given to those that capture major themes in John's Gospel, namely that God was still active in people's lives, that God's actions demonstrated his love toward people, and that Jesus was one with God.

The conversation with Nathanael (1:43-51) built on two Old Testament images. When Jesus' disciple, Philip, introduced Jesus to Nathanael, he was sitting under a fig tree meditating on the Torah. The vision of *"every man...under his fig tree"* was from 1 Kings (4:25), Micah (4:4), and Zechariah (3:10). Nathanael was meditating on Genesis 28, Jacob's vision of God's angels ascending and descending on a ladder. Jacob declared, *"The Lord is in this place"* (Gen 28:17). Jesus tells Nathanael, *"Truly, truly, I say to you, you will see heaven opened and the angels of God ascending and descending upon the Son of Humankind."* The Scripture's vision behind this conversation helps reveal the meaning of Jesus' ministry.

A key image in the Nicodemus story (3:1-17) is the bronze serpent lifted up in the desert that cured Israelites who had been bitten by viper-serpents. *"As Moses lifted up the serpent in the wilderness, so must the Son of Humankind be lifted up, that whoever believes in him may have eternal life"* (3:14-15).

In another event reported by John, Jesus showed who he was by the language he used (6:16-21). Jesus' disciples were crossing the Sea of Galilee to Capernaum in a small boat. A strong wind came up and waves rose higher, frightening the disciples, especially when they saw Jesus walking on the sea. Drawing close to the boat, Jesus said to them, *"It is I; do not be afraid."* The event's force was in the words Jesus used to identify himself, *"It is I (ego eimi)."* In the Septuagint, used in Hellenist synagogues, *"ego eimi"* is the exact phrase by which God identified himself to Moses through the burning bush on the mountainside (Ex 3:13-14). In using this phrase, Jesus gave new meaning to his followers about his relationship to God. The writer John was well aware of this.

Jesus also described himself as the good shepherd, *"I am the good shepherd"* (10:11). All Jews knew Psalm 23, *"The Lord is my shepherd...,"* that detailed what a good shepherd does. They also knew Ezekiel 34 that contains a scathing denunciation of Israel and its kings, princes, priests, and elders as bad shepherds for not caring properly for their "sheep." Ezekiel declared God will replace evil shepherds and become Israel's new good shepherd. Jesus was this person.

Many episodes in Jesus' ministry emphasized "abundance" flowing to humanity from God through Jesus Christ. The wedding at Cana (2:1-12) spoke of abundance of wine due to Jesus' intervention as a sign of the joyous arrival of God's new age. Jesus also fed multitudes with abundance when he took five loaves, gave thanks, and distributed them to those around him. After the meal, Jesus' disciples gathered twelve full baskets of leftovers, true abundance, one basket for each of Israel's twelve original tribes. The Samaritan woman by the well had abundant water. Another time, Jesus healed an official's son—he gave abundance of life. In describing God's gifts to the people, the prophets Amos (9:13) and Joel (3:18) spoke of similar abundance.

Jesus cleansing the temple (Jn 2:13-24) was built on Jeremiah as a Scriptural source; the Lord's house would be destroyed if the people did not mend their ways (7:1-20). Kings Hezekiah and Josiah cleansed the temple of alien icons when they took office. Jesus' "cleansing" initiative was to fulfill Malachi's program, *"The messenger of the Lord coming suddenly to his temple"* (Mal 3:1).

Jesus and Jewish leaders had a continuing discussion over Scriptural sanctity for the Sabbath. Jews considered Sabbath laws sacred—God rested on the Sabbath after creating the universe, so all Jews should do likewise. Jesus was accosted three times because he did something on the Sabbath which Pharisees and priests deemed unlawful. On a Sabbath, Jesus healed a beggar by the pool of Siloam (5:1-18), on a Sabbath Jesus gave sight to the Man Born Blind (9:1-42) and declared,

"I am the light of the world," and a woman was taken in adultery on a Sabbath (8:2-11).

In the event of the man born blind, scribes long recognized that the living God was active on the Sabbath. To reconcile continuing divine activity with the Sabbath's sanctity, rabbis distinguished between God's work as creator and his work as judge. God rests from physical work on the Sabbath but is eternally active in his judgments, condemning the wicked and conferring life on the just. On this issue, Mark had Jesus declare, *"The Sabbath is made for man, not man for the Sabbath"* (Mk 2:27). The writer John carried Jesus' response at least one step farther than Mark when Jesus said, *"My Father is working still and I am working."* God is constantly an active, living, working God, even on the Sabbath.

An issue about Abraham occurred as Jesus said, *"When you have lifted up the Son of Humankind, then you will know that I am he (ego eimi), and that I do nothing on my own authority. I speak as the Father taught me. He who sent me is with me...for I always do what is pleasing to him"* (Jn 8:28-29). The Jews said, *"Abraham died, as did the prophets; and you say, 'If any one keeps my word, he will never taste death. Are you greater than our father Abraham who died...? Who do you claim to be?'"* Jesus answered, *"It is my Father who glorifies me, of whom you say that he is your God. You have not known him. I know him... Your father Abraham rejoiced that he was to see my day. He saw it and was glad."* The Jews said to him, *"You are not yet fifty years old and you have seen Abraham?"* Jesus said to them, *"I say to you, before Abraham was, I am"* (8:52-58). The result of this dialogue was that *"they took up stones to throw at him; but Jesus hid himself, and went out of the temple"* (8:59).

Hostility to Jesus and his interpretations of Scripture also developed during the winter Feast of Dedication in Jerusalem (10:22-42). Jesus was walking in the Temple's Portico of Solomon when Jews gathered around and said, *"How long will you keep us in suspense? If you are the Christ, tell us plainly."* Jesus responded, *"I told you and you do not believe. The works that I do in my Father's name, they bear witness to me. But you do not believe because you do not belong to my sheep. My sheep hear my voice...and they follow me; and I give them eternal life...and no one shall snatch them out of my hand. I and the Father are one."* To this response, *"the Jews took up stones again to stone him."* Jesus said, *"I have shown you many good works from the Father. For which of these do you stone me?"* The Jews responded, *"We stone you for no good work, but for blasphemy because you, being a man, make yourself God"* (see Leviticus 24:10). Jesus responded, *"If I am not doing the works of my Father, then do not believe me. But if I do them, even though you do not believe me, believe the works, that you may know and understand that the Father is in me and I am in the Father."* Again they tried to arrest him, but he again escaped.

John also reported Jesus using Scripture several times in the last meal with *"his friends."* First, Jesus speaks of Judas' pre-determined disloyalty. *"Even my bosom friend in whom I trusted, who ate of my bread, has lifted his heel against me"* (Jn 13:18; Psalm 41:9). Jesus also found it difficult to understand how Judas or the Jewish people could hate him (15:25). For this reason he resorted to Scripture. *"Let not those rejoice over me who are wrongfully my foes, let not those wink the eye who hate me without cause"* (Psalm 35:19).

John reported that Jesus used a vine and vineyard analogy. Isaiah had said that Israel was God's vineyard but that God promised to destroy it when it bore bad fruit (Is 5:1-7). Jesus and his disciples replaced these untrustworthy people. *"I am the true vine and you are the vineyard that bears much fruit"* (Jn 15:1, 8).

Another instance saw the prophet Ezekiel lamenting that Judah was transplanted in a wilderness, in a dry and thirsty land (Ez 19:10-14) (but for Moses and Joshua it was a land of water, milk, and honey; Ex 13:5, 33:3; Numbers 13:27; Deuteronomy 8:5-10, passim). For his disciples, Jesus likened his present time through an image of anguish, of *"travail,"* such as a woman experiences when she bears a child (Isaiah 13:8, Hosea 13:13, Micah 4:9; Jn 16:16-24). Jesus assured his followers that they will not be in travail but rejoice when they see him again.

The writer John also uses Scripture in the passion story to help explain events. When Jesus came to Jerusalem during the Passover Feast, some took palm branches to meet him, chanting *"Hosanna! Blessed is he who comes in the name of the Lord, even the King of Israel!"* (Psalm 118:25). Jesus sat on a donkey's colt. *"Fear not, daughter of Zion; behold, your king is coming, sitting on a donkey's colt!"* (Zechariah 9:9; Jn 12:12-15).

John used another instance of Scripture during Jesus' last days in Jerusalem that reflected Jesus' despair. *"Though he had done so many signs before them, yet they did not believe in him; it was that the word spoken by the prophet Isaiah might be fulfilled. 'Lord, who has believed our report, and to whom has the arm of the Lord been revealed?'"* (Is 53:1). *"Therefore they could not believe. For Isaiah again said, 'He has blinded their eyes and hardened their heart, lest they should see with their eyes and perceive with their heart, and turn for me to heal them'"* (Is 6:10). *"Isaiah said this because he saw his glory and spoke of him"* (Jn 12:37-41).

Words from Scripture were spoken as Jesus hung on the cross. Soldiers who had crucified him made four scrawny piles of his clothes and cast lots to see who would get what. *"This was to fulfil the scripture, 'They parted my garments among them, and for my clothing they cast lots'"* (Psalm 22:18; Jn 19:24).

Another of Jesus' statements from the cross built on Scripture, *"I thirst"* (Jn 19:28). The Psalmist described the kind of thirst that afflicted Jesus, *"I am poured out like water, and all my bones are out of joint; my heart is like wax, it is melted within my breast; my strength is dried up like a potsherd and my tongue cleaves to the roof of my mouth; thou dost lay me down in the dust of death"* (Ps 22:14-15). Psalm 69:21 added, *"For my thirst they gave me vinegar to drink."*

In his account of the resurrection, John made additional statements drawn from Scripture. The first was, *"for as yet they did not know the scripture, that he must rise from the dead"* (Jn 20:9). Followers in the early Jesus movement zealously searched Scriptures to find an indication that he would rise. Jonah was one source they scrutinized. *"Jonah was in the belly of the fish three days and three nights"* (Jonah 1:17), the amount of time Jesus lay in the tomb.

A dramatic use of Scripture in the resurrection story comes in Thomas confessing to Jesus, *"My Lord and my God."* By this Thomas meant that all descriptions of "God" and "Lord" found in Scripture now apply to Jesus Christ. Jesus Christ's words and actions are all that human beings can expect God to say and do.

In John's Gospel, Jesus' life and ministry was informed and shaped by Scripture. John's Gospel reported that Jesus used Scripture in his public ministry at many different times and in many different ways, often in support of his major themes. But Scripture did not *determine* Jesus' ministry. Only a few times did Jesus say he was *"fulfilling Scripture."* Although Luke's Gospel had Jesus say, when in Nazareth's synagogue, that *"this day the Scripture is fulfilled in your ears"* (Lk 4:21), John did not report this incident in this way. Jesus was intimately acquainted with the active, living God. His ministry reflected a response to what God was doing in his life and world. John reported that Jesus made his own decisions regarding God's will for him. Scripture shaped and informed Jesus' ministry but did not *determine* what he did.

Major Theme in John's Gospel: One with the Living, Working, and Loving God

The major theme of John's Gospel, from our perspective, is that Jesus was one with the living, loving and working God who asked his followers to love others as God in Christ loves them. This theme begins with John's prologue and continues through a series of events by using dialogues and monologues explaining Jesus' unique relationship with God in a variety of ways. The last meal concludes with Jesus' praying in Gethsemane, followed by the climax of Jesus' death and resurrection.

John's Prologue

John's prologue previews the Gospel's overall message that exemplifies a Jewish-Hellenist synthesis. Its beginning captures both Jesus' Hebrew heritage and a Hellenist legacy which John's Hellenist-Jewish community brought to the Jesus movement.

The prologue resembles poetry more than prose, even if, to our knowledge, it was not printed as a poem in any extant copy of John's Gospel. Possibly parts of it were first chanted as a hymn by Hellenist Jews in Alexandria, where the Septuagint was translated, and it was later adapted for Hellenist-Christian worship.

About the fourth decade of the first century, when the Jesus movement began in Alexandria, a Jewish philosopher, Philo of Alexandria, recast ancient Judaism into a form acceptable to Hellenist Jews and Christians there. His central concepts were *"the Word of God,"* *"light…, life…, and love,"* and how Jesus related to Moses. The original hymn, sometimes called a "Hymn to Wisdom," may have contained only the first few lines on the creation of the world as Jews understood it. But Hellenist Christians interpreted these ideas as referring to Jesus. This powerful hymn was later taken to Ephesus where it was incorporated as the frontispiece to John's Hellenist Gospel.

*"In the beginning was the Word
and the Word was with God
and the Word was God.*

He was in the beginning with God,
all things were made through him
and without him was not anything made that was made.
In him was life
and the life was the light of men.
The light shines in the darkness
and the darkness has not overcome it.
He was in the world
and the world was made through him
yet the world knew him not.
He came to his own home
and his own people received him not.
But to all who received him
who believed in his name
he gave power to become children of God
who were born
not of blood
nor of the will of the flesh
nor of the will of man
but of God."

These words described God's efforts to deal with recalcitrant Hebrews for almost 2000 years. But in the phrases, *"He was in the world...yet the world knew him not...and his own received him not,"* Hellenist Christians could recognize what happened to their Christ. These Christians then transformed the hymn into an overt Christian expression by incorporating its great climax, *"And the Word became flesh and dwelt among us."*

The Prologue, bathed in the Scriptures of Hellenist Jews, speaks to three cultures, Judaism, Hellenism, and Christianity. Each stanza is a theme in John's Gospel. In contrast with other Gospels, from the start in John's Gospel Jesus is "one with God." This theme was so powerful that not even J. S. Bach, the greatest of all church musicians, gave music and voice to it. This prologue serves many purposes in John's Gospel.

- It outlined how God related to the Word (*Logos;* Jn 1:1-5).
- It put Judeo-Christians in cosmic perspective, *"In the beginning was the* word."
- It was John's Christmas story—instead of shepherds and wise men as in Luke and Matthew, the story says, *"The Word became flesh and dwelt* among us."
- It introduced main themes in John's Gospel.
- It affirmed that Jesus is an historical figure.
- It portrayed Jesus as the revealer of the Father.
- It proclaimed that, through Jesus, salvation comes to people.
- It focused attention on the Gospel's main concepts, *"light, life, grace, truth, witness, glory, world, only son of the father."*
- It served as John's story of the transfiguration. In other Gospels, the glory of God shines on Jesus at a particular moment when, in the presence of several disciples, Jesus is transfigured. In John's Gospel *"the glory"* is upon him from the moment *"the word became flesh and dwelt among us"* (1:14).

"In the beginning was the Word" (Jn 1:1). This sentence immediately recalls the opening words of Genesis, *"In the beginning God"* (Gen 1:1). *"The Word of the Lord"* made heaven and earth, *"and God said…"* (Gen 1:3, 6, 9, 14, 20, 24, 26). The prophets also used the phrase, *"the Word of the Lord."* In Greek, *"Word"* is *logos.* It means "rationale," "root cause," or "in principle." *Logos* was a key concept in Greek thinking—the rational principle, long sought by Greeks, that brings unity and significance to all existing things. To Greeks it inferred "the beginning of history" and "root cause of the universe." Since congregations for which the Gospel was originally addressed were composed of both Greek- and Hebrew-speakers, they each undoubtedly had their own thoughts as they read or heard this prologue. John was saying that *"the Word"* fulfills both Jewish history and Greek philosophy.

This first sentence also tells of the relationship between *"God"* and *"Word."* The Word which God speaks is not separated from God, not another god beside God. The Word infers "in the presence of God" but not subordinate to God. The Word belongs to God. It is God's way of revealing himself to humankind. The Word became flesh in Jesus Christ. Nor is Christ a god beside God or subordinate to God. Jesus Christ is God in action in this world.

"In him was life (zoe)" (1:4). In Jewish usage the word "life" had several meanings.

- *"Life"* contrasted with death.
- *"Life of the age"* contrasted with "life of time," an indefinitely long rather than a finite period.
- *"Life of the age to come"* contrasted with the "life of this age."
- *"Perfect life,"* timeless in quality, thus exempt from death, possible in the here and now but to be realized in its fullness only beyond Christ's grave.

"Life" also brings *"light"* (in Greek, *phos*). John used this term 24 times (see Fig 7). The difference between light and darkness is primarily the difference between security and danger. To both Hebrews and Greeks, "darkness" was a time of danger, distress, dread, terror, a time when evildoers, demons, mischievous things were at work. "Light" was the time when people went about their lawful business in peace and safety. In John's Gospel, *"light"* was a quality that made Jesus Christ attractive to others. Light was in him and this light had an ambience that lit up others' lives. This "light" cannot be overcome by darkness. The word *katelaben,* *"overcome,"* had myriad meanings—to master, to apprehend, to seize, to possess. John, like many Greek writers, delighted in words' double and triple meanings. By using *kataleben,* he meant to express all such denotations. *"The light shines in the darkness and the darkness does not master it"* (1:5), the darkness does not apprehend it, seize it, or take possession of it.

"The world, kosmon," a variation of *kosmos*, pointed to a paradox. It infers both the organized and responsible world of humankind, the object of God's love, but also defines a humankind that rejects Christ, lives in darkness, does evil works, is ignorant of the father, and rejoices over the death of the son (Niebuhr, 1951, uses the word "culture" to stand for *"the kosmos").* Then follow both good news and bad news. The good news was that *"He [God] was in the world."* The bad news was *"yet the world knew him not. He came to his own people and his own people did not accept him"* (1:10-11). These words might refer to Christ but they could just as well refer to God and his earlier work in history when God was trying to make himself known to the world. *"The world"* had become perverted but God still loves the world in his creating and redeeming actions. Yet the world responded to this love by denying its actuality with either ignorance or outright denial of God's Word. Only the Son responded to the Father as all humankind should. He obeyed the Father's will and did the Father's work. He honored and glorified the Father, he loved, bore witness to, and drew his life from the Father.

Another element in the good news was that, to those who did receive him, *elebon* (whose basic meaning is "welcoming a traveler back to his rightful home"), God gave his people the power, *exousian* (also translated as "right" or "authority") to become children of God. The new birth came not from "blood," *aimaton* (Greek physiology said that a father's seed mingled with a mother's blood to produce a child), or "the will of flesh" (the sexual impulses that draw men and women together), or "the will of man" (a father's desire for a child as heir). The new birth occurred because God willed it throughout history as he invited into his family those who had forfeited the relationship because of their all-too-human ignorance, denial, or sin.

Then came the prologue's grand climax, *"The Word became flesh and dwelt among us, and we have seen his glory, the glory as of the only son of the father, full of grace and truth"*

(1:14). When Christians say the name "God," they also think *"the Word became flesh,"* Jesus Christ. Christ is not Christ subordinate to God. Jesus Christ is God in action.

"The Word became flesh (sarx)." "Flesh" gives body to all of life, animal and human. That *"the Word became flesh"* shows God's concern for both humanity and all things God created in this world. This phrase has strong implications for human and environmental relationships. God is so concerned for the whole creation that God sent his son into the world to redeem all of it. *"Flesh"* infers the part of human nature associated with frailty, evil, weakness, mortality—human nature as distinct from God's nature. To send his only son into the world to share fully in the life of the world is the greatest of all God's acts.

"And dwelt (eskenosen) among us." God in Christ *"dwelt"* (more exactly "pitched his tent," "tabernacled") among us. In the Feast of Tabernacles, God and people "temporarily" pitch their tents among one another. A tent put up one day can be taken down the next, and moved to another place, as early Hebrews did with the Ark of the Covenant. *Eskenosen* called to mind the tabernacle in the wilderness (Exodus 25:9 ff, passim), the *"tent of meeting"* (Ex 33:7), where God met with Moses and the people's elders. An implication is that God through Christ is again present temporarily in the flesh with his people. Jesus' ministry will be of short duration. He will be in the world a little while and then return to his father.

"We have seen his glory." The Greek word for "glory" is *"doxan."* The Hebrew word for glory is *shekinah*. The sign of God's *shekinah* is light, all-pervading light, *phos*. The *shekinah* was present with the people of God in a cloud by day and a fire by night. It led Moses and his people through the wilderness. The *shekinah* glistened on the Tent of Meeting. The *shekinah* shone annually inside the Temple at Jerusalem, on the one day of the year when the rising sun blazed over the peak of the Mount of Olives and burst into the Temple to indicate that God had come again to his Temple. Where the *shekinah* is, God is present. When God's *shekinah* is seen in

Jesus Christ, God is present in Christ. In John's Gospel the glory of God is seen most clearly in Jesus Christ.

"As of the only son (monogenous) of the father." The original meaning of the Greek word *monogenous* was "one who bore the power of attorney for another." In the Old Testament it referred to the king who ruled Israel in God's name (Psalm 2:7). God said to the king, *"You are my son, today I have begotten you."* In the New Testament, the word refers to a father granting power of attorney to his eldest son (or anyone so designated) so that the father's business could be carried on properly. Men from Judea and Galilee sometimes had business elsewhere, such as in Jesus' parable about conducting business in *"far countries."* In times of slow communication, how could they do it? They designated someone as their representative with full power of attorney, *monogenous*, to conduct business for them.

Monogenous is a striking image for the relationship between God and Jesus. God, the distant Father needing to conduct business on Planet Earth, sent Jesus and designated him as his *"only son,"* granting him God's power of attorney. Jesus could speak for God, act for God, sign God's name to contracts (covenants). Whatever Jesus did bore the father's power of attorney, because God gave it to him.

"Full of grace and truth." Old Testament counterparts to the Greek *charitos*, grace, and *aletheias*, truth, "removing the veil," are, in Hebrew, *hesed* and *emet*. *Hesed* (grace) describes a relationship of loyalty and mutual responsibility within a covenant and *emet* (truth) stresses the idea of faithfulness and dependability. *"Grace"* means "unmerited good will, a favor to the receiver, love in action, for no reason other than it is love." *"Truth"* implies "revealing what is behind the veil." No longer is God hidden in a cloud. Christ has removed the veil. The more people experience grace, truth, and love, the more confident they become of their source as being outside themselves.

"Truth," *aletheias* in Greek, originally meant "firm, fixed, valid, binding." In legal procedure, it meant first "finding the

facts of a case, then making judgments that corresponded with the facts and legal standards." In religious terms Hebrew *emet, truth,* meant "reality, genuineness, reliability." Truth referred to one's character and conduct, the opposite of being dominated by myths and lies. Christian truth is a divine act of self-manifestation. "To speak the truth" means "to put the Revelation into words, to reveal what is behind the veil." Truth in Hebrew Scripture, in contrast with truth in science, meant "reliance on God, who does not change."

"And from his fulness have we all received, grace upon grace" (2:16). This was the greatest news—grace, *charitos,* was in Jesus Christ. All the grace contained in the fullness of God was poured into Jesus Christ. He in turn pours it into Christians to receive unmerited grace upon grace upon grace, the treasure of the Christian faith.

"The law was given through Moses" contrasts with *"grace and truth came through Jesus Christ"* (Jn 2:17). Moses was particularly important in Alexandria and Egypt, his homeland. Philo of Alexandria wrote extensively about Moses. To Philo, Moses was the "greatest and most perfect" human being and to have come near to God as a family relation. Fully aware that Moses was a real human being, Philo could still speak of Moses' second birth, his association with the *Logos,* and his transition to immortal life. One Philo writing (see 1993: 164-165) was a prayer addressed to Moses. John's Gospel attested to the immense value of God's revelation to the Jews, *"The law was given through Moses."* But John goes on to say, *"Grace and truth came through Jesus Christ."* This statement affirmed that the old revelation was superseded. The old covenant was a gift of grace, John declared, but the new grace in Jesus Christ was superior to the old.

"In the bosom of the father, he has made him known" (1:18). This figure of speech is drawn from banqueting. At banquets both Hebrew and Greek men reclined on couches when they ate, with the most honored position given to the one who lay closest to the host. While reclining, he was directly in front of the host, his head near the host's chest. The two could

talk intimately during a meal. So was the son with the father. The phrase *"has made him known (exegesato)"* had two basic meanings. Greeks used it when a mystery religion's priest interpreted dreams to devotees about life's mysteries. Hebrews used it in interpreting the Torah, the Jewish law. The invisible God was in Christ making manifest his grace, glory, and truth.

Nowhere else is the meaning and mystery of God in Christ more concisely and adequately presented than in this Prologue.

"Signs"

John appears to make special use of the word *"sign,"* semeion in Greek. After turning water into wine at the wedding in Cana, John says, *"This, the first of his signs, Jesus did at Cana in Galilee and manifested his glory; and his disciples believed in him"* (2:11). This is followed by the story of Jesus healing the official's son. After Jesus healed this young man, John remarks, *"This was now the second sign that Jesus did when he had come from Judea to Galilee"* (4:54).

Is John's use of the word *"sign"* unique to this Gospel? According to Arndt & Gingrich in their *Greek-English Lexicon*, a *"sign"* was a distinguishing mark by which something is known, a token, an indication of something else. The word was used extensively in Jewish life, including the Old Testament. Circumcision was a sign of belonging to the covenant (Gen 17:11; Ex 7:3; Deut 4:34, 6:22, 7:19; Is 8:18, 20:3, Jeremiah 39:21). Philo used the word as "a sign of things to come." Josephus (94) used it. Luke included it in the angels' song, *"This will be a sign to you, you will see the babe wrapped in swaddling cloths and lying in a manger"* (Lk 2:12). Luke also talked of Jesus giving a warning sign to his generation as Jonah did to his (Lk 11:29-30). Mark, Luke, and Matthew (Mk 13:3, Mt 24:3, and Lk 21:7) used it to describe *"signs of the end-times."* *"Sign"* was used in Acts (2:43, 4:30, 5:12, 6:8, 7:36, 14:3, 15:12), and the letters to the

Romans (15:19) and Hebrews (2:4). Clearly, "signs" was not a word unique to John.

Yet John used the word *"sign"* in a unique way. John never used the term "miracle." John used the word *"sign"* to refer to what others called Jesus' *"miracles."* For John the significance of an action rested not solely in the act itself but on that to which the event points, to God's activity in the world. A healing is always a *"sign from God"* or a *"sign of God's action."* What Jesus does in a given act always pointed beyond itself to what God was doing.

Jesus performing "signs" and Jews discussing them is a continuing presence in John's Gospel. Following a meal by the Sea of Galilee, John writes, *"A multitude followed Jesus, because they saw the signs which he did on those who were diseased"* (Jn 6:2). This would be understandable in Mark's Gospel, given Jesus' many healings reported there. But to this point, chapter 6 in John's Gospel, Jesus performed only two healings—the nobleman's son and the beggar by the pool of Bethzatha.

When Jesus fed the multitude, extended questions about signs were raised. After the meal, from the five barley loaves the disciples gathered twelve baskets of fragments left by those who had eaten. *"When the people saw the sign which he had done, they said, 'This is indeed the prophet who is to come into the world!'"* (6:12-14). When Jesus left, the crowd followed and found him. Jesus raised the question of "signs." *"'Truly, truly, I say to you, you seek me, not because you saw signs, but because you ate your fill of the loaves.' They said to him, 'What sign do you do, that we may see, and believe you? What work do you perform?'"* (6:22-30). This was followed by a discussion of what Jesus really did in the meal by the sea—was he another Moses giving the Israelites *manna* in the wilderness?

Later, *"the people"* sought to arrest him, but no one laid hands on him *"because his hour had not yet come"* (Jn 7:30). They asked one another, *"When the Christ (the anointed) appears, will he do more signs than this man has done?"* (7:31).

When the blind man by the pool of Siloam is given his sight, again the question of *"signs"* is raised. *"The Pharisees again asked him how he had received his sight. He said to them, 'He put clay on my eyes, and I washed, and I see.' Some of the Pharisees said, 'This man is not from God, for he does not keep the Sabbath.' But others said, 'How can a man who is a sinner do such signs?'"* (9:15-16).

The discussion intensified after Jesus raised Lazarus from the dead (12:18). People and authorities alike considered this event to be a *"sign."* Chief priests and Pharisees gathered the Jewish Council in Jerusalem to make a decision about Jesus. The question before the council concerned Jesus' *"signs."* They asked each other, *"'What are we to do? For this man performs many signs. If we let him go on this way, everyone will believe in him and the Romans will come and destroy both our holy place and our nation.' Caiaphas, who was high priest that year, said to them, 'Do you not understand that it is expedient that one man should die for the people and that the whole nation should not perish.' So from that day on they took counsel how to put him to death"* (11:47-53).

After the Sanhedrin made its decision about Jesus, John's Gospel used the word *"signs"* only twice more. In chapter 12, the writer wondered why, though Jesus had done so many signs before them, Jews on the Sanhedrin did not believe in him. John decided it happened so that *"the word spoken by the prophet Isaiah might be fulfilled"* (Jn 12:38). *"Lord, who has believed our report and to whom has the arm of the Lord been revealed?"* (Is 53:1). Isaiah also said, *"He has blinded their eyes and hardened their heart, lest they should see with their eyes and perceive with their heart and turn for me to heal them"* (Is 6:10). Isaiah said this, the writer John decided, because Isaiah had foreseen Christ's glory and spoke of him (Jn 12:37-43).

The final use of *"signs"* is in the Gospel's summation. *"Now Jesus did many other signs in the presence of the disciples, which are not written in this book; but these are written that you may believe that Jesus is the Christ, the Son of God, and that believing you may have life in his name"* (20:30-31). *"My father is working,"* Jesus said, after a cripple was able to walk again, *"and I am working"* (5:17). The word *"sign"* is a shorthand form for this idea. *"Truly, truly, I say to you,"* said Jesus in concluding a healing story (5:19), *"the Son can do nothing of his own accord, but only what he sees the Father doing; for whatever the Father does, that the Son does likewise."*

Jesus' Final Temptation

"Now among those who went up to worship at the feast were some Greeks. So these came to Philip... and said to him, 'Sir, we wish to see Jesus'... Andrew went with Philip and they told Jesus. And Jesus answered them, 'The hour has come for the Son of humankind to be glorified. Truly, truly, I say to you, unless a grain of wheat falls into the ground and dies, it remains alone; but if it dies, it bears much fruit. He who loves his life loses it and he who hates his life in this world will keep it for eternal life. If any one serves me, he must follow me; and where I am, there shall my servant be also; if any one serves me, the Father will honor him. Now is my soul troubled. And what shall I say? 'Father, save me from this hour?' No, for this purpose I have come to this hour. Father, glorify thy name... Now is the judgment of this world, now shall the ruler of this world be cast out; and I, when I am lifted up from the earth, will draw all men to myself'" (12:20-32).

A key question in interpreting this passage is, Who were these Greeks, and what did they wish to say to Jesus? They could have been Greeks who were Jewish proselytes or Hellenist-Jewish Greeks who came to Jerusalem to celebrate this feast and merely wished to meet him. Or, as some scholars believe, they were Greeks from their homeland who had journeyed to Judea to learn what truths were being taught there. Such Greeks were the humanists of the ancient world and were always looking for the good, the true, and the beautiful. Would they find these things in Jesus, a well-known teacher, and, if so, might they even try to recruit him to join them in teaching in their home country?

This was posed as the final temptation before Jesus—should he go to Greece and teach in the shadowed groves of the Platonists and the pleasant arcades of the Aristotelians, test his ideas against theirs, see who really held the truth? Or should he go to the cross and die? To show the depth of temptation John used the same word that Mark used as he described Jesus' temptation in Gethsemane, *"Now is my soul troubled."*

Jesus made his decision. *"What shall I say? 'Father, save me from this hour?' No, for this purpose I have come to this hour."* He explains his decision, *"Unless a grain of wheat falls into the ground and dies, it remains alone; but if it dies, it bears much fruit. He who loves his life loses it and he who hates his life in this world will keep it for eternal life."* Jesus decided to be like that grain of wheat. He would go forth and die. He could not explain the new life, he could not teach it. He had to give his life to bring new life into being from his crucified and risen life. He asked his Father if he had made the correct decision. *"Father, glorify thy name,"* he said. The Father answered at once. *"A voice came from heaven, I have glorified it, and I will glorify it again."* This was Jesus' final temptation, says John's Gospel, and this is how Jesus answered it (12:20-32).

The long waiting, first intimated at the sign in Cana, was now ending. Three times the writer John used the solemn phrase, *"Has come the hour when the Son of Humankind may be glorified"*—here, at the last supper after Judas left (13:31), and in the high priestly prayer (17:1). *"Glory"* in John's Gospel means the point at which God's glory enters human life.

One thing became clear from this event. In John's Gospel, Jesus' glorification is his death. His death was his *"being lifted up"* from the world. Then *"all (pantos)"*, implying *"all people,"* will be drawn to him. In John's Gospel, Jesus' death, *"being lifted up,"* and glorification are all in this one act. The *"glory"* of God is the cross of Jesus Christ. On the cross—in its stark dreadfulness—the presence of God most clearly shows itself.

Did *"all people"* come to Christ at the cross? No. At the cross only a few of his most intimate friends were with him— his Mother and the Beloved Disciple, a few women watched *"from afar."* The Twelve were not there. But after his resurrection, his followers began to come back. Mary Magdalene, Peter, and the Beloved Disciple were there first. A few other Galilean followers came later. Some Jews from Jerusalem came. Then Jews and Greeks from the world's cities gathered around him. Even a few Romans joined in. Within a century, a cascade of followers flowed to him. *"All people"* have not come to him. But all kinds of people—rich, poor, strong, weak, women, men, slaves, free, ethnics from many races and nations—have come to him. That is fulfillment enough for the words, *"If I be lifted up, I will draw all to me"* (12:32).

The Gospel's prologue said *"the light shines in the darkness and the darkness does not overcome it."* In the Gospel's crucifixion story many people were overcome by the darkness; they did not see the light while the light was there. Jesus' response to this issue is quite sharp. Many still wanted to engage Jesus in debate. But for Jesus, debate was over. He must do what he determined he must do—go to the cross and in this way fulfill his father's will for him. Instead of debating with them over the issue of who is the Son of Humankind, Jesus simply instructs them to walk in the light as they have seen the light, so that the darkness might not overcome them (12:35).

The Meal before Passover

"Now before the feast of the Passover, when Jesus knew that his hour had come to depart out of this world to the Father, having loved his own who were in the world, he loved them to the end. And during supper, when the devil had already put it into the heart of Judas Iscariot, Simon's son, to betray him, Jesus, knowing that the Father had given all things into his hands and that he had come from God and was going to God, rose from supper, laid aside his garments, and girded himself with

a towel. Then he poured water into a basin and began to wash the disciples' feet and to wipe them with the towel with which he was girded" (Jn 13:1-5).

The features in this meal are unique to John's Gospel—no other Gospel even hinted at them. All Gospels agreed that Jesus gathered his Disciples for a meal before Passover. The Twelve from Galilee, led by Peter, were there but John noted that at least one Hellenist attended, the Beloved Disciple, *"who laid at Jesus' breast"* (13:23). John's Gospel gave no hint of a cloak and dagger aspect to the story—no finding a secret place for a meal and no man with a pitcher of water leading furtive disciples to the meal's location. This meal, in John, is not a Passover meal (13:1a)—no such meal was prepared for this occasion.

John's prelude for this meal has to do with Jesus' love for his followers, *"Having loved his own, he loved them to the end"* (13:1b). Figure 7, above, shows that the word *"agape, love"* (or its cognates, such as "loving") is used more often (81 times, 45 in John alone) than any word in all the Gospels except "father"(309 times), "enter" (116 times), and "Son of Humankind," or "Son of Man" (82 times). "Forgive" is used only 48 times.

The meaning of *"love,"* agape—what God wanted all people to do toward one another according to John—is seen in washing the disciples' feet as well as those acts that followed. Jesus loved his own to the end, the end of his life seen in his sacrificial love. John added a second comment about Jesus at the meal, *"Jesus knew that he had come from God and was going to God"* (13:3). For Jesus, the meal represented a critical moment between this life and the next. The Father had been with him in every moment of his life so that Jesus had the confidence to know that God would be with him in what he faced in his next few hours and in his life to come.

When guests arrived for a meal, someone, usually a hired servant or a slave, was always present to wash the guests' feet. In John's account of the Last Supper Jesus is the servant who washes their feet. The Greek word, *doulos,* used throughout this passage for "serve" is a very intimate word. It does not refer to a slave who worked at a distance in the fields or in a shop, out of the master's sight and mind. *Doulos* is a personal servant, who works in close attendance to a master (13:26). Guests wore mainly open sandals to a meal and had just come in from the city's filthy streets. Urine, feces, garbage filled those streets. Someone, usually a *doulos*, had to wash such dirty feet (13:3-4). "Someone" at this meal was not a hired servant or slave. Jesus himself rose from the table, laid off his outer robe, tied a towel around his waist as any *doulos* would do, then washed his disciples' feet.

By this act Jesus' consciously fulfilled the role of God's servant (Is 53). Like any faithful servant, Jesus was bent on doing God's will and work, even when despised and rejected by men, a man of sorrows, acquainted with grief. Washing his disciples' feet stands as a great portrayal of Christian experience—when the greatness and far-reaching presence of God exhibited itself, it came as a *doulos* washing dirt off his disciple's feet. Instead of emphasizing eating, drinking, fellowship, and merriment in this meal, God in Christ does the meal's most menial act performed for another, washing the feet of *"his friends."* John's Gospel emphasized God's act of servitude. *"If I have washed your feet, you ought to wash one another's feet"* (13:14). By this act, Jesus disclosed another clue to a Christian life. Christians serve one another and the world, as Christ has served. Until this happens, a fellowship is not a Christian fellowship.

Simon Peter did not want Jesus to do a servant's work and rebelled against it. *"You will not wash my feet"* (13:6-11). Peter quite misunderstood Jesus' purpose. When Jesus said that only those whose feet he had washed had a share in him, Peter wanted Jesus to wash his hands and head as well, a possible touch of baptismal theology. In baptism, one does not wash; the water is a small symbol of one's total cleansing. *"You are all clean,"* said Jesus, *"except one."*

At the meal, Jesus *"was deeply troubled in spirit"* (13:21). To the writer John, this was again the equivalent of Jesus' prayer in Gethsemane in the other Gospels. In both events, Jesus *"was deeply troubled."* The "deep troubling's" cause is apparent—Jesus announced that one of those sitting at the table will betray him. Somehow Jesus anticipated what Judas was about to do. The disciples were seated on couches, reclining on their left arms, which supported their heads. They used their right arm to reach the dishes on a table placed in the center of the couches. Jesus would have come to the outside of the couches to wash the disciples' feet which were stretched out behind them (Brown, 1979: 511). This position at the table is important to what is about to occur.

When Jesus announced that *"one of you will betray me,"* a puzzled Peter, seated near Jesus but not next to him, inquired of the *"disciple whom Jesus loved"* sitting next to Jesus, who it might be. When the beloved disciple asked the question, *"Jesus answered, 'It is he to whom I will give this piece of bread when I have dipped it.'"* Jesus gave it to Judas and said, *"What you have to do, do quickly."* No one at the table, even at this late date, suspected Judas or knew what he was about to do. Judas took the bread and left. *"And it was night,"* said the Gospel, a sinister time for Judas and for the whole unresponsive world.

Jesus then said, *"Now the Son of Humankind has been glorified and God has been glorified in him."* In saying this, Jesus again was saying that God's glory will be seen on his cross. All the light of God was now to focus on this one act, one that seemed least likely to display God's glory, the stark and bitter cross.

At this point, three key persons need further identification. *"The Son of Humankind"* is one. This epochal figure was to appear at the end of the age and bring in God's new kingdom. When Jesus identified himself as this figure, he was announcing the end of the present age in favor of a new way of life. This new age would be distinguished by how people loved one another. *"Love one another,"* Jesus said, *"as I have loved you"*—with the love of God. The love shown to one another is the love by which God has loved you. The Son of Humankind brings this love into human life.

"Judas" is a second. Here he was called *"son of Simon Iscariot."* No other Gospel identified him this way. Elsewhere he was *"Judas Iscariot."* Thinking that *"Iscariot"* referred to Judas' childhood village, scholars have tried to locate it, without success. More recently, *"Iscariot"* is understood as an Aramaic form of *"sicarii."* *Sicarii* were assassins in Judea dedicated to overthrowing Roman rule by force. Under flowing sleeves they carried a short knife, a *"sicarius"* in Latin. Given an opportunity, sicarii would use this knife on Roman soldiers. If this latter identification is correct, it throws much light on who Judas was. He could follow Jesus loyally because Jesus often questioned conventional ways of understanding and doing things. But Judas probably had another loyalty—to the armed-rebellion goals and means used by his father Simon Iscariot, something quite different from Jesus' loyalties so that Jesus disappointed him (Zeitlin, 1988: 143).

"The disciple whom Jesus loved" (13:23) is the third figure. During the last supper was the first time the writer John reported a disciple with this title. Was the Gospel writer this person? Was *"the beloved disciple"* John the son of Zebedee, the brother of Simon Peter? *"The beloved disciple"* seemed to know a great deal more about Jerusalem than a fisherman from northern Galilee was apt to know. *"The beloved disciple"* was known personally by the high priest and bold enough to stand at the cross which Roman law forbade. In John's Gospel, accounts of the last supper and crucifixion probably derived from him, especially those parts that disagree with the other Gospels. He was a man *"lying close to Jesus' breast,"* an intimate who knew Jesus' heart well and specifics of what happened to Jesus in his final hours.

Who else in the early Jesus movement could *"the beloved disciple"* possibly be? John's Gospel provided several clues that hint at his identity. John's Gospel first mentioned someone *"whom Jesus loved"* in the account of Lazarus' resurrection (Jn 11:2 ff). Lazarus' two sisters, Mary and Martha, sent

Jesus a message, *"Lord, he whom you love is ill."* The evangelist then amplified the remark. *"Now Jesus loved Martha and her sister and Lazarus"* (11:5). These two statements point to a pre-history, not narrated by John, of Jesus' close loving relationship with this family.

Lazarus lived with his sisters Mary and Martha in Bethany, located on the Mount of Olives' east side over the lip of the Mount outside Jerusalem so that Bethany could not be seen from Jerusalem. When Jesus was in Judea or Jerusalem, he appears to have stayed with this family in Bethany. As Jesus made his way from Jericho to Jerusalem to celebrate a last Passover with his followers, the sisters sent a message to him that their brother was very ill. Jesus did not respond immediately to this message. But on arriving in Bethany, he found that Lazarus had died four days earlier. Jesus went with the sisters and a crowd of followers to Lazarus' tomb. On arriving there, *"Jesus was greatly disturbed in spirit and deeply moved."* This same phrase was used to describe Jesus at the last meal before identifying Judas' betrayal and in the Garden of Gethsemane when he prayed that the cup *"be removed from me."* Since John's Gospel did not depict Jesus praying in the Garden, the words *"greatly disturbed, deeply disquieted in spirit, vastly upset"* (the latter being alternate translations) imply that raising Lazarus was equivalent, in John's Gospel, to Jesus facing issues of life and death in Gethsemane.

The moment of Lazarus' deliverance from death is dramatic. Jesus ordered that the large stone in front of the tomb be removed. Martha demurred. *"He has been dead four days. The stench will be overwhelming."* Jesus said, *"If you believe, you will see the glory of God."* Jesus prayed. Then, like the trumpet on the last day, Jesus cried out with a loud voice, *"Lazarus, come out!"* Bound up in the grave clothes of death, Lazarus came out. *"Unbind him,"* Jesus said, *"and let him go."*

This act of resurrection had dire consequences for both Jesus and Lazarus. The Sanhedrin called a quick meeting and sentenced Jesus to death. *"It is expedient for you that one man should die for the people and that the whole nation should not perish,"* said Caiaphas, the high priest and presiding officer of the Sanhedrin. From this day forward the chief priests took counsel how to put Jesus to death (11:49, 53). They also planned to put Lazarus to death. Many Jews believed in Jesus due to Lazarus' resurrection (12:10-11). As long as Lazarus lived, Lazarus was a symbol of Jesus' power and threatened the priests' power.

At this point (after 12:10-11), Lazarus' name disappears from John's Gospel. A main clue to identifying *"the beloved disciple"* comes when Lazarus leaves the story and *the beloved disciple* enters it. After Lazarus' name disappeared, John's Gospel used the title *"the beloved disciple"* four times. He had the choice spot during Jesus' last supper—*"lying close to the breast of Jesus"* (13:23). Probably he was also the *"other disciple known to the high priest"* who, with Simon Peter, heard Jesus' interrogation by the high priest (18:15-24). He could also have been present when Pilate questioned Jesus in the praetorium. He was surely present at Jesus' crucifixion (19:26-27)—at the excruciating moment Jesus bequeathed his mother's care to this disciple. He was the first man to reach Jesus' tomb on resurrection morning (20:3-9) and the first to *"see and believe."* He was in Galilee when Jesus revealed himself by the Sea of Tiberias (21:20-23). We suspect he was also the one of whom it was said, *"This is the disciple who is bearing witness to these things, and who has written these things, and we know that his testimony is true"* (21:24).

The title *"the beloved disciple"* might have been designed to hide Lazarus' identity from those who had sentenced him to death. But possibly this phrase was simply a title of honor given to someone who was very close to Jesus in body and spirit. Although the person behind the title remains a mystery, before Lazarus was given the death sentence by Caiaphas and the Sanhedrin, he was the one *"whom Jesus loved."* After the sentence someone became known to others in the Jesus movement as *"the beloved disciple."* Quite possibly, then, *"the beloved disciple"* was Lazarus. If so, much of John's Gospel can be attributed to Lazarus.

"A new commandment I give you, that you love one another" (13:34). This new commandment extended an old commandment, *"love your neighbor as yourself"* (Leviticus 19:18). What was new was that Christian love is not based on how much people love themselves but on how God loves us all. God's love is not only for a neighbor but is the special love that Jesus showed for *"all men, all people"* (Jn 13:34-36). The commandment was new both because of what it said and because of the person who gave it. Everything Jesus said, everything Jesus did helped to define God's love. Following this commandment by the Teacher and Master may sound simple but it is indeed demanding and difficult (13:31-36; see Romans 7:15, *"For I do not do what I want to do; but what I do not want to do, that I do"*).

This conversation, probably several conversations condensed into one, between Jesus and his close friends was the longest recorded conversation between Jesus and others in the four Gospels. It covers four chapters in John's Gospel, chapters 14 through 17. It was the first recorded time he called his disciples *"his friends."* *"You are my friends, if you do what I command you. No longer do I call you servants; for the servant does not know what his master is doing; but I have called you friends, for all things that I heard from my Father, I have made known to you"* (15:14-15).

Greek practice had precedence for such a conversation in what was called a symposium, an occasion when a dozen or so intimate friends would get together for food, drink, and conversation (Hughes, 2010: Location 5039-5048). Such conversations normally focused on things relevant to the friends' lives. Such symposia were common among Hellenists and probably among Hellenist Christians in their frequent "fellowship meals." The group would discuss matters important to them, such as the meaning of "justice," *dikai,* or *philos,* "brotherly love," *eros,* sexual love, and Christian *agape,* God's love (the word *agape* was seldom used in classical Greek—Greeks had no God of *agape* in their pantheon, even if they had gods of *eros* and *philos*). The meal before Passover in John's Gospel fit very well with a Greek symposium meal. It was the model for symposia later conducted by Hellenist Christians throughout Roman civilization.

Four parts of this long conversation seem most relevant—*"the way"* of Jesus Christ; the coming of the *"Paraclete"*; the branch, the vine, and the *"Son of Humankind"*; and the promise of *"eternal life."*

The Way

"The way" comes from Jesus' long reflection, *"'Let not your hearts be troubled; believe in God, believe also in me. In my Father's house are many rooms; if it were not so, would I have told you that I go to prepare a [resting] place for you? And when I go and prepare a place for you, I will come again and will take you to myself, that where I am you may be also. And you know the way where I am going.' Thomas said to him, 'Lord, we do not know where you are going; how can we know the way?' Jesus said to him, 'I am the way and the truth and the life; no one comes to the Father, but by me. If you had known me, you would have known my Father also; henceforth you know him and have seen him'"* (14:1-7). This statement clarified Jesus' previous theme that *"I and the Father are one"* (10:30).

"Do not let your hearts be troubled. Believe in God, believe also in me." Jesus used the Greek phrase, *kardia tarassestho,* *"hearts be troubled,"* several times in John's Gospel—when standing before Lazarus' tomb and when confronting his own cross. Here these words are commands—his friends are commanded not to be *"troubled." "Do not be troubled,"* but, when you are troubled, come to me, *"believe in me."*

The Greek phrase Jesus used for *"resting place," monai caravaniserais* (14:2), signified a wayside resting-place, a shelter along a road, an ancient rest stop, where travelers, often in caravans, refreshed themselves in their journeys. In the Mideast wealthy travelers usually sent a servant forward to prepare the next resting-place for them. Here the Lord presents himself as a spiritual servant treading the way of faith—the *"pioneer and perfecter of faith"* (Hebrews 12:2)—making resting places ready to welcome his followers.

"The way (hodos)." Jesus as the way shows he thought of himself as the trusted guide through life, through its peaks and valleys, dark streets and pleasant fields, prickling brambles and hidden paths. Hellenist Christians chose the nickname, *"hodos,"* the Way, for expressing their fellowship (Acts 9:2).

"The truth (aletheia)." Jesus' word is built on the bedrock of truthfulness, "revealing what is behind the veil," a solid foundation for people's lives. As God is truthful in all he says, so Jesus always spoke the truth about God.

"The life (zoe)." Jesus did not say "I have the life." He said, *"I am...the life."* Jesus represented authentic life. Paul accurately describes this life, *"To me to live is Christ."*

"The Paraclete"

"I will pray the Father and he will give you another Counselor (paraclete) to be with you for ever, even the Spirit of truth, whom the world cannot receive, because it neither sees him nor knows him; you know him for he dwells with you and will be in you. I will not leave you desolate; I will come to you" (14:16-18). John's Gospel introduces the ambiguous Greek term, *"paraclete."*

In the New Testament's King James version, *paraclete* is translated *"Comforter."* John Wyclif, the first person to translate the Bible into English, used the word *"Strengthener."* He chose this word because the Latin text translated *paraclete* as *cumfortis*, combining two Latin words, *cum* and *fortis*. *Fortis* means "strength," and *cum* is "with." The Comforter strengthens Christians as they face their adversities. The American Standard Version uses *"Helper."* The Revised Standard Version, above, uses *"Counselor."* The New Revised

Standard Version uses *"Advocate."* In Greek, *paraclete* combines two words, *kletos*, meaning "called," and *para* meaning "to," "beside," or "above." The Paraclete, coming from above, calls out to and stands beside Jesus' followers as they face their numerous life situations.

John's Gospel used *Paraclete* five times in this long conversation during his last meal (14:16; 14:25; 15:26; 16:7b-11; 16:12-15). Jesus and the *Paraclete* have different roles. The *Paraclete* comes only after Jesus departs; the *Paraclete* is Jesus' presence when Jesus is absent. Jesus' promise to dwell with his disciples is fulfilled in the *Paraclete*. Jesus will be in heaven with the Father while the *Paraclete* is on earth with the disciples.

If the *Paraclete* has such important functions, why is the word used so infrequently today? The reason probably is that the word *paraclete* was competing with the term *pneuma*, *"Spirit,"* later called *hagion pneuma, "Holy Spirit."* Which term might Jesus have preferred? The writer John used both terms, *paraclete* here and *hagion pneuma* earlier (1:33) and later (20:22). Mark's Gospel, the earliest of the written Gospels, does not use either term. Neither Luke nor Matthew used the word *paraclete*. Brethren communities probably used *Hagion Pneuma*, then later formalized it in Matthew's Gospel. Apostles' communities probably also used *Hagion Pneuma* then formalized it in Luke's Gospel. The writer John was possibly searching for a term that Hellenist Christians would understand more readily than the term *Holy Spirit* and chose the word *paraclete*. Over the next 300 years, Christian leaders recognized that *Paraclete* and *Hagion Pneuma* were one and the same—they had similar descriptions and did the same work. The Nicene and Apostles' Creeds in effect sanctified the term *"Holy Spirit"* to become the church's common language.

The *Paraclete*, the *Holy Spirit*, the successor to Jesus, continues Jesus' ministry. In the Old Testament, Joshua was successor to Moses and carried on Moses' ministry; Elisha was successor to Elijah and continued Elijah's prophetic work.

In the New Testament, Jesus' successor is the Paraclete, the Holy Spirit, who continues his ministry, begun in Judea and Galilee, among all *"ethne,"* the entire world.

Everything said about the *paraclete* has already been said about Jesus.

- Jesus has come; the *paraclete* will come
- Jesus is the first; the *paraclete* is *"another"*
- The disciples were privileged to know Jesus; they are now privileged to know the *paraclete*
- The world did not accept Jesus; the world cannot accept the *paraclete*
- Jesus bore witness against the world; the *paraclete* witnesses in face of the world's opposition
- The *paraclete* will prove the world wrong about Jesus' trial.

"The True Vine," the Branch, and the "Son of Humankind"

"I am the true vine and my Father is the vinedresser. Every branch of the vine that bears no fruit, he takes away and every branch that does bear fruit he prunes that it may bear more fruit. Abide in me and I in you. As the branch cannot bear fruit by itself unless it abides in the vine, neither can you unless you abide in me. I am the vine, you are the branches. He who abides in me and I in him, he it is that bears much fruit for apart from me you can do nothing. If a man does not abide in me, he is cast forth as a branch and withers; and the branches are gathered, thrown into the fire, and burned" (15:1-6).

Only the writer John records this parable. In it Jesus sees the Father as a vinedresser engaging in two different actions. The first is when, as annually in February and March, a vinedresser prunes branches which have no leaves. When the branches begin to bloom, he cuts away those that would bear less fruit. In August he pinches off shoots so that main fruit-bearing branches get as much nourishment as possible.

In the post-harvest period, all branches not attached to the vine are gathered and burned (15:6).

This parable has at least four implications. First, the analogy reflected the ancient symbol of the tree of life, sometimes represented as a vine. Israel was God's vineyard, sometimes fruitful but often unproductive and disappointing to Yahweh. Psalm 80 tells how God brought a vine out of Egypt, planted it, and watched it grow to bring forth great branches and fruit. Then the fence around it broke, ravishing the vine.

Second, the Septuagint posited that *"the vine"* and *"Son of Humankind"* are identical. The vine represented the people of God, exposed to death and destruction but saved by the hand of God who raised them to life again.

Third, Jesus saw himself as the *"true vine"* (Jn 15:1). All persons who were branches from him were the *"true"* people of God. The implied triangular relationship between Father, Son, and Disciples centers on the word *agape,* the Father's love offered by the Son for the life of the world. The Son's love showed perfect obedience to the Father's will by laying down his life for his disciples. The disciples' love stemmed from their obedience to Christ's command to love one another. By their obedience the Father is glorified in the Son.

Fourth, the vine could also be associated with the Last Supper. The eucharistic meaning of the vine's fruit recognizes the lasting union between Christ and his disciples and the union the disciples had among themselves. The communion energizes the love between Jesus and his followers.

"Eternal Life"

"This is eternal life, that they know thee the only true God and Jesus Christ whom thou hast sent" (17:3). John's Gospel presumed that Christ fulfilled what the world sought. Jesus called it *"eternal life."* The love personified by Jesus the Christ provided this eternal life. Greek culture sought "something else" but could not find it; they could hardly even "name" it.

To know God and participate in eternal life required a radical restructuring of first-century Hellenist life and thought. To Hellenists, eternal life was possible only when *"the flesh (sarx),"* physical matter, had no more power over one's life. Obviously this could not take place until death, when the earthly tent was struck for the last time and the soul, refined by discipline in this life, was released into the realm of pure spirit, its "true" home. In Jesus' time, Greek thought had no "reaching-out" feature about life. Trained to believe that the body's hopes, loves, and commitments meant nothing eternally, most Greeks' lives were to be lived in the present, largely fate-ful, hope-less, and in the end meaning-less. T. S. Eliot, educated in the classical tradition, once remarked that life in London in the 20th century reflected life in first-century Athens and Rome. "I did not know that death had undone so many."

Christian beliefs and actions challenged the alienating features of Greek thought and life. For Christians, not "matter" but "will" was the central reality. Self-chosen habits, routines, thoughts, and decisions kept Hellenists from responding to the love of God in Christ. When a person wills to respond to Jesus Christ—to *"know Christ"* to use the Gospel's terms—eternal life begins immediately, and it later passes through the moment of physical death into the "life of the Eternal." In eternal life, hope conquers despair, grace overcomes fate, love toward others outpaces meaninglessness. Lives for the vast majority of Greco-Roman people lacked meaningful existence because they had no vital hope. "Knowing" Jesus Christ and the love of God would change this condition.

In contrast to Hellenist thought, Christian "knowing" is not cognitive alone. Biblical use of "know" has to do with a person's basic commitments. It was first used in Scripture as the act of sexual intercourse as in *"Adam knew his wife and she conceived."* As such, it meant the complete commitment of one person to another in the most intimate way. It was also used in connection with a covenant treaty, "knowing" a vassal indicated that a master was loyal to his vassal and "knowing" the master indicated that a vassal was loyal to his master.

The prophet Amos used "know" to describe God's relationship with Israel, *"You only have I known of all the peoples of the earth"* (3:2). John's Gospel reports that Jesus used the word "know" to describe God's relationship with his followers. Whoever commits to the unconditional love of God as revealed in Christ has eternal life. The present tense needs to be stressed. Eternal life is not introduced into human life at the moment of death; it enters at the moment of full commitment to Christ—to living the loving life of the eternal God. To be committed to his Son, the anointed, Christ, means to make him central in life, seek his approval when in doubt, find in him strength and support, construct life with him as its model, serve the causes he serves, love the people he loves.

No longer do people have to experience alienation from life with its confusions, lonesomeness, lostness. They can conquer these conditions through the love of God as revealed in Jesus Christ. This was John's affirmation of what Jesus meant. Men and women who fear mortality and guilt can respond fully, consciously, to Jesus the Christ. This is to have life, eternal life, in this life and in God's promised life to come.

This hope, says John's Gospel, is no forlorn hope but written into the structure of life itself. *"Before the world was"* the relationship between Father and Son was. One enters into this life by living in tandem with Christ, as husbands live with wives and both know each other. This Christ is not a ghostly spirit but the Christ to whom one turns in extremity, in decisions, for fellowship. His words are known. Every person can have life, eternal life, when he or she lives in consummate relationship with Christ. This bestowal of eternal life is the life the world longs for. *"This is eternal life, that they know thee the only true God and Jesus Christ whom thou hast sent"* (Jn 17:3).

One with a Living, Working, and Loving God— Jesus as the Great "I AM"

Above all, through the *"I am"* statements John incorporates into his Gospel, he proclaims that Jesus is one with God. *"Ego eimi...,"* *"I am...,"* appears at least nine times in John's Gospel as Jesus explains to people who he is. Persons nurtured in Judaism would clearly recognize the phrase's meaning as the name God gave to himself when Moses asked the voice on the mountain. *"'What is your name?' 'I AM WHO I AM,'"* said the voice to Moses. *"Tell the people of Israel, I AM has sent me to you"* (Exodus 3:14). Throughout John's Gospel, Jesus uses this name as he identifies himself to these later Israelites. The "I AM" statements are the clearest indications in the Gospels that Jesus identified himself fully with God.

- *I am the bread of life*
- *I am the light of the world*
- *I am the door of the sheep*
- *I am the good shepherd*
- *I am the resurrection and the life*
- *I am the way, the truth, and the life*
- *I am the true vine*
- *I am the Son of Humankind*
- *I am the Son of God*
- *I and the Father are one.*

As the Father has given these to me, I give sustenance, I give light, I give comfort and guidance, I gather you around me as a vine holds its branches, I am the way, the truth and the life. I am one with God. And I invite you to share these gifts with me.

John's Gospel ends with a fitting benediction that summarizes Jesus' commands to his followers. Jesus said to Thomas, *"Have you believed because you have seen me? Blessed are those who have not seen and yet believe"* (20:29).

In recording these words, the writer John was looking into near and distant futures. Jesus Christ's influence, the influence of the living, loving, working God, was far from over. This influence will extend into unknown places and to generations yet to be born.

Part Four

Who Is the Jesus of the Early Jesus Movement?

The four Gospels are our most enduring legacy of the four parties of the early Jesus movement. They contain Jesus' words and actions filtered through the presuppositions of each party. This filtering included collecting the stories and words, discussing them with members of their own parties and possibly with representatives of the other parties, making judgments about which were most important to them, telling them to each other, refining them, committing the refined statements to memory, changing them as necessary so that their hearers both in and outside their parties might best understand them. Together, and abetted by the letters and papers of the respective parties' representatives, the Gospels provide our most complete portrait of Jesus of Nazareth.

Chapter 11

The Shared Jesus

Certain things about Jesus the parties readily agreed upon. They agreed that Jesus was a forthright prophet who challenged both civil and religious authorities in the name of his God and in behalf of his message. According to every Gospel, Jesus' first act in his ministry was to go to the Temple in Jerusalem and undertake to cleanse it, ridding it of extraneous things that in his view corrupted its worship of God. His challenge was to both priest and king, the king who built the Temple and the priests who presided there. The result? With the connivance of both priests and king, Jesus was condemned and later executed by crucifixion.

Caring and Compassionate Leader, Healer, Teacher, Person

The four major parties of the early Jesus movement agreed that Jesus was a leader of men and women. People were drawn to him. Peter was a small town entrepreneur, a self-employed fisherman on the Sea of Galilee. Levi, also called Matthew, was a tax-collector for Rome. Paul was in training to be a rabbi with a career in teaching before him; Luke was a physician; and the writer John a philosopher in contemporary Hellenism. Mary Magdalene was a woman of means and Lazarus and his sisters, Mary and Martha, were wealthy enough to own a home in Bethany and an apartment in Jerusalem where Jesus last met with his disciples. Each called Jesus "Master" and charted courses for their lives from his.

He was a healer. The lame, blind, and ill sought him out and he healed them. He healed men and women of their infirmities and their diseases. Word of his healing powers spread to all the villages and by-ways of Galilee and Judea.

He was a teacher without peer; more people in diverse cultures have internalized his words than any other teacher in history. To author any one of his parables would be notable but for one person to author all of them is an unimaginable feat of literary creation. Yet he did not compose his stories and teachings as literary productions. They were to effect changes in people's lives and as Jew, Greek, Roman, Egyptian, Ethiopian, and Oriental people heard his teaching, their hearts were warmed and lives changed.

Jesus was a compassionate human being, whose love for beggar, leper, prostitute, and tax collector, as well as prophet, rabbi, merchant, and householder led them to respond with compassion of their own. Even his words of judgment have to be seen in light of this compassion. Knowing the ambiguity of human lives and people's indwelling ability to be blind to the most obvious sins and failures, he sharply called people to become the selves God created them to be. His healings expressed his compassion. Even when reticent to have his therapeutic activities broadcast throughout Galilee and Judea, he was still moved to take restorative action when the deaf, dumb, maimed, and blind came before him.

Above all, Jesus was a person whose words and actions were of one piece—he did what he said he would do and said only that which he would be able to support with his life's commitment. He said he was willing to suffer in order to show love toward others' suffering. He gave up his home to relate to the homeless, his reputation to associate with outcasts, and his life to die beside others condemned to death.

Accepting the Painful and Anguishing Course of His Ministry

The realization that his ministry was to culminate in his death came to him painfully. He saw his compatriot John the Baptist executed at Herod's command and Jesus realized his own fate could not be far different. Given repeated opportunities to escape his death by avoiding Jerusalem during the Passover festival, or by concealing himself on the Mount of Olives from the arresting throng, or by accepting Pilate's offer of clemency, Jesus resolutely faced the cross and trusted that God would use his death to accomplish his own redemptive purposes.

His death was indescribably painful. There was the physical pain—the scourging by leather thongs as the execution detail prepared him for the cross, the sharp puncture of nails through his hands and wrists under the hammer of the executioner, the wrenching of his body as the soldiers rudely dropped the crossbeam into place, the gasping for life-giving breath as his head sank lower onto his chest. The physical pain might have been bearable had it not been for the emotional pain of loss of friends and companions at this critical hour. As he breathed his last, not his disciples but his enemies—priests and scribes, Pharisees and soldiers—encircled his cross. And they jeered his pain.

The spiritual pain was worse. Where was the God whom he had served so buoyantly? Golgotha was a long way from Galilee where on lakeshore and hillside, in the Jews' synagogues and friends' houses, he had spoken confidently of God. Yet it had to happen, this pain, and Jesus knew that. Only he who had suffered all things that human beings suffer could possibly be their savior, because only by such suffering could he comprehend every depth of anguish into which humankind can descend. To witness the suffering of Christ on the cross is to see not only a human being experiencing the depth of physical extremity but also to see the very love of God himself incarnated in this man who participated in every imaginable form of human suffering.

Jesus also said he would rise from the dead to remain forever with those whom he loved and he did what he said he would do. His followers did not understand what he meant. They were not prepared for what occurred. Even under the prodding of many witnesses to his resurrection, some remained uncomprehending. But Jesus, when questioned earlier about the possibility of resurrection, replied that God has the power to raise the dead if God wished and the will to do it because God loved his people. In the interval after his death, the resurrected Jesus showed himself not as a fleeting memory but as a responding presence. He did not recede into the distant past but called his followers to a hopeful future, opening new insights into lifestyles appropriate to those loyal to him. His spirit seeks out those who are not conscious of his near approach. Jesus shared this quality with God—Jesus did what he said he would do and in his life demonstrated a unique identity of word with deed.

This, in part, is the "shared Jesus." All four Gospels include accounts like these.

Enhancing the Portraits of the Shared Jesus

In addition, each Gospel has its own perspective on Jesus' life and ministry. To have the most accurate portrait of him, all these perspectives need to be taken into account.

The Gospel of Mark: "The Healing, Suffering, and Trusting One"

Mark builds his picture of Jesus around two Old Testament scenarios. One is the picture of the Suffering Servant in Isaiah. *"Who has believed what we have heard? And to whom has the arm of the LORD been revealed? For he grew up before him like a young plant and like a root out of dry ground; he had no form or comeliness that we should look at him and no beauty that we should desire him. He was despised and rejected by men; a man of sorrows and acquainted with grief; and as one from whom men hide their faces he was despised and we esteemed him not. Surely he has borne our griefs and carried our sorrows; yet we esteemed him stricken, smitten by God, and afflicted. But he was wounded for our transgressions, he was bruised for our iniquities; upon him was the chastisement that made us whole, and with his stripes we are healed. All we like sheep have gone astray; we have turned every one to his own way; and the LORD has laid on him the iniquity of us all. He was oppressed and he was afflicted, yet he opened not his mouth; like a lamb that is led to the slaughter and like a sheep that before its shearers is dumb, so he opened not his mouth. By oppression and judgment he was taken away.*

"As for his generation, who considered that he was cut off out of the land of the living, stricken for the transgression of my people? And they made his grave with the wicked and with a rich man in his death, although he had done no violence and there was no deceit in his mouth. Yet it was the will of the LORD to bruise him; he has put him to grief; when he makes himself an offering for sin, he shall see his offspring, he shall prolong his days; the will of the LORD shall prosper in his hand" (Isaiah 53:1-10).

The second is Psalm 22, which Mark attributed to Jesus on the cross. *"My God, my God, why hast thou forsaken me? Why art thou so far from helping me, from the words of my groaning? O my God, I cry by day but thou dost not answer; and by night but find no rest. Yet thou art holy, enthroned on the praises of Israel. In thee our fathers trusted; they trusted, and thou didst deliver them. To thee they cried and were saved; in thee they trusted and were not disappointed.*

"All who see me mock at me, they make mouths at me, they wag their heads; He committed his cause to the LORD; let him deliver him, let him rescue him, for he delights in him!

"*Yet thou art he who took me from the womb; thou didst keep me safe upon my mother's breasts. Upon thee was I cast from my birth and, since my mother bore me, thou hast been my God. Be not far from me, for trouble is near and there is none to help. I am poured out like water, and all my bones are out of joint; my strength is dried up like a potsherd and my tongue cleaves to my jaws; thou dost lay me in the dust of death. A company of evildoers encircle me; they have pierced my hands and feet; they stare and gloat over me; they divide my garments among them, and for my raiment they cast lots.*

"*I will tell of thy name to my brethren; in the midst of the congregation I will praise thee: You who fear the LORD, praise him! all you sons of Jacob, glorify him and stand in awe of him all you sons of Israel! For he has not despised or abhorred the affliction of the afflicted and he has not hid his face from him but has heard, when he cried to him. From thee comes my praise in the great congregation; my vows I will pray before those who fear him. The afflicted shall eat and be satisfied; those who seek him shall praise the LORD! May your hearts live for ever!*

"*All the ends of the earth shall remember and turn to the LORD; and all the families of the nations shall worship before him. For dominion belongs to the LORD, and he rules over the nations. Posterity shall serve him; men shall tell of the Lord to the coming generation, and proclaim his deliverance to a people yet unborn, that he has wrought it*" (Psalm 22:1-31, abridged).

With words like these, Mark composed his Gospel. He pictured Jesus withdrawing into Galilee when John the Baptist was arrested. He withdrew farther from the land of his enemy Herod Antipas, west Galilee, into the land of Herod Philip east and north of the Sea of Galilee. He healed many people as he journeyed throughout Galilee. During his journey, he heard Peter call him Messiah, though he himself preferred the title "Son of Humankind." There in a moment of his revealed glory he was transfigured before them. There he announced, *"The Son of Humankind will be delivered into the hands of men and they will kill him and, when he is killed, after three days he will rise"* (Mk 9:31).

During his last night on this earth Jesus said to them, *"'My soul is very sorrowful, even to death; remain here, and watch.' And going a little farther, he fell on the ground and prayed that, if it were possible, the hour might pass from him. And he said, 'Abba, Father, all things are possible to thee; remove this cup from me; yet not what I will, but what thou wilt'"* (14:34-36).

Then it was a matter of entering further into his sufferings—his arrest, trial, sentence, execution. When he was dying, the word of the Lord came to him, *"My God, my God, why hast thou forsaken me?"* The words of Psalm 22 continue but Jesus, nearing death, was too weary to speak them. But every Jew knew them. *"Why art thou so far from helping me, from the words of my groaning? O my God, I cry by day, but thou dost not answer; and by night, but find no rest."* Then the remaining Psalm spoke to him, *"In thee our fathers trusted; they trusted and thou didst deliver them. To thee they cried and were saved; in thee they trusted and were not disappointed. For dominion belongs to the LORD, and he rules over the nations. Posterity shall serve him; men shall tell of the Lord to the coming generation and proclaim his deliverance to a people yet unborn, that he has wrought it."* He died with those words of assurance on his lips, Jesus, the Serving, Healing, Suffering, and Trusting One.

The Gospel of Matthew: "The Righteous and Just One"

Matthew's Old Testament antecedents are built around living in accord with God's laws as delivered in the Torah. In this Gospel, to be righteous means to be on right terms with God, our neighbor, ourselves, and our world around us. To be on right terms with our neighbor means to love our neighbor as God loves us. To be on right terms with the natural and animal world means careful cultivation of earth and sky, flora and fauna, stewardship of the earth and its resources. To be on right terms with the social world means to display justice and compassion to the "*least among us.*" To be on right terms with ourselves means to display a loving integrity. To be on right terms with God means to trust God in every situation of our lives. This is what Matthew meant by "righteousness."

The Greek language used *dikai* and its cognates to describe the great search in Greek civilization for a just society. In its place the New Testament more often uses the word *dikaio-sunai* for justice. Figure 7, above, shows that Matthew used the word just or justice 10 times, only four less than Luke, who used it the most. Snaith (1952: 1, 231) says that this refers to a wider use than the merely ethical. It moves beyond an abstract and intellectual concept of justice to something warmer and more humane. When Jesus describes "righteousness" in his last parable, it follows this latter meaning. "*When the Son of Humankind comes in his glory, and all the angels with him, then he will sit on his glorious throne. Before him will be gathered all the nations, and he will separate them one from another as a shepherd separates the sheep from the goats, and he will place the sheep at his right hand but the goats at the left. Then the King will say to those at his right hand, 'Come, O blessed of my Father, inherit the kingdom prepared for you from the foundation of the world; for I was hungry and you gave me food, I was thirsty and you gave me drink, I was a stranger and you welcomed me, I was naked and you clothed me, I was sick and you visited me, I was in prison and you came to me.' Then the righteous will answer him, 'Lord, when did we see thee hungry and feed thee, or thirsty and give thee drink? And when did we see thee a stranger and welcome thee, or naked and clothe thee? And when did we see thee sick or in prison and visit thee?' And the King will answer them, 'Truly, I say to you, as you did it to one of the least of these my brethren, you did it to me'*" (24:31-40). To act in this manner is to fulfill all righteousness and justice.

The Gospel of Luke:
"The Caringly Compassionate
and Socially Just One"

Fulfilling the charter of the Apostle's party as laid down early by Jesus' followers (Acts 2:44-47) and Paul in his Letter to the Galatians (3:28), Luke pictured Jesus as making no distinction between Jew and Greek, slave and free, man and woman; his healing ministry was freely open to all.

Luke built Jesus' ministry around Biblical statements of caringly compassionate social justice. His stories of the birth of Jesus included the Song of Mary, with its words, *"God's mercy is on those who fear him from generation to generation. He has shown strength with his arm, he has scattered the proud in the imagination of their hearts, he has put down the mighty from their thrones, and exalted those of low degree; he has filled the hungry with good things, and the rich he has sent empty away"* (1:50-53). Luke pictures the message going first to shepherds, then to the poor like Simeon and Anna.

In his home synagogue Jesus quotes a social justice passage from the prophet Isaiah and declares that now this is fulfilled in him. "Compassionate," in Greek *oiktirmones*, is a strong word, but even it is not enough to translate the New Testament term. *Oik* is a Greek stem for "family." "Humane" is not quite strong enough either. "Steadfast love" is used in many New Testament translations, "womb-like compassion" is Terrien's term, compassion for others like that which a mother has for the child in her womb. "Deeply caring, reaching out to bring others into the family" probably comes the closest. This is the Jesus of the Gospel of Luke.

The Gospel of John:
"One with God"

John's Gospel introduces another dimension into the portrait of Jesus—Jesus is One with God. The other Gospels often came close to saying this but John stated it explicitly,

"I and the Father are one" (10:30). The statements which include the phrase *"I am"* are the clearest indications in the Gospels that Jesus identified himself fully with God. In declaring that in these ways he was one with God, Jesus also set the path for his followers.

I am the bread of life – "I will give you the nourishment to be my follower."

I am the light of the world – "Telling others about me will bring them out of their moral darkness (of relativity) into a new meaning for their lives in reaching out to others"

I am the good shepherd – "I will take care of you"

I am the resurrection and the life – "Following me will make you a new creation"

I am the true vine—"My stem, my being, will give you strength and courage in emulating my endeavors"

I am the way, the truth, and the life

> *The way*—"In my ministry I have shown you what to do to be God's people"
>
> *The truth*—"I have revealed, removed the veil from, the true nature of God as a loving Father, working to heal people's ills and supporting them in loving one another"
>
> *The life*— "Following me will bring you new meaning, vision, hope, vitality, and inspiration to your life as you reach out to bring others into our 'family'"

God is all these, says John's Gospel. Jesus is all these, too. His followers are to respond to God in Christ recognizing these ways as their own.

The Benediction
"Blessed are those who have not seen and yet believe."

John's Gospel ends with a benediction. *"Have you believed because you have seen me? Blessed are those who have not seen and yet believe."* In recording these words, the writer John was looking into the near and distant future. The influence of Jesus Christ was far from over. It will extend into unknown places and unborn generations. It extends to those who share in his "shared ministry." It reaches those who participate in his extended ministries. We can know him as the healing and suffering one, the righteous one, the caringly compassionate and socially just one, with him we can be one with God. We can know him in one of these ways, or, better yet, in all of these ways. Karl Barth (1934) sums it up, "Jesus Christ as he is attested to us in Holy Scripture is the one word of God, whom we must hear, and whom we must trust and obey in life and in death."

Afterword

Jesus Christ, Yesterday, Today, and Tomorrow

We, Harry and Paul Eberts, fully subscribe to the statement in the Barmen Declaration: "Jesus Christ, as he is attested for us in Holy Scriptures, is the one Word of God, which we have to hear and which we have to trust and obey in life and in death."

The Jesus Christ in whom we believe is the one who was baptized by John the Baptist, lived in Galilee, cleansed the Temple in Jerusalem, traveled from Galilee to Jerusalem to celebrate the pilgrimage feasts of Judaism, who preached to the people on those occasions about the centrality of love in people's lives, who healed many blind and lame people, who met with crowds on the mountains and by the seaside, who entered Jerusalem in acclaim, who was condemned by religious and secular authorities for his beliefs and behavior, and, as our creeds say, crucified, dead, and buried. He rose from the dead and remains with his followers now and into the distant future.

Each Gospel chose a different view from the others in presenting Jesus to the world. To Matthew, Jesus is the righteous and just one. To Mark, Jesus is the healing, suffering, and trusting one. To Luke, Jesus is the compassionately caring and socially just one. To John, Jesus is one with a living, loving, and working God. All four Gospels are integral to Christian Biblical witness. Taken together, Christ's righteousness, his willingness to suffer to fulfill his aims, his compassion and caring, his oneness with the moral, loving God provide the church's clearest understanding of who Jesus Christ "really" was.

This Christ provides us with our means of engaging our faith with the present culture which surrounds us in all its multiplicities. In our families and other intimate relationships of life, we have before us in Christ the love of God. In our business and economic life, he is Christ the servant of God. In the political realm, he is Christ expressing the social justice of God. In our search for meaning through our schools and universities, our magazines and newspapers, our movies, TV, and internet, our sciences and philosophies, he is Christ, the truthfulness of God. In our relations with the natural and animal world around us, he is Christ the gentle one. In our spiritual endeavors, including life in our churches, he is Christ the revelation of the living, loving, and working God, who inspires us to become caringly compassionate and socially just. All our efforts in all these realms of life are judged and redeemed through his servanthood, his justice, his truthfulness, his gentleness, his love.

1 Jesus was a non-violent, peaceful revolutionary living in tumultuous, contentious, and dangerous times that featured high taxes, land confiscation, and, frequently, violent responses to these imposed conditions.

2 His life was in constant danger from the moment he understood who he was—as one with a living, loving God, still working his caring compassion in this world—and then acting on this understanding.

3 As the Gospels demonstrate, Jesus was familiar with Jewish Scriptural traditions, with Greek and Hellenistic cultures, and with Roman world-domination perspectives. He was also critical of each one. Applying his re-

interpretation of Scriptures (e.g., among other places, in his "beatitudes,"—"*You have heard that it was said… but I say…*") to his understanding of the four worlds he lived in (Jewish, Greek, Roman, and God's), Jesus produced a revolutionary vision about God's moral and loving nature. In doing this, he initiated a revolution that, when continued by many others, has mightily changed lives, history, and culture.

4 The Gospels show that Jesus was "a healer who suffered," "a righteous man seeking social justice for all kinds of disadvantaged people," "compassionate in his caring for others," and "one with the moral and loving God" who wanted his life to be experienced by all persons equally, with freedom for his people to become new persons, "new creations" (Paul's term, Galatians 6:15)—"born anew" was Jesus' phrase (Jn 3:7)—in bringing about a world with people committed to caring, equality, justice, and freedom for all God's people.

5 We also believe that God in Christ continues to work in our recent century as in all centuries past.

Literally thousands and perhaps millions of people in the last one hundred years have been transformed by Christ in working to transform the world and its structures in his spirit (on "structural justice," see Crosson, 1998: 342 f). In general, churches have done a good job in creating "community" for their members. But we believe *the* major challenge to Christians today is to continue structural transformations in our age of worldly abundance so that more people can enjoy an overall more inclusive world of loving relationships and the multiplicity of people who love one another in it. Here we can mention only a few individuals who have met this challenge and, very briefly, what they did, often supported by organizations they helped generate. We encourage our readers to examine what these men and women have done and to add to this list persons (and groups) you know whom you consider to be undertaking such transformations.

Walter Rauschenbusch graduated from seminary and chose to conduct his ministry in Hell's Kitchen, New York City. From his ministry a social-gospel movement rose in the Christian church that applied Christian ethics to social problems, especially issues of social justice such as wealth generally perceived as excessive and not put to use in resolving people's major problems, of poverty, alcoholism, drug abuse, crime, racial tensions, slums, poor hygiene, child labor, inadequate labor union representation, poor schools, the dangers of war, and wages adequate for food, housing, clothing, and transportation.

Albert Schweitzer left his academic studies behind to go to "darkest Africa" (his term) and extend the healing hand of Christ to persons in the nearby neighborhoods of Lambarene, Gabon, to people who had never heard of Christ and had never experienced modern medicine. His example moved countless others into similar missionary work.

Franklin Roosevelt and his colleagues in the White House began the 20th century realignment of political and social life in the United States, a country that he said at that time was "one-third ill-housed, ill-clad, ill-nourished." Then he led the coalition that confronted the powers of darkness embodied in Nazism, fascism, dictatorship, and authoritarianism that threatened to overtake the entire world. His deeds are well known. Not so well known was his motivation for doing all these things. When asked, he simply said, "I am a Christian and a Democrat."

Karl Barth, from a teaching post in Bonn, Germany, challenged growing Nazism in his country and in 1934 became the author of the Barmen Confession, whose statement about Christ we have repeatedly quoted.

Dietrich Bonhoeffer and his brother-in-law Hans von Dohnanyi were part of the World Christian Student Alliance. Through this connection they were drawn into an underground movement in Nazi Germany, called by the code name "Valkyrie," that came just short of assassinating Hitler in 1943. For this they and many others paid with their lives, being hanged on Hitler's orders just days before American troops liberated the prison in which they were held.

Pope John XXIII, in the Second Vatican Council, threw open the closed windows of the Vatican to let new winds blow in. Pope Francis I shows promise in his installation Mass when he pledged to serve "the poorest, the weakest, the least important, those whom Matthew [in his Gospel] lists in the final judgment on love: the hungry, the thirsty, the stranger, the naked, the sick and those in prison."

Roman Catholic Nuns all over the world work daily with and advocate for the poor and "the least" in their societies.

Archbishop Oscar Romero of El Salvador, an advocate for the plight of poor people (and possibly for liberation theology) in his country where at the time 13 families controlled 40 percent of the land, was assassinated near the altar of a hospital's chapel as he celebrated a mass and was subsequently mourned by several hundred thousand people at his burial.

Martin Luther King, Jr., his Southern Christian Leadership Conference (SCLC) and colleagues such as Bayard Rustin, Ella Jackson, A. Philip Randolph, Ralph Abernathy, Fred Shuttlesworth, Joseph Lowery, C.K. Steele, Hosea Williams, and Jesse Jackson, along with John Lewis and others in the Student Nonviolent Coordinating Committee (SNCC) and James Farmer and others in the Congress of Racial Equality (CORE), and many other people and congregations, challenged repressive U.S. racial policies and helped re-write the laws on white-black relations in the United States.

William Sloane Coffin, senior minister of Riverside Church in New York City's East Side, was a major leader in the Peace and Anti-Vietnam-War Movements and an early advocate for gay rights.

Samuel Habib went into the poverty-stricken, illiterate, superstition-filled villages of Egypt and, before his ministry ended, had brought more than 300 villages into renewed well-being.

Bishop Tutu with Nelson Mandela of South Africa initiated a revolution in racial relations in their country that accomplished, without a civil war, what we could only do through a destructive civil war that killed over 750,000 American men.

And there have been "sheep from other than Christ's fold" who have brought his transforming power into their own societies, Mohandas Gandhi, a Hindu in India, and Aung San Suu Kyi, a Buddhist in Myanmar, to mention only two of the most prominent.

None of these persons worked alone. Rauschenbusch brought the Federal Council of Churches into being; Schweitzer was supported by the Mission Society in Germany; Barth and Bonhoeffer along with Martin Niemoller and others were part of the Confessing Church in Germany; Martin Luther King, Jr., was joined by colleagues and congregations in the Southern Christian Leadership Conference, which was supported by many other groups; John XXIII and Oscar Romero with major portions of the Roman Catholic Church; Bishop Tutu with the Anglican Church of South Africa; Mandela with the African National Congress; Mahatma Ghandi with the Indian National Congress; and Aung San Suu Kyi with the National League for Democracy in Myanmar.

Additionally, myriads of unheralded Christian clergy and laity have been and are involved in localities' human rights and community action agencies, in food banks and low-income housing initiatives, in organizations like Planned Parenthood, meals-on-wheels, and church low-income meal services, in community advocacy and service groups, and similar organizations and agencies working to extend health, humanity, and support to poor, disadvantaged, and unrepresented people of any ethnicity.

Our country may no longer be "one-third ill-housed, ill-clad, ill-nourished,"as Roosevelt declared, but grave social problems remain as seen in reports from the U. S. Census and other U.S. government agencies which provide evidence that

- over 50 percent of all births in the United States are to single mothers;

- over 20 percent of children live in poverty;
- as many as 90 percent of children in inner city schools of metropolitan areas are on free-breakfast and free-lunch programs because their parent or parents fall below certain low-income levels;
- about 25 percent of teenagers do not complete high school in four years—those who don't are more likely to live in poverty in their futures; "middle class" incomes have stagnated over the last 20 years;
- 1 percent of all adults owned over 40 percent of total wealth in 2010 and this 1% have total incomes greater than the combined incomes of the bottom 50 percent of people, with the gaps continuing to grow annually;
- the bottom 50 percent, 150 million people, own less than 2 percent of total wealth of the nation;
- 93 percent of new income from 2010 to 2011 went to the top 1 percent (the 99 percent grew by only 7 percent in total income);
- the U.S. as a nation devotes more of its gross national product to military and home-security concerns than do all other nations of the world, combined (Sanders, 2012; U.S. Census Economic Reports, 2011, 2012).

Since its beginning the Jesus movement has been divided on its social policies. The social policies of many vocal religious groups, then as now, would deny equal rights to at least one group of people (now, gays and lesbians, and, in some cases, non-white minorities) and seek to have another group (pregnant single mothers, especially, but even women in general) restricted in having free-and-equal-with-men access to affordable healthcare, contraception, abortions (for women who want or need them), medical control over their own bodies, and equal pay for equal work. Major elected political leaders holding powerful state and national positions have shown they intend to cut back on government-provided services for healthcare (Medicaid and Medicare), welfare (low-income housing, safety nets, even Social Security), food stamps, education, and unemployment programs. Many support state and local programs that restrict voter registrations of people in certain non-white minorities; and, in the name of "free speech," they support the right of all people (wealthy and non-wealthy alike) and corporations (as if they are "persons") to spend as much money as they like in any way they wish in election campaigns, a practice that heavily favors richer people in spending much larger amounts of money in elections for candidates from one party over any other.

In citing statistics such as these, U. S. Senator Bernie Sanders (Independent, Vermont) noted that "the realities underlying many of these conditions are economic issues but they are also moral issues. It is absurd to be talking about austerity for the most vulnerable people in our country—people who are already experiencing great financial hardship—while protecting the interests of the rich and the powerful" (Sanders, 2012). These are things similar to what Jesus found among leaders in his society in his day. The result? Jesus opposed them.

As we note these brutal statistics, we can also note that each of these issues has spawned non-governmental organizations to challenge such brutality and to ameliorate their effects. Many of these organizations draw support from Christian people and their congregations. The transforming spirit of Jesus Christ still lives among us.

What does this transforming spirit of Jesus' God want those of us who are Christian to do today? In his day Jesus asked, through his words and deeds, that his followers serve the poor, heal the sick, care for the disabled and those discriminated against, and visit the prisoners (Mt 25:34-46); he also asked the rich to follow his commandments (*"love one another…"* as he loved his disadvantaged followers), give all they had to the poor, *"then come and follow"* him. He asks no less of his followers today.

Martin Luther King, Jr., thought "the long arc of the universe is bending toward justice" (1958, 2012). Even 750 years before Christ, the prophet Amos demanded that leaders in his society *"let justice flow down like the waters and righteousness like an everlasting stream"* (Amos 5:24). According to Luke 1:50-53, when God brought Jesus into the world, God's declaration was even stronger. *"God has dispersed the proud into the imagination of their hearts, deposed the potentates from their thrones, and exalted the humble. He has filled the hungry with good things and the rich he has dismissed empty-handed."* All our doctrines, all our theologies, all our Bible studies, all our preaching and worship, all our personal and corporate actions need to focus on this one central person, Jesus Christ and the God he revealed who stands behind and before us urging us, from our abundance, to serve the least among us, to love them as well as our neighbors as God loves us, and to bear one another's burdens. To follow Christ today, we can do no less.

Bibliography
and References*

Altar, Robert, 2004. The Five Books of Moses. New York: W.W. Norton & Co.
Antipas, see Herod Antipas.
Arndt, William, and F. Wilbur Gingrich, 1979. Greek-English Lexicon. Chicago: University of Chicago Press.
Ascough, Richard S., 2003. Paul's Macedonian Associations. Tubingen, Germany: J. C. B. Mohr (Paul Siebeck).
Barclay, John M. G., 1996. Jews in the Mediterranean Diaspora: From Alexander to Trajan (53CE to 117CE). Edinburg: T & T Clark, Ltd.
Barmen Declaration, 1934. See Barth, Karl, 1934. (Barth was its primary author.)
Barrett, C.K., 1978. The Gospel according to St. John: An Introduction with Commentary and Notes on the Greek Text. Philadelphia: Westminster Press.
Bartsch, Hans Werner, 1980. "Inhalt und Funktion des Urchristlichen Osterglaubens," New Testament Studies, 26, 2: 180-196.
Barth, Karl, 1934. "The Theological Declaration of Barmen," Barmen, Germany: Confession Church of Germany. (Also in Constitution of the Presbyterian Church, U.S.A.) See <http://en.wikipedia.org/wiki/Barmen_Declaration>, 2012.
ben-Dov, M., 1985. In the Shadow of the Temple: The Discovery of Ancient Jerusalem. New York: Harper and Row.
Bible Knowledge Accelerator, The, 1995-1996. <www.bible-history.com/jesus/jesus. The Synagogue.htm>.

*We wish to thank Ms. Nancy Skipper, Cornell University Reference Librarian (Music) for assistance in putting this bibliography together.

Bishop, Eric Francis Fox, 1964. "Bethlehem And The Nativity: Some Travesties Of Christmas," Anglican Theological Review, 46, 4: 401-413.

Bonhoeffer, Dietrich, 1953. Letters and Papers from Prison. New York: Macmillan.

Bonhoeffer, Dietrich, 1959. The Cost of Discipleship. New York: Macmillan.

Borg, Marcus J., 1994. Meeting Jesus Again for the First Time: The Historical Jesus & the Heart of Contemporary Faith. San Francisco: HarperSanFrancisco.

Branscomb, Bennett Harvie, 1930. Jesus and the Law of Moses. New York: R.R. Smith.

Brown, David L. and Louis E. Swanson, 2003 – see Flora and Flora, 2003.

Brown, R. E., 1979. The Gospel according to John. Garden City, NY: Doubleday & Company.

Brown, R. E., with J. P Meier, 1983. Antioch and Rome. New York: Ramsey/Paulist Press.

Brueggemann, Walter, 1999. "The Liturgy of Abundance, the Myth of Scarcity," The Christian Century, 116, 10 (March 24-31): 342-347.

Buttrick, George A., editor, 1952. The Interpreter's Bible, Vol. 1. New York: Abingdon-Cokesbury Press.

Cahill, Thomas, 1999. Desire of the Everlasting Hills: The World Before and After Jesus. New York: Nan A. Talese.

Campbell, Alan, 2012. "The Woman at the Well in Samaria," in <http://www.ensignmessage.com/archives/samar.html, Pastor Alan Campbell>.

Crosson, John Dominic, 1998. The Birth of Christianity: Discovering What Happened in the Years Immediately After the Execution of Jesus. San Francisco: HarperSanFrancisco.

Culpepper, R. Alan, 2005. The New Interpreter's Bible. Nashville: Abingdon Press.

Dead Sea Scrolls, 1998. Washington, D.C.: Public Broadcasting Service: DVD. (See also Qumran.)

Dodd, C. H., 1952. According to the Scriptures: The Sub-Structure of New Testament Theology. London: Nisbet.

Dodd, C. H., 1953. The Interpretation of the Fourth Gospel. Cambridge, U.K.: Cambridge University Press.

Dodd, C. H., 1961. The Parables of the Kingdom. New York: Scribner.

Dodd, C. H., 1963. Historical Tradition in the Fourth Gospel. Cambridge, U.K.: Cambridge University Press.

Eberts, Harry W., Jr. and Eberts, Paul R., 2009. The Early Jesus Movement and Its Parties. New York: YBK Publishers.

Eberts, Harry W., Jr. and Eberts, Paul R., 2011. The Early Jesus Movement and Its Congregations. New York: YBK Publishers.

Eberts, Paul R., and Kent P. Schwirian, 1968. "Relative Deprivation and Crime Rates," Criminologica, 5, 4 (February 1968): 43-52; and revised for Daniel Glazer (ed.), Crime in the City. New York: Harper and Row, 1969.

Eberts, Paul R., and Sergio Sismondo, 1978. "Designing and Managing Policy Research" in Rural Policy Research Alternatives, pp. 42-77. Ames, IA: Iowa State University Press.

Eliot, T. S., 1952. The Complete Poems and Plays. New York: Harcourt, Brace.

Eusebius, 2nd Century, 2012. <www.wikipedia.org/wiki/Eusebius>.

Fleming, James (Director, Biblical Resources Study Center in Jerusalem), 1996. Akron, OH: Akron Beacon Journal, March 31: A23.

Flora, Cornelia Butler, and Jan L. Flora, 2003. "Social Capital," pp. 214-227, in David L. Brown and Louis E. Swanson, editors, Challenges for Rural America in the Twenty-First Century. University Park, PA: The Pennsylvania State University Press.

Galilee, Spotlight on, 2013. <http://www.welcometohosanna.com/LIFE_OF_JESUS/021_GalileeSpotlight.htm>.

Gilmour, S. Maclean, 1937. The Rise of Church Consciousness among Early Christians. Chicago: University of Chicago, Ph.D. dissertation.

Gilmour, S. Maclean, 1952. In The Interpreter's Bible, 8, George A. Buttrick, editor. New York: Abingdon-Cokesbury Press.

Gilmour, S. Maclean, 1957. The Gospel Jesus Preached. Philadelphia: Westminster Press.

Gospel Parallels, 1949. Edited by Translators, Revised Standard Version, International Council of Religious Education. New York: Thomas Nelson and Sons.

Grant, Michael, 1975. The Twelve Caesars. New York: Scribner.

Grundy-Volk, Judith, 1995. "Spirit, Mercy, And The Other," Theology Today, 51, 4 (Jan.).

Harper's Bible Commentary, 1998. James L. May, editor. San Francisco: Bible Review.

Hay, L. S., 1964. "The Son-of-God Christology in Mark," Journal of Biblical Religion, 32, 2: 6.

Hengel, Martin, 1989. The 'Hellenization' of Judea in the First Century After Christ. Philadelphia, PA: Trinity Press International.

Herod Antipas, 2012. www.wikipedia.org/Herod_Antipas.

Hillel, The. <https://www.hillel.org/jewish/textstudies/>.

Holy Bible, The, 1946 (Revised Standard Version). The International Council of Religious Education. New York: Thomas Nelson and Sons.

New Testament
Book of the Acts of the Apostles
Gospel of John
Gospel of Luke
Gospel of Mark
Gospel of Matthew
First Letter of Paul to the Corinthians

Second Letter of Paul to the Corinthians
Letter of Paul to the Romans
Letter of Paul to the Galatians
Letter to the Hebrews

Old Testament
Apocrypha
Book of Jubilees
Book of Tobit
Testament of Naphtali
Genesis
Exodus
Leviticus
Numbers
Deuteronomy
Joshua
First Samuel
Second Samuel
First Kings
Second Kings
Psalms
Proverbs
Amos
Daniel
Ezekiel
Hosea
Isaiah
Jeremiah
Joel
Jonah
Malachi
Micah
Zechariah

Horsley, Richard A., with John S. Hanson, 1985. Bandits, Prophets, and Messiahs: Popular Movements in the Time of Jesus. San Francisco, CA: Harper and Row.

Horsley, Richard A., 1989. Sociology and the Jesus Movement. New York: Crossroad.

Horsley, Richard A., 1996. Archeology, History, and Society in Galilee: The Social Context of Jesus and the Rabbis. Valley Forge, PA: Trinity International Press.

Horsley, Richard A., 2011. Jesus and the Powers: Conflict, Covenant, and the Hope of the Poor. Minneapolis: Fortress Press.

Hughes, Bettany, 2010. The Hemlock Cup: Socrates, Athens, and the Search for the Good Life. Amazon, New York: Alfred A. Knopf, Kindle Edition.

Interpreter's Bible, The, 1952. See Buttrick.

Jensen, Morten Horning, 2012. "Antipas: The Herod Jesus Knew," Biblical Archeology Review, 38, 5 (September/October): 42-46.

Jerusalem Perspective. 6, 1991.

Jewish Encyclopedia (online), 2011. <http://www.jewishencyclopedia.com>.

Josephus, Flavius, originally c. 78; 1987. War of the Jews. In The Complete Works of Josephus: Complete and Unabridged. Translated by William Whiston. Peabody, MA: Hendrickson Publishers.

Josephus, Flavius, originally c. 94: 1987. Antiquities of the Jews. In The Complete Works of Josephus: Complete and Unabridged. Translated by William Whiston. Peabody, MA: Hendrickson Publishers.

Josephus, Flavius, originally c. 97: 1987. Against Apion. In The Complete Works of Josephus: Complete and Unabridged. Translated by William Whiston. Peabody, MA: Hendrickson Publishers.

Judas the Galilean, 2012. <www.wikipedia.org/Judas_of_Galilee>.

Kamil, Jill, 1987. Coptic Egypt, History and Guide. Cairo, Egypt: American University in Cairo Press.

King, Martin Luther, Jr., 1958, 2012. "The Arc of the Moral Universe... Bends Toward Justice," <http://quoteinvestigator.com/2012/11/15/arc-of-universe/>.

King, Martin Luther, Jr., 1995. In Richard Lischer, The Preacher King: Martin Luther King, Jr. and the Words that Moved America. New York: Oxford University Press.

Kloppenborg, John S., 1996. "Collegia and Thiasoi: Issues in Function, Taxonomy, and Membership," ch. 2, in John S. Kloppenborg and Stephen G. Wilson (editors), 1996. Voluntary Associations in the Graeco-Roman World. London and New York: Routledge.

Kloppenborg, John S. and S. G. Wilson, 1996. Voluntary Associations in the Graeco-Roman World. Canadian Society of Biblical Studies. London and New York: Routledge.

Kraeling, Carl H., 1956. The Synagogue. New York: Klav Publishing House.

Kraeling, Carl H., 1960. "Review: The Excavations of Herodian Jericho, 1951," American Journal of Archeology, 64, 3:302-303.

Lenski, Gerhard, 1966. Power and Privilege: A Theory of Social Stratification. New York: McGraw-Hill.

Lenski, Gerhard E., and Jean Lenski, 1987. Human Societies. New York: McGraw-Hill.

Lightfoot, Joseph B., 1893. Biblical Essays. London: Macmillan.

Lischer, Richard, 1995. The Preacher King: Martin Luther King, Jr. and the Words that Moved America. New York: Oxford University Press.

MacGregor, G. H. C., 1928, 1959. The Gospel of John. New York: Harper and Brothers.

Matthew, Gospel of, 2012a, b. a.:<www.wikipedia.org/Gospel_of_Matthew>; b.:<www.wikipedia.org/Gospel_of_Matthew#Structure>.

May, James L., ed., 1998. Harper's Bible Commentary. San Francisco: Bible Review.

Meeks, Wayne A., 1983. The First Urban Christians. New Haven and London: Yale University Press.

Mishnah, The. <www.chaver.com/Mishnah/TheMishnah.htm>.

Mithra, 2013. <http://en.wikipedia.org/wiki/Mithra>.

Neusner, Jacob, 1975. First Century Judaism in Crisis. Nashville and New York: Abingdon.

Neusner, Jacob, 1984. Judaism in the Beginning of Christianity. Philadelphia, PA: Fortress Press.

Niebuhr, H. Richard , 1951. Christ and Culture. New York , NY: Harper and Brothers.

Niebuhr, H. Richard, Daniel Day Williams, and James Gustafson, 1956. The Purpose of the Church and Its Ministries. New York: Harper and Row.

Ovid, Allen Mandelbaum, 1993. The Metamorphoses of Ovid. New York: Harcourt Brace.

Oxford English Dictionary, 2004. Edited by E. S. C. Weiner and J. A. Simpson. Oxford, U.K: Oxford University Press.

Padfield, David, 2012. <www.Sepphoris In Galilee/Padfield>.

Pharisee, 2012. <www.wikipedia.org/Pharisee>.

Philo of Alexandria (20BCE-50CE), 1993. De Somniiv. In The Works of Philo: Complete and Unabridged. Translated by Charles Duke Yonge. Peabody, MA: Hendrickson Publishers.

Philo of Alexandria, 2013. <http://en.wikipedia.org/wiki/Philo>.

Q, Quelle, 2012. <www.wikipedia.org/wiki/Q_source>.

Qumran, 1998. In Dead Sea Scrolls, DVD, Public Broadcasting Service.

Qumran, 2013. < http://en.wikipedia.org/wiki/Qumran>.

Reed, Jonathan L., 1992. The Population of Capernaum. Occasional Papers of the Institute for Antiquity and Christianity. Claremont, CA: Institute for Antiquity and Christianity.

Reed, Jonathan L., 2007. The Harper Collins Visual Guide to the New Testament. New York, Harper Collins.

Robinson, J. Armitage, 1962. Twelve New Testament Studies. Cambridge, UK: Cambridge University Press.

Sanders, Bernie, U. S. Senator, 2012. <www.sanders.senate.gov/issues/economy>.

Sanders, E. P., 1993. The Historical Figure of Jesus. London: Allen Lane, Penguin Press.

Sanhedrin, 2012. <www.wikipedia.org/Sanhedrin>.

Schweitzer, Albert, 1911. The Quest of the Historical Jesus. London: A & C Black.

Sepphoris, 2012. <www.wikipedia.org/Sepphoris>; See Strange, 2012.

Spong, John Shelby, 1996. Liberating the Gospels: Reading the Bible with Jewish Eyes and Freeing Jesus from 2,000 Years of Misunderstanding. San Francisco, CA: HarperSanFrancisco.

Snaith, Norman H., 1952. In George A. Buttrick, The Interpreter's Bible, Vol. 1.

Strange, James F., 2001, 2012. "Sepphoris." <www.bibleinterp.com/articles/Sepphoris.htm>.

Strong, James, and John R. Kohlenberger, 2001. New Strong's Expanded Exhaustive Concordance of the Bible. Nashville, TN: T. Nelson.

Tacitus, 116 (1983). Annals of Imperial Rome, Book 16. Cited in Brown, R. E., with J. P Meier, 1983. Antioch and Rome. New York: Ramsey/ Paulist Press.

Tacitus, 2013. <http://en.wikipedia.org/wiki/Tacitus_on_Christ>.

Talmud, The. <www.sacred-texts.com/jud/talmud.htm>.

Taylor, Archibald B., Jr., 1960. "Decision in the Desert: The Temptation of Jesus, in the Light of Deuteronomy," Interpretation: Journal of Bible and Theology, Journal of Union Theological Seminary, Richmond, VA.: 300-309.

Temme. J.M., 1991. "The Shepherds' Role," Bible Today, 29, 6: 376-378.

Terrien, Samuel, 1985. Till the Heart Sings: A Biblical Theology of Manhood and Womanhood. Philadelpia, PA: Fortress Press.

Thorley, J., 1979. "The Nativity Census: What Does Luke Actually Say?" Greece and Rome (Oxford): 26, 1.

U.S. Census, 2010. < www.census.gov/2010census/ reports/economy, poverty >.

Veen, Peter van der, 2013. "When Pharoahs Ruled Jerusalem," Biblical Archeological Review, 39, 2: 42-48.

Wahlde, Urban C. Van, 2011. Biblical Archeological Review: Sep/Oct.

Weights and Measures, 2013. <www.jewishvirtuallibrary.org/jsource/History/weightsandmeasures.html>.

Wright, C. Ernest, 1961. Biblical Archaeology. In The Biblical Archeologist Reader, Edited by David Noel Freeman and Edward F. Campbell. Garden City, NY: Anchor Books, 1961.

Yonge, Charles Duke (Translator), 1993. The Works of Philo: Complete and Unabridged. Peabody, MA: Hendrickson Publishing.

Zeitlin, Irving M., 1988. Jesus and the Judaism of His Time. Cambridge, UK: Polity Press (Basil Blackwell, Inc.).

Internet Sites
<http://en.wikipedia.org/wiki/Tacitus_on_Christ>, 2013.
<http://en.wikipedia.org/wiki/Mithra>, 2013.

<http://en.wikipedia.org/wiki/Philo>, 2013.

< http://en.wikipedia.org/wiki/Qumran>, 2013.

<http://www.jewishvirtuallibrary.org/jsource/History/weightsandmeasures.html>, 2013.

<http://www.welcometohosanna.com/LIFE_OF_JESUS/021_GalileeSpotlight.htm>, 2013.

<www.wikipedia.org/wiki/Eusebius>, 2012.

<www.wikipedia.org/Judas_of_Galilee>, 2012.

<www.wikipedia.org/Gospel_of_Matthew>, 2012a.

<www.wikipedia.org/Gospel_of_Matthew#Structure>, 2012b.

<www.wikipedia.org/Pharisee>, 2012.

<www.wikipedia.org/Sanhedrin>, 2012.

<www.wikipedia.org/Sepphoris>, 2012.

<www.wikipedia.org/wiki/Q_source>, 2012.

<www.chaver.com/Mishnah/TheMishnah.htm>, 2012

Topic Index

(Note: Many topics, including references to New and Old Testament books and verses, are found in the "Detailed Outline" at the beginning of the book)

CPSIA information can be obtained at www.ICGtesting.com
Printed in the USA
LVOW07s2145090913

351333LV00009B/4/P